GW00646307

Edited and designed
by David Dew

Contributors

Richard Birch	Pietro Innocenzi	Colin Russell
James Burn	Paul Kealy	Tom Segal
Matthew Butler	Steve Mason	Brian Sheerin
Tom Collins	Kevin Morley	James Stevens
Dave Edwards	Ben Newton	Alan Sweetman
Richard Forristal	Tony O'Hehir	Kitty Trice
Dylan Hill	Dave Orton	Nick Watts
James Hill	Lewis Porteous	Robbie Wilders

Cover artwork by Samantha Creedon
Inside artwork by David Cramphorn and Stefan Searle

Published in 2018 by Racing Post Books, Raceform, 27 Kingfisher Court, Hambridge Road, Newbury, RG14 5SJ

ISBN: 978-1910497555

LOWDOWN FROM THE TRAINERS

Facebook.com/racingpost

RACING POST EXPERTS

THIS SEASON'S KEY HORSES

THE LOWDOWN GORDON ELLIOTT

Recruitment the force behind master plan to lift champion trophy

LAST season was Gordon Elliott's best yet. A remarkable eight winners at the Cheltenham Festival helped him end the week as the leading handler there for the second consecutive year.

He also secured a breakthrough Irish Grand National win with General Principle before completing the lucrative double when Tiger Roll went on to win the Aintree Grand National, 11 years on from when Silver Birch put Elliott's name in lights after providing the then little-known handler with his first victory in the race.

Not only were the big-race successes plentiful last season, but the 40-year-old sent out a colossal 210 winners in a domestic season, confirming his status as one of the best when it comes to placing horses.

All of these achievements, and to think it could have been even better as some of the stable stars weren't firing by the time Punchestown rolled around and Elliott could only watch as Willie Mullins whizzed by and denied him a maiden championship in the dying strides.

Those championship defeats hurt like hell but they stoke the fire in Elliott's belly, and after a busy year recruiting more stars, he believes he has assembled his hottest bunch of winter warmers yet.

"I love going to the sales and we've been very busy all summer buying horses," he says. "I think we came up short with our older horses last year and, if I'm going to become champion trainer one day, I need to be thinking three, four or five years down the line which is why you have to get out there and spot the young talent coming through."

Samcro the hottest of them all

There's no hotter young prospect in Cullentra than **Samcro**. If Elliott had a penny for every time he's been asked what route last year's Ballymore Novices' Hurdle winner will go this season, he'd be going to the sales with deeper pockets than he already is, which is rather apt as he describes future plans for Samcro as the million-dollar question.

He says: "Shane McCann, who rides him out every day, and Keith

....

The returns from Elliott's novices in Britain aren't as great but they boast a higher strike-rate and provide a small profit over hurdles (34-101, 34% +1.78pt) and fences (10-56, 18%, +1.62pt)

 Facebook.com/racingpost

WINNERS IN LAST FIVE SEASONS 210, 193, 123, 92, 56

'I love going to the sales and we've been very busy all summer buying horses'

Elliott is renowned for his raids at Perth but the layers have cottoned on to his exploits at the track (66-237, 28%, -16.70pt). The quality in his yard is evident though as his highest level-stake return comes at Cheltenham (20-128, 16%, +75.85pt)

Donoghue, who was riding him when Shane was on holidays, say he's in unbelievable form and to see him walking around the place, he's come back in looking brilliant.

"We can't wait to get him back started as he's a very exciting horse, but what route we go, I'm not entirely sure.

"If we were to go for the Champion Hurdle with him I'd imagine he'd be starting back in the Grade 2 WKD Hurdle at Down Royal – that's a meeting where I like to start back most of my good horses. If it's chasing, we might look at a beginners' chase on the same weekend up there."

Champion Hurdle clue

But here comes the biggest clue yet from Elliott. "We sent **Mick Jazz** to finish third in last year's Champion Hurdle and I'd have little doubt in my mind that Samcro is a better horse than him. It's not a bad problem to have and I'm privileged to have a horse like him in the yard."

Elliott might keep us guessing on Samcro but fellow Cheltenham Festival winners **Farclas** and **Veneer Of Charm** will stay over hurdles, with the latter set for a lucrative campaign.

The trainer says: "I might keep Farclas [Triumph Hurdle winner] hurdling but I'd say I'll be stepping him up in trip. He'll probably start off in the four-year-old hurdle at Limerick in early October.

"Veneer Of Charm [Fred Winter winner] started back in the Lartigue Hurdle at Listowel and goes for a hurdle race in America in October and he'll continue to mix it here for the season, all being well."

Jade to tread familiar path

Apple's Jade would have been the first horse on many people's list when trying to predict Elliott's Cheltenham Festival winners last season, but the seven-time Grade 1 winner could manage only third in the Mares'

Hurdle behind Benie Des Dieux, before filling the same spot behind that mare at Punchestown.

However, Elliott believes there were genuine reasons why the real Apple's Jade didn't show up in the spring.

He said: "I was very disappointed with the latter part of her campaign last year but she kept coming into season on us as the year went on and hopefully we have that all sorted out now. She's a very good mare and we're looking forward to her.

"She's going to go down the same route this year with all roads leading back to Cheltenham for the Mares' Hurdle."

Diamond Cauchois is also one Elliott is keen to keep onside throughout the winter and he says: "There'll be plenty of races to be won with him and he likes heavy ground. He stays over hurdles as I'm not sure he has the scope for fences."

Tiger heading back to Aintree

The curtain may have come down on the career of Cause Of Causes last season, winner of three Cheltenham Festival races, including the 2017 cross-country race, but **Tiger Roll** stepped up to the plate to take last season's running of that race before securing legendary status at Cullentra by following up in the Grand National at Aintree.

He is being aimed at both races again and Elliott says: "Tiger Roll is a little star and he's in as good form as ever. We'll probably give him one run over hurdles and go back to Cheltenham for the cross-country races before going back to Aintree in the spring.

"**General Principle** will also go for the National. I'd say he wasn't right all last year, but thankfully he sparked on the right day and won the Irish Grand National at Fairyhouse, so touch wood we might see an even better horse this year.

"**Ucello Conti** is going to go cross-country and hunter chasing so he should be a good

Ladbrokes

fun horse for that, while **Folsom Blue** will be geared towards all those staying handicap chases and we might even start him back in the Fixed Brush Hurdle at Haydock."

"**Bless The Wings** was almost retired last year, but he doesn't seem to be slowing down and you could argue his last run, when fifth in the National, was his best yet. We'll have plenty of fun with him again."

'Looking better than ever'

Outlander has been a standing dish in the best staying chases in Ireland in recent years and the three-time Grade 1 winner is likely to reappear in the JNwine.com Champion Chase in November, a race he won last year.

"He's been a great servant for us and he's come back in looking better than ever. He can be very good or very bad, but on his day he's a classy three-mile chaser.

"I'm sure all roads will lead back to Leopardstown as he loves it there. He seems to go best fresh."

Bargain buy **Doctor Phoenix** is also set for more of the same while Cheltenham Festival winners **Shattered Love** and **The Storyteller** could have a big campaign ahead of them.

"Doctor Phoenix has been a star for us and will have a similar campaign. There's great prize-money to be picked up in all those Grade 2 and 3 two-mile chases and you don't necessarily have to win them all to have a great year.

"**Squouateur** has threatened to win a big one but he's been disappointing. I'm hoping he puts it all together one day.

"**Shattered Love** is a very good mare, as we saw when she won the JLT Novices' Chase, and it's going to be interesting to see how the season progresses for her. She'll probably start back in that second-season novice at Down Royal and we'll let her tell us where we go from there.

"**The Storyteller** got the rub of the green at Punchestown when he won the Grade 1 Growise Novice Chase and he'll have to improve a bit to deal with the big boys over fences. He could be well enough handicapped over hurdles though and we might go back and try and exploit that at some stage."

Don Poli in great shape

Providing an update of some of the stable's big names who have been out of action, Elliott says: "We're delighted to have **Don Poli** back in full training and he looks great. **Sutton Place** is back cantering away and I've always thought a fair amount of him. Whether he goes hurdling or chasing this season, I'm not

entirely sure. As for **Death Duty**, he's out for the season, but we're hoping to have him back."

Powerful novice chase squad

There's serious strength in depth in Elliott's novice chase department. He says: "**Mengli Khan** is going to go chasing. I don't think he's good enough to go to the next level over hurdles which is why we're going over fences with him.

"**Cracking Smart** is another classy horse we're looking forward to sending chasing. He looks particularly well.

"You also wouldn't recognise **Flawless Escape** – he's got a lot stronger and I think he'll have a good year.

"**Blow By Blow**, **Dortmund Park** and **Champagne Classic** are others to look forward to over fences, Champagne Classic in particular. His form has worked out really

GORDON ELLIOTT
LONGWOOD, COUNTY MEATH, IRELAND

	Races Run	1st	2nd	3rd	Unpl	Per cent	£1 Level Stake
Non-hcp hurdles	2282	361	362	277	1282	15.8	-779.83
Hcp hurdles	1438	146	135	118	1039	10.2	-486.17
Non-hcp chases	1004	187	204	138	475	18.6	-156.48
Hcp chases	661	64	43	62	492	9.7	-237.09
Hunter chases	23	4	2	0	17	17.4	-1.13
NH Flat	647	144	114	80	309	22.3	-34.00
Totals	**6055**	**906**	**860**	**675**	**3614**	**15.0**	**-1694.70**

BY MONTH

	W-R	Strike-rate (%)	£1 level stake
January	64-474	13.5	-181.61
February	76-444	17.1	-143.04
March	72-412	17.5	-127.58
April	61-613	10.0	-187.59
May	74-559	13.2	-164.62
June	67-435	15.4	-63.89
July	63-544	11.6	-294.65
August	76-579	13.1	-153.00
September	37-260	14.2	-85.68
October	101-449	22.5	-85.07
November	112-609	18.4	-70.39
December	103-677	15.2	-137.58

Statistics relate to all runners in Ireland from 2009-2018

DID YOU KNOW?

Gordon Elliott is a massive *Home and Away* fan and has not missed a single episode of the Australian soap. He says: "I watch it every day. I never miss it. Nobody rings me between half one and two. They know."

well. He's never shown us a lot at home but he's a Cheltenham winner and he's one to look forward to."

Outlining others to keep an eye out for over fences, Elliott says: "**Delta Work** is another fair horse. It was a bit of an afterthought to go for the Pertemps with him and I'd say he improved another 10lb from Cheltenham to Punchestown when going down by only a neck behind Next Destination in a Grade 1. He's come back in very strong and is a great jumper so one to look out for over fences this year.

He adds: "**Glenloe** was a bit unlucky not to win the Pertemps but he's going chasing and he'll make a nice stayer. **Ben Dundee** is another horse whom we like and there will be races to be won with him over fences as well."

Exciting times with youngsters

Elliott won 28 individual bumpers in Ireland alone last season and says he's dealing with his best bunch of young horses yet.

On his novice hurdling team, he says: "**Felix Desjy** is a very strong horse and he did well in bumpers last year. We'll start him off in a maiden hurdle at Down Royal.

"**Getaway John** is a nice horse as well. He was probably at the end of his tether by the time Punchestown came last season but he'll be starting back over hurdles sooner rather than later.

"We had the one-two-three in last year's Land Rover Bumper with **Commander Of Fleet**, **Column Of Fire** and **Santana Plessis** and they all go novice hurdling.

"**Diamond Turf** could be a nice staying novice hurdler. I've no doubt we've assembled the best bunch of young horses we've ever had and I just can't wait to be going to places like Navan during the winter where we'll find out how good they are.

"At the moment, I'm going down through each barn and there looks to be potentially smart novice hurdlers everywhere. **Vision D'Honneur** is a French bumper winner and a really gorgeous horse. He could be exciting."

The mares' novice programme is one Elliott will be targeting with Tintangle and Black Tears, both of whom won bumpers last year.

"**Tintangle** did nothing wrong all last year and she's tough and stays well. **Black Tears** might have a little bit more class and she's a good little mare to have."

Sublime purchase

Elliott landed both juvenile races at the Cheltenham Festival last year and is particularly excited this season about one particular youngster.

"We were delighted to get **Coeur Sublime** at the sales. The horse won a maiden on the Flat and, while he'll go juvenile hurdling this year, I'd say he'll be more than just a juvenile as he looks built for chasing.

"**Elysian Plains** has already won over hurdles but he's going to have to settle a bit better if he's going to progress.

"**Lethal Steps** is also a nice horse and he should do well.

"It was also great to get **Chief Justice** to win first time out at Listowel – he looks a nice horse."

'Everyone loves him'

"We've got lots of nice horses for bumpers this year and when you go down through the list I start pinching myself.

"**Envoi Allen** looks exciting. He's gorgeous and everyone who's ridden him loves him. He won his point-to-point well and we're looking at starting him off in a bumper this side of Christmas.

"**Malone Road** is a nice horse and looks one for the future, as do **Fury Road** and **Feel My Pulse**. There's plenty there."
Interview by Brian Sheerin

SUPER STATS

Elliott's numbers continue to rise and his British winners last year (21-106, 20%, +35.32pt) saw him earn more than £1.3 million in prize-money. Despite pushing Willie Mullins hard for the Irish trainers' championship, he has been unable to wrest the title away, but his tally of 210 Irish winners and €5.1 million in prize-money was a personal best

The hint should be taken on the rare occasions he sends runners to Bangor (2-3, 67%, +5.38pt) and Carlisle (2-3, 67%, +10.00pt). Any hurdlers sent to Sedgefield are well worth watching out for (9-16, 56%, +5.30pt)

Hurdlers sent to Britain are best followed in Graded races (9-59, 15%, +60.22pt) and handicaps (42-198, 21%, +33.27pt). Elliott's chasers also perform well at Graded level (7-45, 16%, +7.25pt)

Richard Johnson rides the majority of Elliott's successful British raiders but the records of Davy Russell (6-20, 30%, +21.28pt) and Jack Kennedy (4-14, 29%, +36.73pt) were more eyecatching last year

In Ireland Thurles is easily the best track to follow Elliott's string, and the only course at which he has provided a level-stake profit over the past five seasons (32-130, 25%, +29.32pt), especially in bumpers (4-9, 44%, +22.50pt)

Statistics for all trainer Super Stats cover the current season and previous four seasons

Delta Work (right) powers home to win last season's Pertemps Hurdle at Cheltenham

THE LOWDOWN HARRY FRY

Determined to raise the bar again with a team packed full of potential

HE finished higher in the trainers' championship table than he had ever done before in 11th place but, such is his ambition, Harry Fry labelled last season's achievements as slightly underwhelming. Yet there were valid reasons for falling beneath the trainer's own high expectations and there is a real sense of optimism brewing from the Dorset-based trainer for this campaign.

Fry says: "After tragically losing Neon Wolf 12 months ago, who was a real potential flagbearer, we didn't quite get into full stride and we weren't entirely happy with the form of the yard at various points of the year. Saying that, we still had over 50 winners and won more than three-quarters of a million pounds in prize-money.

"It did feel like a case of what could have been, with results such as Misterton being beaten a nose in the Greatwood and American finishing second in the Cotswold Chase, but we have a real drive and determination to improve things and put things right this year.

"Our ambition is to get back up to the level we were in 2016-17. We feel like we've got as good a team coming through as we've

WINNERS IN LAST FIVE SEASONS 53, 67, 54, 36, 34

'We have a
real drive and
determination
to improve
things and put
things right
this year'

Follow Fry at Exeter,
the trainer's best track
in terms of winners
and level-stake profit
(26-66, 39%, +49.78pt).
Although his strike-rate
is impressive there, it's
even better at Doncaster
(7-16, 44%, +10.83pt)

ever had, with lots of exciting young horses to look forward to."

If The Cap Fits is one such young horse who could land a telling blow for Fry this season.

The six-year-old is unbeaten in three starts over hurdles and featured towards the business end of last year's Supreme Novices' Hurdle market after an impressive success at Kempton on Boxing Day. He was ruled out of the big spring festivals with an injury, but Fry reports his promising young talent to be fit and firing ahead of a second season over hurdles.

He says: "He's really good and has made a full recovery from the injury. He could start off at Kempton on October 21 in the Listed hurdle, with a view to then going on to maybe the Elite Hurdle at Wincanton, which is a weight-for-age conditions race for the first time. We'll sort of go down that route with him and see how far up the ladder he can go."

'He's schooled brilliantly'

Last winter was a wet one that put back the proposed chasing career of **Minella Awards**, who had announced himself a highly promising individual in 2017, following up a smooth victory in the EBF Final at Sandown with a big-field handicap success at the Punchestown festival. However, following an effort that his trainer believes was a career-best at Galway over the summer, it appears the time has finally come to unleash the seven-year-old over fences.

Fry says: "The novice chasers will be led by the likes of Minella Awards, who prefers top

Minella Awards (right) gave Harry Fry a day to remember when winning at the Punchestown festival in 2017

Facebook.com/racingpost

of the ground, so we won't see him through the depths of the winter.

"He'll be starting off over fences in October, keeping going until the weather worsens and then he'll reappear in the spring.

"He's done well over hurdles and we feel he can become an equally good, if not better, chaser. He's schooled brilliantly at home. He was a winning point-to-pointer in Ireland before he joined me and jumping has always been for him. We're quite excited, as we think he could potentially make a very good chaser."

Chasing plan for Misterton

Greatwood Hurdle second **Misterton** could be another to make his debut over fences in the coming months, but not before returning over hurdles. Fry explains: "He could start off in the Silver Trophy at Chepstow's two-day meeting. He's another we're keen to see over fences. He runs well from anything over two miles to two and a half so we thought we'd give the valuable handicap hurdle a chance first time out and then switch his attention to the bigger obstacles."

Also set to be among the novice chasing ranks is **Onefortheroadtom**, who holds one of the strongest bits of novice hurdle form from last year. His hurdling debut at Exeter saw him defeat future Grade 1 winners Lalor and Kilbricken Storm. "He's still a bit on the raw, immature side," says Fry. "Hopefully he can progress over fences this year after another summer."

Bags Groove finished second on his chasing debut at Uttoxeter in May over an inadequate 2m trip. Fry expects him to be out in October and says: "We know he wants further and there are a number of options to start at Fontwell, Stratford or Uttoxeter. I'd like to think he'd learn plenty from that first run over fences. He's another who can hopefully be a very useful novice chaser."

As for his novice hurdlers, Fry has some exciting bumper horses from last year going over timber. It's been a waiting game with **Bullionaire**, but the trainer highlights him as a standout horse among the crop.

Winner of a valuable Goffs bumper at Newbury the season before last, the five-year-old only ran in a Listed Ascot bumper last season, finishing runner-up to Didtheyleaveuoutto, but an excited Fry says: "What made his Ascot performance even more impressive is he basically tried to bolt the whole way round, even to the point that turning in he was still virtually trying to run away from Noel Fehily, so to still finish second was hugely encouraging.

"We deliberately didn't run him again, because we wanted to save him as a novice for this season. We've spent a lot of time just trying to get him to relax and chill out. If he went back to the racecourse and ran like that again, he'd never give himself the chance to fulfil his potential. He's done really well over the summer and I'm looking forward to seeing him out over hurdles."

Caribert won last year's running of that same Goffs bumper at Newbury won by Bullionaire in 2017, and will also head over hurdles, but his trainer reveals that's where the similarities end.

Fry says: "He's a different model of horse to Bullionaire, he's more of a galloper, a staying type. He'd probably be able to do two and a half plus, but he's a fine, big horse."

From the rest of his novices, Fry highlights **Definitelyanoscar**, whom he expects to show up well in mares' novice hurdles: "She jumps for fun and could be out early on better ground."

Change of scenery for Samuri

New horses are not exclusively young, as the very experienced **The Last Samuri** will have his first season with Harry Fry after being switched from the Kim Bailey yard. The ten-year-old, who finished second in the 2016

Grand National at Aintree, will likely once again have the famous race on his agenda come April, along with several other familiar engagements in the coming months.

Fry says: "I'm delighted to get to train a horse of the calibre of The Last Samuri, but I know how it feels when it happens the other way and Kim Bailey did a very good job with the horse.

"We're only just getting to know the horse, but he ran well to finish third in the cross-country race at Cheltenham in March and everyone knows his liking for the National fences, so I expect that will be the route we go this year, mixing between Cheltenham's cross-country fences, the Becher Chase and seeing how the season pans out."

Plenty of options for Momella

Classy mare **Momella**, previously with Dan Skelton, is another new addition to the Fry ranks. On her final start for Skelton, the six-year-old finished third in the Grade 1 Betway Mersey Novices' Hurdle at Aintree, and it is such form that has Fry purring at the possibility of having a Mares' Hurdle candidate.

He says: "She had some very good form for Dan last year, so she's an exciting addition to the yard. We're going to start off over hurdles initially and see how far she can progress down that route.

"She's got the size and scope to jump a fence as well, so all options are open for her. We've talked about possibly dropping her in trip slightly. On Wetherby's Charlie Hall Chase day, there is a two-mile Listed hurdle for mares, and that's a tentative plan as it stands."

Cotswold plan for American

While it may not have gone to plan for some of Fry's leading lights last season, the trainer is hopeful they can live up to their billing this time around. It is well known how fragile

American is, but the trainer is much happier with the condition of the eight-year-old at present and says: "From where he is now coming into this season we're much happier than we were 12 months ago. We didn't let him down completely over the summer, we decided to keep him in light work as he's so fragile. We didn't want to make a rod for our own back and make it harder to get him back up to full fitness, so we've kept him ticking over quietly. It's made a big difference to him.

"The Ladbrokes Trophy may possibly be on the agenda again this year, but I think the race we'll be gearing towards will be a return to the Cotswold Chase, having gone so well in it last year, as he's more likely to get his slower ground there than at any other time of the year."

Unowhatimeanharry will be 11 in January, but Fry is optimistic he can also return to his best. The trainer says: "He made a good comeback last year and his form just tapered off. He clearly wasn't at his best at Cheltenham in March and we gave him an early break. He could go back to Newbury for a race he won two years ago, the Long Distance Hurdle. He carried a penalty in that last year but I think he escapes a penalty this time."

Test of stamina ideal for Lass

One of last season's success stories, **Acting Lass**, could still have room for improvement over fences. Fry says: "He wants a bit of cut in the ground and it dried out too much at Kempton last time. He'd be one I'd be keen to see again over three miles on soft. There are no immediate plans with him as he was slightly delayed in getting going again this autumn."

Another second-season chaser, **Hell's Kitchen**, is said to be raring to go at home and Fry believes there should be more to come from him over intermediate trips this

Facebook.com/racingpost

Ladbrokes

HARRY FRY
SEABOROUGH, DORSET

	No. of Hrs	Races Run	1st	2nd	3rd	Unpl	Per cent	£1 Level Stake
NH Flat	17	23	5	5	2	11	21.7	-5.42
Hurdles	41	130	30	17	20	63	23.1	-22.26
Chases	22	87	15	12	12	48	17.2	-27.57
Totals	**71**	**240**	**50**	**34**	**34**	**122**	**20.8**	**-55.25**
16-17	87	283	67	42	33	140	23.7	+4.52
15-16	77	239	54	53	30	102	22.6	-11.36

BY MONTH

NH Flat	W-R	Per cent	£1 Level Stake	Hurdles	W-R	Per cent	£1 Level Stake
May	0-1	0.0	-1.00	May	5-11	45.5	+4.83
June	0-0	0.0	0.00	June	0-3	0.0	-3.00
July	0-0	0.0	0.00	July	1-4	25.0	-0.50
August	0-0	0.0	0.00	August	0-2	0.0	-2.00
September	0-0	0.0	0.00	September	1-2	50.0	+4.00
October	0-2	0.0	-2.00	October	6-20	30.0	+4.00
November	1-2	50.0	+0.75	November	9-24	37.5	+3.42
December	0-4	0.0	-4.00	December	2-17	11.8	-10.00
January	0-3	0.0	-3.00	January	2-12	16.7	+0.10
February	0-1	0.0	-1.00	February	0-10	0.0	-10.00
March	3-5	60.0	+3.83	March	1-12	8.3	-9.90
April	1-5	20.0	+1.00	April	3-13	23.1	-3.22

Chases	W-R	Per cent	£1 Level Stake	Totals	W-R	Per cent	£1 Level Stake
May	3-6	50.0	+3.10	May	8-18	44.4	+6.93
June	0-0	0.0	0.00	June	0-3	0.0	-3.00
July	0-2	0.0	-2.00	July	1-6	16.7	-2.50
August	1-4	25.0	-1.25	August	1-6	16.7	-3.25
September	0-2	0.0	-2.00	September	1-4	25.0	+2.00
October	1-8	12.5	-3.00	October	7-30	23.3	-1.00
November	3-14	21.4	-0.67	November	13-40	32.5	+3.50
December	2-12	16.7	+1.00	December	4-33	12.1	-13.00
January	4-13	30.8	-0.75	January	6-28	21.4	-3.65
February	0-10	0.0	-10.00	February	0-21	0.0	-21.00
March	1-7	14.3	-3.00	March	5-24	20.8	-9.07
April	0-9	0.0	-9.00	April	4-27	14.8	-11.22

DISTANCE

Hurdles	W-R	Per cent	£1 Level Stake	Chases	W-R	Per cent	£1 Level Stake
2m-2m3f	17-60	28.3	+5.35	2m-2m3f	4-23	17.4	-5.32
2m4f-2m7f	12-53	22.6	-12.72	2m4f-2m7f	7-32	21.9	-7.25
3m+	1-17	5.9	-14.90	3m+	4-32	12.5	-15.00

TYPE OF RACE

Non-Handicaps	W-R	Per cent	£1 Level Stake	Handicaps	W-R	Per cent	£1 Level Stake
Nov Hrdls	7-35	20.0	-16.63	Nov Hrdls	0-2	0.0	-2.00
Hrdls	6-16	37.5	+0.45	Hrdls	15-75	20.0	-5.25
Nov Chs	3-14	21.4	-5.90	Nov Chs	1-3	33.3	+1.00
Chases	0-10	0.0	-10.00	Chases	5-49	10.2	-28.25
Sell/Claim	1-1	100.0	+0.33	Sell/Claim	0-0	0.0	0.00

RACE CLASS

	W-R	Per cent	£1 Level Stake
Class 1	0-45	0.0	-45.00
Class 2	15-67	22.4	-6.77
Class 3	15-53	28.3	+11.68
Class 4	13-50	26.0	-9.50
Class 5	6-18	33.3	-1.40
Class 6	1-7	14.3	-4.25

FIRST TIME OUT

	W-R	Per cent	£1 Level Stake
Bumpers	4-17	23.5	-2.92
Hurdles	14-35	40.0	+24.19
Chases	6-19	31.6	+2.35
Totals	24-71	33.8	+23.62

DID YOU KNOW?

Fry took out his first licence in October 2012, but by that stage he had already 'trained' a Champion Hurdle winner. His boss Paul Nicholls was happy enough to give the credit for Rock On Ruby's Cheltenham success that year to his assistant, who masterminded the victory from a satellite yard 25 miles away.

Statistics relate to all runners in Britain from May 1, 2017 to April 28, 2018

On the gallops at Harry Fry's Dorset base

Facebook.com/racingpost

campaign, while Galway Plate faller **Drumcliff** will mix and match over hurdles and fences, with the seven-year-old more likely to return to the larger obstacles in the spring.

Air Horse back for more

Admirably consistent grey **Air Horse One** remains set for a continued uphill fight against the handicapper, with a conditions' race at Aintree a possible early target, while the yard will be looking to get Grade 1 winner **Kylemore Lough** back in the winners' enclosure after a disappointing first season with Fry, with a switch to hurdles a possibility before raising his sights.

Jolly's Cracked It, who dead-heated the 2015 Ladbroke Hurdle with Sternrubin, is nearing a return to action after a lengthy lay-off, as is **Any Drama**, who will look to make up for lost time by heading straight over fences.

Asked whether there was a dark horse to follow in his yard, Fry suggests five-year-old French-bred mare **Dalila Du Seuil**, saying: "She won three out of five hurdles in France, including two at Listed level, and will probably go novice chasing. She could be one to keep on side."

Interview by Matthew Butler

SUPER STATS

Although Fry couldn't quite match his personal best figures achieved in the 2016-17 campaign, last season was still a solid one for the Dorset handler with 53 winners on the board and nearly £800,000 in prize-money

Fry's hurdlers do well at Ascot (11-30, 37%, +15.43pt) and Sandown (4-17, 24%, +11.00pt), while his chasers can be backed with confidence at Uttoxeter (6-21, 29%, +13.10pt) and Fontwell (4-8, 50%, +1.99pt)

Fry has his fair share of bumper winners with most of them coming at Wincanton (4-13, 31%, +0.78pt). His record in those races also catches the eye at Bangor (2-3, 67%, +15.00pt) and Market Rasen (2-3, 67%, +2.33pt)

Chasers return a level-stake profit in handicaps (36-164, 22%, +0.18pt) and Listed contests (5-19, 26%, +6.33pt)

March is usually a strong month for the yard and Fry has returned a level-stake profit for this period in each of the last three seasons, including last term (8-29, 28%, +5.43pt)

Fry's hurdlers are best followed over trips ranging from 2m1½f to 2m3f (33-113, 29%, +23.47pt)

He makes good use of amateur riders, with the records of Michael Legg (14-48, 29%, +16.65pt) and Aine O'Connor (10-20, 50%, +30.25pt) standing out

Noel Fehily rides most winners for the yard but it is his record in bumpers that catches the eye (19-73, 26%, +16.71pt)

Altior, Might Bite and Buveur lead vast array of talent for champion

NICKY HENDERSON stops short of saying his current team is the best he has managed, but the underlying message for his rivals is clear as the champion trainer unveils the wealth of talent at his disposal.

Entering the 41st season of his glittering career, Henderson is showing no signs of slowing down and why would he with the favourites for Cheltenham's championship races in Altior, Might Bite and Buveur D'Air.

They were the headline acts in a campaign that provided Henderson with a fifth trainers' title and a personal best of nearly £3.5 million in prize-money.

"Last season was quite special for a lot of reasons," he says. "Obviously there were the big three, but it wasn't just them.

"We had 14 Grade 1 winners among our 141 winners and record prize-money, while the strike-rate was very good as well and we also had 85 individual winners, so they all did their bit, which is important.

"Things can go wrong, which they pretty much did in the first half of last season. It was all about Altior and his wind problem, while Whisper nearly looked like winning the Ladbrokes Trophy, but from Boxing Day onwards, with Might Bite winning the King

George and Buveur winning the Christmas Hurdle, things looked up and then We Have A Dream won the Finale at Chepstow."

Henderson describes his string as being well balanced in all divisions and unsurprisingly has lofty hopes for them.

The sky will remain the limit for **Altior**, who last season added the Queen Mother Champion Chase to his Cheltenham Festival victories in the Sky Bet Supreme Novices' Hurdle and Racing Post Arkle.

"I think it'd be almost certain he'll start in the Tingle Creek and we've been talking about a King George entry," Henderson says of the superstar who is unbeaten in 14 starts over hurdles and fences.

"If it closed today I'd probably put him in it. One day we might need to branch out, but it's very difficult to do that when they put such a good two-mile programme in front of you. I'm pretty sure he'll get further.

"How much I don't know, but unless he gets three miles there's not really any advantage coming out of two miles. It brings you into the Ryanair, which is a great race,

....

December is often a good month for the yard and last season was no different when Henderson sent out more winners than in any other month (26-82, 32%, +19.13pt)

WINNERS IN LAST FIVE SEASONS 141, 154, 81, 129, 124

'Last season was special for a lot of reasons – there were the big three, but it wasn't just them'

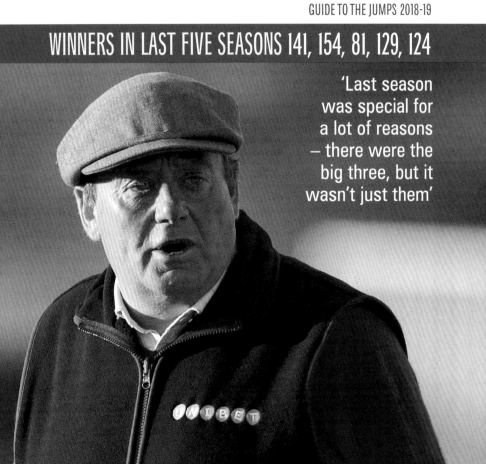

but it's not the Champion Chase or King George."

The master of Seven Barrows, who this summer sent out his 3,000th British jumps winner, does have an ace in the King George VI Chase pack in last year's winner **Might Bite**, who lost nothing in defeat when contributing to an epic Cheltenham Gold Cup with Native River.

He has "grown up a hell of a lot" and Henderson has half an eye on the Jockey Club's £1m Chase Triple Crown, which includes Haydock's Betfair Chase, the King George and the Cheltenham Gold Cup.

"His priority is another King George," he says. "He's got to have a race before that so we'll try to go for the Betfair Chase."

All roads lead to Cheltenham

The third member of Henderson's big three is **Buveur D'Air**, whose season will be geared around Champion Hurdle immortality and emulating the trainer's breakthrough horse See You Then and the mighty Istabraq as three-time winners of hurdling's most prestigious contest.

The Fighting Fifth Hurdle at Newcastle and Kempton's Christmas Hurdle – races the gelding won last term – are inked in again before his historic hurdling bid in March.

A trip to Leopardstown for the Dublin Racing Festival in February is unlikely, however. "I'm not sure he was at his very best at Cheltenham; he's better than that," Henderson says, reflecting on Buveur D'Air's neck victory over Melon.

"I'm full of admiration for that meeting, but I'm not sure an overseas trip and almost certainly a hard race is the right thing when we're trying to get ready for Cheltenham. It's a commendable meeting, but I'm just not sure about the timing as far as we're concerned and his only objective is a third Champion Hurdle."

Terrefort, the horse who shows nothing at home but progressed to Grade 1 victories in the Scilly Isles and Mildmay Novices' Chase at the Grand National meeting, could bid to emulate former Seven Barrows stalwarts Trabolgan and Bobs Worth as second-season chasers to win the Ladbrokes Trophy.

Henderson, who also won his county's most important jumps race with Triolo D'Alene in 2013, is contemplating the Newbury showpiece that used to be known as the Hennessy Gold Cup for Simon Munir and Isaac Souede's five-year-old, whose only defeat in Britain came when he was second in the JLT at Cheltenham.

"He was a big surprise," Henderson says. "He ran in a handicap at Huntingdon off 137 and I was surprised he won that. Two Grade 1s later he made me look rather silly, but I like horses like him – he doesn't show you anything at home. He might start in the intermediate chase at Sandown that Might Bite won last year and then we could have a look at the Ladbrokes Trophy."

'Terrefort was our best novice'

Henderson, who reveals the same owners' L'Ami Serge is out for the campaign, adds: "Terrefort was the best of our novice chasers, while **Brain Power** was second in the Arkle and **Rather Be** was second in the novice handicap chase at the Cheltenham Festival.

"**River Wylde** is also a good horse and won one chase before getting injured, which leaves him in no-man's land, except for intermediate chases, and he'd be good at those. **Divine Spear** is also a lightly raced chaser with improvement in him."

The trainer can also count on Munir and Souede's **Top Notch**, the "amazing" **Theinval**, who won at Ayr in April having run at the track the day before, and the Alan Spence-owned pair **Josses Hill** and **Kilcrea Vale**.

A summer breathing operation may help **O O Seven** win the nice prize he has long threatened to and **Gold Present, Beware**

The Bear and **Vyta Du Roc** could come into the reckoning for the Grand National, a race Henderson is longing to land.

"I haven't got an obvious one for Aintree, but if I can dig one out I will," he says.

Dreaming of Champion Hurdle

Nicky Henderson can have few regrets from the 2017-18 campaign, but **We Have A Dream's** absence from the Triumph Hurdle is perhaps one given what the nascent Champion Hurdle contender went on to do in Aintree's Anniversary 4-Y-O Juvenile Hurdle.

Unbeaten in five starts for Henderson, which also included the Finale at Chepstow, he kick-started a dream Grand National meeting Grade 1 treble for owners Munir and Souede, but there is a sense of what might have been at Cheltenham.

"He won everything he could win, but he got a temperature on the Monday morning of Cheltenham week and that was the end of that, which was pretty bad luck," Henderson says. "The way he won at Aintree makes you think he wouldn't have been far away in the Triumph. He could start in that four-year-old hurdle at Cheltenham in October and then we'll see if he's a Champion Hurdle horse."

Seven years older than We Have A Dream is the popular **My Tent Or Yours**, who has finished second in three Champion Hurdles.

"He's getting on a bit, but he's definitely not retired and I think he'll go for the International Hurdle, which he won so memorably last year," adds Henderson, who labels Grade 2 Select Hurdle winner **Call Me Lord** an "interesting one".

He adds: "The only thing is he has to go right-handed. We could try going left-handed again, but I'm not sure we will. There's the Elite Hurdle, but he proved he stayed two and a half miles at Sandown, which surprised me, and he looked pretty good doing it too."

Soul Emotion, two from two for the stable since arriving from France, could also

Buveur D'Air battles it out with Melon to win the Champion Hurdle for the second time

A stunning sight as Nicky Henderson's string make their way through the woods

be a dark horse for staying hurdles, while the trainer is keeping faith with **Charli Parcs** and also has plenty of belief in **Style De Garde**, who finished a fine second in the Fred Winter under a big weight.

Crack team for novice chases

If there is one department Nicky Henderson is drooling about it is his novice chasers and he thinks the latest innovation to his historic Seven Barrows stable can help them fulfil their potential.

"They could be good fun this season," he says. "We've got a new carpet schooling ground, which we're having a lot of fun on. This time last year I wouldn't have schooled anything because the ground was too quick, but all the novices have been schooled already."

Beat That, **Monbeg Legend** and **Brave**

Eagle got the ball rolling through the summer and are part of an enviable squad covering the 2m speedsters to those with more stamina.

As for the stayers, Henderson says: "**Santini**, who won the Grade 1 Sefton at Aintree, and **Ok Corral**, who was second in the Albert Bartlett, are two cracking big horses who were only messing about over hurdles, while **Chef Des Obeaux** did little wrong.

"**Mr Whipped** could also come into that, although I don't know how far he'll stay. **Thomas Campbell** had a peculiar way of jumping hurdles, but we've done a back operation and I'm optimistic about him."

Over 2m4f, the trainer reckons **On The Blind Side** "could be seriously good", while there are similarly high hopes for **Diese Des**

Bieffes, Pacific De Baune, William Henry, Burrows Edge, Burbank, Champ and Duke Debarry at around that trip.

Pacier types include the soft-ground-loving Whatswrongwithyou "a talented creature who travels so well in his races and wants a strongly run two miles", Claimantakinforgan, Jenkins and Lough Derg Spirit, who is "well schooled and very forward".

Reigning Supreme and Cultivator, a winner in the Bobs Worth colours at Worcester recently, are others expected to fire, as is Caribean Boy.

"He's only four, but he's not a novice over hurdles, so could go chasing and is a fine, big, powerful figure," Henderson adds. "That's a pretty strong team and those three-milers look good, but so do the rest!"

New names to look out for

The summer months can be just as busy for jumps trainers and Henderson spent the off-season stocking up on new talent to go alongside his existing pool of promising youngsters.

"We've got a lot of beautiful young horses," says the trainer, consistently a force in novice hurdles and bumpers.

"Dickie Diver was impressive in his point-to-point in Ireland, while Birchdale won his only point. He's lovely and came from the same academy in Northern Ireland as Rathhill, who was second in his.

"I Can't Explain, who was here last year, is also a point winner and a magnificent-looking beast, and Champagne Platinum and Champagne Mystery are other recruits from Ireland worth looking out for."

Lecale's Article is a "gorgeous horse", while Henderson holds the four-year-old **Angels Breath** in high regard, which also applies to **Beyondthestorm**, who will run in the famous Flat colours of Cheveley Park Stud, and **Falco Blitz.**

Interconnected and **Foxworthy** have come from point-to-points in Britain.

"I think they'll all go over hurdles," says Henderson, who has a bright brigade of bumper horses to join them.

"**Gallahers Cross** is a lovely individual, we like **Morning Vicar** a lot and we've all been waiting for **Pym**. **Before Midnight** is another we think plenty of, while **Laughing Luis** won two bumpers over the summer and you can forget **Mister Fisher**'s last run at Aintree.

"**Palixandre** disappointed on his only start, but he's a nice type and the same goes for **Downtown Getaway**, **Precious Cargo** and **Clarendon Street**."

The good-looking **Dream Du Grand Val**, this season's Million In Mind horse, has arrived from France and **El Kaldoun** is an "exciting prospect for the enthusiastic Middleham Park team".

Humphrey Bogart and **The Cashel Man** are Flat-breds expected to shine over hurdles, while Henderson's three-year-old crop is shaping up nicely.

He says: "At this time of the year I normally don't seem to have a juvenile hurdler in sight, but somehow they appear. I didn't know We Have A Dream or Apple's Shakira were as good as they were at this time last year and was moaning I didn't have any juveniles, but we seem to have a few in place at the moment and they include **Never Adapt**, **Adjali**, **Style De Vole** – a half-brother to **Style De Garde** – **Fusil Raffles** and **Lisheen Castle**."

Mighty mares ready for battle

British racing's attempts to improve the jumping programme for fillies and mares will always be met with approval from

SUPER STATS

Henderson fired in a solid 141 winners last season but of more significance was his prize-money total of nearly £3.5 million, a personal best which saw him comfortably land a fifth trainers' championship

Henderson's northern raids are rare but the hint should be taken when his inmates are sent on the long trek from Lambourn. His strike-rates at Newcastle (3-4, 75%, +2.83pt), Kelso (3-5, 60%, +6.11pt) and Carlisle (1-1, 100%, +0.91pt) over the past five seasons are impressive

He sends out most of his winners at Kempton (50-196, 26%, +27.12pt) but of the tracks where he regularly enjoys success, his strike-rate and level-stake return make for better reading at Sandown (38-128, 30%, +14.97pt), Doncaster (25-72, 35%, +2.17pt) and Aintree (26-119, 22%, +25.11pt)

Henderson's hurdlers perform well at Warwick (11-32, 34%, +17.79pt), while his chasers strike more often than not at Huntingdon (8-15, 53%, +1.54pt)

Henderson sends out plenty of winners in bumpers and boasts an impressive record in such races at Southwell (9-16, 56%, +10.13pt), Market Rasen (5-11, 45%, +8.13pt), Worcester (6-19, 32%, +7.08pt) and Fakenham (4-5, 80%, +3.15pt)

Nico de Boinville's mounts returned a level-stake loss overall last term but his record on the yard's hurdlers made for solid reading (40-125, 32%, +4.46pt)

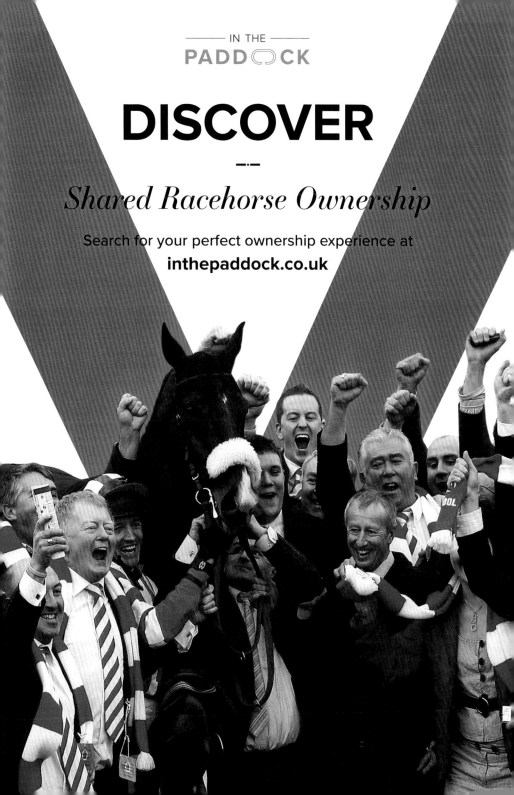

NICKY HENDERSON
UPPER LAMBOURN, BERKS

	No. of Hrs	Races Run	1st	2nd	3rd	Unpl	Per cent	£1 Level Stake
NH Flat	36	51	11	8	9	23	21.6	-20.20
Hurdles	103	327	93	44	28	161	28.4	-17.50
Chases	48	141	36	29	12	64	25.5	-38.79
Totals	**154**	**519**	**140**	**81**	**49**	**248**	**27.0**	**-76.49**
16-17	170	595	149	94	67	283	25.0	-107.37
15-16	151	412	81	53	49	229	19.7	-99.03

BY MONTH

NH Flat	W-R	Per cent	£1 Level Stake	Hurdles	W-R	Per cent	£1 Level Stake
May	2-5	40.0	+1.50	May	4-16	25.0	-3.49
June	3-5	60.0	+3.60	June	5-9	55.6	+1.15
July	0-1	0.0	-1.00	July	3-7	42.9	-0.13
August	0-0	0.0	0.00	August	1-2	50.0	+2.33
September	0-0	0.0	0.00	September	1-3	33.3	-1.09
October	0-3	0.0	-3.00	October	3-17	17.6	-7.75
November	2-7	28.6	-3.17	November	13-47	27.7	-4.16
December	0-4	0.0	-4.00	December	19-51	37.3	+21.08
January	2-7	28.6	+1.00	January	14-38	36.8	+11.70
February	0-8	0.0	-8.00	February	10-44	22.7	-17.15
March	1-3	33.3	-0.75	March	8-43	18.6	-22.90
April	1-8	12.5	-6.38	April	12-50	24.0	+2.93

Chases	W-R	Per cent	£1 Level Stake	Totals	W-R	Per cent	£1 Level Stake
May	3-13	23.1	0.00	May	9-34	26.5	-1.99
June	3-7	42.9	-1.17	June	11-21	52.4	+3.58
July	0-5	0.0	-5.00	July	3-13	23.1	-6.13
August	1-3	33.3	+2.50	August	2-5	40.0	+4.83
September	0-0	0.0	0.00	September	1-3	33.3	-1.09
October	0-5	0.0	-5.00	October	3-25	12.0	-15.75
November	7-27	25.9	-13.53	November	22-81	27.2	-20.86
December	7-27	25.9	+2.05	December	26-82	31.7	+19.13
January	4-13	30.8	-4.31	January	20-58	34.5	+8.39
February	3-8	37.5	-2.51	February	13-60	21.7	-27.66
March	3-16	18.8	-7.60	March	12-62	19.4	-31.25
April	5-17	29.4	-4.22	April	18-75	24.0	-7.670

DISTANCE

Hurdles	W-R	Per cent	£1 Level Stake	Chases	W-R	Per cent	£1 Level Stake
2m-2m3f	44-153	28.8	-26.87	2m-2m3f	13-32	40.6	-6.11
2m4f-2m7f	41-130	31.5	+22.34	2m4f-2m7f	16-70	22.9	-20.80
3m+	7-42	16.7	-12.50	3m+	7-39	17.9	-11.88

TYPE OF RACE

Non-Handicaps	W-R	Per cent	£1 Level Stake	Handicaps	W-R	Per cent	£1 Level Stake
Nov Hrdls	40-113	35.4	+0.17	Nov Hrdls	1-12	8.3	-5.00
Hrdls	30-63	47.6	+21.32	Hrdls	18-132	13.6	-35.04
Nov Chs	14-46	30.4	-15.41	Nov Chs	1-10	10.0	-7.38
Chases	11-19	57.9	+4.67	Chases	9-57	15.8	-14.17
Sell/Claim	0-0	0.0	0.00	Sell/Claim	0-0	0.0	0.00

RACE CLASS

	W-R	Per cent	£1 Level Stake
Class 1	38-146	26.0	-32.31
Class 2	14-79	17.7	-4.61
Class 3	20-98	20.4	-40.13
Class 4	54-152	35.5	+5.11
Class 5	8-30	26.7	-7.48
Class 6	6-14	42.9	+2.93

FIRST TIME OUT

	W-R	Per cent	£1 Level Stake
Bumpers	9-36	25.0	-8.92
Hurdles	25-79	31.6	+17.85
Chases	13-39	33.3	-3.94
Totals	47-154	30.5	+4.99

DID YOU KNOW?

With Nicky Henderson crowned champion trainer for the last two seasons, it's easy to forget he won his first title in 1985-86, his second in 1986-87 and then had to wait 26 years for his third, while David Elsworth (1 title), Martin Pipe (15), David Nicholson (2) and Paul Nicholls (7) made hay.

Statistics relate to all runners in Britain from May 1, 2017 to April 28, 2018

Facebook.com/racingpost

Henderson, who has assembled a typically powerful set of the fairer sex.

"We have a good bunch," says the champion trainer, whose hopes in senior mares' chases will be carried by the capable **Casablanca Mix**, while he is particularly sweet on **With Discretion** and **Kupatana** for novice events over fences.

Henderson continues to think the world of last term's smart juvenile **Apple's Shakira**.

"She's done extremely well over the summer and could go to the very top, while I love **Dame De Compagnie** and **Countister**," he continues.

"**Verdana Blue** will have a Flat prep before a Listed hurdle at Kempton next month and is very good on quick ground over two miles.

"**Sunshade** has also improved a hell of a lot, and will probably stay over hurdles, but she would jump a fence."

Exciting youngsters

A clutch of youngsters are also exciting Henderson, who adds: "Thank god **Daphne Du Clos** is back. She was very good in her bumpers and I thought she'd be one for the Champion Bumper, but she got a leg. She's had a good year off and jumps beautifully. She could be rather useful.

Champion Chase hero Altior powers up the steep gallops at Seven Barrows

I'm absolutely mad about **Lust For Glory**, while **Barbados Blue** and **Sunrise Ruby** were impressive in their bumpers.

"**Epatante** has come from France and is beautiful, as is the gorgeous **Fructine**, who won on the Flat over there.

"Then there's **She Mite Bite**, who is no relation to Might Bite, but some clever Irishman probably thought if he called her that he'd fool that Henderson into buying her and he did!"

Yellow Dockets is another to follow and **Jillythejet** has schooled well recently under none other than ITV presenter Luke Harvey.

Interview by James Burn

THE LOWDOWN PHILIP HOBBS

It's all systems go for improved season with squad in better shape

THE previous jumps season undoubtedly didn't pan out quite as Philip Hobbs would have envisaged, but extenuating circumstances took over. The master trainer's Sandhill Racing Stables fell foul to a bad bug in the height of winter which persisted for some time.

Winners and prize-money were down on what we've come to expect, but so were the quantity of runners, with Hobbs fielding his lowest amount since 2001.

Sandhill still toasted a famous victory in December, though, with Contented's victory at Sedgefield meaning that Hobbs had now saddled a winner at every National Hunt track in Great Britain.

When viruses strike you have no choice but to keep positive, and that is precisely what the Somerset handler has done, who says: "We weren't particularly healthy from Christmas onwards, but the horses seem to be showing they're in better condition now which will be a massive help for the season ahead. We're hoping for much more this time around."

Stable stalwarts back for more

Unfortunately we won't be seeing the likes of Three Faces West and Poppy Kay next season, with both now retired, but Hobbs has welcomed back plenty of familiar faces we have got to know well over the years, with some admittedly more difficult to campaign than others.

There have been few better servants to the yard in recent years than **Village Vic**, an 11-year-old who is being prepared for a hunter chasing campaign under new owner-rider David Maxwell. Hobbs says: "He's a grand old horse who's been struggling with his handicap mark. He'll go hunter chasing and there should be some good opportunities for him there.

"**Royal Regatta** is ten now and not getting any younger, but he's in good form. We'll be looking for a race at Ascot because he always goes well there, or the Old Roan Chase at Aintree in October," says Hobbs. "Although his hurdles mark is far lower [17lb less than his chase mark], at his age I wouldn't want to go in that direction.

The three racecourses at which Hobbs stands out in terms of total winners over the past five seasons are Worcester (30-117, 26%, +36.44pt), Newbury (20-107, 19%, +35.63pt) and Stratford (16-63, 25%, +25.78pt)

Facebook.com/racingpost

WINNERS IN LAST FIVE SEASONS 63, 111, 113, 102, 106

In the north, Hobbs is best followed with his chasers at Wetherby (4-15, 27%, +7.08pt) and Musselburgh (2-2, 100%, +2.53pt)

'The horses seem to be showing they're in better condition now which will be a massive help'

"**Garde La Victoire** is back but remains difficult to place. He's very decent but isn't quite up to level-weight races so we have to target handicaps. There isn't a plan as such. You find races as you go because with his rating there aren't many for him.

"We've decided **Wait For Me** will stay over hurdles, with three miles being his trip. Despite his victory in a chase at Worcester, he never looked happy over fences.

"With **War Sound's** rating of 136, you're stuck between a level-weight novice and a handicap. It was frustrating he didn't win last season but hopefully he'll win a race before too long."

It appears Hobbs will have a few contenders at Chepstow's curtain-raising meeting on October 13, and we could see **Rock The Kasbah**, who was the yard's highest-earning horse last season.

Philip Hobbs with Defi Du Seuil, who could go chasing this season

Hobbs says: "We are looking at Chepstow with him. The race he won last year on the Saturday will be the plan again, I think. He could be a National horse as he stays very well – he definitely wants better ground so I don't imagine he'd be running in the winter.

"I'm looking at the 2m3f handicap chase on Chepstow's opening weekend with **Verni** as well. I was very pleased with his run at Uttoxeter. He's still lightly raced for his age and is in very good form. Now he's won his novice chase he's going to have to go back to handicaps and quite possibly that will be his race.

"**I'm A Game Changer** was progressive last season and seems to be going the right way. He could start off in a hurdle race at Chepstow but, although it's not decided, he's one who could eventually be novice chasing further down the line.

One horse who showed great potential last season for the stable was **Gumball**, and his second to We Have A Dream in Aintree's Grade 1 juvenile hurdle in the spring was a big step forward from previous form. After running into the gifted Apple's Shakira at Cheltenham in October last year, a return to Prestbury Park is being pinpointed again for the Terry Warner-owned gelding.

Hobbs says: "He'll remain over hurdles in the short term. There's a four-year-old conditions hurdle at Cheltenham's October meeting which will be his first aim and we'll plot a route after that."

Ozzie The Oscar is a horse that is progressing nicely through the chasing ranks and put in a fine display when dispatching a useful rival in San Benedeto on his last start, which puts him in the mix for another nice early season pot.

The trainer says: "That was a good performance at Warwick. He's going in the right direction very quickly and the Haldon Gold Cup at Exeter in November is the race we have in

Facebook.com/racingpost

mind for him, but whether he'll run before then I'm not sure. He wouldn't want it too soft."

Returning pack to pay their way

After winning an Aintree Pertemps Handicap Hurdle Series Qualifier in good fashion last November, **Louis' Vac Pouch** looked a horse capable of further improvement. He was kept fresh for a tilt at the Pertemps Final at the Cheltenham Festival when well touted but disappointed that day, likely being among those affected by health issues in the stable.

Hobbs hopes we are yet to see the best of the six-year-old, and says: "He won his handicap at Aintree in good style but we were disappointed with his two runs in the spring at Cheltenham and back at Aintree.

"However, none of our horses were running particularly well at the time so hopefully he will move back in the right direction now. Chasing could be an option but we are yet to decide.

"One who had a setback was **Strong Pursuit**. We had issues with him after his beginners' chase win over Beat That so he didn't run again last season. He's still lightly raced for his age and he should be back around Christmas.

"**Gala Ball** had an issue last November which ruled him out for the season so he hasn't raced since March 2017. He'll be running in the top two-mile and two-and-a-half-mile handicap chases. Soft ground suits him well.

"We were extremely happy with **For Good Measure** after his run behind Cyrname in the Pendil Novices' Chase at Kempton in the spring. He'll probably start off in a two-and-a-half-mile chase and go from there. He wants decent ground and I think he has a good mark over fences."

Westend Story looked a horse with plenty of ability when finishing fifth in the 2016 Champion Bumper behind Ballyandy, and has remarkably started favourite in each of his seven starts since. Despite failing to win in the first four of those, he looks to be putting his talent to better use now with two wins from his last three outings, and Hobbs says: "I'd hope he can make into a decent novice chaser but he's yet to school over fences so he'll run in a hurdle race or two first."

Defi out to bounce back

The sky looked the limit for **Defi Du Seuil** after his outstanding juvenile campaign in 2016-17, which saw him win the Triumph Hurdle and notch seven wins from seven starts including three Grade 1 victories, marking him down as the dominant force of his generation.

We saw him only twice last year, however, with the son of Voix Du Nord well beaten in the Coral Hurdle at Ascot and in the Irish Champion Hurdle at Leopardstown.

Life can be tough for five-year-olds but, although difficult to gauge, the stable virus must have affected Defi Du Seuil in some way.

Hobbs reports his stable star to be going well at home, though, with a novice chasing campaign very much under consideration. He says: "He's in good form again and all is going well. I'm inclined to put a line through last season. We're yet to school him over fences but there's every chance chasing could be on the horizon."

Novice chase possibilities

The yard have plenty of other options at their disposal for novice chases this year, headed by **No Comment**, who retains his novice status after finishing sixth in the National Hunt Chase at the Cheltenham Festival on his most recent start. Quite well fancied by many that day, Hobbs wasn't the only one who expected more from his seven-year-old,

PHILIP HOBBS
WITHYCOMBE, SOMERSET

	No. of Hrs	Races Run	1st	2nd	3rd	Unpl	Per cent	£1 Level Stake
NH Flat	29	47	13	4	5	25	27.7	+34.45
Hurdles	94	265	36	34	39	156	13.6	-100.88
Chases	51	148	14	32	22	80	9.5	-95.51
Totals	**143**	**460**	**63**	**70**	**66**	**261**	**13.7**	**-161.94**
16-17	157	587	107	92	66	322	18.2	-101.41
15-16	144	523	113	82	81	247	21.6	-59.98

BY MONTH

NH Flat	W-R	Per cent	£1 Level Stake	Hurdles	W-R	Per cent	£1 Level Stake
May	1-2	50.0	0.00	May	4-16	25.0	-4.37
June	1-3	33.3	+0.50	June	0-7	0.0	-7.00
July	1-1	100.0	+0.36	July	0-11	0.0	-11.00
August	0-0	0.0	0.00	August	2-6	33.3	+5.00
September	0-0	0.0	0.00	September	3-13	23.1	+4.33
October	1-2	50.0	+4.00	October	6-38	15.8	-16.82
November	2-4	50.0	+10.00	November	7-46	15.2	+21.75
December	0-5	0.0	-5.00	December	1-20	5.0	-18.00
January	1-2	50.0	+5.00	January	4-17	23.5	-7.84
February	1-6	16.7	-4.17	February	0-18	0.0	-18.00
March	2-8	25.0	+1.25	March	3-30	10.0	-21.25
April	3-14	21.4	+22.50	April	6-43	14.0	-27.69

Chases	W-R	Per cent	£1 Level Stake	Totals	W-R	Per cent	£1 Level Stake
May	1-2	50.0	0.00	May	4-16	25.0	-4.37
June	1-3	33.3	+0.50	June	0-7	0.0	-7.00
July	1-1	100.0	+0.36	July	0-11	0.0	-11.00
August	0-0	0.0	0.00	August	2-6	33.3	+5.00
September	0-0	0.0	0.00	September	3-13	23.1	+4.33
October	1-2	50.0	+4.00	October	6-38	15.8	-16.82
November	2-4	50.0	+10.00	November	7-46	15.2	+21.75
December	0-5	0.0	-5.00	December	1-20	5.0	-18.00
January	1-2	50.0	+5.00	January	4-17	23.5	-7.84
February	1-6	16.7	-4.17	February	0-18	0.0	-18.00
March	2-8	25.0	+1.25	March	3-30	10.0	-21.25
April	3-14	21.4	+22.50	April	6-43	14.0	-27.69

Statistics relate to all runners in Britain from May 1, 2017 to April 28, 2018

DISTANCE

Hurdles	W-R	Per cent	£1 Level Stake	Chases	W-R	Per cent	£1 Level Stake
2m-2m3f	12-138	8.7	-48.79	2m-2m3f	4-41	9.8	-23.40
2m4f-2m7f	21-99	21.2	-36.93	2m4f-2m7f	7-61	11.5	-33.86
3m+	3-28	10.7	-15.17	3m+	3-46	6.5	-38.25

TYPE OF RACE

Non-Handicaps	W-R	Per cent	£1 Level Stake	Handicaps	W-R	Per cent	£1 Level Stake
Nov Hrdls	17-80	21.3	+6.97	Nov Hrdls	0-2	0.0	-2.00
Hrdls	5-44	11.4	-33.44	Hrdls	14-135	10.4	-68.42
Nov Chs	6-32	18.8	-13.49	Nov Chs	1-12	8.3	-8.50
Chases	1-7	14.3	-5.00	Chases	6-78	7.7	-49.52
Sell/Claim	0-1	0.0	-1.00	Sell/Claim	0-0	0.0	0.00

RACE CLASS

	W-R	Per cent	£1 Level Stake
Class 1	2-43	4.7	-35.13
Class 2	4-47	8.5	-34.13
Class 3	19-140	13.6	-66.08
Class 4	23-169	13.6	-48.64
Class 5	11-48	22.9	+26.15
Class 6	4-13	30.8	-4.14

FIRST TIME OUT

	W-R	Per cent	£1 Level Stake
Bumpers	8-29	27.6	+11.75
Hurdles	9-77	11.7	-40.10
Chases	5-37	13.5	-16.97
Totals	22-143	15.4	-45.32

DID YOU KNOW?

Philip Hobbs rode winners in point-to-points and as an amateur, then 160 as a professional jockey, but in his day Hobbs was also a decent showjumper. In this respect, however, he was overshadowed by his wife Sarah, who, having been successful pointing and over jumps, also scored on the Flat and was a member of the English team in the European junior three-day eventing championships in Rome in 1974.

and he says: "I was disappointed with him in the four-miler but he did run well at Sandown the time before. He isn't one to give up on just yet. Hopefully he can win a nice novice chase by the end of the season."

The seven-year-old **Sternrubin** has been campaigned openly in recent years, plying his trade over hurdles, fences and on the Flat. He too has preserved his novice status over fences, and that is where he will start off this season according to Hobbs: "He hasn't won a chase yet so that will be his route for the time being. He needs to go right-handed.

"I'd imagine **Jerrysback** will be novice chasing at some point but he hasn't schooled

Philip Hobbs supervises during a schooling session at his stables in Somerset

over fences yet. We'll have to see how he fares.

"Tim Syder has a nice six-year-old called **Springtown Lake**. He should improve this year and is one who could be novice chasing.

"**Steely Addition** won a couple of hurdle races last season and will probably start over hurdles first, but could also be novice chasing after."

Who's My Jockey could be another interesting recruit to fences. The five-year-old is currently rated 136 over hurdles and boasts an eyecatching pedigree as a half-brother to the legendary Hurricane Fly, the winning-most hurdler of all time with 22 Grade 1 successes.

Hobbs says: "He's in good form and we'll start him off in a handicap hurdle before

possibly going novice chasing. He doesn't want the ground too soft."

Next generation of novice hurdlers

Hobbs tasted Listed success at Cheltenham in November last season with **Crooks Peak** following up his debut bumper win at Ffos Las in good style which led to connections seeking top-level riches in the Champion Bumper at the Cheltenham Festival. He finished down the field that day, but remains a promising type and could be one to keep onside in novice hurdles this season.

Hobbs says: "He has plenty of ability and isn't short of speed. He'll be starting off over two miles in the middle of October.

"**Melekhov** will also begin in two-mile novice hurdles," Hobbs adds. "He had two wins and a second from three bumpers last season and looks pretty useful.

"We had another nice bumper winner last season in **Tidal Flow**, who was bred by Richard Johnson and Sarah Hobbs. After his debut victory we were waiting for the ground to dry out and then he ran at Wincanton on ground that had probably quickened up too much. He's a nice horse who should do well in novice hurdles this season. Two and a half miles might be his trip."

"We had one or two health issues with **Dostal Phil** after his debut fourth at Bangor last season where he was beaten at odds-on but he's fine now. We'll start in novice hurdles over a stiff two miles."

Keep Gosheven onside

Gosheven was last seen finishing fifth in a classy Cheltenham novice hurdle behind Nicky Henderson's Diese Des Bieffes. Fergal O'Brien's talented Poetic Rhythm was also in behind that day, and Hobbs says: "He's improved massively in each of his three runs and I'm really looking forward to him. I think he's one of our best youngsters."

Interview by Robbie Wilders

SUPER STATS

The winners dipped for Philip Hobbs last season with just 63 winners on the board and, with a lack of top-class performers at his disposal, he did well to break £700,000 in prize-money

Hobbs hurdlers do well at Newton Abbot (19-77, 25%, +9.83pt) and are also worth watching out for at Perth (4-5, 80%, +7.13pt)

Over hurdles, the mounts of Micheal Nolan (10-72, 14%, +17.87pt) and James Best (4-39, 10%, +2.57pt) often oblige at rewarding odds

Hobbs sends out most of his bumper winners at Warwick (6-22, 27%, -0.35pt) and Newton Abbot (5-13, 38%, +1.86pt) but they have been best followed at Wincanton over the past five seasons (4-17, 24%, +23.25pt)

Hobbs places his string well in graduation chases (3-8, 38%, +7.33pt) and graduation bumpers (5-11, 45%, +4.44pt)

Hobbs has enjoyed a fruitful association with Richard Johnson over the years and their partnership in bumpers more than pays its way (33-114, 29%, +28.04pt)

Although Hobbs's runners returned a level-stake loss in April last year (11-70, 16%, -12.69pt), it was one of his best months in terms of winners and strike-rate. It is typically a strong period for the yard and the yard's runners in that month returned profits in 2017 (14-62, 23%, +7.01pt) and 2015 (15-63, 24%, +5.23pt)

TRAIN ON THE BEST

Established for 30 years

Fully Synthetic Surfaces

We Specialise In
- Gallops   - Lunge Pens
- Arenas   - Turnout Pens

Free Site Visits
& Quotations

 +44 (0)1282 834970   info@equestriansurfaces.co.uk   www.equestriansurfaces.co.uk

Business as usual as Cloudy Dream leads team full of promise

AFTER a couple of relatively quiet years rebuilding his team after the loss of the horses owned by Paul and Clare Rooney, it was nearly business as usual for Donald McCain last season.

He came agonisingly close to reaching a hundred winners for the fifth time in his career, his final tally being 98, but the key to his season was the way his horses ran consistently well throughout and have continued to do so during the summer campaign.

Admittedly he lacked a real star. There were plenty with potential, but no proven top-class performers to go for championship races and few good enough to be competitive in the big Saturday handicaps.

That changed during the summer, however, when Trevor Hemmings – one of McCain's longest-standing owners and a great supporter of northern jumping – made the decision to send him Cloudy Dream and Mount Mews, who were formerly with Malcolm and then Ruth Jefferson.

"The 'boss' has been very good to me and sent me two lovely horses, so I'm very lucky," McCain says.

"Everyone knows about **Cloudy Dream** – he's a very good horse and we'll probably start him off in the Old Roan Chase at Aintree."

Surprisingly the talented eight-year-old has won only three times over fences, but the list of horses who have beaten him reads like a who's who of British chasing. During his short career as a chaser he has come up against the likes of Buveur d'Air, Altior, Fox Norton and in last season's Ryanair was third to Balko Des Flos and Un De Sceaux.

His trainer adds: "After Aintree we'll see what there is for him. He's not short of speed – he showed that when he was an unlucky second in the Scottish Champion Hurdle – so I'd say we'll keep him to less than three miles but nothing is set in stone."

The year-younger **Mount Mews** won three of his eight races over hurdles, including a defeat of Sam Spinner in a 2m novice at Kelso, and was also runner-up in the Grade 1 novice at Aintree in 2017.

Things didn't quite go his way last season. He was short of top-class as a hurdler and so he went chasing, winning a small race at Doncaster on his debut before two good

....

McCain hasn't found it easy in recent years but last season's tally of 98 winners, earning more than £800,000, was a big step back in the right direction

WINNERS IN LAST FIVE SEASONS 98, 80, 53, 99, 142

'He's a very good horse and we'll probably start him in the Old Roan Chase at Aintree'

efforts in defeat at Town Moor and in the Sodexo Reynoldstown Chase at Ascot when third to the prolific winner Black Corton.

That win means he is ineligible for novice chases this season so handicaps or intermediate races now beckon.

McCain says: "His win makes it that bit harder for him as he's into handicaps with only three races over fences under his belt. It will be a matter of getting some practice for him. He's rated 139 over fences so that's a workable mark and I'd expect either he or **Testify** will start off in the Colin Parker Intermediate Chase at Carlisle, although that's two and a half and he'll stay three miles.

One to back first time out

"Testify started off well over fences last season winning three small-field races but things didn't work out for him on the big occasions. He wants soft ground and probably a small field.

"He's always gone well first time out, which is unusual for one of mine as they usually improve for a run. There are a few quirks in his family, his half-brother Wymott was the same as he always went well first time.

"He's best on testing ground and although the Colin Parker at two and a half would be short enough for him as he probably needs three miles now, it would be a suitable race."

Another prolific winner for McCain has been **Dear Sire**, who won seven times over hurdles and then won first time out over fences at Cartmel in July.

His trainer says: "He's done really well for us and he didn't do much wrong when he fell at Cartmel second time over fences as there was a bad patch of ground and they omitted that fence in the later chases.

"We ran him over two and a half because Cartmel did away with their two-mile chases but a strongly run two miles is his trip and he doesn't want to hit the front too soon. I'll back off him a bit as we go into the winter, but hopefully Musselburgh will still have their two-mile novice chases so he'll be going up there later on. He likes the good ground.

"He was a bit unlucky over hurdles at Aintree this year as the horse in front of him fell at the last and then rolled underneath him. He's not the biggest but he's done really well. I bought him from Stuart Crawford after he had finished second in a bumper at Sedgefield. He looked a hardy little horse who could stand some racing and give his owner some fun, but he's turned out to be really good. He is as hard as nails."

Another prolific winning hurdler in the McCain team is **William Of Orange**, who has enjoyed a fine year already with wins in some decent handicaps at Haydock, Kelso and Cartmel.

His trainer says: "He's a bit in and out, he has his good and his bad days – you can often tell saddling him up what sort of mood he's in.

"He doesn't want it too soft, but he'll stay three miles and he needs to go left-handed. He jumps well enough to go chasing, but he has a few aches and pains so I don't know what he'd be like afterwards if I ran him over fences."

Haydock mission

Chti Balko is another decent handicap hurdler in the Bankhouse team but as his trainer says: "He's his own worst enemy as he rarely runs a bad race so just keeps going up in the ratings. He's on 142 now, but he's very effective around Haydock and I expect he'll go for the handicap hurdle at the Betfair meeting.

"I was considering sending him chasing but he was a very average jumper of a hurdle when we first started although he's very slick now so I think we'll stay hurdling with him."

Chasing though is very much on the cards for **Uppertown Prince**, who won two novice

THE RACING POST APP.
HOME TO RACING'S TOP INFORMATION.
HOME TO RACING'S TOP BOOKIES.

Why continually flit between apps when racing's best information
and top bookies are sitting side by side in one app? Better yet, you
can remain logged in to all four bookies at once, and simply switch
account to bet with the best odds. Home sweet home, as they say.

RACING POST

WHEN YOU BET ON RACING,
YOU CAN BET ON RACING POST.

hurdles and ended last season by finishing fourth to Santini in the Doom Bar Sefton Novices' Hurdle at Aintree.

Prince held in high regard

"He's a very smart horse," McCain says. "We probably rode him wrong when he was second in a Grade 2 at Haydock but that was a really good run at Aintree. He's going to make a smart novice staying chaser this season. He's already won a point-to-point, he's a good jumper and he wants slow ground. Apart from Cloudy Dream and Mount Mews he's the one I'm most looking forward to."

"Another going chasing is **Mr McGo**, who was a good novice hurdler two seasons ago but had a slight setback early on so we didn't run him. He'll go over fences. He's won a

point-to-point, he stays well and wants very soft ground. He could be an above average novice over fences in time.

"I could have got him back ready to run last spring, but the ground would have gone so there didn't seem much point."

Another winning hurdler set to go chasing this season is **Fin And Game**, who is a three-parts brother to the trainer's Neptune winner Peddlers Cross, who was also pretty smart over fences.

McCain says: "He won his first novice hurdle in fine style, but he's still immature and learning his job. He's a big horse and, although I haven't schooled him yet, it's highly likely he'll go chasing. He doesn't lack a gear, so two or two and a half will be his trip."

One horse close to the trainer's heart is

Point-to-point winner Mr McGo is a bright prospect for novice chases

Lastbutnotleast, who was the last horse bought by his legendary father Ginger. She showed some smart form as a hurdler and was expected to do even better as a chaser last season, but although she won at Haydock things didn't quite work out for her after that.

McCain explains: "She had a hard race when beating Jonniesofa at Haydock after Christmas and never really got over it. The second is a decent horse, but never ran again and she never seemed to quite get over it.

"Nevertheless, she's won a Listed race over hurdles and got a place in a three-runner Listed chase so she's got her black type. She's a good mare on her day and will go for mares' races and staying handicap chases. She stays well and needs very soft ground."

Promising young guns

In contrast, McCain also has a couple of promising juvenile hurdlers who already have winning form this season, **Ormesher** being unbeaten after wins at Cartmel and Uttoxeter and **Breakfast** winning at Market Rasen on his jumps debut.

Their trainer said: "Ormesher is tiny, but he's won two and coped with the very soft ground when he won at Cartmel. I don't think he wants it that soft, but he stays well. Breakfast won first time and sometimes the early season juvenile form works out so I expect one of the two will be running in the Wensleydale at Wetherby's Charlie Hall meeting."

Although this pair came from the Flat, McCain's normal source of young stock is from the Irish point-to-point field, and as usual he has some new faces from that sphere who will be running this winter.

New names from pointing field

Gaelik Coast was bought for £110,000 at Goffs Aintree Sale and McCain said: "He's a French-bred four-year-old who won his only

SUPER STATS

Many of McCain's winners come at Bangor, where he also enjoys a solid strike-rate and profitable level-stake return (53-278, 19%, +12.43pt)

Bangor aside, McCain's best level-stake returns with his hurdlers come at Stratford (8-34, 24%, +22.00pt) and Cartmel (21-89, 24%, +12.50pt)

Chasers can be backed with confidence at Worcester (7-30, 23%, +19.73pt), Perth (9-35, 26%, +19.13pt) and Haydock (8-24, 33%, +15.03pt)

McCain isn't prolific in bumpers but those sent to Musselburgh are worth a look (2-4, 50%, +4.00pt)

The trainer had a fine record in handicaps last term with 32-220, 15%, +4.25pt over hurdles and 31-145, 21%, +22.25pt over fences

McCain rarely drops his hurdlers into sellers (1-3, 33%, +4.00pt) or claimers (2-10, 20%, +1.00pt) but it should be noted when he does

Last December was good for McCain, with a solid strike-rate and level-stake return (18-68, 26%, +18.08pt)

The mounts of Will Kennedy (25-161, 16%, +3.48pt) and Abbie McCain (7-21, 33%, +6.88pt) provided the best returns over hurdles last season

Kennedy also performed well on the yard's chasers last term (18-99, 18%, +4.53pt), as did Brian Hughes (12-44, 27%, +5.75pt) while Lorcan Murtagh provided the best returns in bumpers (3-11, 27%, +5.75pt)

DONALD McCAIN
CHOLMONDELEY, CHESHIRE

	No. of Hrs	Races Run	1st	2nd	3rd	Unpl	Per cent	£1 Level Stake
NH Flat	20	30	5	7	6	12	16.7	-8.18
Hurdles	79	334	54	47	47	186	16.2	-23.02
Chases	41	168	36	27	21	83	21.4	+14.03
Totals	**113**	**532**	**95**	**81**	**74**	**281**	**17.9**	**-17.17**
16-17	114	570	79	89	95	307	13.9	-129.20
15-16	126	498	54	60	73	311	10.8	-133.27

BY MONTH

NH Flat	W-R	Per cent	£1 Level Stake	Hurdles	W-R	Per cent	£1 Level Stake
May	1-2	50.0	+0.88	May	2-27	7.4	-21.18
June	0-1	0.0	-1.00	June	0-16	0.0	-16.00
July	1-3	33.3	+6.00	July	3-15	20.0	-4.51
August	1-2	50.0	+2.00	August	10-20	50.0	+45.64
September	0-0	0.0	0.00	September	4-13	30.8	+6.75
October	0-2	0.0	-2.00	October	3-35	8.6	-13.00
November	0-6	0.0	-6.00	November	5-39	12.8	+14.50
December	0-4	0.0	-4.00	December	10-39	25.6	+14.33
January	1-2	50.0	+0.20	January	7-39	17.9	-7.25
February	1-1	100.0	+2.75	February	2-26	7.7	-12.50
March	0-1	0.0	-1.00	March	6-33	18.2	-6.81
April	0-6	0.0	-6.00	April	2-32	6.3	-23.00

Chases	W-R	Per cent	£1 Level Stake	Totals	W-R	Per cent	£1 Level Stake
May	4-19	21.1	-7.38	May	7-48	14.6	-27.68
June	1-10	10.0	-7.50	June	1-27	3.7	-24.50
July	2-8	25.0	+2.00	July	6-26	23.1	+15.49
August	2-7	28.6	+7.50	August	13-29	44.8	+55.14
September	1-7	14.3	-3.00	September	5-20	25.0	+3.75
October	2-12	16.7	+7.00	October	5-49	10.2	-8.00
November	4-13	30.8	+13.00	November	9-58	15.5	+21.50
December	8-25	32.0	+7.75	December	18-68	26.5	+18.08
January	8-22	36.4	+4.03	January	16-63	25.4	-3.02
February	2-12	16.7	-0.13	February	5-39	12.8	-9.88
March	2-17	11.8	-5.25	March	8-51	15.7	-13.06
April	0-16	0.0	-16.00	April	2-54	3.7	-45.00

Statistics relate to all runners in Britain from May 1, 2017 to April 28, 2018

DISTANCE

	W-R	Per cent	£1 Level Stake		W-R	Per cent	£1 Level Stake
Hurdles				Chases			
2m-2m3f	27-191	14.1	-77.16	2m-2m3f	12-47	25.5	+2.75
2m4f-2m7f	21-106	19.8	+50.64	2m4f-2m7f	15-61	24.6	+15.41
3m+	6-37	16.2	+3.50	3m+	9-60	15.0	-4.13

TYPE OF RACE

Non-Handicaps	W-R	Per cent	£1 Level Stake	Handicaps	W-R	Per cent	£1 Level Stake
Nov Hrdls	19-82	23.2	-8.80	Nov Hrdls	0-11	0.0	-11.00
Hrdls	3-30	10.0	-16.47	Hrdls	32-209	15.3	+15.25
Nov Chs	5-16	31.3	-1.22	Nov Chs	2-15	13.3	-7.75
Chases	0-6	0.0	-6.00	Chases	23-108	21.3	+21.88
Sell/Claim	0-0	0.0	0.00	Sell/Claim	0-0	0.0	0.00

RACE CLASS

	W-R	Per cent	£1 Level Stake
Class 1	1-24	4.2	-22.47
Class 2	7-35	20.0	+51.50
Class 3	18-92	19.6	-2.63
Class 4	50-291	17.2	-35.67
Class 5	18-79	22.8	+0.23
Class 6	1-11	9.1	-8.13

FIRST TIME OUT

	W-R	Per cent	£1 Level Stake
Bumpers	4-20	20.0	-2.18
Hurdles	6-65	9.2	+4.70
Chases	6-28	21.4	+3.13
Totals	16-113	14.2	+5.65

DID YOU KNOW?

Donald McCain's family has won five Grand Nationals, but ask him who is the best horse he's trained and he'll tell you Peddlers Cross. "I was devastated he got beat 16 lengths [in the Wayward Lad Novices' Chase] at Kempton," he says. "I thought nothing should beat Peddlers Cross like that – I didn't care who it was." The winner was Sprinter Sacre!

 Facebook.com/racingpost

point-to-point. He's not a big horse, but he's an impressive looker and I'd expect we'll start him off in bumpers and then go over hurdles."

Another addition to the team is another winning pointer **Pogue**, about whom McCain said: "We gave good money for him at Cheltenham in May. He's a big grey horse with two white front legs so he's very eye-catching. He just got beat in his first run in a point-to-point but next time won by about a hundred yards. He has plenty of size and scope about him and is just the sort to make up into a staying novice hurdler/chaser.

"One we got last month at Doncaster was **The Con Man**. I tried to buy him after he won his point-to-point in April, but he met with a setback so was off for a while but came up at the sales so we bought him.

"He was a little bit more chancey than the other two but his form was equally as good and I'm looking forward to running him.

"**Lord Springfield** is another winning Irish pointer. We bought him at Punchestown after he'd won his point-to-point. He's by Well Chosen and is a big, strong horse who again should do well in staying novice hurdles and chases."

Pougne Bobbi is another newcomer to the team having been bought out of Nicky Henderson's yard at Doncaster in May.

McCain said: "I'm not trying to improve on Mr Henderson, but he should suit us. He's rated in the mid 130s, is very effective on soft ground and is a two-and-a-half-mile or three-mile chaser so will be ideal for going up to places like Newcastle or Ayr where you get proper soft ground.

Bright novice hurdle hopes

"Two others I like are **Shantaluze** and **The Some Dance Kid**. They are by Shantou, were point-to-pointing in Ireland and won bumpers for me last season. They are the type of horses I like, not overbig, but good hardy, straightforward sorts who should give us some fun in novice hurdles over two and a half plus. They won't take long to get ready and are two solid horses.

"**Nefyn Point** ran in a bumper at the end of last season at Perth. They were raving about the first two and he was the unraced one of the three and finished close up to them so it was promising. He's a half-brother to Nefyn Bay who is only small and has his problems but he's a bigger horse."

All in all it looks a strong, well-balanced team and it should mean McCain not only hits the century again but is up there challenging for some of the main Saturday prizes.

Interview by Colin Russell

THE LOWDOWN WILLIE MULLINS

Quick out of the blocks with wealth of big-race talent ready to unleash

WHATEVER the rest of the season brings for the all-conquering Willie Mullins it is already a campaign with a difference for Ireland's 12 times champion trainer. In 2016-17 and again last season Mullins swooped in the last week of the campaign to twice deny Gordon Elliott a first trainers' championship and successfully reel in and overtake his rival at the Punchestown festival.

What's different about the new season is that Mullins has been making the running in the title race from the beginning. By the end of September he had trained twice as many winners as Elliott and his horses had earned almost double the amount of win and place prize-money won by Elliott-trained horses.

"It's been a different sort of early season for us, that's for sure, and the main reason was that we had more good ground horses than usual to run over the summer months," Mullins explains.

And with most of the big-name performers of the past few years, the heavy artillery, still to make their return, another successful season for Ireland's most powerful jumps operation is very much on the cards.

Of all the yard's high-profile performers last season none was more impressive and consistent than **Footpad**, who went through his first season over fences unbeaten, winning five times and running up a sequence of four consecutive Grade 1 wins including the Racing Post Arkle Trophy at the Cheltenham Festival and culminating with the Ryanair Novice Chase at Punchestown.

Mullins says: "From the first time we schooled Footpad over fences he was electric and he carried that to the track, hardly putting a foot wrong all season. Five lengths was his lowest winning margin and his other wins were all by double-figure margins.

"At one stage we regarded him as a likely type for the JLT or RSA but he was so good

....

Mullins nearly landed the British trainers' championship in the 2015-16 campaign and, while he has sent over fewer runners in the past couple of seasons, they returned a level-stake profit on both occasions with last year's figures reading 10-74 (14%, +8.96pt). He amassed in excess of £1.5 million in prize-money in Britain to go with the €5.9 million which saw him land his 11th consecutive Irish trainers' title and his 12th overall

WINNERS IN LAST FIVE SEASONS 212, 180, 185, 187, 185

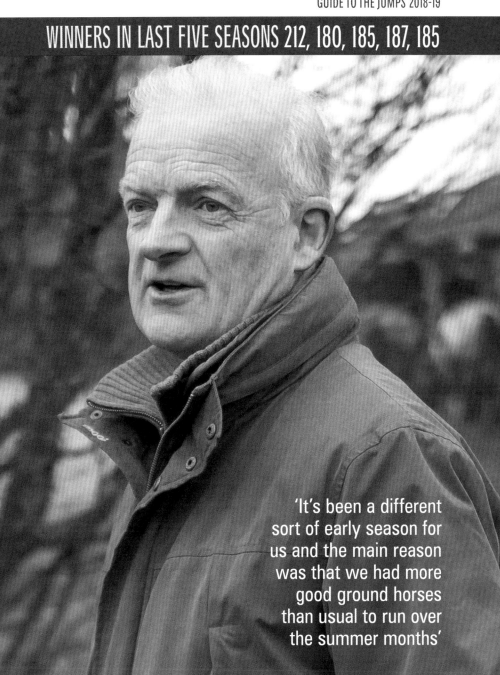

'It's been a different sort of early season for us and the main reason was that we had more good ground horses than usual to run over the summer months'

when we started him off over two miles that we quickly realised we had a Grade 1 horse for the trip.

"I thought his Punchestown festival win was his most impressive performance, even better than his Arkle win at Cheltenham.

"He got two and a half miles well over hurdles and there will be plenty of options for him in terms of distance. I said last season that he could be a Cheltenham Gold Cup horse, if not this season then next. He's back and in good form and, hopefully, he'll have another good campaign whatever plan we draw up for him."

Faugheen could try chasing

One of the most satisfying victories of the season for Mullins was the performance delivered by **Faugheen** in winning the Grade 1 three-mile hurdle at the Punchestown festival by 13 lengths.

Mullins said: "After starting off so well in the Morgiana, his season dipped but when we decided to step him up to three miles at Punchestown he was sensational – back to his very best.

"We haven't decided yet whether we'll concentrate on staying hurdles or send him

novice chasing but he's well and back in training.

"The same applies to **Douvan** who got to run only twice last season, falling four out when leading in the Champion Chase at Cheltenham and then running second to Un De Sceaux in the BoyleSports Champion Chase at Punchestown.

"We're thinking of experimenting with him by stretching him out in distance this season and seeing how things go."

Sceaux back for more

Un De Sceaux has been one of Closutton's top performers in recent seasons and he brought his tally of Grade 1 wins to nine when making all and landing the Champion Chase at the Punchestown festival in April.

His trainer says: "Un De Sceaux is back for another campaign and I'd imagine we'll be targeting the same races as we've done in recent years."

Un De Sceaux scoots home to score at the Punchestown festival

Bellshill could go for gold

Mullins has had several horses placed in the Cheltenham Gold Cup. Djakadam, who twice finished second in the race, is now retired but Bellshill emerged as a likely candidate when landing the Coral Punchestown Gold Cup in April.

Mullins says: "Bellshill had a very light campaign last season and to come out and win at Punchestown so soon after being beaten only a length in gruelling conditions in the Irish Grand National was a very good effort. He'll be aimed at some of the top staying chases and, hopefully, he'll earn a tilt at the Gold Cup."

DID YOU KNOW?

Despite being leading trainer at four of the last six Cheltenham Festivals, Mullins has never won two of the sport's biggest chase prizes – the Gold Cup or Champion Chase.

WILLIE MULLINS

BAGENALSTOWN, COUNTY CARLOW

	Races Run	1st	2nd	3rd	Unpl	Per cent	£1 Level Stake
Non-hcp hurdles	2512	838	501	298	875	33.4	-126.29
Hcp hurdles	725	94	57	54	520	13.0	-135.72
Non-hcp chases	1201	383	189	147	482	31.9	-117.31
Hcp chases	448	46	39	33	330	10.3	-121.39
Hunter chases	29	6	3	2	18	20.7	-5.20
NH Flat	1085	375	214	124	372	34.6	+1.85
Totals	**6000**	**1742**	**1003**	**658**	**2597**	**29.0**	**-504.06**

BY MONTH

	W-R	Strike-rate (%)	£1 level stake
January	211-641	32.9	-41.05
February	192-603	31.8	+40.07
March	104-352	29.5	-18.09
April	184-907	20.3	+51.29
May	134-534	25.1	-129.78
June	54-201	26.9	-3.75
July	131-385	34.0	+25.31
August	125-457	27.4	-124.95
September	76-283	26.9	-50.61
October	75-264	28.4	-24.02
November	205-579	35.4	-43.00
December	251-794	31.6	-185.48

Statistics relate to all runners in Ireland from 2009-2018

Staying chases are also the plan for **Al Boum Photo**, who made a dramatic and bizarre exit at the final fence in the Grade 1 Growise Champion Novice Chase at the Punchestown festival. "He gave us our first win in the Ryanair Gold Cup at Fairyhouse's Easter meeting and he'll be aimed at some of the better staying chases," Mullins says.

Benie heading back over fences

Benie Des Dieux, who achieved a Grade 1 mares' hurdle double by winning at the Cheltenham and Punchestown festivals, was unbeaten in three starts over fences before reverting to hurdles at Cheltenham. "She did very well winning those Grade 1s but it's quite possible we'll concentrate more on chasing with her this season," Mullins says.

Great Field, who was a Grade 1 winner as a novice chaser in 2016-17, made only one appearance last season, landing a Grade 2 at Navan in March and making it five from five over fences.

"He's had training problems but when he's right he's a very exciting chaser at around two miles. He's back in training," the trainer says.

Min, a Grade 1-winning novice chaser two seasons back, was denied a second top-level success at Leopardstown's Christmas meeting last year when relegated to second place in favour of Simply Ned following a stewards' enquiry. He went on to trounce Simply Ned by 12 lengths at the same track in February before finishing second to Altior at Cheltenham and to Politologue at Aintree. He is back in training and Mullins will be following a similar programme with him.

Out to go one better at Aintree

Pleasant Company got to within a head of providing his trainer with a second Grand National victory when failing narrowly to collar Tiger Roll, and the ten-year-old's campaign will again be geared towards another tilt at Aintree.

FIXTURES 2018/19

Taunton RACECOURSE & conference centre

Orchard Portman
Taunton Somerset TA3 7BL
Tel: 01823 337172

SAVE UP TO 20% BY BOOKING ONLINE IN ADVANCE

Wednesday 31st October	- Halloween Meeting
Thursday 15th November	- Autumn Fixture
Thursday 29th November	- Autumn Fixture
Thursday 13th December	- Dave Criddle Travel Festive Meeting
Sunday 30th December	- Christmas Meeting
Wednesday 9th January	- Somerset Sight Charity Day 2 for 1*
Saturday 19th January	- Portman Cup Day
Monday 4th February	- Winter Meeting
Tuesday 19th February	- Bath & West Raceday
Thursday 28th February	- C & S Electrical Raceday
Monday 11th March	- William Hill Free Raceday*
Tuesday 19th March	- RNLI Charity Raceday
Thursday 4th April	- Ladies Day
Wednesday 24th April	- Evening Meeting

*limited offer

www.tauntonracecourse.co.uk

All accompanied children under 18 FREE All car parking FREE
Courtesy bus from Taunton Railway Station

Mullins says: "Pleasant Company has shown he likes Aintree and while we'll be looking at some of the other big handicap chases the National will be his ultimate target."

However, the Aintree spectacular is unlikely to figure in plans for **Total Recall**, who won the Munster National and Newbury's Ladbrokes Trophy on his first two starts for Mullins: "He didn't take to the Aintree fences and I doubt he'll go back there. We'll be looking elsewhere and he could mix it between chasing and hurdling."

Champion plan for Melon

Melon's performance in running Buveur D'Air to a neck in the Champion Hurdle is the performance likely to swing connections towards another tilt at the race in March.

That performance delighted Mullins, who believes the six-year-old will be a better horse this season: "We tried a hood on him in the Irish Champion Hurdle and it didn't work. He ran an awful lot better at Cheltenham and produced the type of performance we thought he was capable of. We have to decide on whether to go novice chasing or go the Champion Hurdle route again and I'd say the latter plan is more likely," Mullins says.

Sharjah, a last-flight faller when looking set to win a Grade 1 novice at Leopardstown's Christmas meeting, went on to win the Galway Hurdle under top weight and might also be aimed at the Champion Hurdle,

Melon delighted Willie Mullins with his Champion Hurdle second last season

while **Limini**, a Cheltenham Festival winner in 2016 and who enjoyed a major Flat handicap win on Irish Champions weekend at Leopardstown in September, will again be campaigned over hurdles.

Light campaign again for Penhill

Penhill did connections proud at Cheltenham in March when landing the Stayers' Hurdle without a run in almost a year and, according to his trainer, a similar preparation is the most likely scenario again.

"We're planning to give Penhill the same type of build-up to Cheltenham as last season and that might mean him going back there for the Stayers' without a prep run," he says.

Among the exciting novice chase prospects in the yard is **Next Destination**, a dual Grade 1 winner over hurdles last season. Third behind Samcro in the Ballymore Novices' Hurdle at Cheltenham, the six-year-old successfully stepped up to 3m at Punchestown, where he landed a Grade 1.

"We're looking forward to sending Next Destination over fences and all the evidence suggests he'll be one for the staying division."

Getabird, who won three times over hurdles, is another of last season's novice hurdlers who will be going chasing.

Laurina, unbeaten in four starts for Mullins and who won the Grade 2 Mares' Novices' Hurdle at the Cheltenham Festival and a Grade 1 mares' novice hurdle at Fairyhouse, is more likely to stay hurdling than go chasing.

"She won all her hurdle races by big margins and, while we haven't made a final call, I'd imagine we'll keep her hurdling this season," the trainer says.

Revved up for hurdles

Among the exciting novice hurdle prospects who will be doing battle for the team are Tornado Flyer, Carefully Selected, Blackbow and Relegate, all of whom performed well in bumpers last season.

Mullins says: "**Tornado Flyer** won two of his three races and showed good improvement after finishing third in the Champion Bumper at Cheltenham to win the Grade 1 at Punchestown. We're looking forward to him doing well over hurdles.

"**Carefully Selected** is in the same category. He made almost all in the Cheltenham Festival bumper only to be caught late on by Relegate and he again performed very well when third behind Tornado Flyer. He's an exciting prospect.

"**Relegate** did very well, winning three in a row, including the Cheltenham bumper in which she got up close home. She lost her unbeaten record at Punchestown at the end of the season and we're looking forward to her going hurdling.

"**Blackbow** won a point-to-point in Britain before we got him. He did well in bumpers, winning two and running well in the Grade 1s at Cheltenham [fifth] and Punchestown [second] and he should do well."

Interview by Tony O'Hehir

SUPER STATS

It's not surprising to learn that most of Mullins' British winners last term came at Cheltenham where they returned a level-stake profit (7-63, 11%, +11.40pt). However, over the last five seasons his returns have been more consistent at Sandown (6-17, 35%, +19.19pt) and Warwick (5-7, 71%, +6.12pt)

Although nowhere near as frequent a visitor to Perth as his compatriot Gordon Elliott, Mullins boasts a fine strike-rate with his select runners at the Scottish track (3-5, 60%, +5.50pt)

While Mullins doesn't have the have greatest strike-rate in British handicap hurdles, they tend to come over for only the most competitive contests with some obliging at surprisingly long odds (6-77, 8%, +33.00pt)

Mullins has a solid record with his British raiders running in Listed hurdles who just about pay their way (3-8, 38%, +£0.02)

Mullins' hurdlers in Britain have fared best over trips ranging from 2m3½f and beyond (20-115, 17%, +20.37pt)

Ruby Walsh rides most of the yard's British winners (31-110, 28%, -24.95pt) but those ridden by Paul Townend provide a greater level-stake return (17-85, 20%, +26.96pt)

It's a similar story in Ireland, with Walsh winning the battle for winners (307-828, 37%, -73.57pt) but Townend doing better in terms of level-stake profit (171-555, 31%, +11.57pt)

THE LOWDOWN PAUL NICHOLLS

Politologue leads the way as ten-time champ builds back to the top

PAUL NICHOLLS is full of excitement for the new season, but is keen to stress it's now all about youth and that it is going to take time to build to the top.

Referring to the trainers' title he has won ten times, Nicholls says: "I'm as hungry for winners as I've ever been, but at the same time I'm realistic. Our team isn't strong enough to beat Nicky Henderson's, unless the likes of Might Bite, Buveur D'Air and Altior underperform for some reason.

"I prefer to stress the positives, and we've managed to finish in the top two in the championship for each of the last 20 seasons, winning ten and runner-up in the other ten, which is a feat I'm really proud of.

"I bet there are not many teams – if any – in the Premier League who have achieved that! And what's more, we've bagged more than £2 million in prize-money for the last 16 of those seasons."

The star of the show this season is **Politologue**, the yard's top-rated chaser on 168, who provided the trainer with welcome Grade 1 victories at the highest level at Sandown and Aintree last season.

Nicholls says: "He had a great campaign but ran a bit below his best in the Champion Chase, where he travelled so well before fading. So we stepped him up to two and a half miles in the Melling Chase, put the tongue-tie on, and bingo – he stayed on strongly from the back of the last.

"I think he's basically a stayer, so we could be brave, step him up to three miles and go straight for the Betfair Chase, which is likely to be his first big target. And if he shows us he stays, the King George would then be the obvious race to aim at. Kempton's flat track would suit him so much better than somewhere like Cheltenham, where he's never won.

"We also have the option of starting off in the Old Roan Chase at Aintree, but at this moment the preferred option is to head straight to Haydock in November."

Of the emerging chasers in the squad, Nicholls singles out **Clan Des Obeaux** as one who "could go all the way".

The trainer says: "He'd thrown a splint

....

Despite an uncharacteristic lack of top-class performers at his disposal last term, Nicholls did incredibly well to accrue just over £2.5 million in prize-money, only slightly below his total in the previous campaign, while a tally of 127 winners was in keeping with his efforts in recent years

Facebook.com/racingpost

WINNERS IN LAST FIVE SEASONS 127, 171, 122, 124, 118

'He's basically a stayer, so we could be brave, step him up to three miles and go straight for the Betfair Chase'

mid-season so we were forced to miss Cheltenham and it was a rush to get him to Aintree. So all things considered he ran a blinder to be third to Might Bite.

"We've got to take on the big boys from now on so the plan is to start off in the Charlie Hall Chase and that should tell us where to go. On Aintree form he's got 10lb to find with Might Bite, but we have to remember he's only six and has very few miles on the clock."

Reflecting on the last few months, Nicholls says: "We went through a quiet spell in late spring when a few of ours weren't quite right, particularly the younger ones we ran."

But any early lost ground should quickly be made up as soon as the season steps up a

Delight as Black Corton scores at Cheltenham last November

gear, and one of the key horses for the yard will once again be **Black Corton**.

Newbury aim for Black Corton

The amazingly tough seven-year-old won eight of his 12 starts last season, and Nicholls reports: "We plan to bring him back in the Rising Stars Chase at Chepstow and use that as a stepping stone to the Ladbrokes Trophy.

"I'm mindful of the fact there's no way he could go out and win the Newbury race from the front, so when he went to Aintree at the backend, which was one run too many really, we deliberately changed tactics and rode him differently, coming from behind. In the RSA Chase he went off in front and set things up for the others, so we want to be doing things slightly differently in a race like the Ladbrokes Trophy."

Art Mauresque showed solid form against some of the best around last winter and Nicholls says: "There's a really nice race to be won with him somewhere. He's very good fresh, he needs quick ground and he's better on a flat track, so something like the Peterborough Chase or Ascot Chase might suit."

Heading for the Haldon Gold Cup is Aintree Grade 1 novice chase winner **Diego Du Charmil**.

"He should get two and a half miles this season, which would open up new avenues, but he has loads of toe, so Exeter looks an ideal starting point," says Nicholls.

'I adore this horse'

The trainer's eyes lit up when outlining plans for **Give Me A Copper**. "I adore this horse,"

PAUL NICHOLLS
DITCHEAT, SOMERSET

	No. of Hrs	Races Run	1st	2nd	3rd	Unpl	Per cent	£1 Level Stake
NH Flat	20	32	4	2	4	22	12.5	-21.46
Hurdles	81	238	45	37	27	129	18.9	-84.31
Chases	79	300	77	52	43	128	25.7	-27.57
Totals	**150**	**570**	**126**	**91**	**74**	**279**	**22.1**	**-133.34**
16-17	161	661	171	90	79	321	25.9	-66.39
15-16	162	568	122	104	74	268	21.5	-73.23

BY MONTH

NH Flat	W-R	Per cent	£1 Level Stake	Hurdles	W-R	Per cent	£1 Level Stake
May	0-0	0.0	0.00	May	1-11	9.1	-9.56
June	0-0	0.0	0.00	June	3-5	60.0	+9.00
July	0-0	0.0	0.00	July	0-2	0.0	-2.00
August	0-0	0.0	0.00	August	0-0	0.0	0.00
September	0-1	0.0	-1.00	September	1-3	33.3	-1.43
October	2-5	40.0	-0.33	October	6-33	18.2	-17.41
November	1-5	20.0	-1.75	November	5-39	12.8	-26.79
December	0-4	0.0	-4.00	December	7-37	18.9	-10.97
January	0-1	0.0	-1.00	January	1-10	10.0	-8.17
February	1-6	16.7	-3.38	February	6-36	16.7	-3.92
March	0-3	0.0	-3.00	March	5-21	23.8	-2.26
April	0-7	0.0	-7.00	April	10-41	24.4	-10.81

Chases	W-R	Per cent	£1 Level Stake	Totals	W-R	Per cent	£1 Level Stake
May	9-19	47.4	+0.11	May	10-30	33.3	-9.45
June	4-12	33.3	-0.70	June	7-17	41.2	+8.30
July	5-10	50.0	+8.32	July	5-12	41.7	+6.32
August	3-9	33.3	-5.19	August	3-9	33.3	-5.19
September	1-2	50.0	-0.60	September	2-6	33.3	-3.03
October	13-34	38.2	+9.63	October	21-72	29.2	-8.11
November	11-46	23.9	-10.95	November	17-90	18.9	-39.49
December	6-46	13.0	-24.97	December	13-87	14.9	-39.94
January	2-18	11.1	-8.59	January	3-29	10.3	-17.76
February	12-34	35.3	-2.70	February	19-76	25.0	-10.00
March	4-28	14.3	+13.57	March	9-52	17.3	+8.31
April	7-42	16.7	-5.50	April	17-90	18.9	-23.31

Statistics relate to all runners in Britain from May 1, 2017 to April 28, 2018

DISTANCE

Hurdles	W-R	Per cent	£1 Level Stake	Chases	W-R	Per cent	£1 Level Stake
2m-2m3f	33-134	24.6	-26.03	2m-2m3f	21-73	28.8	-13.22
2m4f-2m7f	11-77	14.3	-41.28	2m4f-2m7f	35-126	27.8	+0.75
3m+	1-27	3.7	-17.00	3m+	21-101	20.8	-15.10

TYPE OF RACE

Non-Handicaps	W-R	Per cent	£1 Level Stake	Handicaps	W-R	Per cent	£1 Level Stake
Nov Hrdls	27-86	31.4	-2.08	Nov Hrdls	1-6	16.7	-1.50
Hrdls	8-48	16.7	-30.71	Hrdls	9-95	9.5	-47.02
Nov Chs	34-87	39.1	-10.94	Nov Chs	3-16	18.8	-8.63
Chases	17-56	30.4	+16.79	Chases	17-116	14.7	-23.17
Sell/Claim	0-0	0.0	0.00	Sell/Claim	0-0	0.0	0.00

RACE CLASS

	W-R	Per cent	£1 Level Stake
Class 1	20-155	12.9	-60.67
Class 2	15-104	14.4	-34.23
Class 3	34-132	25.8	-29.33
Class 4	48-138	34.8	+13.57
Class 5	3-26	11.5	-19.82
Class 6	6-15	40.0	-1.86

FIRST TIME OUT

	W-R	Per cent	£1 Level Stake
Bumpers	3-20	15.0	-12.71
Hurdles	8-69	11.6	-30.86
Chases	19-61	31.1	-17.88
Totals	30-150	20.0	-61.45

DID YOU KNOW?

He may have started riding out a couple of lots a morning again, but to those of a younger vintage it will come as a surprise to learn that Paul Nicholls once weighed in at 7lb 2oz (when he was born in 1962), rode his first winner at 9st 7lb (in 1981) and could still do 10st 5lb when he won the Hennessy on Broadheath in 1986.

Paul Nicholls keeps a close eye on his string as they return from the gallops

he says. "After he won a two-runner novice chase at Kempton he came back slightly jarred up. He's such a huge talent it wouldn't surprise me if he won a big one somewhere down the line. I could see him running in a National one day."

Talking of the National, the ground went against **Warriors Tale** at Aintree last spring, but Nicholls says: "He's definitely worth taking back to Liverpool, for the Sefton or the Becher, hopefully on better ground."

Nicholls has a real soft spot for another likely Ladbrokes Trophy entry **El Bandit**, who hasn't been sighted since making a winning debut over fences 15 months go.

"I love this horse and rate him highly," he says. "He got a bit jarred up after his last run so we left off him. I know he lacks experience but I think he could be attractively handicapped, so I plan to run him in the Badger Ales Chase at Wincanton, possibly after a little run somewhere to take the freshness out of him."

Those tactics were successfully employed last season with **Present Man**, who won a novice hurdle before capturing the Badger Ales for the Woodhouses, who sponsor the race. And he should be back to try to win the beer money for the second year running.

Smart Cyrname must go right

Few inmates improved as much for fences last winter as **Cyrname**. Nicholls reflects: "We finally got him settled better once he went chasing and bingo – he ran some fantastic races.

"He needs to go right-handed, so something like the Colin Parker Chase at Carlisle would be ideal, but nothing is set in stone yet."

Classy performers **Frodon** and **San Benedeto** "might both be hard to place as they are handicapped to the hilt".

The trainer is itching to try Frodon, who is just shy of Grade 1 level, over the big Aintree fences, while San Benedeto "is better in small-field conditions races and will contest the same sort of races as last season".

An interesting newcomer from France is the precocious **Magic Saint**. Only four, he has already picked up £100,000 in prize-money for winning four times at Auteuil, twice over hurdles and twice over fences.

"I don't know too much about him yet but everything I've seen suggests he's a very nice prospect," says Nicholls. "He could be really interesting in a decent handicap chase with his four-year-old's allowance."

There are no plans just yet for the classy JP McManus-owned pair **Le Prezien** and **Modus**.

'He's a really exciting prospect'

This time last year he was a raw, gangly, unraced six-year-old too backward to get on the racetrack; 12 months on and **Master Tommytucker** has grown into an imposing individual who is unbeaten over hurdles and poised to begin a potentially exciting chasing career.

"He's taken an age to come right, and when he won first time out at Exeter in February we took him there only for a day out," says Nicholls.

"From then on he did nothing but improve and when we went back to Exeter a couple of months later he was very impressive.

"It'll be hard to go chasing on the back of such limited experience, so we could have another run over hurdles, but he's seven rising eight so we probably need to crack on. As a physical model you'd have to go a long way to find anything better. He's a really exciting prospect."

From last season's novice hurdle crop **Mont Des Avaloirs** brings Grade 1-placed form to the table and his trainer predicts: "I hope he can leave his hurdle rating of 139 well behind now he goes over fences.

"Hurdles tended to get in his way last

season and we had babyish issues with him, but he's more settled now and should make some chaser. He's a big horse, totally unlike his brother Le Prezien, so we'll wait for some cut in the ground before he gets going."

Slowly slowly with classy hurdler

On 154, **Topofthegame** is the trainer's highest-rated hurdler going over fences. His chasing CV last season read one run, one fall, but he is expected to do much better at the second attempt.

Despite the horse's undoubted class Nicholls says: "We'll start him low down, to get some chasing experience into him, then work our way up.

"He's a giant and you'd think fences would pose no problem for him, but that isn't always the case with these big horses, who need to use their brain when shortening up at a fence."

Captain could boss novice rivals

There is nothing flashy about **Captain Cattistock**, who quietly went about his business over hurdles last season and won three from six.

"He was very unlucky not to have made that four as he'd have gone close to winning at Cheltenham in April but for making a horlicks of the last," recalls Nicholls.

"He might have one more run over hurdles, possibly in the Silver Trophy at Chepstow, then go chasing. He's a lovely, progressive sort who should do well over fences."

Blu Cavalier, another three-time hurdle winner, came good in the spring and is being aimed at the Persian War Novices' Hurdle at Chepstow in October before going over fences.

Nicholls says he's really looking forward to seeing **Malaya** switch to fences and says: "She's tough and she's good and I have my eye on a novice chase at Newton Abbot in October."

Envoye Special is an interesting French import. A four-year-old half-brother to the brilliant French champion hurdler De Bon Coeur, he has been placed a couple of times over fences and Nicholls says: "He now looks twice the horse he did when he first arrived. He needs to learn to settle better but we like everything we see."

High hopes for improved Kirwan

Among Nicholls' leading hopes for novice hurdles this season is a lightly raced five-year-old who was beaten 59 lengths in a bumper last time out.

Winning pointer **Danny Kirwan** came over from Ireland this time last year with a big reputation and hacked up on his debut in a Kempton bumper but was bitterly disappointing in the Grade 2 at Aintree.

"Six months on and I'm still kicking myself for having run him," says Nicholls.

"As soon as I saw him in the paddock at Aintree he had run up so lean and light I knew he shouldn't be there. So we just have to put a line through it.

"He's grown into a big, strong individual and must be at least 50kg heavier this season. He still needs to fill into his frame so we're going to have to mind him, but he's a high-class individual who has loads of toe."

Point-to-pointers in spotlight

The novice hurdle division boasts a larger number of darker prospects than usual after several youngsters coming through the conveyor belt ran below expectations in the spring when the yard wasn't firing for a time. That puts the spotlight on the ex-Irish pointers; most of them won in that sphere and many have transferred to Ditcheat with expensive price tags.

Nicholls says: "The trouble here is that you don't know how good the Irish point form is,

2018/19
JUMP
SEASON

NEWCASTLE RACECOURSE

12

FIXTURES
NOVEMBER - APRIL

=== INCLUDING ===

| FIGHTING FIFTH HURDLE | NORTHUMBERLAND CHASE | EIDER CHASE | ST PATRICK'S RACEDAY | GRAND NATIONAL RACEDAY |

TICKETS FROM £16*

NEWCASTLE
RACING & EVENTS

NEWCASTLE-RACECOURSE.CO.UK

but you have to pay good money to find out. We hope something among the new intake will turn out to be a gem. Remember, when Denman came to us all he'd done was win a maiden Irish point-to-point."

Danse Idol could be one of the best, in the short term at least. "She won her point before finishing second in a bumper to subsequent Champion Bumper winner Relegate," says Nicholls. "She looks potentially another smart mare for us and will run in another bumper before going novice hurdling."

Corn has to prove his worth

Trevelyn's Corn cost an awful lot of money but Nicholls warns: "He won his Irish point but that's so far all we know about him. As yet we haven't pressed any buttons but we're just starting to get stuck into him."

Of **Silver Forever** the trainer says: "She looked really promising when winning her point-to-point and is a lovely prospect. She'll run in a mares' bumper before going novice hurdling."

And **Brewer's Project** is "a big, scopey sort who we'll know more about soon".

Others showed promise in Irish points without winning, including **King Of Kilmeague**, who missed last season but is well regarded, and four-year-old **Storm Arising**. "Storm Arising scarcely jumped a fence when third on his only run but I liked him a lot," says Nicholls. "When we first schooled him he was clumsy to start with, but by the end of the session he was good. He has loads of pace and I can see him going forward."

Most interesting of the French imports is **My Way**. He is a maiden, but boasts one smart piece of form, beaten five lengths by the brilliant Whetstone at Auteuil, conceding the subsequent champion four-year-old chaser 9lb.

The ex-John Oxx-trained **Birds Of Prey**

has put up three good performances on the Flat this year for Nicholls.

"We've just had his palate re-cauterised and he's the type to go well in a big handicap on the Flat before switching to jumping, where he could be decent," says Nicholls.

Dual hurdle winner **Diamond Guy** progressed nicely in the spring and, being a novice until the end of October, is bound for a Listed novice hurdle at Kempton.

New recruits from overseas

Acquisitions from France and Germany comprise a small team of juveniles that will expand considerably in the coming weeks.

Lisa De Vassy had useful form on the Flat in France, winning twice at Cagnes before finishing third in a Listed fillies' race at Saint-Cloud.

"Harry Cobden went over to France and schooled her before we bought her," says Nicholls. "She's not very big but looks a likely sort for early juvenile hurdles."

Tamaroc Du Mathan should likewise be out fairly early, having won his only start over hurdles at Angers in western France in April, and **Quel Destin** was placed on the Flat in the provinces before getting off the mark over hurdles at the fourth attempt at Auteuil.

"Quel Destin has quite an attractive Flat rating and that gives us another option," pointed out Nicholls.

Ecco arrived from Germany in September. Still a maiden on the

Old Guard could run on the Flat or try fences again

Flat, he wasn't beaten far in a Group 2 and started fourth favourite for the German Derby when down the field. Nicholls sourced smart hurdler Irving from the same country a few years back and will be hoping he has uncovered another German gem.

Old favourite could try the Flat

Old Guard took his career earnings to in excess of £300,000 with three more victories over hurdles last season and could start off in the same Kempton Listed event next month he won 12 months ago.

But Nicholls adds there are other options for the tough seven-year-old.

"He looks to have an attractive Flat mark, which we may try to exploit, and I'm also keen to try him again over fences," he says. "He didn't take to them first time."

Very useful dual-purpose campaigner **Cliffs Of Dover** was a runaway winner on the Flat at Haydock in August and may have one more outing on the Flat before switching back to jumping in the Elite Hurdle at Wincanton.

Nicholls says: "His hurdle mark of 140 looks attractive but he must have decent ground."

There is surely a decent handicap waiting to be won with **Peak To Peak**, who was sidelined with a small injury after his eyecatching third in last season's Silver Trophy at Chepstow. The form of that race worked out brilliantly and he is expected to capitalise on a rating of 130 before his attentions are turned to chasing.

Zubayr is on a long losing run over hurdles, not seeming to enjoy the job since falling in the Elite Hurdle two years ago, but we are advised not to give up on him.

"He's just had his palate re-cauterised and he's definitely capable of winning again, although he may be more of a Flat horse than a jumper nowadays," says Nicholls.

Interview by Ben Newton

SUPER STATS

Most of Nicholls' hurdling winners are sent out close to his base in Ditcheat – Newton Abbot, Taunton, Exeter and Wincanton – but it is his record at the last-named over the last five seasons that catches the eye (50-130, 38%, +10.23pt)

Nicholls' runners are always worth a look at the northern tracks. His best level-stake return is at Ayr (8-40, 20%, +12.88pt) but his rare raids to Carlisle are well worth the trip with a highly impressive strike-rate (5-7, 71%, +6.35pt)

Surprisingly, the track at which Nicholls posts his best level-stake return is Cheltenham (33-296, 11%, +29.26pt), where the strike-rate is also reasonable given the competitive nature of the racing

The yard's chasers are best followed at Haydock (9-21, 43%, +7.60pt) and Fontwell (22-40, 55%, +17.70pt), with his figures at the Sussex track in particular standing out

Most of the Nicholls bumper winners come at Wincanton and Taunton but to a small level-stake loss in recent years. His best returns in this sphere over the last five seasons have come at Cheltenham (3-5, 60%, +5.50pt).

Sam Twiston-Davies rode most winners for the yard last term (47) while Harry Cobden also got the leg up on his fair share (24), but the most impressive strike-rate and level-stakes return were posted by the mounts of Bryony Frost (26-88, 30%, +14.47pt)

All about the future as Jackdaws maestro has eyes fixed on long term

JONJO O'NEILL is looking to the future having made a significant investment in young bloodstock as he searches for the next Taquin Du Seuil, Holywell and More Of That.

In what he hails as the start of a three-year plan, the Gold Cup and Grand National-winning trainer acknowledges he may lack Saturday horses in the short term, while getting anywhere close to 100 winners for the season would be unrealistic, but he is confident his Jackdaws Castle yard will again be competing with the best before too long.

"We won't have a lot of good, Saturday horses but we're lucky we've got nice young horses to build on and this is a three-year plan," O'Neill says.

"When you lose horses like Taquin Du Seuil and More Of That there's a massive hole and it's so hard to fill it, but we've got some lovely horses to look forward to. It takes time but we're positive."

By O'Neill's high standards, last season was a disappointment with 64 winners – his lowest tally since 2001 – while the death of Taquin Du Seuil at Huntingdon in January cast a big shadow over the campaign.

However, with winners already rolling at a decent rate in the current term, he is more than confident his horses are back in top form.

"The weather was really bad and the horses weren't firing last year," he says. "You couldn't put it down to anything but it was clear to see. They've summered really well, though, and the horses have been running to form recently."

With More Of That following Holywell into retirement, **Minella Rocco** has taken on the mantle of flagbearer, with the Grand National the ultimate aim for the strapping JP McManus-owned eight-year-old.

"He was all dressed up with nowhere to go last season as the ground was desperate and it definitely was against him. He went to Aintree last April but there was no point in running him as the rain bucketed down and conditions were very testing so we took him out," says O'Neill.

"He's come back looking brilliant after his good summer holiday. His wind has always been niggling him and he's had a hobday and soft-palate operation.

"Has it fixed it? That's anyone's guess but hopefully it will bring him back to the form of his Gold Cup second and you'd

WINNERS IN LAST FIVE SEASONS 64, 78, 81, 104, 134

'He's come back in looking brilliant. His wind has always been niggling him and he's had a hobday and soft-palate operation'

hopefully have a Grand National horse to look forward to.

"Pre-Christmas we'll look at the big three-mile open handicaps at Ascot and Newbury – with the Ladbrokes Trophy – which used to be the Hennessy Gold Cup – a possibility, although no decision has yet been made as there aren't too many options for horses like him."

Forza back and going chasing

Coming through the ranks, O'Neill is keen on novice chaser **Forza Milan**, who has recovered from an injury sustained when well fancied for the Pertemps Final at Cheltenham in March.

The trainer says: " We thought he had a big chance but it wasn't to be. It might have been the way he jumped but he broke a bone in his back. He seems to be okay again now and I'm really looking forward to him going chasing as I've always thought of him as a chaser."

Above Board is another earmarked for Saturdays after hitting form during the summer, while veteran chaser **Eastlake** will have his season geared towards an incredible sixth tilt at the Topham, a race he won in 2016.

Among the new intake, O'Neill is sweet on three-year-old **Youmzain Star**, whose Flat form ties in with the best of the Classic generation in France and could be a potential Triumph Hurdle contender.

"I love him," says the trainer. "We schooled him recently – it was the first time he'd ever seen a pole – and he was a natural, so that got me excited. He looks like a proper juvenile hurdler for the autumn and winter with Cheltenham hopefully the end game."

Scotland set to brave hurdles

Among the more intriguing horses at Jackdaws Castle is **Scotland**, a regular in Group company on the Flat in the colours of

Fitri Hay and set to try his luck over hurdles at the age of seven.

O'Neill says: "We're still getting to know him but he's in the Cesarewitch at Newmarket in October and that looks a good place to start with him as he has very decent form on the Flat. After that he's likely to be schooled over hurdles with a view to going jumping later on."

Other young hurdlers to note from the yard include Darsi In The Park, Ready And Able, Kitikat and Tedham with O'Neill confidently expecting the quartet to pay their way in novice company over the coming months.

He says: "**Darsi In The Park** looks sure to improve on what he achieved in a bumper at Doncaster last February when switching to jumping hurdles on soft ground, while **Ready And Able** won both his starts over hurdles early in the summer and will have to step up in grade this autumn, but I think he's up to it.

"**Kitikat** was workmanlike when winning a bumper at Southwell in May and stayed on strongly to finish second at Worcester in September on his first start over hurdles, giving the distinct impression that a step up in distance is going to suit him.

"**Tedham** is open to plenty of improvement when sent hurdling as he has the make and shape for the job."

Cake looks a tasty prospect

Besides Forza Milan, O'Neill will have a decent squad of horses in the novice chasing division with Cake De L'Isle, Fleminport, Noble Robin, Oakley Hall and Sky Pirate all at the forefront of the trainer's thoughts as the core jumping season gets under way.

He says: "**Cake De L'Isle** is related to a Listed chase winner in France and, being owned by Trevor Hemmings, it's always safe to assume that jumping fences is going to be the making of him.

JUMP
TO IT

HOME TO THE MIDLANDS GRAND NATIONAL, UTTOXETER RACECOURSE IS FIRMLY ESTABLISHED AS ONE OF THE LEADING NATIONAL HUNT TRACKS IN THE MIDLANDS.

WITH 25 FIXTURES PER YEAR, THE RACING CALENDAR RUNS FROM JANUARY RIGHT THE WAY THROUGH TO 31 DECEMBER FOR NEW YEAR'S EVE RACING.

OCTOBER 2018

SUNDAY 7	OKTOBERFEST RACEDAY
THURSDAY 18	ACCESS ALL AREAS RACEDAY

NOVEMBER 2018

FRIDAY 2	GENTLEMEN'S DAY
SATURDAY 17	MARSTON'S BEER FESTIVAL RACEDAY
SUNDAY 25	AFTERNOON RACING

DECEMBER 2018

TUESDAY 11	CHRISTMAS JUMPER RACEDAY
FRIDAY 21	CHRISTMAS PARTY RACEDAY
MONDAY 31	NEW YEAR'S EVE RACEDAY

JANUARY 2019

SATURDAY 26	LOCALS RACEDAY

FEBRUARY 2019

SATURDAY 9	FEBRUARY HURDLE RACEDAY

MARCH 2019

SATURDAY 16	MIDLANDS GRAND NATIONAL
SATURDAY 30	BEER & GIN JAMBOREE RACEDAY

FOR OUR FULL 2018/19 JUMP SEASON FIXTURES
VISIT UTTOXETER-RACECOURSE.CO.UK

19 07
UTTOXETER
RACECOURSE

🅵 🆈 🅾

JONJO O'NEILL
CHELTENHAM, GLOUCS

	No. of Hrs	Races Run	1st	2nd	3rd	Unpl	Per cent	£1 Level Stake
NH Flat	12	14	1	0	3	10	7.1	-12.50
Hurdles	102	323	34	31	29	229	10.5	-170.60
Chases	60	216	29	21	22	144	13.4	-15.16
Totals	**146**	**553**	**64**	**52**	**54**	**383**	**11.6**	**-198.26**
16-17	156	686	78	84	75	449	11.4	-211.33
15-16	152	559	80	71	44	363	14.3	-118.05

BY MONTH

NH Flat	W-R	Per cent	£1 Level Stake	Hurdles	W-R	Per cent	£1 Level Stake
May	0-1	0.0	-1.00	May	5-29	17.2	-7.13
June	0-0	0.0	0.00	June	4-18	22.2	-7.23
July	0-0	0.0	0.00	July	4-22	18.2	-8.53
August	0-0	0.0	0.00	August	1-14	7.1	-12.09
September	0-0	0.0	0.00	September	2-17	11.8	+3.00
October	1-7	14.3	-5.50	October	8-48	16.7	-9.57
November	0-2	0.0	-2.00	November	2-48	4.2	-35.50
December	0-0	0.0	0.00	December	4-36	11.1	-15.50
January	0-0	0.0	0.00	January	3-36	8.3	-24.63
February	0-3	0.0	-3.00	February	1-15	6.7	-13.43
March	0-0	0.0	0.00	March	0-21	0.0	-21.00
April	0-1	0.0	-1.00	April	0-19	0.0	-19.00

Chases	W-R	Per cent	£1 Level Stake	Totals	W-R	Per cent	£1 Level Stake
May	7-38	18.4	+4.91	May	12-68	17.6	-3.22
June	3-21	14.3	-4.50	June	7-39	17.9	-11.73
July	2-14	14.3	+1.00	July	6-36	16.7	-7.53
August	1-10	10.0	-6.25	August	2-24	8.3	-18.34
September	2-17	11.8	-1.90	September	4-34	11.8	+1.10
October	4-28	14.3	-3.17	October	13-83	15.7	-18.24
November	3-25	12.0	-9.25	November	5-75	6.7	-46.75
December	4-20	20.0	+29.00	December	8-56	14.3	+13.50
January	0-12	0.0	-12.00	January	3-48	6.3	-36.63
February	0-12	0.0	-12.00	February	1-30	3.3	-28.43
March	1-7	14.3	-2.50	March	1-28	3.6	-23.50
April	2-12	16.7	+1.50	April	2-32	6.3	-18.50

Statistics relate to all runners in Britain from May 1, 2017 to April 28, 2018

DISTANCE

Hurdles	W-R	Per cent	£1 Level Stake	Chases	W-R	Per cent	£1 Level Stake
2m-2m3f	10-127	7.9	-80.08	2m-2m3f	6-27	22.2	+8.60
2m4f-2m7f	21-144	14.6	-51.10	2m4f-2m7f	9-72	12.5	-13.92
3m+	2-50	4.0	-39.00	3m+	14-117	12.0	-9.84

TYPE OF RACE

Non-Handicaps	W-R	Per cent	£1 Level Stake	Handicaps	W-R	Per cent	£1 Level Stake
Nov Hrdls	9-80	11.3	-56.31	Nov Hrdls	3-12	25.0	-2.09
Hrdls	5-55	9.1	-36.95	Hrdls	16-168	9.5	-82.25
Nov Chs	3-11	27.3	-4.07	Nov Chs	2-17	11.8	-7.00
Chases	0-2	0.0	-2.00	Chases	21-167	12.6	-10.59
Sell/Claim	0-0	0.0	0.00	Sell/Claim	0-0	0.0	0.00

RACE CLASS

	W-R	Per cent	£1 Level Stake
Class 1	1-21	4.8	-13.00
Class 2	6-54	11.1	-6.50
Class 3	11-136	8.1	-75.17
Class 4	43-274	15.7	-47.09
Class 5	2-62	3.2	-52.00
Class 6	1-6	16.7	-4.50

FIRST TIME OUT

	W-R	Per cent	£1 Level Stake
Bumpers	1-12	8.3	-10.50
Hurdles	11-87	12.6	-23.08
Chases	10-47	21.3	+7.74
Totals	22-146	15.1	-25.84

DID YOU KNOW?

When Jonjo O'Neill broke his right leg in a fall at Bangor in 1980 it was an injury so severe that when he returned to riding too quickly after having it pinned and plated he had to fly to Switzerland for specialist surgery and was asked to sign a consent form for amputation, should it be required. The metalwork was framed and hung on his office wall.

"He might have another run over hurdles before he goes chasing, while **Fleminport** won twice for us over hurdles but going chasing is very likely to see him in an even better light.

"**Noble Robin** seems to want plenty of cut in the ground as his two wins over hurdles came on soft and heavy, so when the rain comes he should pay his way over fences.

"**Oakley Hall** is the type to do well in novice chases, while **Sky Pirate** finished second on his chasing debut at Uttoxeter in September and will benefit for that experience."

Following the King approach

Alan King has made it pay on the Flat during the summer and O'Neill reveals he too will be looking for more winners on the level in the future.

Among a big team of youngsters at Jackdaws Castle are some well-bred store horses but also some bred for the Flat, and O'Neill is hoping they can cut their teeth in that discipline before running over jumps.

"We're buying a few more Flat ones and I think it's the way forward," said the trainer. "You can run them on the Flat as two-year-olds if they're strong enough to take it and then go over hurdles.

"I always did it when I trained in the north and we're getting nice owners who want to do the same thing again, so we're going to buy a few more Flat ones."

Harbour Watch two-year-old **Pop The Cork**, purchased from the breeze-ups, finished third on his debut at Kempton for the yard in August and O'Neill hopes he will make a juvenile hurdler in time.

He adds: "Hopefully you're trying to buy value. We're doing a bit of everything and are getting a lot of new owners."

Interview by Andrew King

Jonjo O'Neill-trained stars of the future climb the rising ground at Jackdaws Castle

SUPER STATS

Since the beginning of 2015 O'Neill is 14-26 (54%, +11.81pt) runners in handicap hurdles over 3m or further that are sent off market leader

Uttoxeter is a track at which you should pay close attention to O'Neill's runners in handicap hurdles who are sent off 4-1 or shorter. The form figures of qualifiers in that sphere since June 2017 read 111411 (83%, +10.62pt)

O'Neill is 1-10 in Warwick bumpers since the start of 2015

Aidan Coleman is 4-10 (40%, +9.25pt) when riding for Jonjo O'Neill at Fontwell since 2016. The form figures are a fairly impressive 1231123144

O'Neill is 2-32 in non-Festival Cheltenham handicap hurdles since the start of 2015

Had you blindly backed all of O'Neill's jumps horses running in the month of November since 2015 you would have backed 21 winners from 247 runners and incurred a level-stake loss of 115.71pt to a £1 stake

Richie McLernon is 1-46 (2%, -31pt) on O'Neill runners in non-handicap hurdles since the start of 2017

O'Neill hasn't had a Grade 1 winner since April 4, 2014 when Holywell scored at Aintree under Tony McCoy. He has saddled 28 runners at the top level since then and all have been beaten

Last December was a good one for O'Neill followers. Backing his hurdlers yielded a profit of 29pt

Positivity everywhere as Pond House team look forward to a big season

FOR David Pipe last season was unfortunate. Unsuitable ground conditions forced by chaotic British weather coupled with a few of his big names off the track through injury meant the trainer didn't quite enjoy the success of previous years, but he is determined and hopeful of changing his fortunes this time.

Pipe's 2017 Cheltenham Festival winner Un Temps Pour Tout missed all of last season and hasn't run since his second victory in the Ultima Handicap Chase, while 2015 Champion Bumper winner Moon Racer was absent until February and the hugely exciting Mr Big Shot didn't return to the track until the Cheltenham Festival – although he did land a valuable handicap at the Grand National meeting on his next start.

There is no negativity at Pond House – in fact the feeling is better than ever with Pipe's stars back in great form and winners for the yard already on the board.

The trainer says: "A lot of our big names had injuries and missed the track last year so this time could be much better. I'm happy with them and they're all in good form and have come back looking great, so it's all systems go.

This year's summer jumpers were in great form with Pipe hitting almost a third of last season's tally before October and he is excited about having his stars back in action and a plethora of unearthed talent behind his stable doors.

"We had a good summer, the horses ran well and we had some winners," Pipe says. "And the horses we've got this year are quite exciting. We haven't got too many novice chasers but we've got a great bunch of novice hurdlers and bumper horses.

"Moon Racer and Mr Big Shot would be our two main novice chasing hopes, but there are quite a few younger horses we're looking forward to seeing."

Duo aimed at National

Pipe's father Martin needs no introduction, and the training master's sole Grand National success came in 1994. It would be somewhat fitting for David to emulate his father in the

....

Chasing success for Pipe is more frequent over longer distances and his runners do particularly well over trips ranging from 2m7f to 3m2½f (61-324, 19%, +52.47pt) but he has a better strike-rate with those running over 2m1½f to 2m3f (10-31, 32%, +10.70pt)

Facebook.com/racingpost

WINNERS IN LAST FIVE SEASONS 33, 59, 80, 116, 90

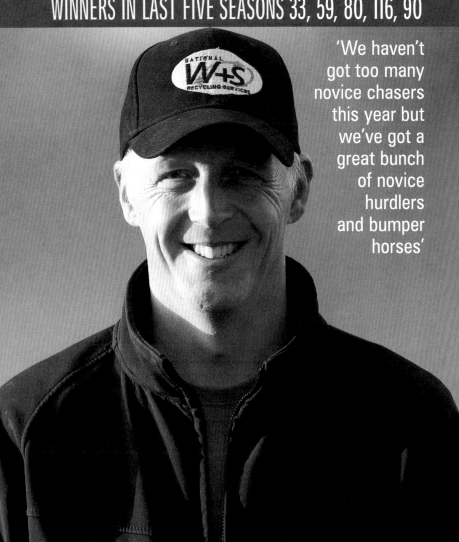

'We haven't got too many novice chasers this year but we've got a great bunch of novice hurdlers and bumper horses'

DAVID PIPE
RACING

Aintree showpiece 25 years on, and he's got two strong representatives being campaigned with Aintree in mind.

Un Temps Pour Tout is a favourite in the yard. He hasn't been seen since his photo-finish success over Singlefarmpayment at the Festival in 2017 but has been given an early season target of the Ladbrokes Trophy.

Pipe, who won the National in 2008 with Comply Or Die, says: "He'll be aimed at the Newbury race for the first part of the season and then we'll be looking at Cheltenham and Aintree after that.

"He had to miss last season but he's in good form at present. It takes a lot of work to get him fit but we're very pleased with him."

One horse who knows the Aintree fences all too well is **Vieux Lion Rouge**. He has had five spins over the National course, winning the Becher Chase in 2016. In the National itself he finished seventh in 2016, sixth in 2017 and ninth in the event last year.

Vieux Lion Rouge will be heading back to Aintree again this season

Facebook.com/racingpost

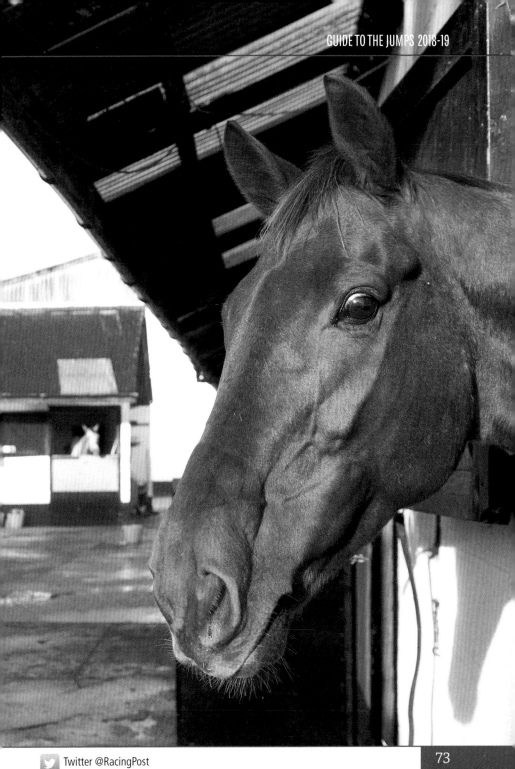

Pipe says of the nine-year-old: "He's another whose long-term target would be the Grand National, but we'll try to run him a bit more this year over hurdles and fences. I thought he was unlucky at Aintree last year – a horse hit him side on and put him out of the race. He seems to jump the fences really well so it's worth another go."

Teillee leads handicap team

Second-season novice **Ramses De Teillee** is among a big team of well-handicapped inmates at the Somerset yard. The six-year-old, who landed two chases last year, is expected to progress from his mark of 141 after summering well.

"He was also placed several times," says the trainer. "He had a wind operation during the summer and he'll have an entry in the BetVictor Gold Cup, but he's a versatile horse who can go two-and-a-half to three miles and he loves soft ground. He's a great jumper of fences, we've always liked him and he's done us proud but there should be a bit more to come."

Among Pipe's ammunition for big-race targets is Moon Racer and What A Moment, a winner at Cheltenham's November Meeting for the last two seasons.

The trainer says: "I think we probably want to step up **Moon Racer** in trip these days. The first two times we ran him last year the ground was too soft and he couldn't cope with it. He does appreciate a better surface these days.

"We'll school him over a fence and see how he goes – if he jumps well then going chasing is an option, although I imagine we'll start him off over hurdles.

"The plan with **What A Moment** is to send him back to Cheltenham in the race he's won for the last two years – the amateur riders' handicap – to try and make it a hat-trick.

"He picked up an injury after last year's win which kept him off for the rest of the season but

Ramses De Teillee cruises to victory in a novice chase at Chepstow last season

he's in good form and he'll go straight to Cheltenham."

Pipe adds: "**Dell' Arca** had a fantastic summer and will mix and match hurdles and fences. He's in the grip of the handicapper a little bit but he's done very well for us.

"**Friday Night Light** ran quite a few times last season and won at Newbury in January. He's summered well and is quite a bit stronger this year. He'll start off over hurdles, probably over two and a half miles, but I'd like to think there's a bit more to come from him.

"I also thought **Daklondike** did quite well last year. He loves soft ground and stays all day – those long-distance chases are what he'll be aimed at. He's young and improving and he stepped up a lot last year and hopefully he can improve a bit more.

"It was a frustrating season for **Vaniteux** but we hope he'll bounce back this year. We'll aim at three-mile chases – he gives the impression he'll stay that trip quite well."

Socks has plenty more to give

One horse in particular it could pay to follow is **King's Socks**. He ran a good race when fifth in the Plate at the Cheltenham Festival before being pulled up at Aintree. Pipe holds him in high regard and says: "I think it's fair to say we expected a lot more from him last year. He travelled very well at the Festival for a long way but just didn't get up the hill.

"He had a wind op during the summer and he'll have an entry in the BetVictor and Haldon Gold Cup. He's still only six so hopefully there should be much more to come."

Ready to be Big Shot over fences

Quite possibly the highlight of the year for Pond House was **Mr Big Shot** winning a valuable Grade 3 handicap hurdle at the National festival. The seven-year-old could be set for a big year as the flagbearer of the yard's novice chasing team.

He says: "We'll probably go novice chasing with him this season – he has bags of potential but isn't the easiest to train. He's related to Philson Run, who was a Midlands National winner, and staying looks one of his fortes."

Huge amount of young talent

Pipe speaks with plenty of enthusiasm about this season's novice hurdling team in which Queens Cave and Remastered look to be the leading hopes after impressive victories in bumpers last season.

"**Queens Cave** is a good mare who won nicely at Uttoxeter. I thought she ran a good race at Sandown, too, but in hindsight she

probably got there a bit sooner than we would've liked. She's summered well, she's talented and we have high hopes for her.

"I like **Remastered**. He won his bumper at Chepstow very nicely and the form of the race worked out very well. It was too late in the season to go novice hurdling so we put him away. He's another who jumps well and he's a relentless galloper who'll be at his best over two and a half miles.

"**Know The Score** won well at Towcester but did too much in the Champion Bumper and paid for it at the end, finishing down the field. He has a really good engine, though, and is one to really look forward to in novice hurdles.

"**Orchard Thieves** won well in a novice hurdle at Worcester in May and I thought it was a very good performance. He's a three-mile stayer in the mud and he'll be kept over hurdles this season. I think he could do well."

High hopes for French recruits

Of the rest of Pipe's young talent, the four-year-old French Grade 2 bumper winner **Ekayburg** gets a favourable mention.

"He'll go novice hurdling," the trainer says. "We had him ready last year but the ground quickened up and we just didn't have him ready in time so we didn't run him. He's summered very well and we're pleased with the work we've seen at home.

There are more new names, too, as Pipe continues: "**Eden Du Houx** is a nice horse. He won a point-to-point in Ireland and could start in a bumper and then go novice hurdling, while **Umbrigado** finished second in an Irish point and is another to look forward to.

"It's early days with **Catch The Swallows**, who was runner-up in an Irish point-to-point in March. Whether he goes in a bumper or straight over hurdles we'll have to discuss with his owner Trevor Hemmings."

Interview by James Stevens

SUPER STATS

Pipe's fortunes haven't been great over the past couple of years and he managed only 33 winners last season, earning just shy of £500,000 which was below his usual standards. However, his figures in the current season strongly suggest he will do much better this term

Pipe is best followed at Haydock, where he registers his highest level-stake return (11-54, 20%, +48pt)

Perth sees Pipe achieve best in terms of strike-rate (12-21, 57%, +17.61pt), while he also fares well at Leicester in that respect (9-25, 36%, +8.90pt)

The yard's chasers do well at Newbury (7-29, 24%, +12.65pt) and Chepstow (5-28, 18%, +12.04pt)

Pipe's hurdlers have a good record at Kempton (6-26, 23%, +13.63pt) and Plumpton (6-25, 24%, +5.98pt), while the odd decent-priced winner over hurdles pops up at Ludlow (4-32, 13%, +12.12pt)

Most of Pipe's bumper winners come at Uttoxeter (3-13, 23%, +5.80pt) and Worcester (4-17, 24%, +2.75pt)

Pipe's string performs solidly in novice chases, enjoying plenty of success and maintaining a high strike-rate and level-stake profit (46-167, 28%, +28.74pt)

Tom Scudamore rides most of the yards winners but does particularly well on Pipe's chasers (85-415, 20%, +26.51pt)

Conor O'Farrell has a good record when called on to ride Pipe-trained chasers (7-49, 14%, +1.55pt)

JUMP SEASON OPENER

SATURDAY 13TH / SUNDAY 14TH OCTOBER
AT CHEPSTOW RACECOURSE

THE WINTER SEASON STARTS AT CHEPSTOW

Oktoberfest Saturday

SILVER TROPHY

FOOD & COUNTRYSIDE SUNDAY

PERSIAN WAR NOVICES' HURDLE

CHEPSTOW
RACING & EVENTS

chepstow-racecourse.co.uk | 01291 622260

SPECIAL FOCUS COLIN TIZZARD

All systems go with big two set to clash early in Betfair Chase thriller

THE Tizzards are eyeing a two-pronged attack on jump racing's triple crown, with reigning Gold Cup hero Native River and a rejuvenated Thistlecrack set for a first career clash in the Betfair Chase at Haydock.

A million-pound bonus has been offered by Jockey Club Racecourses for the last three seasons if a horse can win the Betfair Chase at Haydock on November 24, the King George at Kempton on Boxing Day and the Gold Cup at Cheltenham in March – and the Tizzard team are eyeing Haydock as a likely starting point for **Native River**, who has made a full recovery from a minor injury he encountered towards the end of last season.

The eight-year-old was absent from the first two legs of the jumps triple crown last season, sidestepping Haydock and Kempton for a lower-grade assignment in Newbury's Denman Chase before his victory over Might Bite at the Cheltenham Festival.

Joe Tizzard, assistant and son to trainer Colin, says: "The main aim is to get him to the Gold Cup – last year we couldn't really run him much as he had an injury at the end of the season before.

"We'll likely start him at Haydock for the Betfair Chase, and if he wins that then we'd

be tempted to go for the million-pound bonus. We'd then have to think about going to Aintree or Punchestown.

"If you win at Haydock then it certainly has to come into the equation – there's a lot of time between the races so it's very doable – it's not easy though. We'll have to play it by ear but I'd imagine he'll start back in the Betfair Chase."

Thistlecrack has been on a recovery mission since losing his unbeaten record to the ill-fated Many Clouds in the Cotswold Chase at Cheltenham in January 2017.

The ten-year-old showed glimpses of his former self when fourth in the King George on his most recent start, a race he won in 2016, but he missed a Gold Cup clash with Native River after suffering a stress fracture in January.

The four-time Grade 1-winning hurdler has not been seen since finishing in midfield behind Might Bite at Kempton, and the Charlie Hall Chase at Wetherby on November 3 is a possible early target.

....

While Colin Tizzard narrowly failed to break the £2 million prize-money barrier last term, a feat he achieved for the first time in the 2016-17 campaign, his tally of 79 winners was a personal best

Facebook.com/racingpost

WINNERS IN LAST FIVE SEASONS 79, 57, 50, 38, 26

'We'll likely start him at Haydock for the Betfair Chase, and if he wins that then we'd be tempted to go for the million-pound bonus'

Tizzard says: "Thistlecrack is a little bit older now so things have got to start to happen for him. We'll get him out early and get some runs into him – he'll start in the Charlie Hall and then we'd have a look at the million-pound bonus."

"Although we don't like our horses to clash, there are only so many races to run them in and Native River and Thistlecrack are rated highly enough to deserve to run in those races.

"They've both been in lovely form since we've had them back. They came in around the middle of June and are going through the motions well.

"We couldn't be happier with them, especially Thistlecrack – he's fully over his little problems and we're hoping to have a full and successful campaign with him."

Interview by James Stevens

Thistlecrack is doing well at home and the Tizzards are hopeful all roads will lead to the Gold Cup

EXPERT VIEW

NATIVE RIVER'S owners Brocade Racing must think they have a chance of bagging the big-money bonus if their pride and joy can land the first leg at Haydock, but going right-handed around Sunbury's twisting and turning chase course on Boxing Day might be stretching it, *writes Andrew King.*

At last season's Festival the Tizzard-trained star galloped and jumped his rivals into submission in the Gold Cup before passing the post with over four lengths to spare from Might Bite – and there did not seem to be any fluke about the result.

Confidence is high at Venn Farm Stables that there is more to come from the horse as he has returned from his summer break looking stronger than ever. The obvious first stop of the campaign is Haydock, but it would be no great surprise if he gave Kempton the swerve at Christmas.

Whatever route is chosen by connections this side of the new year it seems a sure bet Native River will warm up for his second tilt at Gold Cup glory in the Betfair Denman Chase at Newbury in February as it perfectly paved the way last season.

If Tizzard has a young chasing star waiting in the wings it might well be **Kilbricken Storm**, who sprang a 33-1 surprise in the Grade 1 Albert Bartlett last season. It will be a shock if his attentions are not turned to fences soon as he won an Irish point before joining current connections and has the make to go to the top of the novice chasing tree.

Anyone looking for a darker horse among the Tizzard team could do worse than **White Moon**, who started well last term by winning at Wincanton and Exeter but then blew out at Sandown. He wasn't seen again but had shown enough to suggest he could prove a cut above average when switched to chasing. He's one to keep on the right side.

SUPER STATS

Tizzard doesn't send many runners north but the hint should be taken when he does, particularly at Newcastle (3-6, 50%, +25.00pt) and Wetherby (4-15, 27%, +8.98pt)

While he doesn't have the amount of ammunition of Nicholls and Henderson, Tizzard regularly competes on quality with his record at Aintree (12-49, 24%, +99.49pt) perfect evidence of that

Although traditionally more associated with staying chasers, Tizzard has a better record with his hurdlers at Cheltenham (7-58, 12%, +4.55pt), while his runners over hurdles also fare well at Kempton (5-27, 19%, +9.25pt)

Tizzard's chasers also do well at Kempton (6-36, 17%, +22.85pt), but they have regular success and better strike-rates at Newbury (10-36, 28%, +13.20pt) and Wincanton (19-80, 24%, +26.58pt)

February is often decent for the yard and it was Tizzard's best month in terms of total winners and strike-rate last season (15-62, 24%, +7.50pt)

It appears the quality in Tizzard's yard is still underestimated by the layers as his strike-rate and level-stake returns are solid in all Graded (41-237, 17%, +94.05pt) and Listed races (9-48, 19%, +12.76pt)

Tizzard knows how to place his up-and-coming types, as his record in graduation chases (5-16, 31%, +3.75pt) and novices hurdles (51-299, 17%, +1.31pt) shows

COLIN TIZZARD
MILBORNE PORT, DORSET

	No. of Hrs	Races Run	1st	2nd	3rd	Unpl	Per cent	£1 Level Stake
NH Flat	26	37	2	2	6	27	5.4	-30.75
Hurdles	65	243	40	38	27	138	16.5	-39.71
Chases	56	256	37	42	48	129	14.5	-88.89
Totals	**111**	**536**	**79**	**82**	**81**	**294**	**14.7**	**-159.35**
16-17	86	402	57	64	54	227	14.2	+11.75
15-16	58	323	50	39	52	182	15.5	-46.75

BY MONTH

NH Flat	W-R	Per cent	£1 Level Stake	Hurdles	W-R	Per cent	£1 Level Stake
May	0-1	0.0	-1.00	May	1-2	50.0	+1.00
June	0-0	0.0	0.00	June	1-2	50.0	-0.39
July	0-0	0.0	0.00	July	0-2	0.0	-2.00
August	0-0	0.0	0.00	August	0-0	0.0	0.00
September	0-0	0.0	0.00	September	0-3	0.0	-3.00
October	1-7	14.3	-4.75	October	8-36	22.2	-5.31
November	0-2	0.0	-2.00	November	8-43	18.6	-7.05
December	0-3	0.0	-3.00	December	6-38	15.8	-8.00
January	0-4	0.0	-4.00	January	1-21	4.8	-18.13
February	1-9	11.1	-5.00	February	7-29	24.1	+1.68
March	0-4	0.0	-4.00	March	7-32	21.9	+32.48
April	0-7	0.0	-7.00	April	1-35	2.9	-31.00

Chases	W-R	Per cent	£1 Level Stake	Totals	W-R	Per cent	£1 Level Stake
May	1-3	33.3	-0.25	May	2-6	33.3	-0.25
June	0-3	0.0	-3.00	June	1-5	20.0	-3.39
July	1-6	16.7	+7.00	July	1-8	12.5	+5.00
August	0-5	0.0	-5.00	August	0-5	0.0	-5.00
September	0-3	0.0	-3.00	September	0-6	0.0	-6.00
October	4-38	10.5	-28.92	October	13-81	16.0	-38.98
November	6-46	13.0	-28.17	November	14-91	15.4	-37.22
December	5-33	15.2	-15.13	December	11-74	14.9	-26.13
January	3-25	12.0	-11.75	January	4-50	8.0	-33.88
February	7-24	29.2	+10.82	February	15-62	24.2	+7.50
March	5-36	13.9	-10.50	March	12-72	16.7	+17.98
April	5-34	14.7	-1.00	April	6-76	7.9	-39.00

DISTANCE

Hurdles	W-R	Per cent	£1 Level Stake	Chases	W-R	Per cent	£1 Level Stake
2m-2m3f	26-136	19.1	-25.02	2m-2m3f	10-57	17.5	-23.82
2m4f-2m7f	11-81	13.6	-34.69	2m4f-2m7f	14-94	14.9	-21.24
3m+	3-25	12.0	+21.00	3m+	13-105	12.4	-43.83

TYPE OF RACE

Non-Handicaps	W-R	Per cent	£1 Level Stake	Handicaps	W-R	Per cent	£1 Level Stake
Nov Hrdls	20-97	20.6	+3.09	Nov Hrdls	1-12	8.3	-8.00
Hrdls	6-29	20.7	-7.18	Hrdls	13-105	12.4	-27.63
Nov Chs	8-49	16.3	-24.38	Nov Chs	3-13	23.1	+0.50
Chases	4-18	22.2	-6.81	Chases	20-155	12.9	-56.20
Sell/Claim	0-0	0.0	0.00	Sell/Claim	0-0	0.0	0.00

RACE CLASS

	W-R	Per cent	£1 Level Stake
Class 1	14-107	13.1	-4.02
Class 2	6-54	11.1	-31.05
Class 3	20-130	15.4	-35.97
Class 4	34-195	17.4	-59.32
Class 5	4-43	9.3	-24.25
Class 6	1-7	14.3	-4.75

FIRST TIME OUT

	W-R	Per cent	£1 Level Stake
Bumpers	2-26	7.7	-19.75
Hurdles	6-39	15.4	-18.18
Chases	8-46	17.4	-27.39
Totals	16-111	14.4	-65.32

DID YOU KNOW?

The Dorset-based trainer most admires Sir Ian Botham, having played cricket with him at school, and watched him achieve huge success as an all-rounder. The Gold Cup-winning trainer is also partial to a tipple of whisky.

Statistics relate to all runners in Britain from May 1, 2017 to April 28, 2018

Native River (right) heads back to base after morning exercise

Facebook.com/racingpost

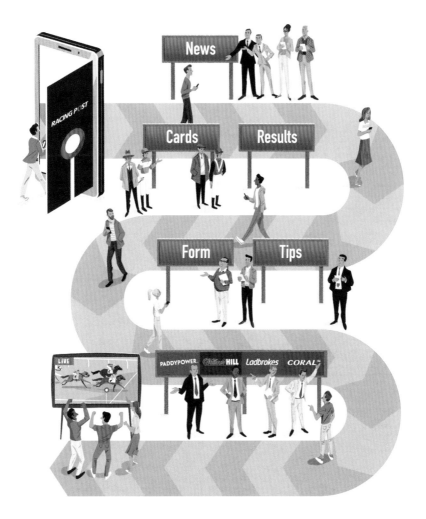

THE RACING POST APP.
EVERYTHING YOU NEED TO INFORM YOUR BET,
AND YOUR CHOICE OF BOOKIE TO PLACE IT.

Why continually flit between apps when racing's best information and top bookies are sitting side by side in one place? It only takes a couple of taps to log in to your account and, to top it all off, you can remain logged in to all four bookies at once. Placing an informed bet with the best odds has never been easier.

RACING POST

**WHEN YOU BET ON RACING,
YOU CAN BET ON RACING POST.**

VIEW FROM IRELAND ALAN SWEETMAN

Mullins in pole position but huge firepower will see Elliott challenging

THE 2017-18 Irish jumps season will be a hard act to follow. A lively domestic campaign reached a fitting conclusion at an action-packed Punchestown festival. Elsewhere, Irish-trained horses made an outstanding contribution at the Cheltenham Festival with a total of 17 wins and filled the first four places in the Randox Health Grand National.

Cheltenham confirmed how the two leading Irish stables have pulled clear of the pack, Gordon Elliott winning the Festival trainers' title from Willie Mullins by a score of 8-7.

Not many negatives were attached to the collective Irish performance at the Festival, although certain weaknesses were implicit in a failure to land the Gold Cup, Champion Hurdle or Champion Chase.

At home, Mullins recorded a tenth consecutive trainers' championship with an earnings margin of around €800,000, and numerically by 210-209. Joseph O'Brien was

Samcro will be a major force whether staying over hurdles or going chasing in a season sure to be dominated by Gordon Elliott and Willie Mullins (facing page)

third on both counts, ahead of Henry de Bromhead, Jessica Harrington and Noel Meade, the other major figures on a scene increasingly dominated by the top half-dozen.

These days only a tiny minority of serious contenders for top-level Irish races will come from outside this narrow cohort. Some of the more significant exceptions are likely to be owned by JP McManus, whose policy of supporting a wide range of trainers provides Irish jump racing with a significant prop.

In a departure from the pattern of two previous seasons characterised by a flying start for Elliott with his summer jumpers, Mullins is setting the pace this time. By the end of the Listowel festival he led Elliott by 82 to 40 with an earnings differential of €650,000.

Given the awesome strength in depth displayed by Mullins in the final months of the last two seasons, he is in pole position to retain the title. Yet Elliott's yard houses Ireland's two highest-profile jumpers – the remarkable **Tiger Roll**, who achieved his third Cheltenham Festival win last March en route to Aintree glory, and last season's outstanding novice hurdler **Samcro**, touted as a possible future Gold Cup winner from the day he won a point-to-point.

Elliott and the Gigginstown strategists face a difficult decision – one that will have a crucial bearing on the narrative of the season – whether to deploy Samcro in the hurdling division or send him straight over fences. His fall at the third-last at Punchestown was a missed opportunity in terms of assessing his likely impact in the senior ranks.

PRESENTING PERCY CAN REACH TOP OVER FENCES

If Jessica Harrington's 2017 hero **Sizing John** fails to make a full recovery from the pelvic injury that put paid to his title defence last season, it will be left to second-season chaser **Presenting Percy** to lead the Irish challenge for the 2019 Cheltenham Gold Cup.

Trained by Pat Kelly, who has kept the flag flying for more modestly resourced stables at recent Cheltenham Festivals, the 2017 Pertemps Final winner confirmed his status as a top-class staying prospect with an emphatic defeat of fellow Irish raider Monalee in the RSA Chase.

Monalee, whose fall at the second-last at Punchestown was overshadowed by the extraordinary incident involving Paul Townend and **Al Boum Photo** at the final fence, is expected to make the grade in the senior ranks for Henry de Bromhead, who has a more established performer in last season's Ryanair winner **Balko Des Flos**.

The Cheltenham Gold Cup continues to elude Mullins.

Djakadam, second in 2015 and 2016 and fourth in 2017, could manage only fifth last season and was beaten by stablemate **Bellshill** in the Punchestown Gold Cup, to whom the big-race baton was passed when Djakadam was retired.

Third to Might Bite in the 2017 RSA Chase and lightly raced last season, Bellshill is probably the pick of the stable's established staying chasers at this stage.

There is no more exciting young chaser around than last season's top 2m novice **Footpad**, five from five over fences, including four Grade 1 events by an aggregate 42-length margin. As things stand, he is a feasible pretender to Altior's crown, yet he also looks ready to take a step up in distance and could mature into a Gold Cup contender.

Un De Sceaux, who failed to repeat his 2017 Ryanair success, was back on top of his game at Fairyhouse and Punchestown, proving too strong for his once-bombproof stablemate **Douvan** in the process. The likes

RETURN OF THE JUMPS

FRI 30	SAT 1	FRI 14	SAT 15	SAT 29
NOVEMBER	DECEMBER	DECEMBER	DECEMBER	DECEMBER

doncaster racing & events

doncaster-racecourse.co.uk

of **Min**, **Great Field** and Al Boum Photo provide further depth for Mullins in the senior chasing division.

Having triumphed at Aintree as an eight-year-old, Tiger Roll could be in the mix again next spring, while runner-up **Pleasant Company**, set to turn 11, will be the same age as three consecutive winners of the great race earlier in the decade. Aintree fourth **Anibale Fly** will be of interest in major conditions races having proved best of nine Irish challengers when third to Native River in the Gold Cup.

Laurina was an impressive winner of the mares' novice hurdle at Cheltenham in March

SO MANY OPTIONS FOR MULLINS AND ELLIOTT

The British-trained and McManus-owned Buveur D'Air was made to work hard for his neck success in last season's Champion Hurdle by the Mullins-trained **Melon**. His perceived vulnerability could be a factor in keeping Samcro and Melon over hurdles.

Mullins has numerous options to weigh up in respect of a strong team of mares, headed by **Benie Des Dieux**, a Grade 1 winner at Cheltenham and Punchestown last season, **Laurina**, a runaway winner of the Mares' Novices' Hurdle at Cheltenham, and **Limini**, who won the same race in 2016 and was back in winning form on the Flat at Leopardstown in September.

Reinvented as a stayer when trouncing stablemate and Stayers' Hurdle winner **Penhill** at Punchestown, former Champion Hurdle winner **Faugheen** is not a back-number. Harrington's **Supasundae**, whose ability to compete at the highest level over a range of distances was a feature of last season, is another force to be reckoned with.

Only when we know the agenda for Samcro and Melon will the novice chase picture become clearer. Whatever happens, Mullins and Elliott will exert a major influence. **Next Destination** and **Delta Work**, who fought out the finish of a 3m Grade 1 novice hurdle for the rival stables at the Punchestown festival, can be rated among the most promising staying novice chasers.

Mullins supplied four out of the first five in the Champion Bumper at Cheltenham, led home by the mare **Relegate** from **Carefully Selected** and **Tornado Flyer**.

At Punchestown, Tornado Flyer headed another one-two-three, completed by **Blackbow** and Carefully Selected. These will provide the nucleus of a powerful novice hurdling squad.

Dorrells Pierji, off the mark over hurdles at Listowel after two bumper wins, should also make the grade. Sidelined by injury last season, **Annamix** will be a fascinating novice prospect if he makes it back.

Elliott has a good bunch of bumper winners and Gigginstown-owned point-to-point graduates for his novice hurdling team. **Commander Of Fleet**, wide-margin winner of the Goffs Land Rover, could be the pick of them. Big things are naturally expected of **Dlauro**, a £410,000 purchase to join Joseph O'Brien after a maiden point win.

Among the mares, John Queally's Aintree winner **Getaway Katie Mai** and the Mullins-trained **Colreevy** are names to note.

With Samcro so short it's worth siding with Bellshill at long odds

CHELTENHAM GOLD CUP

Perhaps the horse who interests me most going into the heart of this jumps season is the Willie Mullins-trained **Bellshill**.

That might seem odd. Most people are wanting to know where Samcro runs – but whatever he does this season he won't be a backable price so from that point of view he doesn't really do it for me.

So why Bellshill? Well, last season he gave a glimpse of what he is truly capable of over fences, and if he has summered well there is no reason why he can't play a big part in all the top staying chases.

He won a Grade 3 on his belated return at Fairyhouse in February and was next seen running an extraordinary race in the Irish National under top weight. He looked like he had everything cooked turning for home after a bold display of jumping and front-running. But, apparently put off by a racecourse steward in a luminous jacket approaching the last, he veered all over the place, just scrambled over, lost all momentum, yet was still beaten only a length at the line.

That was impressive, but so too was his win in the Punchestown Gold Cup, his fourth strike at Grade 1 level. It may have been perennial bridesmaid Djakadam he beat, but Road To Respect, Killultagh Vic and Edwulf were all well beaten and it was a mature effort.

His Cheltenham record can be held up as a stick to beat him with, as in three Festival appearances his form figures are 003 – but it is possible to view them positively.

A tenth place in the Cheltenham bumper of 2015 wasn't awful, while the next year he ran in the Supreme Novices – completely the wrong race for him. His last appearance at the track came when third in the RSA behind Might Bite and Whisper – beaten ten lengths, and he went there on the back of a bad fall at Leopardstown so his effort can be upgraded.

Therefore, the Gold Cup (25-1 with Betfair) shouldn't be out of bounds for connections, and nor too should the King George (25-1 generally) and I could see him going very well at Kempton.

CHAMPION HURDLE

The Champion Hurdle this season is an interesting betting heat as I am keen to take on Buveur D'Air in his hat-trick bid.

He scraped home last season from Melon,

Bellshill looks the Gold Cup value at 25-1

and on the face of it that doesn't set a high standard. Nicky Henderson opined that lack of match practice almost brought about his charge's undoing, but the trainer can have no excuses when he spurned a trip to Ireland in February in favour of the Contenders Hurdle at Sandown which is invariably a penalty kick.

Trainers being creatures of habit, Buveur D'Air is likely to travel down a similar route again which could leave him vulnerable. Henderson could still be sitting pretty, however, with **We Have A Dream** a more than interesting second string.

The four-year-old missed the Cheltenham Festival, but was still unbeaten in five races, two of them Grade 1s. His performance at Aintree's Grand National meeting was impressive and, while he has to step up, his jumping is very good and he travels like a top-class horse.

Defi Du Seuil served as a timely reminder last season of how juveniles can quickly unravel in their second season, but there is something about this horse that impresses, and if Henderson can nurse him into the season, then a race like the International at Cheltenham in December could be a good way to go for him.

CHAMPION CHASE

The Champion Chase is all about Altior. If he sticks at 2m, and there is every indication he will, then he will prove hard to stop. It looked like he had been stopped at Cheltenham in March as he wasn't going well for much of the race but, once switched out turning in, he made Min look very slow.

Douvan doesn't look quite the horse he was as a novice, but the one I do like from a

MY FIVE TO WATCH Pietro Innocenzi

●Benie Des Dieux ●Black Op ●Cracking Smart ●Lalor ●Topofthegame

speculative angle is the Mullins-trained **Great Field** – if he can be kept fit.

He managed only one run last season, but it was still a winning one, as he beat the useful Doctor Phoenix in a Grade 2 at Navan. The latter may well have taken Un De Sceaux's scalp had he stood up at Fairyhouse, so there was merit in the performance and he was giving the runner-up 4lb to boot.

The only way Altior can be beaten in this division is if something goes off fast and gets him out of his comfort zone. Great Field could be that horse. If he pings the first three or four, gets a nice lead, while Altior is a bit sticky at one or two, then things could get tasty. That's getting ahead of ourselves a bit – at this stage let's hope Great Field is fit and well, and can pick up a few domestic 2m chases before he takes on bigger things.

STAYERS' HURDLE

The Champion Chase is, like the Gold Cup, a race that has eluded Mullins, but his

Stayers' Hurdle record is much better and he was won the last two runnings.

Last year Penhill put up a great performance to win on his seasonal debut and he could be value to do it again. Not running a lot doesn't seem to bother him at all, and it doesn't bother Mullins, who nursed Quevega through her entire career while barely running her.

It was a strange Stayers' last season – the gallop was modest and most horses had a chance at the last, where it was Penhill's Flat speed that proved decisive.

He couldn't follow up at Punchestown, but then he couldn't a year earlier after winning the Albert Bartlett at Cheltenham, and it could be that he has one big run in him per year, hence Mullins treading very carefully with him.

If he does make Cheltenham again, punters need have no concern over an absence, and he may always have too many weapons for his rivals in this division as he is far from a grinder – he is a stayer with a bright turn of foot – a potent combination.

Penhill (blue colours) could pull off Stayers' Hurdle repeat

RPRS AND TOPSPEED STEVE MASON AND DAVE EDWARDS

Five to follow from our time and ratings experts

ON THE FIGURES

ALTIOR Despite a curtailed campaign, he took his unbeaten record over obstacles to 14 last season with a hat-trick including a third successive Cheltenham Festival success and a career-best Racing Post Rating of 183. The best jumper in training.

CLAN DES OBEAUX Posted four 160+ RPRs last season, most notably finishing an excellent third to Might Bite in a Grade 1 at Aintree. Still young enough to make an impact at the top level and an official mark of 157 looks generous.

MS PARFOIS Rounded off an excellent first season over fences with second-place finishes behind top-class novices at Cheltenham and Aintree and looks one for the big staying handicaps. The Welsh National looks a likely target.

TERREFORT French import who thrived in the testing ground last season, landing Grade 1s at Sandown and Aintree. Already boasts a RPR of 164 and this five-year-old has the potential to reach the top level.

THOMAS PATRICK Committed, bold-jumping front-runner who impressed when landing decent handicaps at Newbury and Aintree. The Ladbrokes Trophy looks a logical early season target.

ON THE CLOCK

CLAN DES OBEAUX Scored at Haydock last November and earned a personal best time-wise when second at Cheltenham the following month. Also finished third in the Aintree Bowl behind Might Bite in April and he could mix it with the elite staying chasers this season.

ELGIN Improved over a stone on the ratings last term and finished fifth in the Champion Hurdle, justifying the decision to supplement him for the race. Landed valuable handicaps at Ascot and Cheltenham and is effective at 2m on decent ground.

NUBE NEGRA Won a couple of times over hurdles last term and was a creditable third in the Fred Winter. Also fifth in the Anniversary Hurdle at Aintree, he could exploit a favourable handicap mark.

VISION DES FLOS Won only one of his seven races last year but ran some fine races in defeat at the big festivals. Cut underfoot brings out the best in him and he is effective between 2m and 2m4f.

WAITING PATIENTLY Confirmed his star quality when defeating Cue Card at Ascot in February. Refreshingly, Cheltenham is not his Holy Grail and there are other big prizes to be won with him.

Determined and intent Bowen looks every inch like a future champion

THERE will never be another AP McCoy. We are simply deluded to think otherwise. Having said that, incredibly talented teenager James Bowen has made an explosive start to his career, and at times last season it was mighty difficult not to draw parallels with the 20-time champion.

Bowen's refusal to accept defeat when

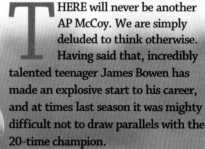

James Bowen pushes out Raz De Maree to win last season's Welsh Grand National

Facebook.com/racingpost

many other riders would have given up on several of his winners around the gaff tracks evoked memories of McCoy at his greatest and hungriest.

Of course, Bowen has a long way to go. We know he is gifted with a tremendous talent, but how will he cope with the pressure and spotlight that is bound to intensify as he gets onto a better calibre of horse?

My hunch is that Bowen *(right)* will be the next champion jockey after Richard Johnson. It won't be this season, but he will be looked after by Nicky Henderson and gradually given more opportunities.

At some stage – probably in the next 12 months – it will be hard for Henderson not to promote him to first jockey and then Johnson will face a bigger battle than Harry Skelton is currently giving him.

WHICH TRAINERS DO WE LOOK OUT FOR IN 2018-19?

Away from the elite three or four, I predict **Anthony Honeyball** and **Jamie Snowden**, who have laid rock-solid foundations over the past few years, will take significant further forward steps.

Both place their horses particularly well – pay particular attention to Honeyball's runners at Fontwell and Plumpton, especially when entering handicaps for the first time equipped with a tongue tie – and just need a couple of high-profile Saturday horses to take them to the next level.

MY FIVE TO WATCH Tom Collins

●Etamine Du Cochet ●Lust For Glory ●Master Tommytucker ●Seddon ●Topofthegame

THREE HORSES TO FOLLOW

When previewing the new campaign it would be easy to write about the likes of Samcro, Kalashnikov, Buveur D'Air, Altior, Penhill, Might Bite, Footpad, Native River, and all those other horses who feature prominently in ante-post lists for the Cheltenham Festival.

I'm going to focus on three horses who should provide lucrative returns if followed to level stakes throughout the campaign that many people will not have heard of.

Glittering Love is a six-year-old owned by Paul and Clare Rooney and trained by Nicky Richards.

He cut little ice in novice hurdles in the early part of 2017, and was next seen in point-to-points under the supervision of the trainer's daughter Joey.

The son of Winged Love – which suggests Glittering Love will need deep mud to be seen to best advantage – duly landed four of his starts between the flags before running in a 2m4f Sedgefield novice hurdle in April.

The second in that race, Knockrobin, competed with an official mark of 132, so it is fair to assume the handicapper hasn't been harsh in allocating Glittering Love, who finished a staying-on fourth to Just Bobby, an opening rating of 92.

It will be a bigger surprise than Leicester City's Premier League title success if Richards cannot win a string of handicaps this winter with Glittering Love off that basement mark.

I am sure he will start off at around 2m4f and show further improvement when stepped up in trip.

The stable's Baywing had a strikingly similar profile when he first graduated to handicap company, and look where he has ended up – an impressive winner of the Eider with the definite potential to win a Grand National at Aintree if the ground came up soft.

Yalltari, winner of three of his five starts for Venetia Williams over hurdles, promises to make up into a terrific 2m4f handicap chaser this term.

Unbeaten in handicaps, the son of Kayf Tara signed off for the latest campaign with a hard-fought success over Applesandpierres at Uttoxeter in January.

Relishing the heavy ground – as so many Williams-trained runners do – Yalltari set out to make all and forged on at the top of the straight.

Joined by Applesandpierres approaching the final flight, he needed to show a mixture of class and determination to win the race, and duly produced an abundance of both.

He has the stamp and physique of a horse who will not fulfil his potential until sent over fences, and will start his chasing career off a mark of 130.

Deep ground looks important to him, so expect Williams to plot a campaign around the months of December to February, during which period he could land a valuable event at around 2m4f.

Snazz Man, my other horse to follow, is much lower-rated than Yalltari, but make sure you keep a close eye on him when he reappears.

A late-maturing sort trained by Sue Gardner, the eight-year-old put a string of blanks firmly behind him on his second start in handicap hurdles at Fontwell in May.

Facebook.com/racingpost

Glittering Love: point-to-point winner looks highly likely to notch up a sequence this season

Dropped 5lb for a heavy Chepstow defeat, Snazz Man started a well-backed 6-1 shot at the Sussex track, and those who had taken part in the gamble were always on fine terms with themselves, apart from one anxious moment after the second-last when Lucy Gardner's saddle slipped.

Snazz Man travelled supremely well at Fontwell and surged clear when shaken up on the flat to slam Howlongisafoot by seven lengths.

The Beat All gelding will start 2018-19 off a mark of just 89 – only 10lb higher than for that win – and is strongly fancied to rack up a sequence from such an attractive low rating.

He seemed much more professional throughout his race at Fontwell, and looks the type who has just taken time to grow up and learn what is required of a racehorse.

It is also relevant that his first start on genuinely good ground coincided with such a leap forward in terms of form. Four of his other five starts had been on going officially described as soft or heavy.

Now the penny has finally dropped his followers are likely to have plenty of fun over the months ahead.

Blackbow to showcase talent in novice hurdles

ANNAMIX

This grey five-year-old was forced to miss last season due to sustaining a pelvis injury. Reports leaking out of his all-conquering stable suggest he is ready to strut his stuff again now though and it will be fascinating to see whether he lives up to the high hopes expected of him after joining Willie Mullins, having finished second on his hurdling debut when trained in France. Winter ground should pose no issues and the Supreme Novices' at Cheltenham is the plan.

BLACKBOW

A point-to-point winner in 2017, this racy five-year-old impressed when making it two from two for Willie Mullins in a Grade 2 bumper at Leopardstown last term. Jockey Patrick Mullins then overdid the waiting tactics when bidding for a hat-trick in the Champion Bumper and, back under more positive handling, he looked sure to resume winning ways when easing to the front in Ireland's equivalent at the Punchestown Festival. However, Blackbow markedly idled and was made to pay where it matters by classy stable companion Tornado Flyer. With another summer on his back Mullins will have learned more about the highly talented performer and he could well prove the cream of the crop over hurdles.

Blackbow: very smart performer in bumpers last season

CALL ME LORD

Stepping up from the minimum distance to 2m5½f at Sandown in Grade 2 company on his final outing last season did the trick with this classy hurdler. He oozed class moving off a slower tempo, and the manner in which he sprinted away from Lil Rockerfeller to win by 16 lengths was most impressive. That marked him down as a leading player in an open-looking Stayers' Hurdle division. His issue is that he needs to race on right-handed circuits, thus making a trip to Cheltenham a real worry for his leading connections. Nicky Henderson is sure to have trained him with that in mind during his summer break, however, and if he overcomes the test then expect his ante-post odds for the big one at the Festival in March to tumble.

CAREFULLY SELECTED

A top bumper performer last season for team Mullins, Carefully Selected heads into the new season with the Albert Bartlett at the Cheltenham Festival very much the plan. The Irish point winner rates a proper stayer in the making, with most ground coming alike to him, and we know the six-year-old likes the course after a near miss in last term's Champion Bumper. Expect him to make his way up through the grades without fuss.

COMMANDER OF FLEET

Each spring the Goffs Land Rover Bumper at the Punchestown festival provides a veritable source of future stars and last season Commander Of Fleet went into the 'could be anything' category when recording a huge RPR of 132 with an impressive success. It is still early days for his Ascot Gold Cup-winning sire Fame And Glory in this sphere, but he has unearthed a top-notcher capable of going all the way to the Cheltenham Festival as a novice hurdler in the shape of

this scopey four-year-old. Stepping up to around 2m4f will suit and his dam won on heavy, so winter ground shouldn't be an issue.

DANNY KIRWAN

Irish point-to-point handler Pat Doyle is widely regarded as one of the best of all time in that sphere, so when he described Danny Kirwan as potentially the most exciting horse to have gone through his hands after an easy maiden win at Lisronagh, it wasn't too surprising the son of Scorpion subsequently joined Paul Nicholls for a whopping price tag. He got his career under rules off to an impressive start when taking a good-ground Kempton bumper and it was just too bad to be true when he flopped on deeper going at Aintree in Grade 2 company when signing off. A sound surface could prove the key over hurdles this season.

GLOBAL CITIZEN

Global Citizen prospered when switched to Ben Pauling last term, slamming rivals in the Grade 2 Dovecote Hurdle at Kempton in February on his second outing for the trainer. He skipped Cheltenham for the Grade 1 Top Novice Hurdle at Aintree's Grand National meeting and was sent off 5-2 favourite. However, rain got into the ground big time that day and it saw him bogged down when the race became serious. With an official rating of 145 connections can think about hitting top 2m handicaps this season – if he encountered a sound surface that mark would be lenient as the best is still to come.

JUST IN TIME

This very useful Flat handicapper is one to keep close tabs on for an impending switch to jumps for the Alan King stable. His owners have long dreamed about a novice hurdle campaign and have some valuable spring targets in mind. Going beyond 2m will really suit and he is versatile as regards underfoot conditions, so could well shake up some of the leading Irish hopes come Festival time.

KLOUD GATE

This ex-French Flat stayer could prove one of the handicap snips of the season when returning to hurdles for Gary Moore. He failed to take to jumps last term but ran over inadequate trips and when he is given further he is sure to shine. Looking at his form on the Flat, an opening handicap mark of 108 is extremely attractive and Moore will have a plan mapped out.

MR BIG SHOT

This well-named son of top jumps sire Flemensfirth landed a big gamble in a Grade 3 Handicap Hurdle at Aintree's Grand National meeting last season. That was his first outing over 3m and, with few miles on the clock for a seven-year-old, he is unexposed as a stayer. Right at home when the mud is flying, it will be fascinating to see whether he tries his luck against the big boys before heading over fences this term – which has always been the plan.

THOMAS PATRICK

This late-maturing six-year-old took his form to a completely new level at Newbury and Aintree on his

final two outings last season. He kicks off this season from an official mark of 148 and trainer Tom Lacey will rightly have valuable targets – such as the Ladbrokes Trophy back at Newbury – in mind. There's also the Welsh National to consider and, still unexposed as a chaser, he ought to provide decent value wherever he rocks up.

WE HAVE A DREAM

Forced to miss the Triumph Hurdle due to a setback, this ex-French four-year-old gained compensation in style when sent to Aintree's Grand National meeting, slamming rivals under a positive ride in the Grade 1 Anniversary Hurdle. That made it five wins from as many outings since joining Nicky Henderson and, while he does handle deep ground, switching to sounder surfaces made a big difference to him. His hurdling technique is slick and, although a chasing career beckons, he could well improve further to prove a dark one for the Champion Hurdle division considering he is already rated as high as 156.

We Have A Dream: interesting Champion Hurdle contender

FESTIVAL FANCIES PAUL KEALY

A dozen names who have what it takes for the season's big races

PRESENTING PERCY

Shares top billing with Might Bite in the Cheltenham Gold Cup market, but is surely a far more realistic winner. Top-class jump racing these days is simply too competitive for horses as old as ten to be considered for the ultimate Cheltenham prize and even horses of the class of Kauto Star and Denman couldn't do it at such an advanced age.

Presenting Percy simply oozed class when switched to fences last year, so much so that I backed him for the Gold Cup a year early just in case connections decided to 'do a Coneygree'. It wouldn't surprise me at all if he'd have won either, so well did he travel and jump to win the RSA Chase.

He had an unusual prep, having run in a 3m5f handicap chase under top weight on only his third chase start, then dropped back to hurdles, then to 2m4f when second to Our Duke at Gowran Park, but for the second year running Presenting Percy was produced to perfection at Cheltenham by Pat Kelly, having won the Pertemps Final easily a year earlier.

What was most impressive was that he raced all last season on soft or heavy ground – there was no choice given the wettest of wet winters endured on both sides of the Irish Sea – yet he'd always been considered much better on a decent surface, his Pertemps win having come on ground more usually associated with Cheltenham in March. That versatility is some weapon to have in the armoury and, while I'm no fan of ante-post betting this early in the season, I really can't see a more likely Gold Cup winner on the horizon.

KALONDRA

This list is going to be a little bit heavy with chasers as that is what I like most, and Kalondra is potentially one of the best-handicapped British chasers at around 2m4f after just six starts over the larger obstacles for Neil Mulholland.

The seven-year-old got off the mark on his chase debut at Sedgefield last October and two outings later

Gold standard: Presenting Percy (right) has the ideal attributes for victory in the main event at Cheltenham

MY FIVE TO WATCH Tom Segal

●Douvan ●Kalashnikov ●Saldier ●Santini ●Willoughby Court

beat subsequent Festival winner Coo Star Sivola at Cheltenham, but it was his final outing in April last term and his return at Galway this term that marked him out as a horse to follow.

Although only third in a 16-runner handicap at Cheltenham in April, Kalondra travelled like by far the best horse in the race and surely just hit the front too soon. He was coming back at the second on the line, but had no answer to the late burst of Traffic Fluide, who had Grade 1 form but had dropped to a very tasty mark of 140 if he could be persuaded to put it in.

Mulholland had toyed with running Kalondra in the Galway Plate, but instead chose a conditions chase at the track in which he was terribly badly off at the weights, having to concede at least 7lb all round, including to winner Sub Lieutenant, who carried a rating of 158. Still, Kalondra travelled and jumped nicely and had moved into a closing third still going well when

disaster struck and he fell two out. Falls are not nice, but that might prove a blessing in disguise as Kalondra is still rated 147 and you can bet your life he would be at least 10lb higher had he stayed on his feet.

MISTER WHITAKER

It is always hard to tell which Cheltenham Festival races will work out well and handicaps are among those least likely to, but I have a feeling the Close Brothers Novices' Handicap Chase was a good one and that at least the front two are worth following, starting with winner Mister Whitaker.

Mick Channon is not exactly renowned for training chasers, but he has won some good prizes with the few he has handled from Tim Radford, and Mister Whitaker may prove the best of those who started life with Channon rather than the retired Henrietta Knight.

Kalondra (2): looks very well handicapped

MY FIVE TO WATCH James Hill

●Blackbow ●Footpad ●Kalashnikov ●Might Bite ●Santini

He certainly had a cracking first season over fences, improving the best part of 30lb on his hurdles performances with three wins in five starts. He was always said to have preferred quickish ground, but the jury has to be out on that now as he has shown his best form on very soft ground on trials day at Cheltenham in January and again at the Festival in March.

In the latter event he showed real courage to get up on the line to beat Rather Be, who was pulling away from the third, and it was a long way back to the fourth and fifth who both have rock-solid Cheltenham Festival handicap hurdle form to their names.

Mister Whitaker: best years to come

Channon didn't want to overrace him last season, so stumps were drawn straight afterwards, and this six-year-old surely has his best years still ahead of him after just ten starts. Most of sire Court Cave's best progeny are best at up to 2m5f, but given the way he finishes he must be worth a try at 3m at some point – and he is a half-brother to Broadway Buffalo, who got 4m.

RATHER BE

As with Channon and Mister Whitaker, Nicky Henderson decided to end Rather Be's season at Cheltenham rather than go in search of some more handicap pots and that is a good sign he has loftier plans this season for the seven-year-old, who won two small-field novice chases by wide margins before his runner-up spot at the Festival.

Also similar to Mister Whitaker, he was considered better on better ground before his March heroics but, unlike his slightly less exposed rival, there was plenty of pre-race evidence to back that up. Indeed, he had already tasted some Festival success as a hurdler, winning a Grade 3 handicap at Aintree in 2017 on good ground, and it would not be a great surprise to see him stepped up to Graded company over fences at some point this term.

He clearly handles soft ground, but he has got plenty of speed and can leave that form behind on a decent surface, while I wouldn't worry at all about him dropping back to 2m.

BALKO DES FLOS

I've never been entirely convinced Un De Sceaux really stays 2m5f on soft ground, but even so there are very few horses who have done to him what Balko Des Flos did in last season's Ryanair Chase at Cheltenham.

Balko Des Flos simply travelled all over his illustrious rival and had him in trouble long before stamina should have become an issue and that was a top-drawer performance.

Horses running over the intermediate trip don't often get the same credit as Champion Chase or Gold Cup contenders, but Balko Des Flos is top class and certainly proved his 66-1 second to Road To Respect in the Christmas Chase at Leopardstown was no fluke.

He flopped at Aintree in April, but horses who shoot the lights out at Cheltenham can often do that and one of my golden rules is to take any form lines post-Cheltenham with a pinch of salt. Make no mistake, this is a very decent chaser yet one quite likely to be underestimated at the top level again.

SANTINI

Some novice chasers now, starting with Santini, who is already among the favourites for the RSA Chase and, all being well, will have that as his obvious long-term target.

He made his debut over hurdles only in

December and all his form is remarkably strong as he thumped favourite and stablemate Chef Des Obeaux on that debut, followed up by beating subsequent Ballymore Hurdle runner-up and Aintree winner Black Op on trials day at Cheltenham and then ran an honourable third in the Albert Bartlett at the Festival itself.

Although a beaten favourite at the Festival, I wouldn't hold that against him as it is a brutal race for those with little experience. He soon bounced back, though, winning at Aintree, and everything about him tells you he is going to be a top-class chaser.

That is exactly how trainer Nicky Henderson saw him in January this year, saying: "You'd think of him as an RSA horse and if he improves as much as he did from last year to this year then he'll be an absolute machine – he's a proper horse."

TOPOFTHEGAME

Pickings at the top table have not been as easy to come by as they used to be for Paul Nicholls but if he has another top-class horse on his hands it could easily be Topofthegame, a horse he describes as "huge, bigger than Denman".

He has got a long way to go before there can be any further comparisons to Denman, but he did look to be in the process of making a fine debut over fences at Newbury last November, only to fall at the 13th.

Having suffered a slight knock to a knee and missed a couple of months, it was decided to keep him over hurdles for the remainder of the season and that hardly backfired as he ran a cracker when said to need the run in the Lanzarote at Kempton (fourth), stepped up on that to win a far more valuable handicap at Sandown three weeks later and then finished an excellent neck second to Bleu Berry in the Coral Cup. That showed he has the pace for 2m5f as well

facebook.com/racingpost

as the stamina for 3m and there's a fair amount of courage to boot so there is a lot to be excited about.

VISION DES FLOS

This five-year-old set connections back €270,000 following his Goffs Land Rover Bumper win from the highly regarded Hollowgraphic at Punchestown in April 2017, but he looked a bit of a dud on his first three starts, especially when beaten at odds of 1-4 on the third of them.

That all changed after wind surgery, though, as he romped home by 31 lengths on his first start of 2018 and, while he was well held when sixth behind Samcro in the Ballymore, runner-up spots in two further Grade 1s at Aintree and Punchestown confirm he has serious potential. You can see him taking high rank among the novice chasers.

KALASHNIKOV

Horses with small stables are often underrated but there has never been much secret over how highly Amy Murphy rates Kalashnikov.

The five-year-old accounted for three of the trainer's eight jumping winners last season, hacking up by ten lengths on his first two and winning the valuable Betfair Hurdle on his penultimate start in February.

Either side of that he was second to Summerville Boy in the Grade 1 Tolworth Hurdle and Supreme Novices' Hurdle, getting much closer on the second occasion despite the ground being heavy both times.

He is yet another considered likely to be better on a decent surface, although there is no evidence to back it up as his two wins on good to soft (the quickest he has raced on) came in the weakest events he has contested.

Whatever the case, there has to be a chance he'll prove even better over fences given his size and scope.

SHARJAH

After falling at the final obstacle with the Grade 1 Future Champions Novice Hurdle at his mercy last December, I was convinced Sharjah was the best of the Willie Mullins/Rich Ricci 2m hurdlers, but he appeared to be doing his level best to prove otherwise as he suffered heavy defeat after heavy defeat.

The penny seems to have finally dropped, however, and the answer is almost certainly better ground as he was an excellent third in a Grade 3 at Tipperary in July and then won the Galway Hurdle in commanding fashion by three lengths in August.

Rated 154, he is now officially the best of those Mullins/Ricci novices and I wouldn't have much doubt that there is more to come. Whether he can make the sizeable leap to Champion Hurdle class is another matter, but the division is as weak as it has been for a while.

PALOMA BLUE

I've liked this one since I saw him win a bumper at Fairyhouse in January 2017, not least because Henry de Bromhead does not have many first-time-out bumper winners.

He has kept very strong company ever since, running second to ill-fated Champion Bumper winner Fayonagh at Punchestown later that season and then filling the frame behind the likes of Next Destination, Samcro and Summerville Boy (fourth to him in the Supreme).

He blew out on his final start last season, but had an excuse and once he learns to settle he is going to turn into a very useful performer, whether over hurdles or fences.

COMMANDER OF FLEET

I like to put a bumper horse in this list and there is no more obvious one than Commander Of Fleet. I made my first visit to Punchestown for the festival in April and you could not have found a much more impressive winner at the meeting.

He earned a Racing Post Rating of 132 for that imperious performance and, to put that into context, it took Samcro three runs to get that high.

The form hasn't been seriously tested, but the near 20-length fifth was second in a bumper next time and the sixth picked up a maiden hurdle in the summer, so there were horses of ability in the field. It will be disappointing if he is not a festival contender come the spring.

Vision Des Flos (left): set to be a big player in novice chase ranks

THE KEY HORSES

By Weekender editor Dylan Hill

A Great View (Ire)

7 b/br g Kayf Tara - Liss A Chroi (Exit To Nowhere)

Denis Cullen (Ir)   John P McManus

PLACINGS: 31132/55518P/642561-   RPR **141+h**

Starts	1st	2nd	3rd	4th	Win & Pl
17	4	2	2	1	£67,616
131	4/18	Punc	3m 119-142 Hdl Hcap yld-sft		£31,327
	1/17	DRoy	2m Nov Ch soft		£7,885
	12/15	Punc	2m Nov Hdl heavy		£8,558
	11/15	Limk	2m Mdn Hdl 4-5yo soft		£6,686

Lost his way over fences after winning a beginners' chase in 2017 but progressed well back in handicap hurdles last season, winning at Punchestown after a short-head defeat earlier in the campaign; unlucky not to finish closer than sixth in the Pertemps Final (blundered two out).

A Toi Phil (Fr)

8 b g Day Flight - Lucidrile (Beyssac)

Gordon Elliott (Ir)   Gigginstown House Stud

PLACINGS: 6515124/45142421423-   RPR **162c**

Starts	1st	2nd	3rd	4th	Win & Pl
26	8	5	1	5	£258,087
	1/18	Thur	2m4f Gd3 Ch heavy		£23,496
	9/17	Gowr	2m4f Gd2 Ch sft-hvy		£22,692
	3/17	Navn	2m4f Gd2 Ch heavy		£21,432
143	1/17	Leop	2m5f 126-154 Ch Hcap good		£50,427
	11/16	Punc	2m6¹/₂f Nov Gd2 Ch soft		£18,438
	11/16	DRoy	2m3¹/₂f Ch good		£5,653
	1/16	Leop	2m4f Nov Gd2 Hdl soft		£18,529
	12/15	Leop	2m2f Mdn Hdl heavy		£6,953

Consistent in good chases at around 2m4f last season, winning Graded races at Gowran Park and Thurles; has looked a strong stayer at that trip but yet to convince over 3m and outran his odds when dropped all the way back to 2m to finish third to Un De Sceaux at Punchestown.

Acapella Bourgeois (Fr)

8 ch g Network - Jasmine (Valanjou I)

Willie Mullins (Ir)   Slaneyville Syndicate

PLACINGS: /31211/4F341165/F2P-   RPR **152c**

Starts	1st	2nd	3rd	4th	Win & Pl
19	6	2	2	2	£101,259
	2/17	Navn	3m Nov Gd2 Ch sft-hvy		£21,432
	1/17	Navn	2m4f Ch soft		£6,833
	3/16	Fair	2m4f Nov Gd2 Hdl yield		£19,522
	2/16	Thur	2m4f Gd2 Hdl soft		£19,522
	12/15	Leop	2m4f Mdn Hdl heavy		£6,953
	10/14	Rcpp	1m4f NHF 4-5yo gd-sft		£4,197

Impressive Grade 2 winner for Sandra Hughes in 2017 but fell well short of big expectations after

switch to Willie Mullins last season (sent off favourite in every run, including just 7-4 when falling in the Troytown); broke blood vessels when pulled up on final run.

Acey Milan (Ire)

4 b g Milan - Strong Wishes (Strong Gale)

Anthony Honeyball   Owners For Owners: Acey Milan

PLACINGS: 21114-   RPR **129b**

Starts	1st	2nd	3rd	4th	Win & Pl
5	3	1		1	£32,146
	2/18	Newb	2m¹/₂f Cls1 List NHF 4-6yo soft		£11,390
	1/18	Chel	1m6f Cls1 List NHF 4yo heavy		£14,238
	12/17	Winc	1m7¹/₂f Cls6 NHF 3yo soft		£1,949

Won three bumpers last season, most impressively when storming to a second Listed victory by 11 lengths at Newbury; beaten favourite in the Champion Bumper at Cheltenham but ran another fine race in fourth (best of the British-trained runners).

Acting Lass (Ire)

7 b g King's Theatre - Darrens Lass (Montelimar)

Harry Fry   Nigel & Barbara Collison

PLACINGS: 124/1119-   RPR **154+c**

Starts	1st	2nd	3rd	4th	Win & Pl
7	4	1			£69,716
143	1/18	Asct	2m5f Cls2 133-143 Ch Hcap soft		£47,571
141	1/18	Leic	2m4f Cls3 Nov 127-141 Ch Hcap soft		£8,295
135	11/17	MRas	2m5¹/₂f Cls3 Nov 125-135 Ch Hcap gd-sft		£7,988
	11/16	Hrfd	2m3¹/₂f Cls4 Nov Hdl soft		£3,639

Took really well to fences last season, winning first three chases including an open handicap at Ascot on soft ground; reportedly unsuited by good ground when a disappointing favourite in the Betdaq Chase at Kempton (also first run beyond 2m5f).

Adrien Du Pont (Fr)

6 b g Califet - Santariyka (Saint Des Saints)

Paul Nicholls   Mrs Johnny De La Hey

PLACINGS: 1/1211/43UP/13232F-   RPR **150c**

Starts	1st	2nd	3rd	4th	Win & Pl
15	5	3	3	1	£127,126
	10/17	Font	2m5¹/₂f Cls4 Nov Ch good		£4,549
139	4/16	Asct	1m7¹/₂f Cls2 116-139 Hdl 4yo Hcap gd-sft		£25,024
	1/16	Chep	2m Cls1 Gd1 Hdl 4yo heavy		£28,475
	10/15	Chep	2m Cls4 Hdl 3yo good		£3,899
	4/15	Engh	2m¹/₂f Hdl 3yo v soft		£17,860

Grade 1 winner over hurdles who has been

Form figures correct to September 9, 2018

Twitter @RacingPost

slightly disappointing since that juvenile campaign; twice beaten at short odds when unable to add to win on chasing debut last season; still only six, though, and looks the type who may have plenty more to offer.

Agrapart (Fr)

7 b/br g Martaline - Afragha (Darshaan)

Nick Williams   The Gascoigne Brookes Partnership III

PLACINGS: 521316/74139/77212-   RPR **162**h

Starts	1st	2nd	3rd	4th	Win & Pl
16	4	3	2	1	£207,314
	1/18	Chel	3m Cls1 Gd2 Hdl heavy.............................£34,170
	1/17	Chel	2m4¹/₂f Cls1 Gd2 Hdl soft.........................£22,887
137	2/16	Newb	2m¹/₂f Cls1 Gd3 128-153 Hdl Hcap heavy...........£88,273
	12/15	Aint	2m1f Cls3 Nov Hdl soft...............................£6,279

Has won Grade 2 hurdles at Cheltenham in each of the last two seasons, outstaying the opposition in testing conditions both times; beaten favourite in the Rendlesham Hurdle at Haydock both times subsequently, suggesting that form shouldn't be taken literally elsewhere; not sighted after February last season.

Ainchea (Ire)

5 b g Flemensfirth - Lady Petit (Beneficial)

Colin Tizzard   Ann & Alan Potts Limited

PLACINGS: 212F-   RPR **136+**h

Starts	1st	2nd	3rd	4th	Win & Pl
4	1	2	-	-	£13,688
	12/17	Sand	2m Cls3 Nov Hdl gd-sft.............................£6,498

Second in a Cheltenham bumper last October and did well in just three races over hurdles last season; would have won for a second time at Sandown but for falling at the final flight; had run well for one so inexperienced when second in a Listed race at Cheltenham in between; looks a fine prospect for fences.

Al Boum Photo (Fr)

6 b g Buck's Boum - Al Gane (Dom Alco)

Willie Mullins (Ir)   Mrs J Donnelly

PLACINGS: F/3115/1F2F10-   RPR **163**c

Starts	1st	2nd	3rd	4th	Win & Pl
11	4	1	1	-	£107,036
	4/18	Fair	2m4f Nov Gd1 Ch sft-hvy.............................£52,212
	11/17	Navn	2m1f Ch sft-hvy......................................£8,950
	4/17	Fair	2m4f Nov Gd2 Hdl sft-hvy.........................£21,432
	1/17	Thur	2m Mdn Hdl 4-5yo yld-sft...........................£5,256

Caused to run out at the final fence when set to win at the Punchestown festival last season but deserved more headlines for the quality of his performance in what may well have been a second Grade 1 victory, although he had looked just short of the best in the RSA; equally effective at 2m4f and 3m.

Allysson Monterg (Fr)

8 b g Network - Mellyssa (Panoramic)

Richard Hobson   D W Fox

PLACINGS: 4/2216/7/1P31-   RPR **147+**c

Starts	1st	2nd	3rd	4th	Win & Pl
10	3	2	1	1	£32,205
137	4/18	Prth	3m Cls3 123-137 Ch Hcap soft...........£12,086
	2/18	Extr	2m3f Cls3 Nov Ch heavy..................£7,408
	2/16	Leic	2m4¹/₂f Cls3 Nov Hdl 4-7yo heavy.........£6,498

Ran just once in nearly two years after sixth in the 2016 Albert Bartlett but made an impressive winning return on chasing debut last season; found the RSA Chase beyond him next time but confirmed himself a useful recruit to fences with win at Perth in April.

Alpha Des Obeaux (Fr)

8 b g Saddler Maker - Omega Des Obeaux (Saint Preuil)

Gordon Elliott (Ir)   Gigginstown House Stud

PLACINGS: /35113P486/2414646F-   RPR **161**c

Starts	1st	2nd	3rd	4th	Win & Pl
27	5	8	2	4	£246,611
	11/17	Clon	2m4¹/₂f Gd2 Ch sft-hvy...................£25,299
	11/16	Cork	2m4f Nov Gd3 Ch good..................£17,353
	10/16	Thur	2m6f Ch good............................£4,974
	1/16	Gowr	3m Gd2 Hdl heavy.......................£18,750
	11/14	Punc	2m4f Mdn Hdl 4yo yield.................£5,750

Has a very patchy record, not helped by tendency to break blood vessels, but has been a smart chaser on his day; ran a huge race when second to Total Recall in last season's Munster National and beat A Toi Phil in a Grade 2 at Clonmel; fell in the Grand National.

Altior (Ire)

8 b g High Chaparral - Monte Solaro (Key Of Luck)

Nicky Henderson   Mrs Patricia Pugh

PLACINGS: 3/611111/111111/111-   RPR **183+**c

Starts	1st	2nd	3rd	4th	Win & Pl
17	15	-	1	-	£697,466
	4/18	Sand	1m7¹/₂f Cls1 Gd1 Ch gd-sft.............£74,383
	3/18	Chel	2m Cls1 Gd1 Ch soft...................£228,872
	2/18	Newb	2m¹/₂f Cls1 Gd2 Ch soft.................£28,475
	4/17	Sand	1m7¹/₂f Cls1 Gd1 Ch good..............£71,188
	3/17	Chel	2m Cls1 Nov Gd1 Ch gd-sft.............£99,663
	2/17	Newb	2m¹/₂f Cls1 Gd2 Ch soft.................£28,475
	12/16	Kemp	2m Cls1 Nov Gd2 Ch good..............£22,780
	12/16	Sand	1m7¹/₂f Cls1 Nov Gd1 Ch gd-sft.........£25,628
	11/16	Kemp	2m2f Cls4 Nov Ch soft....................£4,549
	3/16	Chel	2m¹/₂f Cls1 Nov Gd1 Hdl gd-sft.........£68,340
	12/15	Kemp	2m Cls2 Nov Hdl gd-sft.................£11,696
	11/15	Chel	2m¹/₂f Cls1 Nov Gd2 Hdl gd-sft.........£17,286
	10/15	Asct	1m7¹/₂f Cls3 Nov Hdl good..............£7,798
	10/15	Chep	2m Cls4 Nov Hdl good....................£3,899
	5/14	MRas	2m¹/₂f Cls6 NHF 4-6yo good..............£1,560

Outstanding performer who is unbeaten in 14 runs over obstacles and a winner at three successive Cheltenham Festivals, last season storming home in the Champion Chase to add to victories in the Arkle and Supreme Novices' Hurdle; returned from a wind operation as good as ever towards the end of last term.

American (Fr)

8 b g Malinas - Grande Sultane (Garde Royale)

Harry Fry   The Jago Family Partnership

PLACINGS: 1/316/111/P29-   RPR **156c**

Starts	1st	2nd	3rd	4th	Win & Pl
9	4	1	1	-	£77,543

148	3/17	Uttx	3m Cls2 Nov 122-148 Ch Hcap soft	£18,768
	1/17	Wwck	3m Cls1 Nov List Ch soft	£14,305
	11/16	Extr	3m Cls3 Nov Ch soft	£9,495
	11/15	Asct	2m5¹/₂f Cls2 Nov Hdl gd-sft	£12,512

Unbeaten in three runs as a novice chaser two seasons ago but disappointed in the face of stiff tasks in the Ladbrokes Trophy and Cheltenham Gold Cup last term; again showed plenty of promise when second in the Cotswold Chase in between; needs soft ground.

Altior in the Cheltenham Festival winner's enclosure for a third time

Ami Desbois (Fr)

8 b g Dream Well - Baroya (Garde Royale)

Graeme McPherson   EPDS Racing Partnership 12 & Partner

PLACINGS: /42238/1123151/11PP-   RPR **143+c**

Starts	1st	2nd	3rd	4th	Win & Pl
18	6	3	2	2	£47,849

	12/17	Weth	2m3¹/₂f Cls3 Nov Ch soft	£6,256
	11/17	Weth	1m7f Cls4 Nov Ch gd-sft	£3,994
	4/17	Newc	2m4¹/₂f Cls4 Nov Hdl good	£3,249
137	2/17	Weth	3m Cls3 115-137 Hdl Hcap soft	£5,523
126	11/16	Hayd	2m7f Cls3 110-130 Hdl Hcap soft	£6,498
	5/16	Hexm	2m7¹/₂f Cls5 Mdn Hdl good	£2,464

Very useful hurdler who took well to fences last season, winning twice over trips arguably short of his best (peaked over 3m as a hurdler); twice flopped subsequently but may not have been suited by conditions on those occasions as they were his only runs on heavy ground since a bumper defeat in November 2015.

Anibale Fly (Fr)
8 b g Assessor - Nouba Fly (Chamberlin)

Tony Martin (Ir)   John P McManus

PLACINGS: 1346/112P142/591F34-   RPR **170c**

Starts	1st	2nd	3rd	4th	Win & Pl
20	3	3	2	3	£359,807

148	12/17	Leop	3m¹/₂f 126-150 Ch Hcap yield	£94,017
	1/17	Naas	3m Nov Gd3 Ch yld-sft	£22,692
	11/16	Navn	2m1f Ch yld-sft	£7,235
135	4/16	Punc	2m4f 125-149 Hdl Hcap yield	£43,382
	12/15	Navn	2m Mdn Hdl heavy	£7,488
	4/15	Fair	2m NHF 4-7yo soft	£7,221
	3/15	Navn	2m NHF 5-7yo heavy	£4,814

Progressed into a high-class chaser last season, finishing third in the Cheltenham Gold Cup and fourth in the Grand National; thorough stayer who now needs to prove himself in shorter Grade 1 races (only win last season off what proved a very good mark in the Paddy Power Chase).

Annamix (Fr)
5 gr g Martaline - Tashtiyana (Doyoun)

Willie Mullins (Ir)   Mrs S Ricci

PLACINGS: 2/

Starts	1st	2nd	3rd	4th	Win & Pl
1	-	1	-	-	£3,705

Bought by Rich Ricci after finishing second over hurdles in France in 2016 and described by the owner as the pick of his novice team last season before suffering a pelvis injury in November; again figures among the favourites for the Supreme Novices' Hurdle but has yet to race outside of France.

Any Second Now (Ire)
6 b g Oscar - Pretty Neat (Topanoora)

Ted Walsh (Ir)   John P McManus

PLACINGS: 113U/22238-   RPR **152+c**

Starts	1st	2nd	3rd	4th	Win & Pl
9	2	3	2	-	£58,676

| | 1/17 | Punc | 2m Nov Gd2 Hdl soft | £22,440 |
| | 12/16 | Navn | 2m Mdn Hdl 4yo yld-sft | £5,426 |

Won a Grade 2 novice hurdle in 2017 but came up just short in top novice chases when switched to fences last season; sent off favourite on his handicap debut at the Cheltenham Festival but finished only eighth behind Mister Whitaker, although he had been runner-up to Footpad in Grade 1 company at Leopardstown over Christmas.

Facebook.com/racingpost

Apple's Jade (Fr)

6 b m Saddler Maker - Apple's For Ever (Nikos)

Gordon Elliott (Ir)   Gigginstown House Stud

PLACINGS: 1121/1221211/11133-   RPR **157+h**

Starts	1st	2nd	3rd	4th	Win & Pl
16	10	4	2	-	£483,897

12/17	Leop	3m Gd1 Hdl soft		£42,863
12/17	Fair	2m4f Gd1 Hdl soft		£50,427
11/17	Navn	2m4f Gd2 Hdl sft-hvy		£21,432
4/17	Punc	2m4f Gd1 Hdl gd-yld		£50,427
3/17	Chel	2m4f Cls1 Gd1 Hdl gd-sft		£61,897
12/16	Fair	2m4f Gd1 Hdl gd-yld		£43,382
4/16	Punc	2m Gd1 Hdl 4yo yield		£43,382
4/16	Aint	2m1f Cls1 Gd1 Hdl 4yo soft		£56,437
12/15	Leop	2m Gd2 Hdl 3yo heavy		£21,415
5/15	Vich	2m¹/₂f Hdl 3yo soft		£7,814

Brilliant mare who took her Grade 1 tally to seven last season with a second successive victory in the Hatton's Grace and a first win over 3m at Leopardstown; had a poor spring, though, failing to retain her Mares' Hurdle crown at Cheltenham and again beaten at odds-on at Punchestown.

Apple's Jade (below) powers to another victory at the top level

Apple's Shakira (Fr)

4 b f Saddler Maker - Apple's For Ever (Nikos)

Nicky Henderson   John P McManus

PLACINGS: 111143-   RPR **137+h**

Starts	1st	2nd	3rd	4th	Win & Pl
6	4	-	1	1	£73,659

1/18	Chel	2m1f Cls1 Gd2 Hdl 4yo soft		£18,224
12/17	Chel	2m1f Cls2 Hdl 3yo soft		£12,512
11/17	Chel	2m¹/₂f Cls1 Gd2 Hdl 3yo soft		£17,085
5/17	Vich	2m¹/₂f Hdl 3yo v soft		£8,615

Bought after winning over hurdles in France last season and added three more victories at Cheltenham, two at Grade 2 level, to go off a short-priced favourite for the Triumph Hurdle; couldn't get away with keen-going tendencies in the highest grade.

Art Mauresque (Fr)

8 b g Policy Maker - Modeva (Valanour)

Paul Nicholls   Mrs Johnny De La Hey

PLACINGS: 31677P2/11787P/F242-   RPR **159c**

Starts	1st	2nd	3rd	4th	Win & Pl
28	9	4	2	1	£160,229

150	10/16	Chep	2m3¹/₂f Cls2 140-160 Ch Hcap good	£25,320
144	5/16	NAbb	2m5f Cls2 126-144 Ch Hcap good	£15,640
	10/15	Chel	2m4f Cls2 Nov Ch good	£12,628
	5/15	Kemp	2m4¹/₂f Cls3 Nov Ch good	£6,498
	4/15	Tntn	2m Cls4 Nov Ch gd-fm	£4,549
135	3/15	Kemp	2m Cls3 Nov 122-135 Ch Hcap good	£9,747
	8/13	Claf	2m1f Hdl 3yo v soft	£13,268
	6/13	Nanc	2m1f Hdl 3yo good	£7,024
	6/13	Stra	2m Hdl 3yo heavy	£7,024

Paid the price with the handicapper for a fine run

of form in 2016 but has finally slipped below his last winning handicap mark despite running well in defeat last season; finished second to top-class pair Waiting Patiently and Top Notch either side of a good fourth in the Betdaq Chase at Kempton.

Aso (Fr)

8 b/br g Goldneyev - Odyssee Du Cellier (Dear Doctor)

Venetia Williams   The Bellamy Partnership

PLACINGS: /22213561/4218434/5-   RPR **145c**

Starts	1st	2nd	3rd	4th	Win & Pl
25	7	5	4	3	£175,318
145	12/16	Chep	2m3¹/₂f Cls3 127-149 Ch Hcap soft...................£25,320
	4/16	NAbb	2m5f Cls3 Nov Ch soft...£7,280
	1/16	MRas	2m5¹/₂f Ch soft...£12,777
	1/15	Hayd	2m Cls1 Nov Gd2 Hdl heavy £15,661
	12/14	Tntn	2m3f Cls4 Nov Hdl soft...£3,574
	11/14	Wwck	2m Cls4 Nov Hdl soft...£3,899
	7/13	Gran	1m4f NHF 3yo gd-fm...£4,065

Progressive handicap chaser two seasons ago, winning at Chepstow and running well in several bigger races (second in the Caspian Caviar Gold Cup); coped well with step up to Grade 1 level when third in the Ryanair Chase; missed nearly all of last season through injury.

Audacious Plan (Ire)

9 b g Old Vic - North Star Poly (Presenting)

Dr Richard Newland   valueracingclub.co.uk

PLACINGS: /264P0F/P330P9/2111-   RPR **142+c**

Starts	1st	2nd	3rd	4th	Win & Pl
27	5	4	6	3	£58,801
127	12/17	Ludl	3m1¹/₂f Cls3 118-130 Ch Hcap good £11,394
122	11/17	Sedg	3m5f Cls2 117-134 Ch Hcap good....................£18,768
112	10/17	Hntg	3m1f Cls4 84-112 Hdl Hcap good.........................£3,574
115	4/15	Ffos	3m Cls4 112-122 Ch Hcap good............................£5,198
112	10/14	Ffos	3m Cls4 105-120 Hdl Hcap gd-sft...........................£3,119

Much improved following switch from Rebecca Curtis last season and won his last three for new connections, all on good ground including the Durham National over 3m5f at Sedgefield; missed the second half of the season but back in training this summer.

Aye Aye Charlie

6 b g Midnight Legend - Trial Trip (Le Moss)

Fergal O'Brien   All Four One

PLACINGS: 3614/3F4374-   RPR **146h**

Starts	1st	2nd	3rd	4th	Win & Pl
10	1	-	3	3	£13,056
	1/17	Sthl	1m7¹/₂f Cls6 Mdn NHF 4-6yo soft £1,326

Failed to win in six runs over hurdles last season but was very highly tried and showed his quality when beaten less than five lengths into fourth in a Grade 1 at Aintree; finished best of all over 2m4f that day and should be suited by 3m; still eligible for novice hurdles.

Bacardys (Fr)

7 b g Coastal Path - Oasice (Robin Des Champs)

Willie Mullins (Ir)   Shanakiel Racing Syndicate

PLACINGS: F1/131/3F11P1/3FF0-   RPR **155h**

Starts	1st	2nd	3rd	4th	Win & Pl
13	5		3	-	£145,235
	4/17	Punc	2m4f Nov Gd1 Hdl gd-yld.....................................£50,427
	2/17	Leop	2m2f Nov Gd1 Hdl soft...£45,385
	12/16	Leop	2m Mdn Hdl yield..£6,331
	4/16	Aint	2m1f Cls1 Gd2 NHF 4-6yo soft £22,508
	12/15	Leop	2m NHF 4yo heavy...£5,349

Was expected to take high rank as a novice chaser last season having won two Grade 1 novice hurdles in 2017 but was a beaten favourite first time out and fell on his second run; was going well when reverting to the smaller obstacles in the Stayers' Hurdle only to fall again at the last; talented but starts the season with something to prove.

Bachasson (Fr)

7 gr g Voix Du Nord - Belledonne (Shafoun)

Willie Mullins (Ir)   Edward O'Connell

PLACINGS: 611/111128U/F21/11F-   RPR **165+c**

Starts	1st	2nd	3rd	4th	Win & Pl
16	9	2	-	-	£102,958
	1/18	Tram	2m5f List Ch heavy £16,327
	11/17	Thur	2m6f List Ch sft-hvy...£14,981
	2/17	Gowr	2m4f Ch heavy £7,371
	10/15	Tipp	2m Nov Gd3 Hdl good...£15,116
	9/15	Gway	2m2f Nov Hdl good...£9,093
	7/15	Gway	2m Nov Hdl 4yo yield £10,078
	7/15	Slig	2m Mdn Hdl 4yo good..£5,616
	9/14	Stra	1m4f NHF 3yo v soft...£5,000
	7/14	Vitt	1m4f NHF 3yo gd-sft...£4,583

Very lightly raced since going chasing two seasons ago, running just six times over fences, but comfortably won two Listed chases last season before falling at the second when thrown in at the deep end in the Cheltenham Gold Cup; yet to win beyond 2m6f.

Baie Des Iles (Fr)

7 gr m Barastraight - Malownia (Smadoun)

Ross O'Sullivan (Ir)   Mrs Z Wentworth

PLACINGS: 6F/71246/0513/6630-1   RPR **146c**

Starts	1st	2nd	3rd	4th	Win & Pl
25	7	2	5	1	£259,044
	6/18	Autl	2m6f Gd2 Ch v soft £87,611
141	2/17	Punc	3m4f 126-154 Ch Hcap soft £25,214
130	1/16	Punc	3m1f 106-130 Am Ch Hcap heavy..........................£8,625
	10/14	Autl	2m1¹/₂f Ch 3yo heavy...£34,000
	9/14	Autl	2m2f Hdl 3yo v soft..£26,000
	8/14	Roya	1m6¹/₂f NHF 3yo gd-sft..£4,167
	5/14	Vich	2m¹/₂f Hdl 3yo good...£8,400

Tough staying mare who gave connections a special day when winning a big prize at Auteuil this summer; likely to be aimed at a return trip for the Grand Steeple-Chase de Paris but also loves Punchestown, finishing first and third in the last two Grand National Trials there.

facebook.com/racingpost

Down Royal Racecourse

Every Revolution
NEEDS A
Hero

Down Royal
Festival of Racing, 20 Year Celebration

Friday 2nd & Saturday 3rd November 2018

Billecart-Salmon Most Stylishly dressed Lady – Saturday 3rd November
Winner will receive a year's supply of Billecart-Salmon, a trip to the Champagne
House and vineyards and an overnight in Paris.

Featuring the Grade 1 JNwine.com Champion Chase,
The MyCarNeedsA.com (Grade 2) Steeplechase, Grade 2 WKD Hurdle
and the EBF Lough Construction Ltd Mares Hurdle (Grade 3),
The Billecart-Salmon Handicap Hurdle (Grade C)

Hospitality packages from £65
bespoke Private Corporate Entertaining options available.

Book now at www.downroyal.com

#20years #downroyal

Balko Des Flos (Fr)
7 ch g Balko - Royale Marie (Garde Royale)

Henry de Bromhead (Ir)   Gigginstown House Stud

PLACINGS: 0154/72133F3/123214-   RPR **174**+c

Starts	1st	2nd	3rd	4th	Win & Pl
19	6	3	4	2	£425,803

	3/18	Chel	2m5f Cls1 Gd1 Ch soft	£200,263
146	8/17	Gway	2m6¹/₂f 137-160 Ch Hcap good	£126,068
	1/17	Fair	2m5¹/₂f Ch soft	£5,879
	1/16	Punc	2m4f Mdn Hdl sft-hvy	£6,088
	5/15	Slig	2m2f NHF 4yo yield	£5,349
	1/15	Leop	2m NHF 4yo soft	£4,279

Hugely progressive last season and bridged the gap from handicap to Grade 1 level when winning the Ryanair Chase to add to his Galway Plate success; felt to need better ground prior to that win and earlier 3m Grade 1 second to Road To Riches perhaps still his best form.

Ball D'Arc (Fr)
7 b g Network - Pretty Moon (Moon Madness)

Gordon Elliott (Ir)   Gigginstown House Stud

PLACINGS: 62U21423111233/31U5-   RPR **160**+c

Starts	1st	2nd	3rd	4th	Win & Pl
28	9	5	5	1	£207,388

	11/17	Naas	2m Gd3 Ch sft-hvy	£17,083
	3/17	Naas	2m4f Nov Gd3 Ch sft-hvy	£17,083
	2/17	Navn	2m1f Nov Gd3 Ch sft-hvy	£21,432
133	1/17	Fair	2m1f 127-142 Ch Hcap soft	£50,243
	10/16	Wxfd	2m Ch good	£5,200
	2/16	Naas	2m Nov Gd2 Hdl sft-hvy	£20,173
	1/16	Punc	2m Nov List Hdl sft-hvy	£14,338
	12/15	Limk	2m Mdn Hdl 4yo heavy	£6,686
	11/15	Thur	2m NHF 4-7yo yield	£4,814

Not far off the best novice chasers two seasons ago and won a Grade 3 at Naas early last term only to disappoint subsequently; has won three times at Grade 3 level (two of them at Naas over 2m and 2m4f) but now 0-6 in higher grades.

Ballyandy
7 b g Kayf Tara - Megalex (Karinga Bay)

Nigel Twiston-Davies   Options O Syndicate

PLACINGS: 112114/23214/14P-   RPR **143**c

Starts	1st	2nd	3rd	4th	Win & Pl
14	6	3	1	3	£187,852

	9/17	Prth	2m4f Cls3 Nov Ch heavy	£7,507
135	2/17	Newb	2m¹/₂f Cls1 Gd3 126-146 Hdl Hcap soft	£88,273
	3/16	Chel	2m¹/₂f Cls1 List NHF 4-6yo good	£39,865
	2/16	Newb	2m¹/₂f Cls1 List NHF 4-6yo heavy	£11,390
	11/15	Chel	2m¹/₂f Cls1 List NHF 4-6yo gd-sft	£11,390
	10/15	Worc	2m Cls6 NHF 3-5yo gd-sft	£1,560

Won the Champion Bumper at Cheltenham in 2016 and did well over hurdles the following season, landing the Betfair Hurdle and finishing

fourth in the Supreme; disappointing in just three runs over fences last term despite a successful chasing debut.

Ballyarthur (Ire)
8 b g Kayf Tara - Ariels Serenade (Presenting)

Nigel Twiston-Davies   Graham & Alison Jelley

PLACINGS: 1/2/24F1322/3P2311-5   RPR **143**+c

Starts	1st	2nd	3rd	4th	Win & Pl
15	3	5	3	1	£36,776

129	4/18	Prth	2m4f Cls3 Nov 110-129 Ch Hcap soft	£10,137
126	4/18	Uttx	2m4f Cls3 Nov 126-139 Ch Hcap heavy	£7,408
	1/17	Leic	2m4¹/₂f Cls4 Nov Hdl soft	£5,198

Took time to find his feet over fences last season but really flourished in the spring, winning novice handicaps at Perth and Uttoxeter in impressive fashion; well beaten when favourite to win again at Haydock in May but may have been unsuited by quicker ground.

Ballydine (Ire)
8 ch g Stowaway - Bealaha Essie (Denel)

Charlie Longsdon   Alan Halsall

PLACINGS: 25/21129/231-   RPR **140**+c

Starts	1st	2nd	3rd	4th	Win & Pl
9	3	3	1	-	£57,760

131	2/18	Sand	3m Cls2 124-146 Ch Hcap good	£31,280
	11/15	Newc	2m6f Cls2 Nov Hdl soft	£11,261
	10/15	Strf	2m6f Cls5 Mdn Hdl soft	£2,599

Won a good handicap chase at Sandown last season when stepped up to 3m for the first time over fences; had pushed Barters Hill close in a Grade 2 novice hurdle over that trip in 2016 before missing 18 months through injury; open to progress after just three chases.

Ballymoy (Ire)
5 b g Flemensfirth - John's Eliza (Dr Massini)

Nigel Twiston-Davies   Simon Munir & Isaac Souede

PLACINGS: 4/335111-   RPR **138**+h

Starts	1st	2nd	3rd	4th	Win & Pl
5	3	1	1	-	£70,316

132	4/18	Sand	2m Cls2 Nov 118-137 Hdl Hcap gd-sft	£61,900
	3/18	Bang	2m¹/₂f Cls4 Nov Hdl soft	£4,094
	2/18	Uttx	2m Cls4 Mdn Hdl heavy	£4,094

Hugely progressive in the second half of last season following a breathing operation and completed a hat-trick in the novice handicap hurdle final at Sandown on the final day of the campaign; seems sure to stay at least 2m4f; could go novice chasing.

Ballyoisin (Ire)
7 b g Presenting - Regal Force (King's Ride)

Enda Bolger (Ir)   John P McManus

PLACINGS: 1/31/F1FF/31212F8-11   RPR **162+c**

Starts	1st	2nd	3rd	4th	Win & Pl
15	6	2	2	-	£111,606

	6/18	Punc	2m5f Ch good	£11,429
	5/18	Klny	2m4¹/₂f Gd3 Ch good	£20,885
150	10/17	Cork	2m1f 122-150 Ch Hcap yld-sft	£25,214
144	7/17	Klny	2m1f 129-157 Ch Hcap good	£25,214
	1/17	Fair	2m1f Ch soft	£8,410
	9/15	Navn	2m Mdn Hdl good	£6,419

Progressed nicely in 2017 and pushed Disko close in a Grade 2 chase at Down Royal last November; looked even better when easing to wide-margin wins at Killarney and Punchestown early this summer; could exploit a much lower hurdles mark at some stage.

Ballyoptic (Ire)
8 b g Old Vic - Lambourne Lace (Un Desperado)

Nigel Twiston-Davies   Mills & Mason Partnership

PLACINGS: 111/1F2F4P5/5124142-   RPR **158c**

Starts	1st	2nd	3rd	4th	Win & Pl
18	6	3	-	3	£212,442

	2/18	Weth	3m Cls1 Nov Gd2 Ch heavy	£20,284
	11/17	Extr	3m Cls2 Nov Ch soft	£14,206
148	10/16	Chep	2m3¹/₂f Cls1 Gd3 131-148 Hdl Hcap good	£28,475
	4/16	Aint	3m³/₄f Cls1 Nov Gd1 Hdl soft	£56,270
	3/16	Uttx	2m4f Cls4 Nov Hdl soft	£5,064
	2/16	Ffos	2m4f Cls4 Nov Hdl 4-7yo heavy	£4,549

Thorough stayer who made steady progress over fences last season and ran a huge race to finish a close second in the Scottish Grand National; may have benefited from a flatter track after finishing fourth in the RSA Chase (0-4 at Cheltenham including odds-on defeat).

Ballyoisin flies to victory at Killarney in May

Ballyward (Ire)

6 b g Flemensfirth - Ifyoucouldseemenow (Saddlers' Hall)

Willie Mullins (Ir)   Andrea & Graham Wylie

PLACINGS: 2/1/4144-   RPR **148+h**

Starts	1st	2nd	3rd	4th	Win & Pl
5	2	-	-	3	£24,989
	1/18	Naas	2m3f Mdn Hdl sft-hvy		........£8,722
	12/16	Leop	2m4f NHF 4-7yo yield		........£4,974

Thrown in at the deep end when running in the Albert Bartlett at Cheltenham after winning only a maiden hurdle but acquitted himself very well when beaten only six lengths in fourth; unable to build on that when a far more remote fourth at Punchestown next time.

Baltazar D'Allier (Fr)

7 br g Malinas - Kinoise D'Allier (Roi De Rome)

Gordon Elliott (Ir)   John P McManus

PLACINGS: 1/12F/   RPR **144h**

Starts	1st	2nd	3rd	4th	Win & Pl
3	1	1	-	-	£14,200
	11/16	Naas	2m3f Mdn Hdl yld-sft		........£5,653

Very lightly raced over hurdles and missed last season through injury but had been a fine second in the Challow Hurdle in 2016 before falling early when odds-on for his only subsequent outing; big, fine horse who was always likely to make a much better chaser anyway.

Bapaume (right) could prove a smart recruit to the novice chasing ranks this season

Bamako Moriviere (Fr)

7 b g Califet - Halladine (Passing Sale)

Willie Mullins (Ir)   Mrs S Ricci

PLACINGS: 1/3P0/461101/F23F11-   RPR **153+c**

Starts	1st	2nd	3rd	4th	Win & Pl
18	7	4	3	1	£75,975

	11/17	Cork	2m4f Nov Gd3 Ch soft	£20,171
	10/17	Fair	2m Ch gd-yld	£6,318
	8/16	Cork	2m Hdl 4-5yo good	£6,783
	7/16	Bell	2m4f Hdl yield	£5,879
133	6/16	Punc	2m 110-135 Hdl Hcap good	£10,853
	1/15	Pau	2m1¹/₂f Hdl 4yo heavy	£11,907
	10/14	Pmnl	1m4f NHF 3yo gd-sft	£4,167

Gradually got his act together over fences last season until ruled out by injury following a 16-length thrashing of Jury Duty at Cork in November; confirmed liking for soft ground having largely been kept to better conditions in the summer prior to that.

Bapaume (Fr)

5 b g Turtle Bowl - Brouhaha (American Post)

Willie Mullins (Ir)   Mrs S Ricci

PLACINGS: 61/21231/2383P5-21   RPR **156+h**

Starts	1st	2nd	3rd	4th	Win & Pl
15	4	4	3	-	£312,169

6/18	Autl	2m3¹/₂f Gd2 Hdl 4yo v soft	£69,690
4/17	Punc	2m Gd1 Hdl 4yo gd-yld	£50,427
12/16	Leop	2m Gd2 Hdl 3yo yield	£19,522
4/16	Fntb	1m7f Hdl 3yo v soft	£7,059

Struggled to build on a high-class juvenile campaign last season when finishing third in the Triumph and winning a Grade 1 at Punchestown in 2017; got back on track when winning the Prix la Barka at Auteuil in June; could go novice chasing.

Barney Dwan (Ire)

8 b g Vinnie Roe - Kapricia Speed (Vertical Speed)

Fergal O'Brien   Paul & Clare Rooney

PLACINGS: 311413/2BU427/3114F-   RPR **153+c**

Starts	1st	2nd	3rd	4th	Win & Pl
18	5	2	3	3	£87,564

2/18	Muss	2m4f Cls3 Nov Ch gd-sft	£8,255
12/17	MRas	3m Cls4 Nov Ch gd-sft	£5,198
129	3/16	Sand	2m4f Cls1 Nov Gd3 120-135 Hdl 4-7yo soft £34,170
12/15	Sedg	2m1f Cls4 Nov Hdl heavy	£3,769
11/15	MRas	2m2¹/₂f Cls4 Nov Hdl gd-sft	£3,899

Second in the Pertemps Final in 2017 but aim of going one better at last season's Cheltenham Festival hit by the rain, finishing fourth in the novice handicap chase on ground softer than ideal; had won over 2m4f and 3m and will have more good handicaps on his agenda.

Baron Alco (Fr)

7 ch g Dom Alco - Paula (Network)

Gary Moore   John Stone

PLACINGS: 134086/11120/312122/   RPR **156c**

Starts	1st	2nd	3rd	4th	Win & Pl
18	5	5	2	1	£99,830

1/17	Plum	2m1f Cls3 Nov Ch soft	£7,988
11/16	Plum	2m3¹/₂f Cls3 Nov Ch good	£6,657
127	12/15	Kemp	2m5f Cls3 118-135 Hdl Hcap gd-sft	£9,747
123	11/15	Font	2m1¹/₂f Cls3 110-124 Hdl Hcap soft	£6,330
116	10/15	Strf	2m2¹/₂f Cls3 107-129 Hdl Hcap good	£6,330
11/14	Sand	2m Cls3 Hdl 3yo soft	£6,498

Very smart novice chaser two seasons ago; gained both wins at Plumpton and ran consistently well in stronger company, finishing second in a Grade 1 at Sandown and a red-hot Cheltenham Festival handicap; missed last season through injury.

Barters Hill (Ire)

8 b g Kalanisi - Circle The Wagons (Commanche Run)

Ben Pauling   Circle Of Friends

PLACINGS: 1111/1114/P/6-   RPR **153h**

Starts	1st	2nd	3rd	4th	Win & Pl
10	7	-	-	1	£81,862

1/16	Donc	3m¹/₂f Cls1 Nov Gd1 Hdl good	£17,165
12/15	Newb	2m4¹/₂f Cls1 Nov Gd1 Hdl soft	£22,780
11/15	Hntg	2m3¹/₂f Cls4 Nov Hdl gd-sft	£3,899
4/15	Aint	2m1f Cls1 Gd2 NHF 4-6yo gd-sft	£16,881
2/15	Newb	2m1f Cls1 List NHF 4-6yo soft	£11,390
12/14	Wwck	2m Cls6 NHF 4-6yo gd-sft	£1,560
11/14	Hntg	2m Cls6 NHF 4-6yo gd-sft	£1,560

Brilliant novice hurdler three seasons ago who took winning streak to seven (including the Challow Hurdle) before finishing fourth in the Albert Bartlett; suffered a tendon injury on chasing debut two seasons ago and has run only once since when pulled up at Newbury last season.

Baywing (Ire)

9 br g Winged Love - Cerise De Totes (Champ Libre)

Nicky Richards   David & Nicky Robinson

PLACINGS: 65/1111P/414/3F5312-   RPR **154c**

Starts	1st	2nd	3rd	4th	Win & Pl
18	6	1	2	2	£101,830

140	2/18	Newc	4m¹/₂f Cls2 123-149 Ch Hcap heavy	£50,048
2/17	Weth	3m Cls1 Nov Gd2 Ch soft	£18,546
125	1/16	Hayd	2m7f Cls3 124-137 Hdl Hcap heavy	£6,498
112	12/15	Uttx	2m7¹/₂f Cls4 105-112 Hdl Hcap heavy	£3,509
104	12/15	Uttx	2m4f Cls4 104-119 Hdl Hcap heavy	£3,509
89	11/15	Carl	2m4f Cls4 Nov 89-110 Hdl Hcap heavy	£3,249

Mudlover and thorough stayer who made the most of ideal conditions when showing an

impressive turn of foot to win the Eider Chase at Newcastle last season; raised 9lb for that win but ran well off his new mark when second at Kelso next time.

Beer Goggles (Ire)
7 br g Oscar - Tynelucy (Good Thyne)

Nicky Martin   Bradley Partnership

PLACINGS: 70711/3VPF311/21315-   RPR **160**h

Starts	1st	2nd	3rd	4th	Win & Pl
23	6	3	3	2	£70,459

	12/17	Newb	3m Cls1 Gd2 Hdl soft	£28,475
145	10/17	NAbb	3m2¹/₂f Cls2 131-157 Hdl Hcap good	£15,358
122	4/17	Ayr	3m¹/₂f Cls3 97-127 Hdl Hcap gd-sft	£7,798
113	3/17	Newb	3m Cls4 105-116 Hdl Hcap gd-sft	£4,549
104	3/16	Hexm	2m7¹/₂f Cls5 77-104 Hdl Hcap heavy	£2,601
97	3/16	Sedg	3m3f Cls4 94-110 Hdl Hcap soft	£4,159

Shock winner of the Long Distance Hurdle at Newbury last season for the late Richard Woollacott; may well prove flattered by that win and only fifth in the Cleeve next time but had been progressive prior to that, winning three of his last five handicaps.

Beggar's Wishes (Ire)
7 b g Oscar - Strong Wishes (Strong Gale)

Peter Bowen   Roddy Owen & Paul Fullagar

PLACINGS: 542/4426P117/15421-1   RPR **149**+c

Starts	1st	2nd	3rd	4th	Win & Pl
17	5	3	-	4	£48,846

132	5/18	Hayd	2m4¹/₂f Cls2 126-145 Ch Hcap good	£18,768
127	4/18	MRas	2m5¹/₂f Cls3 Nov 116-128 Ch Hcap heavy	£9,747
119	11/17	Sedg	2m¹/₂f Cls4 Nov 100-120 Ch Hcap good	£3,899
106	3/17	Sthl	1m7¹/₂f Cls4 85-110 Hdl Hcap soft	£3,899
97	2/17	Bang	2m¹/₂f Cls4 97-111 Hdl Hcap soft	£6,498

Took a while to build on victory on chase debut last season but made rapid progress during the

spring, winning in April and May; particularly impressive when following up by six lengths at Haydock on good ground, underlining versatility after previous win on heavy.

Bel Ami De Sivola (Fr)
7 b g Network - Notting Hill (Garde Royale)

Noel Meade (Ir)   Gigginstown House Stud

PLACINGS: 1115P8/235342813-36P   RPR **137**+c

Starts	1st	2nd	3rd	4th	Win & Pl
21	4	3	5	1	£72,019

129	4/18	Fair	2m¹/₂f Nov 120-140 Ch Hcap sft-hvy	£26,106
	12/16	Fair	2m4f Nov Hdl yield	£7,235
	11/16	DRoy	2m Mdn Hdl 4-6yo good	£6,331
	10/16	Punc	2m NHF 5-7yo gd-yld	£4,522

Had become slightly disappointing until getting off the mark over fences in a good novice handicap chase at Fairyhouse over Easter; fair third at Punchestown next time over 2m4f but may be better back at 2m; ran at Grade I level over hurdles and may well have more to offer.

Belami Des Pictons (Fr)
7 b g Khalkevi - Nina Des Pictons (Denham Red)

Venetia Williams   Hills Of Ledbury (Aga)

PLACINGS: 533111/4111/2-   RPR **152**c

Starts	1st	2nd	3rd	4th	Win & Pl
11	6	1	2	1	£56,149

	2/17	Leic	2m6¹/₂f Cls3 Nov Ch soft	£9,495
	2/17	Wwck	3m Cls3 Nov Ch heavy	£9,419
132	12/16	Newb	2m6¹/₂f Cls3 Nov 124-144 Ch Hcap gd-sft	£6,498
	3/16	Bang	2m Cls4 Nov Hdl soft	£3,249
	3/16	Wwck	2m Cls4 Nov Hdl soft	£3,249
	10/15	Vich	2m2¹/₂f Hdl 4yo v soft	£8,186

Won three out of four as a novice chaser two seasons ago, though kept to a modest level with

Benatar: very smart novice chaser last season and sure to prove a force again

Facebook.com/racingpost

last victory coming at 1-4 in a two-runner race; second to Waiting Patiently on sole start last term before being ruled out; trainer feels he'll be fine on better ground (all wins on soft or heavy).

Bellshill (Ire)
8 b g King's Theatre - Fairy Native (Be My Native)

Willie Mullins (Ir)   Andrea & Graham Wylie

PLACINGS: 2/1111302/111F3/14d1-   RPR **172+c**

Starts		1st	2nd	3rd	4th	Win & Pl
19		10	3	2	-	£415,407
	4/18	Punc	3m¹/₂f Gd1 Ch yield			£143,584
	2/18	Fair	3m1f Gd3 Ch soft			£23,496
	12/16	Limk	2m3¹/₂f Nov Gd2 Ch heavy			£19,305
	11/16	Gowr	2m4f Ch yld-sft			£7,235
	4/16	Punc	3m Nov Gd1 Hdl gd-yld			£43,382
	1/16	Naas	2m4f Nov Gd1 Hdl heavy			£39,706
	12/15	Navn	2m4f Nov Gd2 Hdl heavy			£20,155
	11/15	Cork	2m Mdn Hdl heavy			£7,488
	4/15	Punc	2m Gd1 NHF 4-7yo gd-yld			£44,186
	11/14	Thur	2m NHF 4-7yo soft			£4,313

Lightly raced chaser who looked much improved last season, winning twice including the Punchestown Gold Cup with sole defeat a huge effort under top weight in the Irish Grand National; yet to prove as effective left-handed and well beaten on three trips to Cheltenham.

Benatar (Ire)
6 b g Beneficial - Carrigeen Lily (Supreme Leader)

Gary Moore   Ashley Head

PLACINGS: 11424/1113-   RPR **154+c**

Starts		1st	2nd	3rd	4th	Win & Pl
8		4	1	1	2	£63,220
	12/17	Asct	2m5f Cls1 Nov Gd2 Ch gd-sft			£19,933
	11/17	Plum	2m3¹/₂f Cls3 Nov Ch gd-sft			£6,975
142	11/17	Asct	2m3f Cls3 Nov 126-142 Ch Hcap good			£9,747
	1/17	Font	2m3f Cls5 Mdn Hdl soft			£2,274

High-class novice chaser last season, winning first three races over fences, including a Grade 2 at Ascot when beating Finian's Oscar, and suffered only defeat when third in the JLT at Cheltenham; pulled hard that day and should prove capable of better.

Benie Des Dieux (Fr)
7 b m Great Pretender - Cana (Robin Des Champs)

Willie Mullins (Ir)   Mrs S Ricci

PLACINGS: 141/633/1/1111-   RPR **152+h**

Starts		1st	2nd	3rd	4th	Win & Pl
11		7	-	2	1	£229,658
	4/18	Punc	2m4f Gd1 Hdl yld-sft			£52,212
	3/18	Chel	2m4f Cls1 Gd1 Hdl heavy			£67,582
	2/18	Naas	2m List Ch heavy			£17,688
	12/17	Carl	2m4f Cls1 List Ch soft			£17,286
	12/16	Limk	2m3¹/₂f Ch sft-hvy			£6,105
	4/15	Autl	2m2f Hdl 4-5yo v soft			£22,326
	10/14	Autl	2m2f Hdl 3yo heavy			£22,000

Unbeaten in five races since moving from France, winning three times over fences before switching to hurdles to achieve a Grade 1 double at Cheltenham

and Punchestown last season; expected to be suited by step up to 3m and should have lots of options.

Bentelimar (Ire)
9 ch g Beneficial - Montel Girl (Montelimar)

Charlie Longsdon   Swanee River Partnership

PLACINGS: 262533F/13U26032271-   RPR **150+c**

Starts		1st	2nd	3rd	4th	Win & Pl
38		7	7	6	3	£152,594
135	4/18	Aint	2m Cls1 Gd3 129-153 Ch Hcap soft			£50,517
	6/17	Wxfd	2m4f Nov Ch soft			£7,897
	2/15	Punc	2m Nov List Hdl soft			£15,116
126	12/14	Leop	2m4f Nov 98-126 Hdl Hcap soft			£14,083
	6/14	WxfR	2m2f Nov Hdl gd-fm			£5,750
	5/14	Klny	2m1f Mdn Hdl yld-sft			£4,888
	4/14	Tram	2m NHF 5-7yo yld-sft			£4,313

Picked out by his trainer as one to follow last season and finally justified that billing with an impressive win in the Red Rum Chase at Aintree; raised 10lb for that win but expected to prove even better on good ground and runner-up Theinval franked the form by winning at Ayr.

Beware The Bear (Ire)
8 b g Shantou - Native Bid (Be My Native)

Nicky Henderson   G B Barlow

PLACINGS: 22/2431/11174/1P4P-   RPR **157+c**

Starts		1st	2nd	3rd	4th	Win & Pl
13		5	1	1	3	£70,214
145	12/17	Newc	2m7¹/₂f Cls1 List 126-150 Ch Hcap soft			£40,053
136	12/16	Newb	2m7¹/₂f Cls3 Nov 116-136 Ch Hcap gd-sft			£6,498
130	11/16	Asct	3m Cls3 Nov 122-135 Ch Hcap gd-sft			£7,148
	5/16	Sthl	3m Cls4 Nov Hdl good			£3,899
	4/16	Bang	2m7f Cls5 Mdn Hdl heavy			£3,139

Finished notably well when getting up to win last season's Rehearsal Chase and ran a similar race when a staying-on fourth in the Ultima at Cheltenham; seems sure to relish extreme trips on that evidence but was pulled up in the Welsh and Scottish Grand Nationals.

Beyond The Clouds
5 ch g Peintre Celebre - Evening (Mark Of Esteem)

Kevin Ryan   Guy Reed Racing

PLACINGS: 12/11110-   RPR **139h**

Starts		1st	2nd	3rd	4th	Win & Pl
7		5	1	-	-	£24,996
	2/18	Muss	1m7¹/₂f Cls2 Nov Hdl soft			£12,996
	11/17	Muss	1m7¹/₂f Cls4 Nov Hdl good			£3,249
	10/17	Kels	2m Cls4 Nov Hdl good			£3,899
	9/17	Worc	2m Cls5 NHF 4-6yo good			£1,949
	1/17	Muss	1m7¹/₂f Cls6 NHF 4-6yo good			£1,949

Dual wide-margin bumper winner who also won first three novice hurdles last season, with his biggest success coming at Musselburgh when coping better than expected with soft ground (every other run on good); flopped when well fancied for the Scottish Champion Hurdle.

Black Corton: winner of eight races over fences last season in a tremendous campaign

Big River (Ire)

8 b g Milan - Call Kate (Lord America)

Lucinda Russell   Two Black Labs

PLACINGS: 221/1/21521/1P312-   RPR **150c**

Starts	1st	2nd	3rd	4th	Win & Pl
13	6	4	1	-	£60,566

	2/18	Kels	2m7½f Cls2 Ch heavy	£16,025
	10/17	Kels	2m7½f Cls4 Nov Ch good	£4,549
132	3/17	Kels	3m2f Cls2 132-149 Hdl Hcap heavy	£14,621
115	12/16	Ayr	2m5½f Cls3 112-127 Hdl Hcap heavy	£7,148
	10/15	Kels	2m Cls4 Mdn Hdl good	£3,249
	3/15	Kels	2m Cls6 NHF 4-6yo gd-sft	£1,625

Did really well in novice chases last season, with only poor effort coming when suffering from a fibrillating heart; bounced back to gain a fifth course win at Kelso and ran a cracker when second conceding 23lb to a progressive rival at Uttoxeter; should stay beyond 3m.

Bigmartre (Fr)
7 b g Montmartre - Oh La Miss (Le Balafre)

Harry Whittington   P J Dixon

PLACINGS: 2/121433/1860/11271-   RPR **154c**

Starts	1st	2nd	3rd	4th	Win & Pl
20	6	3	2	1	£95,514

	4/18	Ayr	2m4½f Cls1 Nov Gd2 Ch good	£30,247
137	12/17	Newb	2m½f Cls3 Nov 130-139 Ch Hcap gd-sft	£12,974
132	10/17	Ludl	2m Cls3 Nov 123-134 Ch Hcap gd-fm	£9,082
133	12/16	Kemp	2m Cls3 124-139 Hdl Hcap good	£12,512
	12/15	Hayd	1m7½f Cls4 Nov Hdl 4-6yo heavy	£3,899
	10/15	Font	2m1½f Cls4 Nov Hdl good	£5,198

Won three times when sent novice chasing last season, though probably flattered by his Grade 2 success at Ayr when only two finished; had been well beaten when up in grade in the JLT at Cheltenham but may have found 2m4f on soft ground too far that day.

Binge Drinker (Ire)
9 b g Spadoun - Our Honey (Old Vic)

Paul Nicholls   Corsellis & Seyfried

PLACINGS: 231/111541/9/1/8-   RPR **116c**

Starts	1st	2nd	3rd	4th	Win & Pl
12	6	1	1	1	£24,457

	11/16	Ffos	2m3½f Cls4 Nov Ch good	£5,198
133	3/15	Bang	2m7f Cls3 122-135 Hdl Hcap gd-sft	£6,498
	12/14	Chep	2m7½f Cls4 Nov Hdl gd-sft	£3,119
	11/14	Ffos	3m Cls4 Nov Hdl soft	£3,119
	10/14	Worc	2m4f Cls5 Mdn Hdl good	£1,949
	2/14	Chep	2m Cls6 Am Mdn NHF 4-6yo heavy	£1,560

Fragile horse who has run just twice since April

2015, including when well beaten on debut for Paul Nicholls last season; clearly talented, though, having beaten Might Bite on his chasing debut in 2016 (runner-up made mistakes) and won three times over hurdles.

Black Corton (Fr)
7 br g Laverock - Pour Le Meilleur (Video Rock)

Paul Nicholls   The Brooks, Stewart Families & J Kyle

PLACINGS: 311214/121111121154-   RPR **160+c**

Starts	1st	2nd	3rd	4th	Win & Pl
24	13	4	4	2	£196,528

	2/18	Asct	3m Cls1 Nov Gd2 Ch soft	£22,780
	12/17	Kemp	3m Cls1 Nov Gd1 Ch soft	£43,466
	11/17	Chel	3m½f Cls2 Nov Ch soft	£15,640
	10/17	Chel	3m½f Cls2 Nov Ch good	£16,218
	10/17	NAbb	2m5f Cls2 Ch good	£18,705
	8/17	Font	2m5½f Cls4 Nov Ch gd-fm	£3,899
	7/17	Worc	2m7f Cls4 Nov Ch good	£3,899
	6/17	Font	2m1½f Cls4 Nov Ch gd-sft	£3,899
135	4/17	Tntn	2m3f Cls3 124-135 Hdl Hcap good	£7,280
	10/16	Kemp	2m Cls1 Nov List Hdl good	£11,390
	10/16	NAbb	2m2½f Cls4 Nov Hdl 4-6yo good	£4,549
	4/16	Extr	2m1f Cls5 Mdn Hdl good	£2,599
	5/15	Pina	1m7f NHF 4yo gd-sft	£5,426

Tough and prolific novice chaser last season; won eight of his first ten races over fences, including the Kauto Star at Kempton and the Reynoldstown at Ascot, though may have had his limitations exposed against the very best when well beaten at Cheltenham and Aintree.

Black Op (Ire)

7 br g Sandmason - Afar Story (Desert Story)

Tom George   R S Brookhouse

PLACINGS: 1/19/41221-   RPR **155+h**

Starts	1st	2nd	3rd	4th	Win & Pl
7	3	2		1	£95,237

	4/18	Aint	2m4f Cls1 Nov Gd1 Hdl soft	£56,141
	1/18	Donc	2m5f Cls5 Mdn Hdl soft	£3,119
	2/17	Donc	2m¹/₂f Cls6 NHF 4-6yo good	£1,949

Developed into a top-class novice hurdler last season, winning a Grade 1 at Aintree having just been outstayed by Santini and outclassed by Samcro when second in his previous two races; expected to come into his own as a novice chaser by connections.

Blackbow (Ire)

5 b g Stowaway - Rinnce Moll (Accordion)

Willie Mullins (Ir)   Roaringwater Syndicate

PLACINGS: 1/1152-   RPR **142+b**

Starts	1st	2nd	3rd	4th	Win & Pl
4	2	1	-	-	£63,511

	2/18	Leop	2m Gd2 NHF 4-7yo soft	£39,159
	12/17	Leop	2m NHF 4yo yield	£5,528

Top of the pecking order among his trainer's bumper performers last season according to market moves (shortest price among Cheltenham team and favourite at Punchestown despite coming only fifth at the Festival); good second in the latter race and a top prospect for novice hurdles.

Blaklion

9 b g Kayf Tara - Franciscaine (Legend Of France)

Nigel Twiston-Davies   S Such & CG Paletta

PLACINGS: 4F12113/45324/212BP-   RPR **166+c**

Starts	1st	2nd	3rd	4th	Win & Pl
27	9	6	3	4	£411,166

153	12/17	Aint	3m2f Cls1 Gd3 133-159 Ch Hcap heavy	£81,443
	3/16	Chel	3m1¹/₂f Cls1 Gd1 Ch good	£85,425
	2/16	Weth	3m Cls1 Nov Gd2 Ch heavy	£19,221
	12/15	Chel	3m1¹/₂f Cls2 Nov Ch soft	£14,442
	12/14	Chel	3m Cls1 Nov Gd2 Hdl gd-sft	£17,085
	10/14	Chep	2m3¹/₂f Cls1 Nov Gd2 Hdl soft	£17,085
	9/14	Prth	2m4f Cls4 Nov Hdl good	£3,119
	4/14	Hayd	1m7¹/₂f Cls5 NHF 4-6yo good	£1,949
	3/14	Ffos	2m Cls6 NHF 4-5yo soft	£1,625

Has looked a natural over the Grand National fences over the last two seasons, winning last season's Becher Chase, but was brought down at the first in the big race in April; produced perhaps his best run over regulation fences when second to Bristol De Mai in the Charlie Hall.

Bleu Berry (Fr)

7 b g Special Kaldoun - Somosierra (Blushing Flame)

Willie Mullins (Ir)   Luke McMahon

PLACINGS: 512/7F/1115/0143-0   RPR **149+h**

Starts	1st	2nd	3rd	4th	Win & Pl
14	5	1	1	1	£138,490

143	3/18	Chel	2m5f Cls1 Gd3 135 153 Hdl Hcap soft	£56,950
	4/17	Fair	2m Nov Gd2 Hdl sft-hvy	£22,692
	3/17	Naas	2m Nov List Hdl sft-hvy	£14,455
	2/17	Fair	2m Mdn Hdl sft-hvy	£6,844
	9/14	Clun	1m4f NHF 3yo v soft	£4,167

Missed much of last season through injury but made up for lost time when winning the Coral Cup at Cheltenham on just his second run outside novice company; seemed to have limitations exposed in Graded company, although was badly hampered when finishing third at Punchestown.

Bleu Et Rouge (Fr)

7 gr g Charming Groom - Lady Du Renom (Art Francais)

Willie Mullins (Ir)   John P McManus

PLACINGS: 22/141F5/1U4/042049-   RPR **153h**

Starts	1st	2nd	3rd	4th	Win & Pl
16	3	3	-	4	£105,348

	12/16	Leop	2m3f Ch yield	£6,331
	2/16	Leop	2m2f Nov Gd1 Hdl sft-hvy	£39,044
	11/15	Cork	2m Mdn Hdl 4yo heavy	£6,419

Lightly raced since winning a Grade 1 novice hurdle in February 2016 but suggested he retains all his ability when second in last season's Betfair Hurdle under a big weight; has also won over fences but lost his way after impressing on that chasing debut.

Blow By Blow (Ire)

7 ch g Robin Des Champs - Shean Rose (Roselier)

Gordon Elliott (Ir)   Gigginstown House Stud

PLACINGS: 211/1/32161147-   RPR **152+h**

Starts	1st	2nd	3rd	4th	Win & Pl
12	6	2	1	1	£134,530

144	3/18	Chel	2m4¹/₂f Cls2 136-144 Cond Hdl Hcap soft	£43,792
	2/18	Thur	2m4f Nov Gd3 Hdl soft	£23,496
	12/17	Navn	2m7f Mdn Hdl heavy	£7,108
	4/16	Punc	2m Gd1 NHF 4-7yo gd-yld	£43,382
	3/16	Fair	2m NHF 4-7yo yld-sft	£5,879
	2/16	Navn	2m NHF 5-7yo heavy	£4,070

Won a Grade 1 bumper in 2016 before spending 18 months out; not quite up to that level in novice hurdles last season but still proved thrown in off a mark of 144 when running away with the Martin Pipe Hurdle at Cheltenham; likely to go novice chasing.

facebook.com/racingpost

Racing to a new career at ror.org.uk

rorsourceahorse.org.uk

A new website for selling or loaning a horse directly out of a trainer's yard and for all former racehorses.

Bloodstock Sales

In addition to Horses In Training sales, RoR holds auctions dedicated to horses leaving racing.

Rehoming Direct

RoR has compiled a checklist to safeguard your horse's future when moved directly into the sport horse market.

Retrainers

RoR has a list of retrainers recommended by trainers who can start the retraining process and assess each horse.

Visit
ror.org.uk
for rehoming options and advice

Equine Charities

Retrain former racehorses for a donation, as well as care for vulnerable horses with the help of RoR funding.

RoR is British horseracing's official charity for the welfare of horses retired from racing.

Blu Cavalier

8 b g Kayf Tara - Blue Ride (King's Ride)

Paul Nicholls   Mrs Angela Tincknell & W Tincknell

PLACINGS: 414/244111-2   RPR **142+h**

Starts	1st	2nd	3rd	4th	Win & Pl
10				4	£22,052
	4/18	Winc	2m4f Cls4 Nov Hdl gd-sft		£5,133
	4/18	Tntn	2m3f Cls4 Nov Hdl heavy		£5,458
	3/18	Winc	1m7¹/₂f Cls4 Mdn Hdl heavy		£4,354
	11/15	Tntn	2m¹/₂f Cls5 Mdn NHF 4-6yo good		£2,738

Blotted his copybook with defeat at 2-13 at Newton Abbot in May (possibly unsuited by drop in trip and quicker ground when beaten a neck) but had gone there on a four-timer after winning three novice hurdles, impressing over longer trips; likely to go novice chasing.

Bonbon Au Miel (Fr)

7 b g Khalkevi - Friandise II (Mistigri)

Willie Mullins (Ir)   Andrea & Graham Wylie

PLACINGS: 231/21P/41F-   RPR **151+c**

Starts	1st	2nd	3rd	4th	Win & Pl
9			1	1	£35,299
	1/18	Navn	2m4f Ch heavy		£7,904
	3/17	Cork	2m Hdl heavy		£10,530
	9/14	Fntb	2m2f Hdl 3yo v soft		£9,200

Lightly raced and inconsistent since moving from France but looked a fine prospect in the second of three runs in novice chases last season, winning easily at Navan; well beaten when falling at the last in the RSA Chase next time; suited by heavy ground.

Brace Yourself (Ire)

5 ch g Mahler - Angelica Garnett (Desert Story)

Noel Meade (Ir)   Mrs Patricia Hunt

PLACINGS: 2132-   RPR **132+b**

Starts	1st	2nd	3rd	4th	Win & Pl
3	1	1	1	-	£14,618
	12/17	DRoy	2m NHF 4-7yo heavy		£5,265

Point-to-point runner-up and a brilliant 24-length winner on his bumper debut last season; lost little in defeat subsequently, finishing third behind high-class pair Blackbow and Rhinestone before chasing home Getaway John (pulled 24 lengths clear of the third) when favourite at Fairyhouse; bright novice hurdle prospect.

Brahma Bull (Ire)

7 ch g Presenting - Oligarch Society (Moscow Society)

Willie Mullins (Ir)   Mrs S Ricci

PLACINGS: 111196-   RPR **140+h**

Starts	1st	2nd	3rd	4th	Win & Pl
6	4	-	-	-	£28,525
	11/17	Thur	2m7¹/₂f Mdn Hdl yield		£5,791
	10/17	Tipp	2m NHF 4-7yo sft-hvy		£6,844
	9/17	List	2m NHF 4-7yo heavy		£9,477
	7/17	Baln	2m1¹/₂f NHF 5-7yo good		£5,528

Won three bumpers and maintained unbeaten record with an impressive win at Thurles on his hurdling debut; suffered a setback after that, though, and perhaps paid for lack of experience when thrust straight back into Grade 1 company at Cheltenham and Punchestown.

Bristol De Mai: tough high-class chaser who goes particularly well at Haydock

Facebook.com/racingpost

Brain Power (Ire)

7 b g Kalanisi - Blonde Ambition (Old Vic)

Nicky Henderson   Michael Buckley

PLACINGS: 10/121/381185/1UF2F-   RPR **162c**

Starts	1st	2nd	3rd	4th	Win & Pl
16	6	2	1	-	£185,093

	11/17	Kemp	2m2f Cls4 Nov Ch gd-sft	£4,660
149	12/16	Asct	1m7¹/₂f Cls1 Gd3 125-150 Hdl Hcap gd-sft	£85,425
142	12/16	Sand	2m Cls1 List 120-144 Hdl Hcap gd-sft	£33,762
	3/16	Kemp	2m Cls4 Nov Hdl good	£3,249
	11/15	Kemp	2m Cls4 Nov Hdl 4-6yo gd-sft	£3,899
	2/15	Newc	2m¹/₂f Cls6 NHF 4-6yo gd-sft	£1,560

Smart hurdler who looked to have a big future over fences when making a winning novice chase debut at Kempton last November but failed to strike again; failed to complete three times, twice when running well before tiring; finished second in the Arkle at Cheltenham in between on first run after wind surgery; could yet take high rank among the top-class chasers.

Bristol De Mai (Fr)

7 gr g Saddler Maker - La Bole Night (April Night)

Nigel Twiston-Davies   Simon Munir & Isaac Souede

PLACINGS: 211122/221375/11632-   RPR **182+c**

Starts	1st	2nd	3rd	4th	Win & Pl
26	9	8	4	1	£454,396

	11/17	Hayd	3m1¹/₂f Cls1 Gd1 Ch heavy	£113,072
	11/17	Weth	3m Cls1 Gd2 Ch soft	£57,218
154	1/17	Hayd	3m Cls1 Gd2 142-162 Ch Hcap soft	£28,475
	2/16	Sand	2m4f Cls1 Nov Gd1 Ch gd-sft	£25,628
	1/16	Hayd	2m4f Cls1 Nov Gd2 Ch heavy	£18,438
	12/15	Leic	2m Cls3 Nov Ch soft	£6,330
	11/15	Wwck	2m Cls3 Nov Ch 4-5yo gd-sft	£9,384
	12/14	Chep	2m Cls1 Gd1 Hdl 3yo heavy	£19,933
	9/14	Autl	2m2f Hdl 3yo v soft	£19,200

Won last season's Betfair Chase in remarkable circumstances, galloping his rivals into the ground to win by 57 lengths; now 3-3 at Haydock and yet to prove as effective elsewhere, though he showed high-class form when second to Might Bite in the Bowl at Aintree.

Buveur D'Air (Fr)

7 b g Crillon - History (Alesso)

Nicky Henderson   John P McManus

PLACINGS: 124/1131/11111/1111-   RPR **167+h**

Starts	1st	2nd	3rd	4th	Win & Pl
17	14	1	1	1	£865,845

	3/18	Chel	2m¹/₂f Cls1 Gd1 Hdl heavy	£266,384
	2/18	Sand	2m Cls1 List Hdl soft	£17,085
	12/17	Kemp	2m Cls1 Gd1 Hdl soft	£68,340
	12/17	Newc	2m¹/₂f Cls1 Gd1 Hdl soft	£61,897
	4/17	Aint	2m4f Cls1 Gd1 Hdl good	£112,260
	3/17	Chel	2m¹/₂f Cls1 Gd1 Hdl gd-sft	£227,800
	2/17	Sand	2m Cls1 List Hdl heavy	£14,238
	12/16	Wwck	2m Cls1 Nov Gd1 Hdl soft	£5,198
	12/16	Hayd	1m7¹/₂f Cls2 Nov Ch soft	£11,574
	4/16	Aint	2m¹/₂f Cls1 Nov Gd1 Hdl soft	£42,203
	1/16	Hntg	2m Cls4 Nov Hdl gd-sft	£3,249
	11/15	Newb	2m¹/₂f Cls3 Mdn Hdl soft	£6,498
	10/14	Nant	1m4f NHF 3yo gd-sft	£6,250
	8/14	Sjdm	1m5f NHF 3yo	£4,167

Has won the last two runnings of the Champion

Hurdle as part of an unbeaten seven-race run since being switched back to hurdles after an aborted chase campaign; won very weak runnings of the Fighting Fifth and Christmas Hurdles last term before just beating Melon at Cheltenham.

Cadmium (Fr)

6 b g Early March - Mirquille (Passing Sale)

Willie Mullins (Ir)   Supreme Horse Racing Club & Kenneth Sharp

PLACINGS: 9/4/1/3141-15   RPR **153+c**

Starts	1st	2nd	3rd	4th	Win & Pl
9	4	-	1	2	£59,636

	6/18	Rosc	2m Nov Ch good	£7,632
133	4/18	Punc	2m 122-150 Ch Hcap yld-sft	£33,938
	2/18	Fair	2m1¹/₂f Ch soft	£9,267
	12/16	Limk	2m3f Mdn Hdl yield	£4,522

Back from a long absence last season after winning his sole start over hurdles and eventually proved himself a very smart novice chaser when running away with a 2m handicap chase at Punchestown; patchy record otherwise and doesn't seem to get anything beyond 2m.

Calett Mad (Fr)

6 b/br g Axxos - Omelia (April Night)

Nigel Twiston-Davies   Simon Munir & Isaac Souede

PLACINGS: 43/1212952/11541P1-9   RPR **145+h**

Starts	1st	2nd	3rd	4th	Win & Pl
18	6	3	2	2	£99,585

	4/18	Prth	3m Cls1 Nov List Hdl soft	£15,575
138	2/18	Muss	3m2f Cls2 117-142 Hdl Hcap soft	£12,996
	10/17	Chel	3m Cls3 Nov Hdl good	£6,343
	9/17	Prth	3m Cls4 Nov Hdl heavy	£3,399
138	1/17	Tntn	2m7f Cls3 128-138 Ch Hcap good	£8,229
130	11/16	Newc	2m7¹/₂f Cls3 Nov 124-135 Ch Hcap soft	£9,986

Sent chasing as a four-year-old in 2016 and did well to win twice and finish second at Grade 2 level; proved equally adept when reverting to novice hurdles last term, winning three times up to 3m2f; beaten favourite back over fences in the Summer Plate and may be best over further.

Calino D'Airy (Fr)

6 ch g Anzillero - Monita D'Airy (Oblat)

Henry de Bromhead (Ir)   Gigginstown House Stud

PLACINGS: 1716F/11303-0F   RPR **154c**

Starts	1st	2nd	3rd	4th	Win & Pl
11	3	-	2	-	£36,250

	10/17	Gway	2m2f Nov Ch heavy	£9,740
	10/17	Gway	2m Nov Ch soft	£7,371
	12/16	DRoy	2m Mdn Hdl soft	£4,522

Lightly raced youngster who won his first two runs over fences last season and belatedly built on that promise when third at 33-1 behind Finian's Oscar at Aintree (first run over 2m4f); had previously shown his best form on a slower surface, including heavy.

Call Me Lord (Fr)
5 b/br g Slickly - Sosa (Cape Cross)

Nicky Henderson			Simon Munir & Isaac Souede

PLACINGS: 5111/31321-   RPR **164+h**

Starts	1st	2nd	3rd	4th	Win & Pl
9	5	1	2	-	£135,144

	4/18	Sand	2m5¹/₂f Cls1 Gd2 Hdl gd-sft.................................£31,323
143	1/18	Sand	2m Cls2 117-143 Hdl Hcap heavy £15,640
135	4/17	Sand	2m Cls2 109-135 Hdl 4yo Hcap good...............£31,280
	3/17	Comp	2m2f Hdl 4yo heavy...£19,692
	12/16	Cagn	2m¹/₂f Hdl 3yo soft..£11,294

Progressed nicely over hurdles last season and was particularly impressive when stepped up to 2m5½f on his final start at Sandown having finished a close second under a big weight in the Imperial Cup; deliberately kept to right-handed tracks so far so may have options reduced.

Campeador (Fr)
6 gr g Gris De Gris - Royale Video (Video Rock)

Gordon Elliott (Ir)			John P McManus

PLACINGS: 2/14F/F/1F3-   RPR **154+h**

Starts	1st	2nd	3rd	4th	Win & Pl
8	2	1	1	1	£35,954

	10/17	Punc	2m Hdl yld-sft...£10,530
	6/15	Claf	2m1f Hdl 3yo v soft...£12,651

Unlucky not to have a far more impressive record having twice fallen at the last in big handicaps in 2016, including when sure to win at Fairyhouse; won easily on his first run since then last season but twice disappointing when stepped up in class subsequently.

Cap Soleil (Fr)
5 b m Kapgarde - Move Again (Noir Et Or)

Fergal O'Brien			Mrs S A Noott

PLACINGS: 111/1212-   RPR **134h**

Starts	1st	2nd	3rd	4th	Win & Pl
7	5	2	-	-	£74,411

	12/17	Hayd	2m3f Cls1 Nov List Hdl heavy £11,390
	11/17	Newb	2m¹/₂f Cls2 Nov Hdl gd-sft.................................£12,996
	3/17	Sand	2m Cls1 List NHF 4-6yo soft...............................£11,390
	1/17	Chel	1m6f Cls1 List NHF 4yo soft................................£11,888
	12/16	Newb	1m4¹/₂f Cls6 NHF 3yo gd-sft..................................£1,949

Tough and consistent performer in top mares' races over the last two seasons; won two Listed bumpers in 2017 and added a novice hurdle in that grade at Haydock over 2m3f; lacked the speed to lay up when down in trip at Cheltenham but stayed on for second behind Laurina.

Capitaine (Fr)
6 gr g Montmartre - Patte De Velour (Mansonnien)

Paul Nicholls			Martin Broughton & Friends

PLACINGS: 21/12124P1/11F5-0   RPR **156+c**

Starts	1st	2nd	3rd	4th	Win & Pl
14	6	3	-	1	£62,834

	10/17	MRas	2m1f Cls3 Nov Ch good.......................................£7,798
	5/17	NAbb	2m¹/₂f Cls3 Ch good..£7,656
	4/17	Winc	1m7¹/₂f Cls4 Nov Hdl gd-fm.................................£3,899
	12/16	Asct	1m7¹/₂f Cls1 Nov Gd2 Hdl gd-sft.........................£18,224
	11/16	Winc	1m7¹/₂f Cls3 Nov Hdl 4-6yo good..........................£6,498
	4/16	Winc	1m7¹/₂f Cls6 NHF 4-6yo gd-sft...............................£1,625

Won his first two races over fences last season but missed much of the campaign after a heavy fall at Sandown (held but running a good race behind Sceau Royal at the time); reverted to hurdles when back in the spring and disappointed when favourite for the Swinton.

Captain Cattistock
5 b g Black Sam Bellamy - Pearl Buttons (Alflora)

Paul Nicholls			Peter Hart

PLACINGS: 1/411414-   RPR **143+h**

Starts	1st	2nd	3rd	4th	Win & Pl
6	3	-	-	3	£19,626

	3/18	Winc	2m5¹/₂f Cls4 Nov Hdl heavy £4,224
130	2/18	Winc	2m4f Cls3 115-130 Hdl Hcap heavy.....................£8,814
	11/17	Winc	2m5¹/₂f Cls4 Nov Hdl soft £4,224

Won three hurdle races last season, all at Wincanton; gained all those victories on soft or heavy ground but coped well with quicker when set to go close in stronger company at Cheltenham until blundering at the last; likely to go novice chasing.

Captain Redbeard (Ire)
9 ch g Bach - Diesel Dancer (Toulon)

Stuart Coltherd			S Coltherd

PLACINGS: 411/434311P2/36121U-   RPR **151+c**

Starts	1st	2nd	3rd	4th	Win & Pl
25	7	3	6	4	£89,480

139	3/18	Ayr	2m4¹/₂f Cls3 118-139 Hdl Hcap heavy £10,657
135	12/17	Hayd	2m7f Cls2 118-144 Ch Hcap heavy.....................£15,698
131	3/17	Hayd	2m4f Cls3 Nov 126-136 Ch Hcap gd-sft................£9,747
124	1/17	Weth	2m3¹/₂f Cls3 116-131 Ch Hcap gd-sft....................£6,498
124	3/16	Kels	2m5f Cls3 113-130 Hdl Hcap gd-sft......................£5,848
114	3/16	Carl	2m4¹/₂f Cls4 94-117 Am Hdl Hcap soft..................£3,249
106	1/16	Sedg	2m4f Cls4 101-117 Hdl Hcap gd-sft......................£3,899

Climbed just 6lb in the handicap last season despite generally progressive form; won the Tommy Whittle at Haydock and bumped into a handicap blot when second in the Peter Marsh

Facebook.com/racingpost

next time; also won over hurdles before unseating his rider early in the Grand National.

Carefully Selected (Ire)

6 b g Well Chosen - Knockamullen Girl (Alderbrook)

Willie Mullins (Ir)   Miss M A Masterson

PLACINGS: **21**/1123-   RPR **142b**

Starts	1st	2nd	3rd	4th	Win & Pl
4	2	1	1	-	£37,396
2/18	Naas	2m NHF 4-7yo soft			£7,087
12/17	Leop	2m4f NHF 4-7yo soft			£6,318

Won two bumpers last season (up to 2m4f) and went close to a hat-trick in the Champion Bumper at Cheltenham; possibly flattered by that bare form (stole a five-length lead at the start and had an easy time in front) but again ran well when third at Punchestown.

Carter McKay

7 gr g Martaline - Saxona (Jade Robbery)

Willie Mullins (Ir)   Pearl Bloodstock

PLACINGS: **21**/1106/1330-   RPR **140h**

Starts	1st	2nd	3rd	4th	Win & Pl
8	3	-	2	-	£30,348
11/17	Gowr	2m Mdn Hdl heavy			£7,897
2/17	Naas	2m3f NHF 5-7yo soft			£5,791
12/16	Leop	2m NHF 4-6yo yield			£4,296

Slightly disappointing since well fancied for the 2017 Champion Bumper, proving less effective on quicker ground in that sphere and winning only a maiden hurdle last season; has already

won a point-to-point and may do better in novice chases.

Casablanca Mix (Fr)

6 ch m Shirocco - Latitude (Kadalko)

Nicky Henderson   Rutland Rascals

PLACINGS: 3411/114513P4/321F-   RPR **150+c**

Starts	1st	2nd	3rd	4th	Win & Pl
16	6	1	3	3	£89,292
11/17	Hntg	2m4f Cls4 Nov Ch gd-sft			£5,198
9/16	Autl	2m2f Hdl 4yo v soft			£18,353
5/16	Autl	2m2f Hdl 4yo heavy			£16,941
4/16	Mlns	2m2f Hdl 4-5yo gd-sft			£6,353
11/15	Pari	1m4f NHF 3yo heavy			£11,628
10/15	Fntb	1m5f NHF 3yo v soft			£5,814

Exciting mare who missed the second half of last season but had already looked a smart recruit to fences; thrashed the useful Theatre Territory when off the mark at the third attempt and well clear when falling at the last at Exeter next time.

Castlegrace Paddy (Ire)

7 b g Flemensfirth - Thunder Road (Mtoto)

Pat Fahy (Ir)   Clipper Logistics Group

PLACINGS: 2/42415/115-   RPR **154+c**

Starts	1st	2nd	3rd	4th	Win & Pl
8	3	1	-	2	£35,366
3/18	Thur	2m2f Nov List Ch soft			£16,327
12/17	Fair	2m Ch heavy			£7,897
3/17	Gowr	2m Mdn Hdl sft-hvy			£6,844

Made a big impression when sent chasing last season despite running only three times, winning twice including a Listed chase at Thurles; only fifth when stepped up in class at Punchestown (no match for Footpad) but possibly unsuited by quicker ground.

Call Me Lord (right): smart performer over hurdles last season

Ch'Tibello (Fr)

7 b g Sageburg - Neicha (Neverneyev)

Dan Skelton — The Can't Say No Partnership

PLACINGS: 1/2231/35132/42280- RPR **156**h

Starts	1st	2nd	3rd	4th	Win & Pl
15	3	5	3	1	£203,535

	11/16	Hayd	2m Cls2 Hdl heavy	£61,900
135	4/16	Ayr	2m Cls1 Gd2 133-147 Hdl Hcap gd-sft	£57,520
	4/15	Comp	2m1f Hdl 4yo heavy	£8,186

Hasn't won since 2016 but has been mixing it in top company since then, including when second in the Champion Hurdle Trial at Haydock and Kingwell Hurdle at Wincanton last season; failed to fire back in handicap company off a falling mark in the Scottish Champion Hurdle.

Champ (Ire)

6 b g King's Theatre - China Sky (Definite Article)

Nicky Henderson — John P McManus

PLACINGS: 12/2-11 RPR **138**+h

Starts	1st	2nd	3rd	4th	Win & Pl
5	3	2	-	-	£13,573

	5/18	Wwck	2m5f Cls4 Nov Hdl gd-sft	£4,549
	5/18	Prth	2m4f Cls4 Mdn Hdl good	£4,224
	1/17	Sthl	1m7¹/₂f Cls6 Mdn NHF 4-6yo soft	£2,053

Beaten a neck by subsequent Listed winner Vinndication on his only run over hurdles last season at Ascot; retained novice status for this campaign and has already taken advantage with two smooth wins in May; could be a leading novice.

Champagne Classic (Ire)

7 b g Stowaway - Classical Rachel (Shahanndeh)

Gordon Elliott (Ir) — Gigginstown House Stud

PLACINGS: 1/212321311/ RPR **153**

Starts	1st	2nd	3rd	4th	Win & Pl
9	4	3	2	-	£109,938

	4/17	Punc	3m Nov Gd1 Hdl gd-yld	£50,427
138	3/17	Chel	2m4¹/₂f Cls2 135-145 Cond Hdl Hcap good	£40,664
	2/17	Thur	2m6¹/₂f Mdn Hdl soft	£5,791
	11/16	Fair	2m4f NHF 4-7yo soft	£4,070

Big improver when encountering quicker ground for the first time in the spring of 2017, winning the Martin Pipe at Cheltenham and beating Penhill in a 3m Grade 1 at Punchestown having landed only a maiden from first five hurdle runs; missed last season through injury.

Charbel (Ire)

7 b g Iffraaj - Eoz (Sadler's Wells)

Kim Bailey — Mrs Julie Martin & David R Martin

PLACINGS: 11/412215/512F3/44F- RPR **163**c

Starts	1st	2nd	3rd	4th	Win & Pl
16	5	3	1	3	£95,092

	10/16	Uttx	2m Cls3 Ch good	£9,384
	2/16	Muss	1m7¹/₂f Cls2 Nov Hdl gd-sft	£14,389
	10/15	Strf	2m¹/₂f Cls3 Nov Hdl 4-6yo soft	£6,498
	3/15	Limk	2m List NHF 4yo heavy	£12,597
	2/15	Leop	2m NHF 4yo soft	£5,349

Very talented chaser and even looked like giving Altior his biggest scare over fences when falling two out in the 2017 Arkle; reportedly lost his confidence after that and fell at Cheltenham again in last season's Champion Chase but wasn't beaten far in the Tingle Creek.

Charli Parcs (Fr)

5 b g Anabaa Blue - Ella Parcs (Nikos)

Nicky Henderson — John P McManus

PLACINGS: 11F6/200P4- RPR **147**+h

Starts	1st	2nd	3rd	4th	Win & Pl
9	2	1	-	1	£48,115

	12/16	Kemp	2m Cls2 Hdl 3yo good	£12,512
	11/16	Engh	2m1¹/₂f Hdl 3yo v soft	£17,647

Yet to live up to big early expectations but was a fair sixth in the Triumph Hurdle in 2017 and ran well in a couple of good handicaps last season; twice flopped on soft ground but finished a close fourth in the Scottish Champion Hurdle back on a faster surface.

Chef Des Obeaux (Fr)

6 b g Saddler Maker - O Dame De Gene (Passing Sale)

Nicky Henderson — Sullivan Bloodstock

PLACINGS: 57/2/2111PP- RPR **153**+h

Starts	1st	2nd	3rd	4th	Win & Pl
9	3	2	-	-	£28,737

	2/18	Hayd	2m7f Cls1 Nov Gd2 Hdl heavy	£16,972
	1/18	Kemp	3m¹/₂f Cls3 Nov Hdl good	£6,238
	12/17	Uttx	2m4f Cls5 Am Mdn Hdl soft	£2,469

Dented his reputation when pulled up at Cheltenham and Aintree but had already shown himself to be a high-class staying novice hurdler last season, winning three in a row including a decent Grade 2 at Haydock by 15 lengths; likely to go novice chasing.

Facebook.com/racingpost

Chesterfield (Ire)
8 ch g Pivotal - Antique (Dubai Millennium)

Seamus Mullins   The Rumble Racing Club

PLACINGS: 1211F/80211/00443-2   RPR **147**h

Starts	1st	2nd	3rd	4th	Win & Pl
16	5	3	1	2	£154,383

	3/18	Kemp	2m Cls4 NHF std-slw £4,874
143	4/17	Ayr	2m Cls1 Gd2 135-155 Hdl Hcap gd-sft £59,798
132	4/17	Aint	2m¹/₂f Cls2 120-140 Am Hdl Hcap good £30,950
123	11/14	Chel	2m¹/₂f Cls3 Nov 100-130 Hdl Hcap soft £7,507
	10/14	Hntg	2m Cls4 Nov Hdl good £3,899
	7/14	Worc	2m Cls4 Nov Hdl good £3,249

Has a terrific record in big 2m handicap hurdles, winning at Aintree and Ayr (Scottish Champion Hurdle) in 2017; found life tougher off higher marks since then but still second in the Swinton, third in the Scottish Champion and fourth in the County Hurdle.

Chris's Dream (Ire)
6 b g Mahler - Janebailey (Silver Patriarch)

Henry de Bromhead (Ir)   Robcour

PLACINGS: 010/62119-   RPR **149+**h

Starts	1st	2nd	3rd	4th	Win & Pl
7	2	1	-	-	£28,486

2/18	Clon	3m Nov Gd3 Hdl heavy £20,409
12/17	Limk	2m3f Mdn Hdl soft £5,791

Bought for £175,000 after winning a maiden hurdle at Limerick last season and looked money well spent when hacking up in a Grade 3 at Clonmel next time; sent off just 6-1 for the Albert Bartlett at Cheltenham after that but trailed home a distant ninth.

Cilaos Emery (Fr)
6 b g Califet - Queissa (Saint Preuil)

Willie Mullins (Ir)   Luke McMahon

PLACINGS: 11251/42-   RPR **155**h

Starts	1st	2nd	3rd	4th	Win & Pl
7	3	2	-	1	£90,470

4/17	Punc	2m¹/₂f Nov Gd1 Hdl gd-yld £50,427
12/16	Navn	2m Mdn Hdl sft-hvy £6,331
4/16	Punc	2m NHF 4yo gd-yld £5,426

Perhaps flattered by Grade 1 win as a novice

hurdler in 2017 (main rivals went too fast in front) but proved not far off the best last season when second to subsequent Champion Hurdle third Mick Jazz; didn't appear to stay 2m4f when fourth in the Hatton's Grace.

Claimantakinforgan (Fr)
6 b g Great Pretender - Taquine D'Estrees (Take Risks)

Nicky Henderson   Grech & Parkin

PLACINGS: S1/16235/11352-   RPR **150**h

Starts	1st	2nd	3rd	4th	Win & Pl
10	3	2	2	-	£65,623

12/17	Asct	1m7¹/₂f Cls1 Nov Gd2 Hdl soft £19,933
11/17	Newb	2m¹/₂f Cls4 Nov Hdl gd-sft £4,549
11/16	Hayd	1m7¹/₂f Cls4 NHF 4-6yo heavy £3,249

Third and fifth at Grade 1 level at the Cheltenham Festival in the last two seasons, most recently in the Supreme Novices' Hurdle; connections felt he would have preferred quicker ground that day and duly stepped up on good when second in the Scottish Champion Hurdle.

Clan Des Obeaux (Fr)
6 b g Kapgarde - Nausicaa Des Obeaux (April Night)

Paul Nicholls   Mr & Mrs PK Barber, G Mason & Sir A Ferguson

PLACINGS: 1/126/412514/2123-   RPR **164**c

Starts	1st	2nd	3rd	4th	Win & Pl
14	5	4	1	2	£136,545

11/17	Hayd	2m5¹/₂f Cls2 Ch heavy £32,490
3/17	Extr	2m3f Cls3 Nov Ch gd-sft £7,148
11/16	Newb	2m4f Cls1 Nov Gd2 Ch gd-sft £19,933
12/15	Newb	2m¹/₂f Cls4 Hdl 3yo soft £3,249
4/15	Lrsy	1m4f NHF 3yo £3,876

Showed smart form in all four runs last season, including a good third behind Might Bite in the Bowl at Aintree when stepped up in distance and class; may be capable of better having been off for nearly four months prior to that run and still only six years old.

Cliffs Of Dover
5 b g Canford Cliffs - Basanti (Galileo)

Paul Nicholls   Mr & Mrs J D Cotton

PLACINGS: 1311111/P-   RPR **138**h

Starts	1st	2nd	3rd	4th	Win & Pl
8	6	-	1	-	£56,739

	12/16	Donc	2m¹/₂f Cls1 Gd2 Hdl 3yo good £22,780
	10/16	Weth	2m Cls1 List Hdl 3yo good £11,390
129	10/16	Chst	2m¹/₂f Cls3 110-136 Cond Hdl Hcap good £6,256
	10/16	Kemp	2m Cls3 Hdl 3yo good £5,525
121	10/16	Winc	1m7¹/₂f Cls3 120-129 Hdl Hcap gd-fm £5,848
	8/16	Worc	2m Cls4 Mdn Hdl 3yo good £3,509

Went from strength to strength when winning six hurdle races as a juvenile two seasons ago before missing the spring through injury; pulled up on only run since then over hurdles (conditions too soft to run as planned in big 2m handicaps) but did well back on the Flat.

Cloudy Dream (Ire)
8 gr g Cloudings - Run Away Dream (Acceglio)

Donald McCain   Trevor Hemmings

PLACINGS: 3112/1122221/222235-   RPR **162c**

Starts		1st	2nd	3rd	4th	Win & Pl
20		7	9	3	-	£249,856
	4/17	Ayr	2m4¹/₂f Cls1 Nov Gd2 Ch good			£26,283
	11/16	Hayd	2m¹/₂f Cls2 Ch soft			£12,996
	10/16	Carl	2m Cls4 Ch soft			£3,899
122	3/16	MRas	2m2¹/₂f Cls3 115-129 Hdl Hcap soft			£9,384
	11/15	Donc	2m3¹/₂f Cls4 Nov Hdl 4-6yo good			£3,899
	10/15	Carl	2m1f Cls6 NHF 4-6yo good			£1,560
	4/15	Hexm	2m Cls6 NHF 4-5yo good			£1,711

Has been something of a nearly horse in the last two seasons, winning just once since his first two chases in 2016 and finishing second eight times during that period; has looked a weak finisher at times and the step up to around 3m last season didn't help; twice disappointing in the spring; has since left Ruth Jefferson and is set to start his campaign in the Old Roan Chase at Aintree.

Clyne
8 b g Hernando - Lauderdale (Nebos)

Evan Williams   David M Williams

PLACINGS: 35/311/1123/2324413-   RPR **155h**

Starts		1st	2nd	3rd	4th	Win & Pl
17		6	3	5	2	£136,345
146	3/18	Uttx	2m4f Cls2 123-146 Hdl Hcap heavy			£12,512
140	12/16	Hayd	2m3f Cls2 114-140 Hdl Hcap soft			£12,512
132	11/16	Hayd	1m7¹/₂f Cls3 106-132 Hdl Hcap heavy			£12,996
119	2/16	Wwck	2m Cls4 104-119 Hdl Hcap soft			£3,899
115	12/15	Ffos	2m Cls3 107-132 Hdl Hcap heavy			£6,498
	12/14	Ffos	2m Cls4 Nov Hdl soft			£3,119

Continued to progress over hurdles last season; followed a series of good runs in defeat by defying top weight in a handicap at Uttoxeter before a fine third in the Aintree Hurdle; has run only once on ground quicker than soft when below par at Fontwell.

Cobra De Mai (Fr)
*6 b g Great Pretender - Miria Galanda (Ut*chef De Clan)*

Dan Skelton   Norman Lake & Susan Carsberg

PLACINGS: 42/45442/111P154122-   RPR **149c**

Starts		1st	2nd	3rd	4th	Win & Pl
22		7	5	2	5	£78,650
133	2/18	Wwck	2m4f Cls2 131-144 Ch Hcap gd-sft			£18,768
	10/17	Sedg	2m¹/₂f Cls4 Nov Ch good			£3,899
	5/17	Hntg	2m¹/₂f Cls4 Nov Ch good			£4,534
116	5/17	Worc	2m Cls4 97-117 Hdl Hcap gd-fm			£3,379
116	5/17	Wwck	2m Cls4 Nov 99-119 Ch Hcap good			£4,549
	2/16	Weth	2m Cls5 Mdn Hdl 4yo heavy			£2,599
	6/15	Nanc	1m4f NHF 3yo good			£4,264

Won three times when sent chasing last season; patchy record otherwise but got back on an upward curve after wind surgery, earning biggest win at Warwick and twice finishing a good second including in a Grade 2 novice chase at Ayr behind Bigmartre.

Coney Island (Ire)
7 b g Flemensfirth - Millys Gesture (Milan)

Edward Harty (Ir)   John P McManus

PLACINGS: 32151/2212/1PP-   RPR **167+c**

Starts		1st	2nd	3rd	4th	Win & Pl
12		4	4	1	-	£115,306
	12/17	Asct	2m5f Cls2 Ch gd-sft			£16,245
	12/16	Fair	2m4f Nov Gd1 Ch gd-yld			£36,875
130	3/16	Fair	3m Nov 109-131 Hdl Hcap yield			£23,860
	12/15	Leop	2m Mdn Hdl 4yo heavy			£6,953

Won the Drinmore as a novice in 2016 before finishing a half-length second to Our Duke in another Grade 1 that Christmas but has run just three times since due to injury and was pulled up the last twice; also won well at Ascot last season, though, and could yet have a big future.

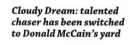

Cloudy Dream: talented chaser has been switched to Donald McCain's yard

Facebook.com/racingpost

Coneygree
11 b g Karinga Bay - Plaid Maid (Executive Perk)

Mark Bradstock — The Max Partnership

PLACINGS: 8/1113/1111/1/23/PP- — RPR **178+c**

Starts	1st	2nd	3rd	4th	Win & Pl
15	9	1	2	-	£520,223

11/15	Sand	3m Cls1 List Ch gd-sft		£17,085
3/15	Chel	3m2½f Cls1 Gd1 Ch soft		£313,225
2/15	Newb	2m7½f Cls1 Gd2 Ch soft		£28,475
12/14	Kemp	3m Cls1 Nov Gd1 Ch gd-sft		£42,047
11/14	Newb	2m4f Cls1 Nov Gd2 Ch soft		£18,184
12/12	Chel	3m Cls1 Nov Gd2 Hdl heavy		£14,238
11/12	Chel	2m5f Cls1 Nov Gd2 Hdl soft		£14,238
11/12	Uttx	2m4f Cls4 Nov Hdl soft		£2,534
11/11	Uttx	2m Cls6 NHF 4-6yo gd-sft		£1,365

Brilliant winner of the Gold Cup as a novice in 2015 but has suffered a string of injury problems since then, running just five times; twice pulled up last season but had been a close third behind Sizing John in the 2017 Punchestown Gold Cup and connections keen to keep going.

Constantine Bay
7 b g Kayf Tara - Alina Rheinberg (Waky Nao)

Nicky Henderson — Grech & Parkin

PLACINGS: 21/11144/ — RPR **147h**

Starts	1st	2nd	3rd	4th	Win & Pl
5	3	-	-	2	£37,995

1/17	Donc	3m1½f Cls1 Nov Gd2 Hdl good		£17,085
1/17	Chep	2m3½f Cls4 Nov Hdl heavy		£3,574
11/16	Hayd	2m3f Cls3 Nov Hdl 4-7yo soft		£5,393

Smart novice hurdler two seasons ago, winning a Grade 2 at Doncaster and fourth in 3m Grade 1 events at Cheltenham and Aintree; all those runs came on good ground but believed by connections to prefer softer (has won on heavy); missed last season through injury.

Coo Star Sivola (Fr)
6 b g Assessor - Santorine (Della Francesca)

Nick Williams — Babbit Racing

PLACINGS: /233/281614/532411P- — RPR **151+c**

Starts	1st	2nd	3rd	4th	Win & Pl
18	4	3	3	2	£129,762

I42	3/18	Chel	3m1f Cls1 Gd3 137-155 Ch Hcap heavy		£62,645
I35	2/18	Extr	3m Cls3 Nov 116-135 Ch Hcap soft		£9,846
	2/17	Wwck	2m3f Cls4 Nov Hdl 4-7yo soft		£3,899
	1/17	Chel	2m4½f Cls1 Nov List Hdl gd-sft		£11,390

Won the Ultima Handicap Chase at last season's Cheltenham Festival, keeping up a fine record at the meeting having finished third and fourth in competitive handicap hurdles there previously;

progressing well over fences but pulled up in Grade 1 company at Aintree.

Coquin Mans (Fr)
6 b g Fragrant Mix - Quissisia Mans (Video Rock)

Willie Mullins (Ir) — George Creighton

PLACINGS: 1/1/1122S14-P — RPR **159+h**

Starts	1st	2nd	3rd	4th	Win & Pl
10	5	2	-	1	£91,539

4/18	Fair	2m4f Gd2 Hdl heavy		£36,549
8/17	Cork	3m Hdl yield		£11,038
6/17	Wxfd	3m Hdl soft		£6,844
12/16	Limk	2m Mdn Hdl 4yo sft-hvy		£5,653
3/15	Pmnl	1m4f NHF 3yo v soft		£4,264

Ran only once as a novice two seasons ago and got better with experience last term, proving himself a high-class hurdler when winning a 2m4f Grade 2 at Fairyhouse in April; has also shown fair form at 2m and 3m, though well beaten at Grade 1 level at each of those trips.

Cracking Smart (Fr)
6 b g Great Pretender - Maya Du Frene (Le Pommier D'Or)

Gordon Elliott (Ir) — Gigginstown House Stud

PLACINGS: F21/1122- — RPR **153+h**

Starts	1st	2nd	3rd	4th	Win & Pl
7	3	3	-	-	£56,781

11/17	Cork	3m Nov List Hdl soft		£20,171
10/17	Punc	2m4f Mdn Hdl yld-sft		£7,108
4/17	Fair	2m NHF 4-7yo gd-yld		£5,265

Twice beaten by Next Destination last season but looked full of promise when a length second in a Grade 1 at Navan, finishing strongly; always expected to improve when stepped up to 3m and was favourite for the Albert Bartlett before meeting with a setback.

Crievehill (Ire)
6 b g Arcadio - Ma Douce (Mansonnien)

Nigel Twiston-Davies — Highclere T'Bred Racing – Crievehill

PLACINGS: 6/2413008/71324212- — RPR **147c**

Starts	1st	2nd	3rd	4th	Win & Pl
15	3	4	2	2	£49,011

I29	3/18	Sand	2m4f Cls3 106-129 Ch Hcap soft		£9,419
I27	11/17	Ling	2m Cls3 112-127 Ch Hcap soft		£12,660
I22	1/17	Ling	2m Cls4 103-122 Hdl Hcap heavy		£3,249

Went chasing last season and got better with practice, finishing with three fine runs including a 20-length win at Sandown; beaten a short head prior to that and a close second again when

THE JOCKEY CLUB
Since 1750

—— 2018 ——
FIXTURE LIST

SEASON OPENER | Thu 4 Oct
GO RACING RACEDAY | Tue 16 Oct
ANNUAL BEER FESTIVAL | Sun 4 Nov
GO RACING RACEDAY | Tue 13 Nov
WINTER LADIES DAY[*] | Sat 24 Nov
THE PETERBOROUGH CHASE[*] | Sun 9 Dec
BOXING DAY[*] | Wed 26 Dec

RACE ON

BOOK NOW **HUNTINGDON.THEJOCKEYCLUB**.CO.UK

HUNTINGDON
A Jockey Club Racecourse

conceding 26lb to the winner on his final run; still going the right way.

Crosshue Boy (Ire)

8 b g Brian Boru - Gluais Linn (Supreme Leader)

Sean Doyle (Ir)   N J Heffernan

PLACINGS: 92190/9983450611131-   RPR **145+c**

Starts	1st	2nd	3rd	4th	Win & Pl
29	7	2	3	3	£128,705

136	4/18	Ayr	3m Cls2 Nov 124-143 Ch Hcap good £64,980
	3/18	DRoy	2m3¹/₂f Nov Ch heavy £8,722
118	3/18	Wxfd	2m Nov 101-118 Ch Hcap heavy £8,995
	3/18	Leop	2m1f Nov Ch yield £11,973
	3/17	Wxfd	2m4¹/₂f Hdl sft-hvy £8,687
114	9/16	Kbgn	2m3¹/₂f 104-119 Hdl Hcap good £8,366
	5/16	Punc	3m Mdn Hdl good £5,426

Massive improver last spring, winning four out of five in a remarkable six-week spell (only defeat when a close third at Fairyhouse); had shown most of his form on heavy ground but stepped forward again on good when winning a novice handicap chase at Ayr.

Cyrname (Fr)

6 b g Nickname - Narquille (Passing Sale)

Paul Nicholls   Mrs Johnny De La Hey

PLACINGS: 521/56/7121214-   RPR **162+c**

Starts	1st	2nd	3rd	4th	Win & Pl
12	4	3	-	1	£90,218

	2/18	Kemp	2m4¹/₂f Cls1 Nov Gd2 Ch good £18,224
	12/17	Kemp	2m Cls1 Nov Gd2 Ch soft £23,491
130	11/17	Hntg	2m1¹/₂f Cls3 123-131 Ch Hcap good £7,798
	1/16	Pau	2m1¹/₂f Hdl 4yo v soft £11,294

Smart novice chaser last season, winning three times and finishing a neck second to Terrefort in the Scilly Isles; all those runs on right-handed tracks and yet to prove as effective going the other way, managing only a below-par fourth when favourite for a Grade 1 at Aintree.

Cyrus Darius

9 b g Overbury - Barton Belle (Barathea)

Colin Tizzard   Mr & Mrs G Calder & PM Warren

PLACINGS: 4/3111/1/419/14315-   RPR **150+**

Starts	1st	2nd	3rd	4th	Win & Pl
14	7	-	4	3	£107,905

	2/18	Kels	2m2f Cls2 Hdl heavy £16,245
137	11/17	Ayr	2m4¹/₂f Cls3 112-138 Ch Hcap heavy £11,696
	2/17	Kels	2m2f Cls2 Hdl heavy £16,643
	9/15	Prth	2m4f Cls3 Nov Ch gd-sft £6,882
	4/15	Aint	2m¹/₂f Cls1 Nov Gd2 Hdl gd-sft £33,762
	3/15	Hexm	2m Cls4 Nov Hdl gd-sft £3,285
	3/15	Newc	2m1¹/₂f Cls4 Nov Hdl good £3,249

Huge talent who has struggled to fulfil his potential since suffering a serious injury after his chasing debut in 2015; still won twice last season, hacking up by 12 lengths in the Morebattle Hurdle; has since left Ruth Jefferson and may have more to offer as a chaser after just four runs over fences.

Daklondike (Ire)

6 b g Gold Well - Strong Irish (Corrouge)

David Pipe   Prof Caroline Tisdall

PLACINGS: 1/43164/41411P-   RPR **143+c**

Starts	1st	2nd	3rd	4th	Win & Pl
11	4	-	1	4	£31,467

133	12/17	Newb	3m2f Cls3 129-135 Ch Hcap heavy £11,696
126	12/17	Winc	3m1f Cls3 108-126 Ch Hcap soft £9,583
114	11/17	Wetl	3m Cls4 98-122 Ch Hcap soft £3,899
	11/16	Ling	2m Cls4 Nov Hdl heavy £4,549

Progressive staying novice chaser last season, winning for the third time in a valuable handicap at Newbury over Christmas; missed subsequent targets due to minor niggles and below par when back at Punchestown (pulled up despite going off favourite).

Dame De Compagnie (Fr)

5 b m Lucarno - Programmee (Kahyasi)

Nicky Henderson   John P McManus

PLACINGS: 1/322/1521-   RPR **130+h**

Starts	1st	2nd	3rd	4th	Win & Pl
8	3	3	1	-	£41,050

	4/18	Chel	2m4¹/₂f Cls1 Nov List Hdl good £14,238
	11/17	Uttx	2m Cls4 Mdn Hdl good £3,249
	4/16	Lrsy	1m4f NHF 3yo £3,676

Didn't quite live up to promise of win on British debut last season but got back on track by landing a Listed mares' novice hurdle at Cheltenham; had been beaten at odds-on in a Grade 2 and then may just have needed first run back from a break; likely to go novice chasing.

Danny Kirwan (Ire)

5 b g Scorpion - Sainte Baronne (Saint Des Saints)

Paul Nicholls   Mrs Johnny De La Hey

PLACINGS: 110-   RPR **108+b**

Starts	1st	2nd	3rd	4th	Win & Pl
2	1	-	-	-	£3,119

	2/18	Kemp	2m Cls5 NHF 4-6yo good £3,119

Well backed ahead of bumper debut at Kempton last season having earned rave reviews at home and duly won impressively; sent off favourite again for Aintree's Grade 2 bumper at the Grand National meeting but disappointed in much softer conditions.

Daphne Du Clos (Fr)

5 b m Spanish Moon - Katarina Du Clos (Panoramic)

Nicky Henderson   Sullivan Bloodstock Limited

PLACINGS: 121/   RPR **111b**

Starts	1st	2nd	3rd	4th	Win & Pl
3	1	2	-	-	£20,621

	2/17	Newb	2m1¹/₂f Cls1 List NHF 4-6yo soft £11,390
	10/16	Sbri	1m4f NHF 3yo gd-sft £4,779

Among the leading fancies for the Champion

Bumper at Cheltenham in 2017 before being ruled out and had already beaten eventual fifth Western Ryder in a Listed contest at Newbury; hasn't run since through injury but should make a good novice hurdler.

Debece

7 b g Kayf Tara - Dalamine (Sillery)

Tim Vaughan   Robert Kirkland

PLACINGS: 441/123313/4-F   RPR **141**h

Starts	1st	2nd	3rd	4th	Win & Pl
11	3	1	3	3	£28,252

121	3/17	Newb	2m4¹/₂f Cls4 99-121 Hdl Hcap soft	£4,549
	5/16	Kemp	2m Cls4 Nov Hdl good	£3,249
	3/16	MRas	2m1¹/₂f Cls6 Mdn NHF 4-6yo soft	£1,560

Held in very high regard by his trainer and went some way to justifying the faith with a half-length third in a Grade 1 at Aintree in 2017 (first run over 3m); out of action for a year subsequently but returned with a fair fourth back at Aintree in April before falling early on at Haydock the following month; set to go novice chasing.

Debuchet (Fr)

5 gr g Smadoun - Luzerne Du Poitou (Royal Charter)

Mags Mullins (Ir)   Force Eight Syndicate

PLACINGS: 2121/469F-3   RPR **141**h

Starts	1st	2nd	3rd	4th	Win & Pl
9	2	2	1	1	£45,220

	4/17	Limk	2m List NHF 4yo soft	£20,171
	1/17	Leop	2m NHF 4yo good	£4,731

Finished second in the 2017 Champion Bumper at Cheltenham; failed to run up to the same level of form in novice hurdles last season due to jumping issues but still a fair ninth in the Supreme and still in front when falling two out at Punchestown; retains novice status.

Defi Du Seuil (Fr)

5 b g Voix Du Nord - Quarvine Du Seuil (Lavirco)

Philip Hobbs   John P McManus

PLACINGS: 2/11111111/47-   RPR **139**h

Starts	1st	2nd	3rd	4th	Win & Pl
11	8	1	-	1	£218,699

	4/17	Aint	2m1f Cls1 Gd1 Hdl 4yo good	£56,181
	3/17	Chel	2m1f Cls1 Gd1 Hdl 4yo good	£71,188
	1/17	Chel	2m1f Cls1 Gd2 Hdl 4yo soft	£17,085
	12/16	Chep	2m Cls1 Gd1 3yo soft	£28,475
	12/16	Chel	2m1f Cls2 Hdl 3yo gd-sft	£12,512
	11/16	Chel	2m Cls1 Gd2 Hdl 3yo gd-sft	£17,165
	10/16	Ffos	2m Cls5 Mdn Hdl 3yo good	£2,599
	4/16	Pari	1m4f NHF 3yo v soft	£5,882

Outstanding juvenile hurdler two seasons ago, winning all seven races including the Cheltenham-Aintree double; aimed at the Champion Hurdle last term but flopped twice and was given an extended summer break; likely to go novice chasing.

Definitly Red (Ire)

9 ch g Definite Article - The Red Wench (Aahsaylad)

Brian Ellison   Phil & Julie Martin

PLACINGS: 2122F1/131U1P/3116U-   RPR **169**+c

Starts	1st	2nd	3rd	4th	Win & Pl
25	12	4	2	-	£294,455

	1/18	Chel	3m1¹/₂f Cls1 Gd2 Ch heavy	£56,950
	12/17	Aint	3m1f Cls1 Gd2 Ch heavy	£28,135
149	3/17	Donc	3m2f Cls2 137-161 Ch Hcap soft	£34,408
141	12/16	Weth	3m Cls1 Gd3 131-153 Ch Hcap gd-sft	£22,780
140	10/16	Carl	2m4f Cls2 122-148 Hdl Hcap gd-sft	£12,512
137	4/16	Ayr	2m4¹/₂f Cls1 List 132-148 Ch Hcap good	£25,628
	1/16	Catt	3m1f Cls4 Nov Ch soft	£7,148
	2/15	Hayd	2m7f Cls1 Nov Gd2 Hdl soft	£15,735
	1/15	Catt	2m3¹/₂f Cls4 Nov Hdl gd-sft	£4,874
	11/14	Chel	2m¹/₂f Cls1 List NHF 4-6yo soft	£11,390
	2/14	Newb	2m1¹/₂f Cls1 List NHF 4-6yo heavy	£11,390
	12/13	Uttx	2m Cls6 Mdn NHF 4-6yo heavy	£1,949

Proved himself a very smart staying chaser last season with a pair of Grade 2 victories, most notably in the Cotswold Chase at Cheltenham (both on heavy ground but won the 2016 Rowland Meyrick on good to soft); limitations exposed when sixth in the Cheltenham Gold Cup.

Delta Work (Fr)

5 br g Network - Robbe (Video Rock)

Gordon Elliott (Ir)   Gigginstown House Stud

PLACINGS: 213324312-   RPR **150**+h

Starts	1st	2nd	3rd	4th	Win & Pl
9	2	3	3	1	£99,987

139	3/18	Chel	3m Cls1 Gd3 135-155 Hdl Hcap soft	£56,950
	5/17	Punc	2m1¹/₂f Mdn Hdl good	£6,844

Progressed throughout last season and ran out a narrow winner of the Pertemps Final at Cheltenham; had come up short in Graded races earlier in the season but underlined his improvement when a neck second to Next Destination at Punchestown.

Diakali (Fr)

9 gr g Sinndar - Diasilixa (Linamix)

Gary Moore   Nick Peacock

PLACINGS: 11343/34/10/41/66-11   RPR **159**+c

Starts	1st	2nd	3rd	4th	Win & Pl
21	9	2	3	4	£355,304

	6/18	NAbb	2m¹/₂f Cls3 Nov Ch good	£9,357
	6/18	Font	2m2f Cls4 Nov Ch good	£4,614
	4/17	Fair	2m Hdl gd-yld	£11,564
	7/15	Tipp	2m Gd3 Hdl good	£31,492
	11/13	Naas	2m Gd3 Hdl 4yo yld-sft	£14,533
	6/13	Autl	2m3¹/₂f Gd1 Hdl 4yo v soft	£98,780
	4/13	Punc	2m Gd1 Hdl 4yo heavy	£40,325
	1/13	Punc	2m Gd1 Hdl 4yo heavy	£14,533
	11/12	Gowr	2m Mdn Hdl 3yo heavy	£5,750

One-time high-class hurdler for Willie Mullins, winning a Grade 1 juvenile hurdle in 2013 and third in the following year's Aintree Hurdle; barely raced in subsequent years but back on track over fences this summer for new connections; could be an exciting novice chaser.

Diamond Cauchois (Fr)

7 b g Crillon - Diamond Turtle (Limnos)

Gordon Elliott (Ir)　　　　Danny & Eamon Partnership

PLACINGS: P/040P842P01/313126-　　　　RPR **155h**

Starts	1st	2nd	3rd	4th	Win & Pl
23	5	7	3	3	£105,081

	2/18	Navn	2m5f Gd2 Hdl sft-hvy.................................£23,496
128	12/17	Navn	2m4f 120-140 Hdl Hcap heavy..................£25,214
119	3/17	Thur	2m7f 90-121 Hdl Hcap sft-hvy..................£8,424
108	1/16	Thur	2m4f 102-129 Hdl Hcap soft.......................£8,371
	5/15	Dax	2m1¹/₂f Hdl 4yo good.................................£6,326

Massive improver following move to Gordon Elliott last season, developing into a high-class staying hurdler; beaten off 126 on his yard debut yet soon hacked up in the Boyne Hurdle and was a close second to Coquin Mans in another Grade 2 at Fairyhouse.

Didtheyleaveuoutto (Ire)

5 ch g Presenting - Pretty Puttens (Snurge)

Nick Gifford　　　　John P McManus

PLACINGS: 10-　　　　RPR **128b**

Starts	1st	2nd	3rd	4th	Win & Pl
2	1	-	-	-	£17,085

	12/17	Asct	1m7¹/₂f Cls5 List NHF 4-6yo gd-sft.............£17,085
	11/17	Ling	2m Cls6 NHF 4-6yo stand............................£1,949

Impressed in winning two bumpers last season, most notably in a Listed race at Ascot; long-time favourite for the Champion Bumper at Cheltenham but drifted close to the day due to conditions (believed to need quicker ground) and finished only tenth.

Diego Du Charmil (Fr)

6 b g Ballingarry - Daramour (Anabaa Blue)

Paul Nicholls　　　　Mrs Johnny De La Hey

PLACINGS: 32214/19010/132F15-　　　　RPR **164+c**

Starts	1st	2nd	3rd	4th	Win & Pl
16	5	3	2	1	£181,473

	4/18	Aint	2m Cls1 Nov Gd1 Ch soft............................£56,130
	9/17	NAbb	2m1¹/₂f Cls3 Nov Ch gd-sft...........................£7,121
140	2/17	Muss	1m7¹/₂f Cls1 List 117-143 Hdl Hcap good....£28,475
138	10/16	Chep	2m Cls2 120-140 Hdl 4yo Hcap good...........£12,996
133	3/16	Chel	2m1¹/₂f Cls1 Gd3 128-142 Hdl 4yo Hcap good....£42,713

Had his progress over fences held up by a

ON THE FIGURES

DIEGO DU CHARMIL Although he added only one more win to a Newton Abbot chasing debut success last September, the fact it came in Grade 1 company at Aintree bodes well for a successful second season over fences. Expected to stay further, but heads initially for Exeter's Haldon Gold Cup. [Steve Mason, Racing Post Ratings]

setback last autumn but came good when winning a Grade 1 at Aintree; probably flattered by that win (main rival Petit Mouchoir boiled over in preliminaries) but bodes well that he did it on soft ground having been seen as needing quicker.

Diese Des Bieffes (Fr)

5 gr g Martaline - Chanel Du Berlais (Saint Preuil)

Nicky Henderson　　　　Sullivan Bloodstock

PLACINGS: 5/112551-　　　　RPR **140h**

Starts	1st	2nd	3rd	4th	Win & Pl
7	3	1	-	-	£26,828

	4/18	Chel	2m4¹/₂f Cls2 Nov Hdl good........................£12,512
	11/17	Tntn	2m¹/₂f Cls4 Nov Hdl good............................£4,549
	11/17	Font	2m1¹/₂f Cls4 Nov Cond Hdl good..................£3,249

Won three novice hurdles last season, most notably a competitive race at Cheltenham in April; back to winning ways that day after a couple of tries in handicaps, running well enough when fifth in the Lanzarote and the Martin Pipe; could go novice chasing.

Dingo Dollar (Ire)

6 ch g Golden Lariat - Social Society (Moscow Society)

Alan King　　　　M Warren, J Holmes, R Kidner & J Wright

PLACINGS: 1/20171/4F112-　　　　RPR **150c**

Starts	1st	2nd	3rd	4th	Win & Pl
10	4	2	-	1	£37,845

	2/18	Donc	3m Cls4 Nov Ch gd-sft..................................£4,494
130	12/17	Newb	2m7¹/₂f Cls3 Nov 125-137 Ch Hcap soft.......£6,498
	4/17	Font	3m1¹/₂f Cls4 Nov Hdl good.............................£3,249
	1/17	Bang	2m7f Cls4 Mdn Hdl gd-sft..............................£3,249

Progressive novice chaser last season, winning twice and doing remarkably well to finish a length second at Ayr last time given he lost a shoe and finished lame; had been considered a Cheltenham Festival contender until ruled out because of soft ground.

Disko (Fr)

7 gr g Martaline - Nikos Royale (Nikos)

Noel Meade (Ir)　　　　Gigginstown House Stud

PLACINGS: 1/221/6133131/1-　　　　RPR **168c**

Starts	1st	2nd	3rd	4th	Win & Pl
12	6	2	3	-	£177,433

	11/17	DRoy	2m3¹/₂f Gd2 Ch soft....................................£25,214
	4/17	Punc	3m¹/₂f Nov Gd1 Ch gd-yld..........................£50,427
	2/17	Leop	2m5¹/₂f Nov Gd1 Ch soft.............................£42,863
	10/16	Punc	2m4f Ch yield...£5,879
	11/15	Naas	2m4f Mdn Hdl soft.......................................£6,686
	2/15	Punc	2m NHF 4yo yield..£4,814

Won two Grade 1 novice chases two seasons ago and looked to have improved again when making an impressive winning return at Down Royal last term; missed the rest of the campaign with a small stress fracture but should still have plenty more to offer.

f Facebook.com/racingpost

Divine Spear (Ire)
7 b g Oscar - Testaway (Commanche Run)

Nicky Henderson   Middleham Park Racing LXII

PLACINGS: 121308/13225/112-   RPR **142+c**

Starts	1st	2nd	3rd	4th	Win & Pl
14	5	4	2	-	£45,125

133	12/17	Asct	2m1f Cls3 Nov 122-133 Ch Hcap soft	£9,747
	11/17	Catt	2m3f Cls4 Ch gd-sft	£4,549
123	12/16	Font	2m1½f Cls3 110-126 Hdl Hcap gd-sft	£6,330
	2/16	Ludl	2m Cls5 Mdn Hdl soft	£2,599
	5/15	Towc	2m Cls6 Mdn NHF 4-6yo good	£1,949

Won first two chases last season, including a ten-length stroll in a novice handicap at Ascot; had excuses for defeat at 1-3 in only subsequent race when jockey caught out tactically off slow pace; missed intended run in the novice handicap at the Cheltenham Festival through injury.

Doctor Phoenix (Ire)
10 br g Dr Massini - Lowroad Cross (Anshan)

Gordon Elliott (Ir)   Nick Bradley Racing Club

PLACINGS: 1185/2P244/210112F5-   RPR **166+c**

Starts	1st	2nd	3rd	4th	Win & Pl
24	7	5	2	3	£148,361

	2/18	Naas	2m Gd3 Ch soft	£24,279
146	1/18	Fair	2m1f 132-153 Ch Hcap soft	£52,212
139	11/17	Cork	2m1½f 113-139 Ch Hcap sft-hvy	£13,141
	11/15	Hayd	2m½f Cls2 Ch soft	£12,996
132	11/15	Ling	2m Cls3 115-132 Ch Hcap soft	£6,963
	3/15	Uttx	2m4f Cls4 Nov Hdl soft	£3,899
	2/15	Newc	2m½f Cls4 Mdn Hdl heavy	£3,249

Went from strength to strength after moving to Gordon Elliott last season, winning three times and climbing 19lb in the handicap; threatened a big upset against Un De Sceaux at Fairyhouse until falling two out and may not have fully recovered when disappointing at Punchestown.

Dolos (Fr)
5 b g Kapgarde - Redowa (Trempolino)

Paul Nicholls   Mrs Johnny De La Hey

PLACINGS: 313330212/2013272-   RPR **155c**

Starts	1st	2nd	3rd	4th	Win & Pl
16	3	5	5	-	£94,585

	11/17	Asct	2m3f Cls3 Ch gd-sft	£9,986
	4/17	Chep	2m Cls4 Nov Hdl good	£3,899
	10/16	Chep	2m Cls4 Hdl 3yo good	£3,899

Sent chasing last season and proved himself a smart recruit, finishing a half-length second in good 2m handicaps at Sandown and Ayr; let down by his jumping when only seventh in the Grand Annual (only run in a big field).

Domesday Book (USA)
8 br g Street Cry - Film Script (Unfuwain)

Stuart Edmunds   J Humberstone

PLACINGS: 22162/3130/456831/P-   RPR **145+**

Starts	1st	2nd	3rd	4th	Win & Pl
16	3	3	3	1	£70,346

137	3/17	Chel	3m2f Cls2 133-145 Am Ch Hcap good	£40,233
	12/15	Limk	2m1f Ch heavy	£7,221
	12/14	Navn	2m Mdn Hdl yld-sft	£6,900

Moved from Ireland in early 2017 and won the Kim Muir at Cheltenham on his second run for new yard, relishing stepping up to that trip for the first time (fair sixth in the Troytown on only run over 3m); out for a year and pulled up in the bet365 Gold Cup on only run last term.

Don Poli (Ire)
9 b g Poliglote - Dalamine (Sillery)

Gordon Elliott (Ir)   Gigginstown House Stud

PLACINGS: 111/2111/51132/3P23/   RPR **168c**

Starts	1st	2nd	3rd	4th	Win & Pl
18	8	5	3	-	£447,584

	12/15	Leop	3m Gd1 Ch heavy	£69,767
	12/15	Aint	3m1f Cls1 List Ch soft	£22,780
	3/15	Chel	3m½f Cls1 Gd1 Ch good	£85,425
	12/14	Leop	3m Nov Gd1 Ch sft-hvy	£40,625
	11/14	Gowr	2m4f Ch heavy	£8,625
143	3/14	Chel	2m4½f Cls2 133-146 Cond Hdl Hcap good	£31,280
	2/14	Clon	3m Nov Gd3 Hdl heavy	£17,063
	1/14	Thur	2m6f Mdn Hdl sft-hvy	£6,325

Without a win since the 2015 Lexus Chase but had continued to run well in top Irish staying chases until missing last season, most notably when second in the Lexus again in 2016; enjoys good ground but probably needs softer to slow others down at 3m; may do better over further.

Donna's Diamond (Ire)
9 gr g Cloudings - Inish Bofin (Glacial Storm)

Chris Grant   D & D Armstrong

PLACINGS: 1541/331P44/U4/1102-   RPR **149h**

Starts	1st	2nd	3rd	4th	Win & Pl
23	6	3	2	5	£69,645

	2/18	Hayd	2m7f Cls1 Gd2 Hdl heavy	£23,048
129	1/18	Hayd	2m7f Cls3 119-140 Hdl Hcap heavy	£8,123
130	1/16	Muss	3m2f Cls3 105-130 Hdl Hcap gd-sft	£7,798
124	3/15	Newc	3m Cls3 109-131 Hdl Hcap soft	£5,458
	1/15	Kels	2m6½f Cls4 Nov Hdl 4-7yo soft	£3,249
	2/14	Muss	1m7½f Cls6 NHF 4-6yo soft	£1,949

Better than ever on his return from more than a year out last season, running away with a handicap at Haydock and winning the Grade 2

Rendlesham Hurdle back there; had departed early on his only attempt over fences before his layoff.

Dortmund Park (Fr)

5 b g Great Pretender - Qena (Le Balafre)

Gordon Elliott (Ir)   Gigginstown House Stud

PLACINGS: 1/1611481-   RPR **152+h**

Starts	1st	2nd	3rd	4th	Win & Pl
8	5	-	-	1	£86,555

4/18	Punc	2m4f Nov Gd1 Hdl soft		£52,212
1/18	Thur	2m6½f Nov Hdl heavy		£7,904
1/18	Fair	2m4f Mdn Hdl heavy		£7,087
6/17	Nant	1m4f NHF 4-5yo good		£10,684
4/17	Le L	1m3½f NHF 4yo soft		£5,128

Won three novice hurdles last season, most notably a 2m4f Grade I at Punchestown; helped by main rivals failing to get round and had twice disappointed at Grade I level beforehand but also seemed to benefit from a wind operation in between; likely to go novice chasing.

Double Shuffle (Ire)

8 b g Milan - Fiddlers Bar (Un Desperado)

Tom George   Crossed Fingers Partnership

PLACINGS: /24135/2P512P/22274-   RPR **170c**

Starts	1st	2nd	3rd	4th	Win & Pl
20	4	6	1	2	£160,486

143	12/16	Kemp	3m Cls2 126-143 Ch Hcap good	£25,024
134	12/15	Ludl	2m4f Cls3 Nov 120-134 Ch Hcap soft	£11,372
	3/15	Newb	2m½f Cls4 Nov Hdl gd-sft	£3,422
	2/15	Donc	2m½f Cls4 Nov Hdl 4-7yo good	£3,574

A revelation when a length second to Might Bite in last season's King George at 50-1; excels over that course and distance but yet to back up the form elsewhere after a couple of disappointing runs in the spring.

Dounikos (Fr)

7 b g Smadoun - Baby Sitter (Nikos)

Gordon Elliott (Ir)   Gigginstown House Stud

PLACINGS: 1/P9/211249/114PPP-   RPR **155c**

Starts	1st	2nd	3rd	4th	Win & Pl
14	4	2	-	2	£47,345

12/17	Limk	2m3½f Nov Gd2 Ch heavy	£22,440
11/17	Gowr	2m4f Ch heavy	£8,950
11/16	Thur	2m7f Mdn Hdl good	£4,522
10/16	Dpat	2m2f NHF 4-7yo yld-sft	£4,070

Pulled up in each of his last three runs last season but had already proved himself a smart novice chaser; won his first two races before a close fourth to Monalee in the Flogas; looked likely to improve over further and ran in the Irish National subsequently.

Douvan (Fr)

8 b g Walk In The Park - Star Face (Saint Des Saints)

Willie Mullins (Ir)   Mrs S Ricci

PLACINGS: 111/111111/11117/F2-   RPR **170c**

Starts	1st	2nd	3rd	4th	Win & Pl
18	14	2	-	-	£569,969

2/17	Punc	2m Gd2 Ch soft	£22,692
12/16	Leop	2m1f Gd1 Ch yield	£43,382
12/16	Cork	2m1f Gd2 Ch sft-hvy	£21,691
4/16	Punc	2m Nov Gd1 Ch yield	£49,890
4/16	Aint	2m Cls1 Nov Gd1 Ch gd-sft	£56,270
3/16	Chel	2m Cls1 Gd1 Ch gd-sft	£85,827
1/16	Leop	2m1f Nov Gd1 Ch soft	£39,706
12/15	Leop	2m1f Nov Gd1 Ch heavy	£42,558
11/15	Navn	2m1f Ch soft	£8,558
4/15	Punc	2m Nov Gd1 Hdl gd-yld	£44,186
3/15	Chel	2m1½f Cls1 Nov Gd1 Hdl gd-sft	£68,340
1/15	Punc	2m Nov Gd2 Hdl soft	£20,155
11/14	Gowr	2m Nov Hdl 4yo heavy	£7,475
6/14	Comp	2m1f Hdl 4yo v soft	£8,800

Once looked invincible, winning his first 13 starts for Willie Mullins including two Cheltenham

Festival triumphs, but has been beset by physical problems since; fell when going well in last season's Champion Chase and below his best when second to Un De Sceaux at Punchestown.

Draconien (Fr)

5 br g Linda's Lad - Holding (Useful)

Willie Mullins (Ir)   Clipper Logistics Group

PLACINGS: 4/12U21-   RPR **152+h**

Starts	1st	2nd	3rd	4th	Win & Pl
6	2	2	-	1	£72,622

4/18	Punc	2m¹/₂f Nov Gd1 Hdl yld-sft	£52,212
12/17	Clon	2m3¹/₂f Mdn Hdl sft-hvy	£5,791

Surprise winner of a 2m Grade 1 novice hurdle at Punchestown last season; probably flattered by that win (produced late off an overly strong gallop and favourite Getabird disappointed) but had also been a respectable second to Getabird at Fairyhouse before that.

Drumcliff (Ire)

7 b g Presenting - Dusty Too (Terimon)

Harry Fry   John P McManus

PLACINGS: 138/6225B/0114P-1F   RPR **150+c**

Starts	1st	2nd	3rd	4th	Win & Pl
15	4	2	1	1	£55,685

139	5/18	Uttx	2m4f Cls2 128-153 Ch Hcap good	£24,864
129	1/18	Asct	2m3f Cls3 117-133 Am Ch Hcap soft	£9,608
123	11/17	Winc	1m7¹/₂f Cls3 Nov 116-124 Ch Hcap soft	£9,097
	12/15	Tntn	2m¹/₂f Cls4 NHF 3-5yo gd-sft	£3,422

Won first two novice chases last season and got back on track when winning a good handicap at Uttoxeter in May; well suited by good ground that day according to his trainer but had gained previous chase wins on soft; fell when prominent in the Galway Plate.

Douvan: suffered a disappointing season having previously looked invincible

Duc Des Genievres (Fr)

5 gr g Buck's Boum - Lobelie (Round Sovereign)

Willie Mullins (Ir) | Sullivan Bloodstock

PLACINGS: 132556- | RPR **149+h**

Starts	1st	2nd	3rd	4th	Win & Pl
6	1	1	1	-	£36,486
	5/17	Mlns	2m2f Hdl 4yo v soft		.....£7,385

Moved from France having already won over hurdles last season and was highly tried subsequently; twice placed at Grade 1 level and beaten only nine lengths when fifth in the Ballymore at Cheltenham but form tailed off in two runs after that.

Edwulf

9 b g Kayf Tara - Valentines Lady (Zaffaran)

Joseph O'Brien (Ir) | John P McManus

PLACINGS: 2/7F1F/3U21F1P/P187- | RPR **169+c**

Starts	1st	2nd	3rd	4th	Win & Pl
15	4	1	1	-	£143,057
	2/18	Leop	3m Gd1 Ch soft		£100,000
145	2/17	Naas	2m4f Nov 124-145 Ch Hcap heavy		£25,214
	1/17	Punc	2m4f Ch sft-hvy		£7,359
	1/16	Naas	2m3f Mdn Hdl sft-hvy		£7,610

Completed a miracle recovery when winning the Irish Gold Cup last season having almost lost his life when collapsing at the 2017 Cheltenham Festival; probably got lucky in a moderate Grade 1 but still very capable on soft ground when stamina is at a premium.

El Bandit (Ire)

7 b/br g Milan - Bonnie Parker (Un Desperado)

Paul Nicholls | Colm Donlon, Barry Fulton & Chris Giles

PLACINGS: 6/831/1111710/1- | RPR **143c**

Starts	1st	2nd	3rd	4th	Win & Pl
12	7	-	1	-	£69,173
	5/17	Wwck	3m1½f Cls2 Nov Ch good		£13,436
139	2/17	Muss	3m2f Cls2 120-146 Hdl Hcap good		£14,296
	10/16	Chel	2m5f Cls2 Nov Hdl good		£10,635
	10/16	Chep	2m3½f Cls1 Nov Gd2 Hdl good		£19,933
	6/16	Font	2m5½f Cls4 Nov Hdl good		£3,899
112	5/16	Wwck	2m5f Cls4 95-120 Hdl Hcap gd-sft		£3,249
	4/16	Wwck	2m5f Cls4 Mdn Hdl good		£3,249

Won five times over hurdles two seasons ago, including the Persian War at Chepstow, and looked an even better chaser when hacking up on his debut over fences in May 2017; missed the rest of last season but back in training this summer.

Elegant Escape (Ire)

6 b g Dubai Destination - Graineuaile (Orchestra)

Colin Tizzard | J P Romans

PLACINGS: 2/114577/2212133- | RPR **156c**

Starts	1st	2nd	3rd	4th	Win & Pl
13	4	3	2	1	£108,525
	2/18	Extr	3m Cls2 Ch heavy		£12,512
	12/17	Newb	2m7½f Cls1 Nov Gd2 Ch gd-sft		£23,048
	11/16	Asct	2m5½f Cls2 Nov Hdl gd-sft		£12,512
	10/16	Chep	2m3½f Cls4 Mdn Hdl gd-sft		£3,899

Very useful staying novice chaser last season, finishing placed in three Grade 1 contests including when best of the British runners in the RSA Chase at Cheltenham; versatile regarding ground (won on good to soft and heavy) and should stay longer trips.

Empire Of Dirt (Ire)

11 b g Westerner - Rose Of Inchiquin (Roselier)

Gordon Elliott (Ir) | Gigginstown House Stud

PLACINGS: /4F32F1F/F2P11/124P/ | RPR **167c**

Starts	1st	2nd	3rd	4th	Win & Pl
25	6	5	1	3	£240,220
148	11/16	Navn	3m 125-150 Ch Hcap yld-sft		£43,382
142	3/16	Chel	2m5f Cls1 Gd3 135-157 Ch Hcap good		£56,950
133	1/16	Leop	2m5f 125-153 Ch Hcap soft		£44,118
125	2/15	Naas	2m4f Nov 119-134 Ch Hcap sft-hvy		£25,194
	3/14	Naas	2m Nov List Hdl yld-sft		£13,542
	10/13	Punc	2m Mdn Hdl yld-sft		£5,610

Late developer who flourished in 2016 and 2017, winning the Troytown two seasons ago to add to his 2016 Cheltenham Festival success and subsequently excelling at Grade 1 level when second to Sizing John in the Irish Gold Cup; missed last season through injury.

Espoir D'Allen (Fr)

4 b g Voix Du Nord - Quadanse (Maille Pistol)

Gavin Cromwell (Ir) | John P McManus

PLACINGS: 1/11114- | RPR **140+h**

Starts	1st	2nd	3rd	4th	Win & Pl
6	5	-	-	1	£64,074
	12/17	Leop	2m Gd2 Hdl 3yo yield		£22,692
	12/17	Fair	2m Gd3 Hdl 3yo soft		£17,083
	11/17	DRoy	2m Hdl 3yo soft		£7,897
	10/17	Punc	2m Hdl 3yo yld-sft		£8,161
	4/17	Lign	1m4f NHF 3yo good		£4,701

Bought from France after winning a bumper and added first four races over hurdles last season, taking the scalp of subsequent Triumph Hurdle winner Farclas; beaten at odds-on in a Grade 1

Facebook.com/racingpost

at Leopardstown when racing too keenly and missed the rest of the season.

Euxton Lane (Ire)

6 b g Getaway - Local Hall (Saddlers' Hall)

Oliver Sherwood — Trevor Hemmings

PLACINGS: 3572117- — RPR **141h**

Starts	1st	2nd	3rd	4th	Win & Pl
7	2	1	1	-	£11,536
	3/18	Newb	2m4½f Cls3 Nov Hdl soft		£6,238
	3/18	Font	2m1½f Cls5 Mdn Hdl soft		£3,119

Much improved in the spring having had problems in the first half of last season, winning novice hurdles at Fontwell and Newbury on soft ground; fair seventh at Aintree when stepped up to Grade 1 level; likely to go novice chasing.

Fabulous Saga (Fr)

6 b g Saint Des Saints - Fabalina (Dear Doctor)

Willie Mullins (Ir) — Sullivan Bloodstock

PLACINGS: 13/12211231177- — RPR **147+h**

Starts	1st	2nd	3rd	4th	Win & Pl
12	5	3	2	-	£77,111
	12/17	Limk	3m Nov Gd2 Hdl heavy		£22,440
	12/17	Cork	3m Nov Gd3 Hdl heavy		£18,397
	9/17	List	2m4f Nov Hdl heavy		£11,827
	8/17	Baln	2m5½f Mdn Hdl yield		£5,791
	5/17	Tipp	2m2f NHF 4-7yo good		£5,528

Exciting front-running novice hurdler last season; won four times over hurdles, most notably in a Grade 2 at Limerick from subsequent Cheltenham winner Delta Work; beaten twice subsequently but lost second only in the final 100 yards of the Albert Bartlett after setting a strong gallop.

Fagan

8 gr g Fair Mix - Northwood May (Teenoso)

Alex Hales — R A Bartlett

PLACINGS: 34111/111224/P/122P- — RPR **147c**

Starts	1st	2nd	3rd	4th	Win & Pl
12	4	4	1	1	£51,107
	7/17	Prth	3m Cls4 Nov Ch good		£5,004
	12/15	Muss	1m7½f Cls4 Nov Hdl 4-6yo soft		£3,899
	10/15	Ayr	2m Cls6 NHF 4-6yo good		£1,711
	9/15	Prth	2m Cls6 NHF 4-6yo gd-sft		£2,053

Second to Unowhatimeanharry in the 2016 Albert Bartlett at Cheltenham but very lightly raced since then; got off the mark over fences last summer and twice ran well in defeat after that but was pulled up when favourite for the Scottish National; has since left Gordon Elliott.

Edwulf: marvellous staying chaser recovered from injury last season for an emotional Irish Gold Cup triumph

Fair Mountain (Ger)
6 b g Tiger Hill - Fair Breeze (Silvano)

Dan Skelton					Mark Adams
PLACINGS: 2112					RPR **139h**

Starts	1st	2nd	3rd	4th	Win & Pl
4	2	2	-	-	£18,326

7/18	Uttx	2m Cls4 Nov Hdl good	£4,159
6/18	Bang	2m¹/₂f Cls4 Mdn Hdl good	£4,094

Smart Flat performer in Germany (Listed winner and placed five times at a higher level, twice in Group I races); began hurdling in May and made a rapid impression, winning twice and finishing second when favourite for the Summer Hurdle; sets a good standard among novices.

Farclas (Fr)
4 gr g Jukebox Jury - Floriana (Seattle Dancer)

Gordon Elliott (Ir)					Gigginstown House Stud
PLACINGS: 2215-					RPR **149+h**

Starts	1st	2nd	3rd	4th	Win & Pl
4	1	2	-	-	£97,079

3/18	Chel	2m1f Cls1 Gd1 Hdl 4yo soft	£71,188

Broke his duck on the biggest stage of all last season when winning the Triumph Hurdle, appearing to relish a stiffer test of stamina as he reversed previous form with runner-up Mr Adjudicator; below his best at Punchestown next time; bred to appreciate quicker ground.

Faugheen: celebrations after his success over 3m at the Punchestown festival

Faugheen (Ire)
10 b g Germany - Miss Pickering (Accordion)

Willie Mullins (Ir)					Mrs S Ricci
PLACINGS: 111/1111/1211/1P261-					RPR **171h**

Starts	1st	2nd	3rd	4th	Win & Pl
18	14	2	-	-	£913,593

4/18	Punc	3m Gd1 Hdl yld-sft	£143,584
11/17	Punc	2m Gd1 Hdl sft-hvy	£42,863
1/16	Leop	2m Gd1 Hdl soft	£48,529
12/15	Kemp	2m Cls1 Gd1 Hdl gd-sft	£56,950
5/15	Punc	2m Gd1 Hdl gd-yld	£93,023
3/15	Chel	2m¹/₂f Cls1 Gd1 Hdl gd-sft	£227,800
12/14	Kemp	2m Cls1 Gd1 Hdl gd-sft	£57,218
11/14	Asct	2m3¹/₂f Cls1 Hdl soft	£50,643
4/14	Punc	2m Nov Gd1 Hdl gd-yld	£46,500
3/14	Chel	2m5f Cls1 Nov Gd1 Hdl good	£68,340
12/13	Limk	3m Nov Gd3 Hdl heavy	£15,061
12/13	Navn	2m4f Nov Hdl gd-yld	£7,293
11/13	Punc	2m6f Mdn Hdl yield	£7,293
5/13	Punc	2m NHF 5yo yield	£4,488

Brilliant 2015 Champion Hurdle winner who returned from long-term injury by winning the Morgiana Hurdle last season but subsequently looked short of speed over 2m; suggested he could yet have a future as a stayer, though, when winning easily at Punchestown over 3m.

Felix Desjy (Fr)
5 ch g Maresca Sorrento - Lamadoun (Smadoun)

Gordon Elliott (Ir)					Gigginstown House Stud
PLACINGS: 1/1165-					RPR **135b**

Starts	1st	2nd	3rd	4th	Win & Pl
4	2	-	-	-	£15,937

11/17	DRoy	2m NHF 4-7yo soft	£7,897
10/17	Punc	2m NHF 4-7yo soft	£5,265

Impressive winner of a point-to-point (by 15 lengths) and first two bumpers last season; did well to finish sixth in the Champion Bumper at Cheltenham despite racing too keenly in a first-time hood but below that level when only fifth at Punchestown.

Facebook.com/racingpost

Moorcroft
Racehorse Welfare Centre

PROVIDING THE
VERY BEST
OF CARE
FOR OUR WONDERFUL
HORSES AWAITING A NEW
HOME AND A NEW LIFE

This centre in the south of England was set up to ensure that retired racehorses whatever age, can be re-trained to find another career in life. Much care and attention is given to each individual horse and when fully retrained new homes are found. The centre retains ownership for life and visits these horses every year to ensure that all is well.

This charity depends on generous donations from horse lovers. Many horses need a time for rehabilitation due to injury etc and start to enjoy an easier life after their racing careers. Visits by appointment are welcomed. Please ring Mary Frances, Manager, on 07929 666408 for more information or to arrange a visit.

Huntingrove Stud, Slinfold, West Sussex. RH13 0RB
Tel: 07929 666408 | Email: moorcroftracehorse@gmail.com | www.moorcroftracehorse.org.uk

First Flow (Ire)

6 b g Primary - Clonroche Wells (Pierre)

Kim Bailey   A N Solomons

PLACINGS: 4/4111P-   RPR **146+**h

Starts	1st	2nd	3rd	4th	Win & Pl
6	3	-	-	2	£27,094

1/18	Hayd	1m7¹/₂f Cls1 Nov Gd2 Hdl heavy	£17,085
12/17	Newb	2m¹/₂f Cls4 Hdl heavy	£4,549
11/17	Ling	2m Cls4 Nov Hdl soft	£5,198

Won first three novice hurdles last season, including a ten-length thrashing of Scottish Champion Hurdle winner Midnight Shadow, but was pulled up in the Supreme Novices'; may not appreciate good ground.

Flying Angel (Ire)

7 gr g Arcadio - Gypsy Kelly (Roselier)

Nigel Twiston-Davies   R J Rexton

PLACINGS: 53123/1FP161P/54380-   RPR **158**c

Starts	1st	2nd	3rd	4th	Win & Pl
20	5	2	4	1	£179,906

	4/17	Aint	2m4f Cls1 Nov Gd1 Ch good	£56,130
	2/17	Wwck	2m Cls1 Nov Gd2 Ch heavy	£22,780
	9/16	Prth	2m4f Cls3 Nov Ch soft	£7,611
133	3/16	Sand	2m Cls1 Gd3 123-149 Hdl Hcap soft	£39,865
	10/15	Worc	2m4f Cls4 Nov Hdl good	£3,249

Won a Grade 1 novice chase at Aintree two seasons ago; well below that level last season but dropped 12lb in the handicap during just five runs; was given wind surgery in February and has run only once subsequently when tenth in the Topham.

Folsom Blue (left): big improver won last season's Grand National Trial at Punchestown

Facebook.com/racingpost

Folsom Blue (Ire)

1 1 b g Old Vic - Spirit Leader (Supreme Leader)

Gordon Elliott (Ir)   Core Partnership

PLACINGS: /4PP00871208/144140-   **RRPR 148+c**

Starts	1st	2nd	3rd	4th	Win & Pl
45	7	6	5	10	£216,577

133	2/18	Punc	3m4¹/₂f 118-146 Ch Hcap heavy	£52,212
123	11/17	Clon	3m 104-132 Hdl Hcap sft-hvy	£13,141
127	3/17	Navn	3m 113-139 Ch Hcap heavy	£11,038
127	2/14	Punc	3m4f 122-150 Ch Hcap heavy	£17,333
	2/12	Clon	2m6f Nov List Hdl heavy	£14,354
	1/12	Thur	2m6f Nov Hdl soft	£8,050
	12/11	Limk	2m Mdn Hdl 4yo heavy	£5,948

Improved massively in his first campaign for Gordon Elliott last season; won the Grand National Trial at Punchestown and was unlucky not to follow up in the Irish National (brought to a standstill at the last and beaten just a length).

Footpad (Fr)

6 b g Creachadoir - Willamina (Sadler's Wells)

Willie Mullins (Ir)   Simon Munir & Isaac Souede

PLACINGS: 3113F/1124243/11111-   **RPR 172+c**

Starts	1st	2nd	3rd	4th	Win & Pl
20	10	3	3	2	£583,358

4/18	Punc	2m Nov Gd1 Ch yld-sft	£60,044
3/18	Chel	2m Cls1 Nov Gd1 Ch heavy	£99,663
2/18	Leop	2m1f Nov Gd1 Ch soft	£52,212
12/17	Leop	2m1f Nov Gd1 Ch yield	£45,385
11/17	Navn	2m1f Ch sft-hvy	£8,950
6/16	Autl	2m3¹/₂f Gd1 Hdl 4yo soft	£89,338
5/16	Autl	2m3¹/₂f Gd3 Hdl 4yo v soft	£44,669
2/16	Leop	2m Gd1 Hdl 4yo sft-hvy	£36,875
1/16	Gowr	2m Hdl 4yo heavy	£10,037
11/15	Gowr	2m Mdn Hdl 3yo soft	£6,419

Smart hurdler who has already proved even better over fences, going unbeaten in five races last season; obliterated his rivals from the front most often but proved tactical versatility under a more patient ride when a brilliant winner of the Racing Post Arkle at Cheltenham.

Forest Bihan (Fr)
7 ch g Forestier - Katell Bihan (Funny Baby)

Brian Ellison   Phil & Julie Martin

PLACINGS: 42P36/U121152/1P346-   RPR **160+c**

Starts	1st	2nd	3rd	4th	Win & Pl
23	5	4	4	2	£130,324

	3/18	Newc	2m1/2f Cls3 NHF stand.................................£6,498
154	10/17	Kels	2m1f Cls2 128-154 Ch Hcap good.................£18,582
	1/17	Donc	2m1/2f Cls1 Nov Gd2 Ch good....................£20,554
	1/17	Newc	2m1/2f Cls4 Nov Ch soft..............................£4,549
	11/16	Towc	2m Cls3 Nov Ch good..................................£7,220
	11/14	Engh	2m1/2f Hdl 3yo heavy................................£20,000

Slightly disappointing last season after a winning return at Kelso; had shown smart form as a novice prior to that but only subsequent win came at 3-10 in a jumpers' bumper; dropped 2lb below last winning mark following latest well-beaten effort at Ayr.

Forge Meadow (Ire)
6 b m Beneficial - Ballys Baby (Bob Back)

Jessica Harrington (Ir)   Joseph M Doyle

PLACINGS: 1/2152184/6551221PP-   RPR **154h**

Starts	1st	2nd	3rd	4th	Win & Pl
17	4	4	-	1	£141,495

	2/18	Gowr	2m Gd3 Hdl heavy.....................................£23,496
	11/17	Punc	2m2f List Hdl sft-hvy..................................£15,769
	2/17	Naas	2m Nov Gd2 Hdl sft-hvy.............................£23,449
	11/16	Wxfd	2m Mdn Hdl sft-hvy....................................£5,879
	3/16	Fair	2m NHF 4-5yo yield....................................£43,382

Twice disappointed last spring but had looked to be progressing into a high-class mare prior to that; gained a notable win over subsequent Grade 1 winner Identity Thief in the Red Mills Trial Hurdle having pushed the ill-fated Sandsend to a neck in another Grade 3 at Naas.

Forza Milan (Ire)
6 b g Milan - Nonnetia (Trempolino)

Jonjo O'Neill   Deep Sea Partnership

PLACINGS: 6221/622P-   RPR **141+h**

Starts	1st	2nd	3rd	4th	Win & Pl
8	1	4	-	-	£16,110

	2/17	Chep	2m3½f Cls4 Mdn Hdl soft...........................£3,899

Lightly raced hurdler who progressed well despite not winning last season, finishing second in good staying handicaps at Aintree and Newbury; subsequently laid out for the Pertemps Final at Cheltenham but pulled up after going lame; back in training this summer.

....

'He's always dangerous in good handicaps and starts the season just 4lb above his last winning mark'

Fox Norton (Fr)
8 b g Lando - Natt Musik (Kendor)

Colin Tizzard   Ann & Alan Potts Limited

PLACINGS: 11233331/112211/12P-   RPR **172+c**

Starts	1st	2nd	3rd	4th	Win & Pl
25	11	5	5	1	£593,520

	11/17	Chel	2m Cls1 Gd2 Ch soft..................................£42,713
	4/17	Punc	2m Gd1 Ch gd-yld.....................................£126,068
	4/17	Aint	2m4f Cls1 Gd1 Ch good............................£112,310
	11/16	Chel	2m Cls1 Gd2 Ch soft..................................£42,713
146	10/16	Chel	2m Cls2 131-157 Ch Hcap good..................£31,280
	4/16	Chel	2m1/2f Cls2 Nov Ch good.............................£12,512
	10/15	MRas	2m1f Cls3 Nov Ch good................................£7,798
	5/15	Hntg	2m1/2f Cls4 Nov Ch good..............................£3,769
140	2/15	Tntn	2m Cls2 129-145 Hdl Hcap soft...................£11,078
	12/13	Donc	2m1/2f Cls1 Gd2 Hdl 3yo good.....................£15,876
	4/13	Fntb	2m Hdl 3yo soft..£8,585

Dual Grade 1 winner in the spring of 2017 but missed that period last season after a leg injury; had earlier won a second successive Shloer Chase at Cheltenham but just lost out to Politologue in the Tingle Creek; looked a non-stayer over 3m in the King George.

Foxtail Hill (Ire)
9 b g Dr Massini - Flynn's Girl (Mandalus)

Nigel Twiston-Davies   Options O Syndicate

PLACINGS: 4P/F13511F92/186800-   RPR **150c**

Starts	1st	2nd	3rd	4th	Win & Pl
25	5	2	2	1	£94,377

140	10/17	Chel	2m Cls2 132-158 Ch Hcap good...................£31,280
133	1/17	Chel	2m5f Cls1 Gd3 131-156 Ch Hcap soft...........£34,170
124	1/17	Kemp	2m4½f Cls2 Ch 115-136 Ch Hcap gd-sft...........£6,279
115	10/16	Worc	2m1/2f Cls4 101-118 Ch Hcap good.................£5,064
	10/14	Strf	2m1/2f Cls5 Mdn Hdl good............................£2,599

Has won good handicap chases at Cheltenham in each of the last two seasons from 2m to 2m5f, most recently beating subsequent Grand Annual winner Le Prezien; lost his way after that but dropped back below his last winning mark.

Frodon (Fr)
6 b g Nickname - Miss Country (Country Reel)

Paul Nicholls   P J Vogt

PLACINGS: /11101F115/32321350-   RPR **173+c**

Starts	1st	2nd	3rd	4th	Win & Pl
26	9	2	5	1	£296,116

154	1/18	Chel	2m5f Cls1 Gd3 131-154 Ch Hcap heavy..........£42,713
	2/17	Kemp	2m4½f Cls1 Nov Gd2 Ch good.....................£18,793
	2/17	Muss	2m4f Cls3 Nov Ch good.................................£7,798
149	12/16	Chel	2m5f Cls1 Gd3 132-158 Ch Hcap soft............£56,950
	11/16	Winc	2m4f Cls1 Nov Gd2 Ch good........................£28,486
	9/16	Font	2m5f Cls4 Nov Ch good................................£5,198
	9/16	NAbb	2m1/2f Cls3 Nov Ch good..............................£7,187
	2/16	Hayd	1m7½f Cls2 Hdl 4yo heavy.............................£9,747
	4/15	Autl	1m7f Hdl 3yo heavy...................................£20,465

Tends to come up short in top company but always dangerous in good handicaps, with runaway victory at Cheltenham in January adding to his 2016 Caspian Caviar Gold Cup win; has run in only one other handicap in that time and starts the season just 4lb above last winning mark.

facebook.com/racingpost

Garde La Victoire (Fr)
9 b g Kapgarde - Next Victory (Akarad)

Philip Hobbs   Mrs Diana L Whateley

PLACINGS: 541/111FF/12318/240-   RPR **142c**

Starts	1st	2nd	3rd	4th	Win & Pl
26	12	3	2	3	£217,642

154	1/17	Sand	1m7¹/₂f Cls2 134-154 Ch Hcap soft....................	£15,640
148	10/16	Ffos	2m Cls2 135-148 Hdl Hcap gd-sft...................	£18,768
	1/16	Ludl	2m Cls3 Nov Ch heavy	£6,657
	11/15	Chel	2m Cls1 Nov Gd2 Ch gd-sft	£18,224
	10/15	Uttx	2m Cls4 Ch soft	£3,833
	1/15	Sand	2m Cls1 List Hdl soft	£14,238
144	11/14	Chel	2m¹/₂f Cls1 Gd3 121-147 Hdl Hcap soft.........	£56,950
	4/14	Chel	2m4¹/₂f Cls2 Nov Hdl good	£10,010
	4/14	Tntn	2m3f Cls4 Nov Hdl good	£4,106
	11/13	Wwck	2m Cls4 Nov Hdl gd-sft............................	£3,899
	10/13	Aint	2m¹/₂f Cls4 Mdn Hdl gd-sft......................	£4,549
	10/12	Extr	1m5f Cls6 NHF 3yo gd-sft..........................	£1,365

High-class 2m chaser/hurdler at his peak who won the Welsh Champion Hurdle and reverted to fences to strike off 154 at Sandown two seasons ago; disappointing last term but was dropped 7lb by the handicapper.

General Principle (Ire)
9 b g Gold Well - How Provincial (Be My Native)

Gordon Elliott (Ir)   Gigginstown House Stud

PLACINGS: 26/322F26115/470461-   RPR **146+c**

Starts	1st	2nd	3rd	4th	Win & Pl
20	5	4	1	2	£302,002

139	4/18	Fair	3m5f 135-163 Ch Hcap heavy	£238,938
	3/17	Limk	3m Nov Gd3 Ch soft..................................	£21,432
	3/17	Gowr	2m4f Ch heavy	£7,897
	2/16	Navn	2m Mdn Hdl sft-hvy.................................	£5,426
	2/15	Punc	2m NHF 5-7yo soft	£4,814

Fortuitous winner of last season's Irish Grand National after final-fence carnage but still took form to a new level stepping up beyond 3m for only the second time (fifth in the race as a novice in 2017); should continue to run well in long-distance handicap chases.

Getabird (Ire)
6 b g Getaway - Fern Bird (Revoque)

Willie Mullins (Ir)   Mrs S Ricci

PLACINGS: 01/11/11017P-   RPR **153+h**

Starts	1st	2nd	3rd	4th	Win & Pl
8	5	-	-	-	£67,088

	4/18	Fair	2m Nov Gd2 Hdl heavy...........................	£26,106
	1/18	Punc	2m Nov Gd2 Hdl sft-hvy..........................	£23,235
	12/17	Punc	2m4f Mdn Hdl heavy...............................	£6,844
	1/17	Gowr	2m NHF 5-7yo heavy................................	£6,833
	12/16	Fair	2m NHF 4yo gd-yld.................................	£4,070

Finished last season with a patchy record having

gone to Cheltenham unbeaten in bumpers and over hurdles; raced too keenly that day but won brilliantly at Fairyhouse next time and had excuses for two defeats at Punchestown (struck into in first race and then badly hampered).

Getaway John (Ire)
5 ch g Getaway - Present Your Own (Presenting)

Gordon Elliott (Ir)   John F Doyle

PLACINGS: 3/2110-   RPR **136+b**

Starts	1st	2nd	3rd	4th	Win & Pl
5	2	1	1	-	£18,822

	4/18	Fair	2m NHF 4-7yo heavy...............................	£10,903
	2/18	Punc	2m NHF 5-7yo heavy...............................	£5,451

Generally progressive in bumpers last season, winning at Fairyhouse and Punchestown after just being beaten by subsequent Grade 1 winner Tornado Flyer; well beaten behind that horse when stepped up to the top level (quickest ground ever encountered after wins came on heavy).

Gino Trail (Ire)
11 br g Perugino - Borough Trail (Woodborough)

Kerry Lee   Mrs Jan Smith

PLACINGS: 3P/P1122216/3112123-   RPR **157c**

Starts	1st	2nd	3rd	4th	Win & Pl
19	7	6	3	-	£131,247

148	2/18	Sand	1m7¹/₂f Cls2 126-152 Ch Hcap soft.............	£18,768
145	12/17	Chel	2m¹/₂f Cls2 133-159 Ch Hcap soft..............	£18,768
140	11/17	Weth	1m7f Cls3 114-140 Ch Hcap soft................	£6,498
	3/17	Ludl	2m Cls3 Nov Ch soft.................................	£8,546
134	12/16	Hayd	2m1¹/₂f Cls3 122-140 Ch Hcap soft............	£7,798
129	11/16	Ludl	2m Cls3 Nov 123-129 Ch Hcap good...........	£6,975
	1/15	Towc	2m Cls4 Nov Hdl soft................................	£3,249

Evergreen 2m chaser who has been remarkably consistent in good handicaps since moving to Kerry Lee in 2016, winning six times and finishing second or third in seven of his other eight races since his yard debut; prefers soft or heavy ground.

Give Me A Copper (Ire)
8 ch g Presenting - Copper Supreme (Supreme Leader)

Paul Nicholls   Done, Ferguson, Kyle, Mason & Wood

PLACINGS: 11/161/U1-   RPR **144+c**

Starts	1st	2nd	3rd	4th	Win & Pl
6	4	-	-	-	£22,577

	11/17	Kemp	3m Cls3 Nov Ch good...............................	£8,133
	4/17	Ayr	2m4¹/₂f Cls3 Nov Hdl gd-sft......................	£6,498
	12/16	Extr	2m7f Cls4 Mdn Hdl soft............................	£3,249
	3/16	Cork	2m3f NHF 5-7yo heavy..............................	£4,296

Beaten only once in four completed runs since

moving from France, though not stretched to make all in a two-runner race when off the mark over fences last season; RSA Chase mentioned by his trainer after that win but missed the rest of the season.

Glenloe (Ire)

7 br g Kayf Tara - Mandys Native (Be My Native)

Gordon Elliott (Ir)					John P McManus
PLACINGS: 7/6515/22325-					RPR **146+h**

Starts	1st	2nd	3rd	4th	Win & Pl
10	1	3	1	-	£46,839

12/16 Navn 2m7f Mdn Hdl sft-hvy..........................£5,653

Progressive staying hurdler last season and very nearly landed a monster gamble in the Pertemps Final at Cheltenham when second to Delta Work; unlucky to bump into one that day but keeps climbing the handicap without winning, including after latest fifth at Punchestown.

Global Citizen (Ire)
6 b g Alkaadhem - Lady Willmurt (Mandalus)

Ben Pauling — The Megsons

PLACINGS: 1/152116- — RPR **145+h**

Starts	1st	2nd	3rd	4th	Win & Pl
6	3	1	-	-	£25,327

2/18	Kemp	2m Cls1 Nov Gd2 Hdl good	£17,085
2/18	Sthl	1m7½f Cls4 Nov Hdl soft	£4,094
10/17	Worc	2m Cls6 NHF 4-6yo gd-fm	£1,689

Bought for £275,000 after winning an Irish point-to-point and won two novice hurdles last season, including a runaway victory in the Dovecote at Kempton; slightly worrying that the form took such a hit at Aintree, including his own tame sixth in the 2m Grade 1 at the meeting.

Go Conquer (Ire)
9 b g Arcadio - Ballinamona Wish (Kotashaan)

Jonjo O'Neill — Paul & Clare Rooney

PLACINGS: 23/461/2F2250/11U58- — RPR **158+c**

Starts	1st	2nd	3rd	4th	Win & Pl
19	5	4	1	1	£109,339

142	11/17	Asct	3m Cls1 Gd3 128-150 Ch Hcap good	£56,950
135	10/17	Font	2m5½f Cls2 117-143 Ch Hcap good	£11,711
122	4/16	Winc	2m4f Cls3 118-129 Ch Hcap gd-sft	£6,498
	12/14	Kels	2m Cls4 Nov Hdl soft	£3,249
	4/14	Carl	2m1f Cls6 NHF 4-6yo gd-sft	£1,560

Bold front-running chaser who showed career-best form early last season, winning handicap chases at Fontwell and Ascot, but found life a lot harder after going up 16lb; best on good ground and missed Cheltenham and Aintree due to unsuitable conditions.

Go Conquer: showed fine form early last season, winning handicap chases at Fontwell and Ascot

God's Own (Ire)
10 b g Oscar - Dantes Term (Phardante)

Tom George · Crossed Fingers Partnership

PLACINGS: F/3241/1233553/6333- · RPR **166c**

Starts	1st	2nd	3rd	4th	Win & Pl
33	7	7	10	2	£547,253

	4/16	Punc	2m Gd1 Ch gd-yld £86,765
	4/16	Aint	2m4f Cls1 Gd1 Ch gd-sft £112,788
155	11/14	Extr	2m1¹/₂f Cls1 Gd2 152-172 Ch Hcap gd-sft......... £35,594
	5/14	Punc	2m Nov Gd1 Ch yield.. £56,833
129	11/13	Kemp	2m5f Cls2 129-155 Hdl Hcap gd-sft................... £11,574
	2/13	Muss	2m3¹/₂f Cls4 Nov Hdl good................................. £3,899
	11/12	Donc	2m¹/₂f Cls4 Nov Hdl good................................... £3,899

Without a win since a Grade 1 double at Aintree and Punchestown in 2016 but has continued to run well in top 2m-2m5f chases, including when third in last season's Champion Chase (fourth and fifth in previous two runnings); prefers good ground.

Gold Present (Ire)
8 br g Presenting - Ouro Preto (Definite Article)

Nicky Henderson · Mr & Mrs J D Cotton

PLACINGS: 2211/P60/1522F/11PP- · RPR **159+c**

Starts	1st	2nd	3rd	4th	Win & Pl
16	5	4	-	-	£126,491

147	12/17	Asct	3m Cls1 List 130-156 Ch Hcap gd-sft................. £56,950
142	12/17	Newb	2m6¹/₂f Cls2 124-144 Ch Hcap gd-sft................. £25,024
130	11/16	Donc	2m3f Cls3 Nov 120-134 Ch Hcap gd-sft.............. £12,512
	4/15	MRas	2m2¹/₂f Cls4 Nov Hdl good................................. £3,899
	3/15	Strf	2m2¹/₂f Cls4 Mdn Hdl gd-sft............................... £3,249

Won good handicaps at Newbury and Ascot last season; aimed at the Grand National (had been going well when falling at the Canal Turn in 2017 Topham) but withdrawn due to soft ground after flopping in similar conditions at Cheltenham and pulled up again in the Scottish National.

Got Away (Fr)
5 b m American Post - Hideaway Girl (Fasliyev)

Oliver Sherwood · B McDonald & B Mellon

PLACINGS: 3212F1253/4147F1PF- · RPR **143+c**

Starts	1st	2nd	3rd	4th	Win & Pl
17	4	3	2	2	£134,252

	1/18	Leic	2m6¹/₂f Cls1 List Ch soft............................... £17,085
	6/17	Autl	2m2¹/₂f Ch 4yo v soft.................................. £21,333
	11/16	Autl	2m1¹/₂f Hdl 3yo heavy................................. £19,412
	9/16	Vich	2m1¹/₂f Hdl 3yo heavy.................................. £7,096

Hurdle and chase winner in France (placed at Listed level) who put a fall on her British debut behind her when winning a Listed mares' chase at Leicester; pulled up next time but running much better (still in contention) when falling four out at Punchestown.

. . . .

'He's won all five starts over fences and more valuable pots are likely to come his way'

Great Field (Fr)
7 b g Great Pretender - Eaton Lass (Definite Article)

Willie Mullins (Ir) · John P McManus

PLACINGS: 2/11/1P/1111/1- · RPR **170+c**

Starts	1st	2nd	3rd	4th	Win & Pl
10	8	1	-	-	£145,287

	3/18	Navn	2m Gd2 Ch heavy... £23,496
	4/17	Punc	2m Nov Gd1 Ch gd yld.................................. £57,991
	3/17	Thur	2m2f Nov List Ch yld-sft............................... £15,769
	3/17	Leop	2m1f Nov Ch sft-hvy.................................... £11,038
	1/17	Gowr	2m Ch soft... £7,096
	2/16	Leop	2m2f Hdl soft... £9,496
	11/14	Pari	2m1f Hdl 3yo gd-sft...................................... £8,400
	9/14	Pari	2m1f Hdl 3yo gd-sft...................................... £8,000

Exciting front-running chaser who has won all five starts over fences; missed nearly all of last season but impressed again when beating Doctor Phoenix on his only run at Navan in March; coped well with heavy ground on that occasion having produced his best run as a novice on good to yielding; more valuable pots are likely to come his way.

Guitar Pete (Ire)
8 gr g Dark Angel - Innishmore (Lear Fan)

Nicky Richards · Mrs P Sloan

PLACINGS: P/090652/0222191U68- · RPR **143+c**

Starts	1st	2nd	3rd	4th	Win & Pl
35	8	8	4	-	£282,918

134	12/17	Chel	2m5f Cls1 Gd3 134-155 Ch Hcap soft............... £68,340
127	11/17	Weth	2m3¹/₂f Cls1 List 127-152 Ch Hcap gd-sft.......... £15,661
	8/15	Kbgn	2m4f Ch yield... £5,884
	4/14	Aint	2m1f Cls1 Gd1 Hdl 4yo good......................... £56,270
	2/14	Leop	2m Gd1 Hdl 4yo sft-hvy............................... £40,667
	12/13	Leop	2m Gd2 Hdl 3yo soft.................................... £21,138
	11/13	DRoy	2m Hdl 3yo yld-sft... £7,854
	9/13	List	2m Hdl 3yo good... £8,415

Nicely progressive in the first half of last season following move from Sandra Hughes in Ireland in April 2017; landed the Caspian Caviar Gold Cup at Cheltenham, albeit in fortuitous circumstances as Starchitect sadly broke down; finished strongly when sixth in the Plate in March; looks fairly well treated on mark of 137.

Gumball (Fr)
4 gr g No Risk At All - Good Time Girl (Slickly)

Philip Hobbs · Terry Warner

PLACINGS: 3/1122P21- · RPR **139h**

Starts	1st	2nd	3rd	4th	Win & Pl
8	3	3	1	-	£48,755

	4/18	Ludl	2m Cls4 Nov Hdl good.................................... £4,874
	10/17	Chep	2m Cls4 Hdl 3yo good.................................... £5,198
	10/17	Strf	2m¹/₂f Cls4 Hdl 3yo good................................ £3,899

Had become disappointing after winning twice early last season but bounced back with a fine second behind We Have A Dream at Aintree and won again at Ludlow; may not like Cheltenham (twice disappointing there) and only other defeat came on unsuitably soft ground.

facebook.com/racingpost

Happy Diva (Ire)
7 b m King's Theatre - Megans Joy (Supreme Leader)

Kerry Lee   Will Roseff

PLACINGS: 2/325114222/3221121-   RPR **143+c**

Starts	1st	2nd	3rd	4th	Win & Pl
21	5	9	2	1	£78,609

	3/18	Asct	2m5f Cls3 Nov Ch soft	£10,007
	2/18	Bang	2m4¹/₂f Cls4 Nov Ch heavy	£5,458
	1/18	Ludl	2m4f Cls3 Nov Ch gd-sft	£7,722
121	1/17	Weth	3m Cls4 100-121 Hdl Hcap gd-sft	£3,899
114	12/16	Font	2m5¹/₂f Cls4 94-117 Hdl Hcap gd-sft	£3,899

Won three small-field novice chases last season (no more than four runners), with most notable victory coming over Adrien Du Pont at Ascot; yet to score at Listed level (second twice last season as well as over hurdles in 2017) but may well be up to that grade and beyond.

Hell's Kitchen
7 b g Robin Des Champs - Mille Et Une (Trempolino)

Harry Fry   John P McManus

PLACINGS: 312/3/2U1P-   RPR **153+c**

Starts	1st	2nd	3rd	4th	Win & Pl
8	2	2	2	-	£23,571

137	12/17	Kemp	2m4¹/₂f Cls3 Nov 118-137 Ch Hcap gd-sft	£13,814
	3/16	Newb	2m4¹/₂f Cls4 Nov Hdl soft	£4,549

Held in high regard by his trainer and has shown glimpses of big potential, notably when beating Cheltenham Festival winner Mister Whitaker in a novice handicap chase at Kempton last December; pulled up when favourite for a big Leopardstown handicap on only subsequent outing.

Highway One O One (Ire)
6 br g Stowaway - High Accord (Accordion)

Chris Gordon   Anthony Ward-Thomas

PLACINGS: 5B3/311221012-   RPR **141h**

Starts	1st	2nd	3rd	4th	Win & Pl
8	4	3	-	-	£33,106

4/18	Kemp	2m Cls4 Nov Hdl gd-sft	£4,094
12/17	Font	2m1¹/₂f Cls4 Nov Hdl soft	£3,574
10/17	Plum	2m Cls5 Mdn Hdl gd-sft	£3,249
9/17	NAbb	2m1f Cls6 NHF 4-6yo gd-sft	£1,711

Consistent and progressive performer in novice hurdles last season, with sole flop coming in the

ON THE FIGURES

HOGAN'S HEIGHT Enjoyed a successful first season over fences and, with an official mark of 139, should not be too difficult to place with his trainer also having the option to exploit his novice status over hurdles. [Steve Mason, Racing Post Ratings]

---

fiercely competitive Imperial Cup at Sandown; got back on track with a good win at Kempton and followed up with a close second in the novice handicap final at Sandown; likely to go novice chasing.

Hogan's Height (Ire)
7 b g Indian River - Electre Du Berlais (Royal Charter)

Jamie Snowden   Foxtrot Racing: Hogan's Height

PLACINGS: 32526/2721116-   RPR **146+c**

Starts	1st	2nd	3rd	4th	Win & Pl
10	3	3	-	-	£30,932

131	3/18	Hayd	2m4¹/₂f Cls3 Nov 118-131 Ch Hcap soft	£9,747
	1/18	Weth	2m3¹/₂f Cls4 Nov Ch soft	£4,679
	12/17	Ludl	2m4f Cls3 Nov Ch gd-sft	£11,078

Landed three successive novice chases last season, including a novice handicap off a mark of 131 at Haydock, but was later found out at Grade 1 level at Aintree; looks the type for the Ladbrokes Trophy at Newbury, a race eyed by his trainer, who warns he doesn't want quick ground.

Hunters Call (Ire)
8 b g Medaaly - Accordiontogelica (Accordion)

Olly Murphy   Holloway, Clarke & Black

PLACINGS: PO/4141/54639/4531-   RPR **138+h**

Starts	1st	2nd	3rd	4th	Win & Pl
13	3	-	2	4	£101,403

128	12/17	Asct	1m7¹/₂f Cls1 Gd3 125-151 Hdl Hcap gd-sft	£85,425
	11/15	Naas	2m Mdn Hdl soft	£6,419
	6/15	Gowr	2m4f NHF 5-7yo good	£4,814

Bought from Ireland last summer having failed to win since his hurdling debut but made an instant impact for new connections when landing a valuable 2m handicap at Ascot just before Christmas; hasn't run since but being aimed at the Greatwood at Cheltenham.

I Just Know (Ire)
8 b g Robin Des Pres - Desperado Queen (Un Desperado)

Sue Smith   M B Scholey & The Late R H Scholey

PLACINGS: 7636P/12211P3/3412F-   RPR **148+c**

Starts	1st	2nd	3rd	4th	Win & Pl
18	4	3	4	1	£43,469

131	1/18	Catt	3m6f Cls3 111-133 Ch Hcap soft	£15,890
125	2/17	Catt	3m1f Cls3 115-133 Ch Hcap soft	£7,798
114	1/17	Donc	3m Cls4 Nov 110-122 Ch Hcap gd-sft	£3,899
105	11/16	Hexm	3m Cls4 Nov 79-105 Ch Hcap soft	£5,064

Progressive staying chaser who was backed down to 14-1 for last season's Grand National but fell when in front at Becher's on the first circuit; had taken form to another level with a wide-margin win at Catterick (previous chase win also at that track) before adding a novice hurdle.

Identity Thief (Ire)

8 b g Kayf Tara - Miss Arteea (Flemensfirth)

Henry de Bromhead (Ir)　　　　　Gigginstown House Stud

PLACINGS: 1126/211PU460/62414-　　　　RPR 165+h

Starts	1st	2nd	3rd	4th	Win & Pl
22	4	7	4	1	3	£326,748

4/18	Aint	3m¹/₂f Cls1 Gd1 Hdl soft	£101,204
11/16	Punc	2m Nov Gd2 Ch soft	£19,305
10/16	Punc	2m Ch yield	£5,879
11/15	Newc	2m¹/₂f Cls1 Gd1 Hdl soft	£63,585
10/15	DRoy	2m Gd2 Hdl yld-sft	£23,256
12/14	Leop	2m4f Mdn Hdl 4yo soft	£6,325
11/14	Fair	2m NHF 4yo yield	£4,600

Had badly lost his way since winning the 2015 Fighting Fifth Hurdle, especially when sent chasing, but bounced back over hurdles last season; stayed on into fourth in the Champion Hurdle and proved a revelation when stepped up to 3m, winning easily at Aintree.

If The Cap Fits (Ire)

6 b g Milan - Derravaragh Sayra (Sayarshan)

Harry Fry　　　　　Paul & Clare Rooney

PLACINGS: 114/111-　　　　RPR 145+h

Starts	1st	2nd	3rd	4th	Win & Pl
6	5	-	-	1	£26,853

12/17	Kemp	2m Cls2 Nov Hdl gd-sft	£12,512
11/17	Bang	2m¹/₂f Cls4 Nov Hdl soft	£3,249
10/17	Extr	2m2¹/₂f Cls4 Nov Hdl good	£3,899
2/17	Tntn	2m¹/₂f Cls5 Am NHF 4-6yo good	£3,184
11/16	Plum	2m1¹/₂f Cls6 NHF 4-5yo gd-sft	£1,625

Has won five out of six races, including all three novice hurdles last season; put himself firmly in the picture for the Supreme at Cheltenham with an impressive win at Kempton only to miss the meeting after a setback; should stay further.

Imperial Presence (Ire)

7 ch g Presenting - Penneyrose Bay (Karinga Bay)

Philip Hobbs　　　　　Sir Christopher & Lady Wates

PLACINGS: 1247/25512/52-111　　　　RPR 153+c

Starts	1st	2nd	3rd	4th	Win & Pl
14	5	4	-	1	£62,895

142	7/18	Uttx	2m4f Cls2 139-159 Ch Hcap soft	£15,640
135	6/18	Strf	2m3¹/₂f Cls3 123-139 Ch Hcap good	£7,343
128	5/18	Kemp	2m2f Cls2 126-143 Ch Hcap good	£14,442
127	3/17	Newb	2m¹/₂f Cls3 124-131 Ch Hcap gd-sft	£6,498
	11/15	Kemp	2m Cls4 Nov Hdl good	£3,899

Went from strength to strength this summer and won a good handicap by eight lengths off 142 at the end of July to complete a hat-trick; gained that win on soft ground but unproven on bad winter ground; could continue to progress granted suitable conditions.

Invitation Only (Ire)

7 b g Flemensfirth - Norabelle (Alamo Bay)

Willie Mullins (Ir)　　　　　Andrea & Graham Wylie

PLACINGS: 1/1/1136/F113P3U-　　　　RPR 159c

Starts	1st	2nd	3rd	4th	Win & Pl
12	5	1	3	-	£66,479

1/18	Punc	2m4f Nov Gd3 Ch sft-hvy	£23,235
12/17	Navn	2m4f Ch soft	£7,634
11/16	Gowr	2m Mdn Hdl gd-yld	£5,426
4/16	Punc	2m NHF 4-7yo yield	£6,783
3/16	Navn	2m NHF 5-7yo sft-hvy	£4,296

Long held in high regard and began to justify his reputation last season in novice chases having disappointed over hurdles; still came up just short at the top level but was twice going well when let down by his jumping, including when pulled up in the JLT after a bad blunder.

Isleofhopendreams

11 b g Flemensfirth - Cool Island (Turtle Island)

Willie Mullins (Ir)　　　　　Kilbroney Racing Partnership

PLACINGS: 35P/1/3F/1210/PP222-　　　　RPR 150c

Starts	1st	2nd	3rd	4th	Win & Pl
18	3	5	2	-	£140,441

120	2/17	Punc	3m 120-148 Hdl Hcap soft	£13,929
	11/16	Cork	2m5f Ch sft-hvy	£7,235
86	2/14	Thur	2m6f 80-92 Hdl Hcap heavy	£4,313

Second in three big staying handicaps last season, including when caught on the line in the Irish Grand National; very lightly raced for his age (ran only once between 2012 and 2016) and still far from exposed after just five runs over fences.

Jenkins (Ire)

6 b g Azamour - Aladiyna (Indian Danehill)

Nicky Henderson　　　　　Pump & Plant Services

PLACINGS: 1/2141/77110P0-　　　　RPR 151+h

Starts	1st	2nd	3rd	4th	Win & Pl
143	5	4	1	-	£61,997

143	1/18	Asct	2m3¹/₂f Cls1 Gd3 121-147 Hdl Hcap soft	£28,475
132	1/18	Kemp	2m Cls3 119-139 Hdl Hcap soft	£6,238
	4/17	Ffos	2m Cls4 Nov Hdl good	£3,899
	11/16	Newb	2m¹/₂f Cls3 Mdn Hdl soft	£6,498
	4/16	Newb	2m¹/₂f Cls6 NHF 4-6yo good	£1,689

Long held in high regard but was becoming disappointing until helped by the application of blinkers in January, winning good handicaps at Kempton and Ascot in the space of just a week; well below that level in three subsequent runs, albeit off higher marks.

facebook.com/racingpost

Grade 1 meets
Delicious treats
Dublin beats

Celebrate the best of our proud and famous city, in one famous city venue.

Two days of exhilarating racing, including the BHP Insurance Irish Champion Hurdle and the

Unibet Irish Gold Cup, with over €1.5 million in prize money, performances from the best Dublin

Entertainment and Dublin's finest food, all for only €30 each day.

February 2nd & 3rd. **Book now at leopardstown.com**

Jetz (Ire)
6 b g Flemensfirth - Miss Squiff (Saddlers' Hall)

Jessica Harrington (Ir)   G McGrath

PLACINGS: 433/31234228-   RPR **146h**

Starts	1st	2nd	3rd	4th	Win & Pl
11	1	3	4	2	£47,332
	11/17	Fair	2m4f Mdn Hdl soft..£5,791

Half-brother to Grade 1 winners Jezki and Jetson who very nearly upheld family tradition when beaten a head by Tower Bridge at Leopardstown last season; made the frame in four more Graded novice hurdles; can race keenly and should improve if learning to settle.

Joe Farrell (Ire)
9 b g Presenting - Luck Of The Deise (Old Vic)

Rebecca Curtis   M Sherwood, N Morris & R Curtis

PLACINGS: 127/1/17620/424311-   RPR **146+c**

Starts	1st	2nd	3rd	4th	Win & Pl
15	5	3	1	2	£143,114
135	4/18	Ayr	4m Cls1 Gd3 129-155 Ch Hcap good...........£122,443
124	3/18	Newb	2m7¹/₂f Cls3 Nov 117-131 Ch Hcap soft.............£7,343
	11/16	Ffos	2m4f Cls5 Mdn Hdl good................................£2,274
	7/15	Worc	2m Cls6 NHF 4-6yo gd-fm................................£1,754
	11/14	Hntg	1m5¹/₂f Cls6 Mdn NHF 4-6yo soft.....................£1,625

Failed to win in first four chases early last season but much improved when back from a break in the spring, getting off the mark by 17 lengths in a novice handicap at Newbury and following up in the Scottish Grand National; lightly raced and open to further improvement.

Jolly's Cracked It (Fr)
9 b g Astarabad - Jolly Harbour (Rudimentary)

Harry Fry   GDM Partnership

PLACINGS: 42/1/112596/31/0/   RPR **147h**

Starts	1st	2nd	3rd	4th	Win & Pl
12	4	2	1	1	£99,084
141	12/15	Asct	1m7¹/₂f Cls1 Gd3 131-150 Hdl Hcap gd-sft.........£58,740
	11/14	Asct	1m7¹/₂f Cls3 Hdl soft.....................................£6,882
	11/14	Asct	1m7¹/₂f Cls3 Nov Hdl good.............................£10,635
	1/14	Winc	1m7¹/₂f Cls6 NHF 4-6yo heavy..........................£1,625

Dead-heated for the Ladbroke in 2015 but has run only once since then when disappointing in the same race 12 months later; had been seen as a high-class chasing prospect and should finally get his chance over fences after two seasons of injury problems.

Jury Duty (Ire)
7 b g Well Chosen - Swan Heart (Broken Hearted)

Gordon Elliott (Ir)   Sideways Syndicate

PLACINGS: 4413/21236/12122U3-3   RPR **157c**

Starts	1st	2nd	3rd	4th	Win & Pl
19	4	5	6	2	£140,588
	11/17	Punc	2m6¹/₂f Nov Gd2 Ch sft-hvy..........................£22,440
	10/17	Limk	2m6f Ch soft...£8,161
126	11/16	Navn	2m6¹/₂f 118-146 Hdl Hcap yld-sft....................£21,691
111	2/16	Navn	2m4f 88-116 Hdl Hcap sft-hvy.........................£5,426

Useful staying hurdler who took to fences well last season, beating Shattered Love in a Grade 2 at Punchestown and twice placed at Grade 1 level; disappointing favourite for the National Hunt Chase at Cheltenham (well beaten when unseated rider) but third in the Galway Plate this summer.

Kalashnikov (Ire)
5 br g Kalanisi - Fairy Lane (Old Vic)

Amy Murphy   Paul Murphy

PLACINGS: 1/11212-   RPR **153h**

Starts	1st	2nd	3rd	4th	Win & Pl
6	4	2	-	-	£137,691
141	2/18	Newb	2m1¹/₂f Cls1 Gd3 129-148 Hdl Hcap soft..............£88,273
	12/17	Donc	2m1¹/₂f Cls4 Nov Hdl 4-6yo gd-sft....................£3,899
	11/17	Weth	2m Cls3 Nov Hdl soft....................................£5,523
	3/17	Weth	2m Cls5 NHF 4-6yo gd-sft...............................£2,599

Beaten only by Summerville Boy in six runs in bumpers and over hurdles, winning four times, including the Betfair Hurdle at Newbury in comprehensive fashion, before narrow defeat in the Supreme; expected to benefit from quicker ground by connections; likely to go novice chasing.

Kalondra (Ire)
7 b g Spadoun - Mystic Vic (Old Vic)

Neil Mulholland   J Henderson

PLACINGS: /63112315104/12143-F   RPR **153c**

Starts	1st	2nd	3rd	4th	Win & Pl
21	6	3	3	4	£73,496
	12/17	Chel	2m5f Cls2 Nov Ch soft.................................£15,640
	10/17	Sedg	2m3¹/₂f Cls4 Ch gd-sft...................................£3,899
135	2/17	Hntg	2m3¹/₂f Cls2 121-147 Hdl Hcap soft..................£15,640
127	12/16	Asct	2m5¹/₂f Cls3 110-127 Cond Hdl Hcap gd-sft............£6,498
	7/16	Worc	2m4f Cls4 Nov Hdl good.................................£3,379
	7/16	Worc	2m4f Cls4 Nov Hdl good.................................£3,509

Very useful novice chaser last season who beat

facebook.com/racingpost

Cheltenham Festival winner Coo Star Sivola at Cheltenham in December; fine third in a big handicap chase back there in April, bouncing back from a poor run when stepped up to Grade I level at Sandown; best off a fast pace.

Keeper Hill (Ire)
7 b g Westerner - You Take Care (Definite Article)

Warren Greatrex				McNeill Family
PLACINGS: 13/211176/121FFP-				RPR **143+c**

Starts	1st	2nd	3rd	4th	Win & Pl
14	6	2	1	-	£55,660

	12/17	Donc	3m Cls1 Nov Gd2 Ch good	£20,554
	11/17	Strf	2m6¹/₂f Cls4 Nov Ch good	£4,431
	2/17	Hntg	2m3¹/₂f Cls1 Nov List Hdl gd-sft	£17,085
	1/17	Hrfd	2m3¹/₂f Cls4 Nov Hdl soft	£3,379
	11/16	Bang	2m3¹/₂f Cls4 Nov Hdl soft	£3,899
	11/15	MRas	2m¹/₂f Cls6 NHF 4-6yo gd-sft	£1,643

Lost his way as last season went on but had looked a potentially smart chaser early in the campaign, winning a Grade 2 novice chase at Doncaster; going well in front when fell next time at Musselburgh; fell again early at Cheltenham and pulled up on final outing.

Kemboy (Fr)
6 b g Voix Du Nord - Vitora (Victory Note)

Willie Mullins (Ir)			Supreme Horse Racing Club
			Brett T Graham & K Sha
PLACINGS: 1257/214F11-			RPR **162+c**

Starts	1st	2nd	3rd	4th	Win & Pl
10	4	2	-	1	£107,575

	4/18	Punc	2m5f Nov 126-147 Ch Hcap soft	£52,212
	4/18	Limk	3m Nov Gd3 Ch heavy	£22,190
	1/18	Fair	2m5¹/₂f Ch heavy	£7,632
	12/16	Limk	2m3f Mdn Hdl yield	£4,522

Progressive young chaser who put up a top-class performance to defy top weight in a novice handicap at Punchestown in April; had run a cracker to finish fourth in the JLT on just his third run over fences and built on that when winning a Grade 3 at Limerick.

Kilbricken Storm (Ire)
7 b g Oscar - Kilbricken Leader (Supreme Leader)

Colin Tizzard				A Selway & P Wavish
PLACINGS: 45/1311313-				RPR **154+h**

Starts	1st	2nd	3rd	4th	Win & Pl
6	3	-	3	-	£114,107

	3/18	Chel	3m Cls1 Nov Gd1 Hdl soft	£77,600
	12/17	Chel	3m Cls1 Nov Gd2 Hdl soft	£17,085
	11/17	Winc	1m7¹/₂f Cls3 Nov Hdl 4-6yo soft	£6,498

Proved underrated throughout last season, winning the Albert Bartlett Hurdle at 33-1 and showing that was no fluke with a half-length third behind Next Destination at Punchestown; had been wrong when well beaten in the Challow; likely to go novice chasing.

Kildisart (Ire)
6 br g Dubai Destination - Princess Mairead (Blueprint)

Ben Pauling				Simon Munir & Isaac Souede
PLACINGS: 2/2/212519-				RPR **143+h**

Starts	1st	2nd	3rd	4th	Win & Pl
7	2	3	-	-	£35,153

135	3/18	Kemp	2m5f Cls2 122-135 Hdl Hcap soft	£21,896
	11/17	Asct	2m3¹/₂f Cls3 Mdn Hdl gd-sft	£6,498

Ran well in several good handicap hurdles as a novice last season, finally winning the Cheltenham Festival consolation race at Kempton after a blunder two out had stopped him going close at Ascot; came up short in Grade I company at Aintree; likely to go novice chasing.

Killultagh Vic (Ire)
9 b g Old Vic - Killultagh Dawn (Phardante)

Willie Mullins (Ir)			Mrs R Boyd, Mrs MJ Armstrong & JB Anderson
PLACINGS: 116/51231/111/1FP5-P			RPR **168+c**

Starts	1st	2nd	3rd	4th	Win & Pl
17	8	2	1	-	£148,184

	12/17	Punc	2m4f Hdl sft-hvy	£10,530
	1/16	Leop	2m3f Nov Gd2 Ch soft	£18,529
	12/15	Fair	2m Ch heavy	£7,488
	4/15	Punc	3m Nov Gd1 Hdl gd-yld	£44,186
135	3/15	Chel	2m4¹/₂f Cls2 135-144 Cond Hdl Hcap soft	£31,280
	11/14	Clon	2m4f Mdn Hdl heavy	£6,325
	2/14	Naas	2m NHF 4-7yo sft-hvy	£7,763
	1/14	Naas	2m3f NHF 5-7yo sft-hvy	£4,600

Top-class performer at his best; won a Grade I over hurdles in 2015 and may well have followed suit over fences but for falling at the last in the Irish Gold Cup in first chase since getting injured in January 2016; patchy form since as jumping struggles persisted.

King's Odyssey (Ire)
9 b g King's Theatre - Ma Furie (Balleroy)

Evan Williams				Mr & Mrs William Rucker
PLACINGS: /2421/311/3F30/3333-				RPR **145c**

Starts	1st	2nd	3rd	4th	Win & Pl
16	3	3	7	1	£67,663

139	1/16	Chel	2m5f Cls2 Nov 126-152 Ch Hcap heavy	£15,640
	12/15	Winc	2m4f Cls3 Nov Ch soft	£6,657
	3/15	Wwck	2m5f Cls4 Mdn Hdl heavy	£3,249

Hasn't won since a novice handicap chase at

ON THE FIGURES

KALASHNIKOV A leading novice last season, he won the Betfair Hurdle on only his fourth run over obstacles en route to finishing runner-up in the Supreme Novices'. Has the physique to excel over fences and should take high rank in the 2m division. [Steve Mason, Racing Post Ratings]

Cheltenham in early 2016 but hasn't run often since then; finished third in three more handicaps back at that track last season, including the Plate in March, yet continued to creep slowly down the weights.

King's Socks (Fr)
6 b g King's Best - Alexandrina (Monsun)

David Pipe   Bryan Drew

PLACINGS: 21/42122/152/35P-   RPR **143**c

Starts	1st	2nd	3rd	4th	Win & Pl
13	3	5	1	1	£189,684

5/16	Engh	2m2f List Hdl 4yo v soft	£30,000
3/16	Engh	2m1f Ch 4yo v soft	£18,706
4/15	Engh	2m¹/₂f Hdl 3yo v soft	£18,605

Bought from France after winning a chase and finishing second to Footpad in a Grade 1 hurdle; had British debut delayed by setbacks but got started late last season and ran an eyecatching race when fifth in the Plate at Cheltenham; disappointing when down to 2m at Aintree.

Kylemore Lough
9 b g Revoque - One Of The Last (Supreme Leader)

Harry Fry   M J McMahon & Denis Gallagher

PLACINGS: PP/311111/2554/P32P-   RPR **160**c

Starts	1st	2nd	3rd	4th	Win & Pl
20	8	2	3	1	£147,111

	3/16	Fair	2m4f Nov Gd1 Ch yield	£43,382
151	3/16	Sand	1m7¹/₂f Cls3 Nov 132-151 Ch Hcap soft	£6,498
147	2/16	Hayd	2m4f Cls3 Nov 128-147 Ch Hcap heavy	£8,123
	12/15	Extr	2m1¹/₂f Cls2 Ch heavy	£12,820
132	11/15	Uttx	2m4f Cls3 Nov 117-132 Ch Hcap soft	£6,343
	1/15	Weth	2m5¹/₂f Cls4 Nov Hdl soft	£3,249
	1/15	Weth	2m3¹/₂f Cls4 Nov Hdl 4-7yo gd-sft	£3,769
	12/14	Wwck	2m5f Cls4 Mdn Hdl soft	£3,249

Hasn't won since the Ryanair Gold Cup in 2016 but has been lightly raced in that time and slipped slightly in the weights; good second at Warwick on his penultimate run last season and rated lower than when favourite for the BetVictor Gold Cup (pulled up after bad blunder).

L'Inganno Felice (Fr)
8 br g Librettist - Final Overture (Rossini)

Iain Jardine   A Dawson & Mrs K Campbell

PLACINGS: 31-111   RPR **142**+h

Starts	1st	2nd	3rd	4th	Win & Pl
5	4	1	-	1	£35,256

135	7/18	MRas	2m¹/₂f Cls1 List 118-142 Hdl Hcap good	£22,780
	6/18	Uttx	2m Cls4 Nov Hdl good	£4,094
	5/18	MRas	2m¹/₂f Cls4 Nov Hdl good	£4,549
	4/18	MRas	2m¹/₂f Cls5 Mdn Hdl good	£3,119

Late starter over hurdles but soon made up for lost time this summer, completing a four-timer when making all in the Summer Hurdle at Market Rasen; third win over that course and distance and seems best going right-handed; loses novice status in November.

La Bague Au Roi (Fr)
7 b m Doctor Dino - Alliance Royale (Turgeon)

Warren Greatrex   Mrs Julien Turner & Andrew Merriam

PLACINGS: 1/117/111761/11177-   RPR **153**+h

Starts	1st	2nd	3rd	4th	Win & Pl
15	10	-	-	-	£99,218

1/18	Asct	2m7¹/₂f Cls1 Gd2 Hdl soft	£28,810
11/17	Kemp	3m¹/₂f Cls1 List Hdl gd-sft	£14,238
11/17	Weth	2m Cls1 List Hdl soft	£12,529
4/17	Hntg	2m4¹/₂f Cls4 Nov Hdl good	£3,899
11/16	Newb	2m¹/₂f Cls1 Nov List Hdl gd-sft	£13,968
11/16	Weth	2m Cls4 Nov Hdl gd-sft	£3,574
10/16	Uttx	2m Cls4 Mdn Hdl good	£3,379
12/15	Hntg	2m Cls1 List NHF 4-6yo gd-sft	£11,390
10/15	Aint	2m Cls4 NHF 4-6yo good	£3,249
4/15	NAbb	2m1f Cls6 NHF 4-6yo good	£1,711

Prolific mare who added a further three victories to her CV last season, including a demolition job in a Grade 2 hurdle at Ascot; has struggled in stronger races, though, and was well beaten at Cheltenham for the second year in a row in the Mares' Hurdle before disappointing again at Punchestown.

Label Des Obeaux (Fr)
7 b g Saddler Maker - La Bessiere (Loup Solitaire)

Alan King   David Sewell & Terry Warner

PLACINGS: 1320/2321101/83P686-   RPR **156**c

Starts	1st	2nd	3rd	4th	Win & Pl
24	4	6	5	-	£93,833

148	4/17	Ayr	3m¹/₂f Cls2 Nov 126-148 Ch Hcap good	£16,245
141	2/17	Extr	3m Cls3 Nov 119-141 Ch Hcap gd-sft	£9,495
	2/17	Ludl	3m Cls4 Nov Ch soft	£4,660
	12/15	Sand	2m4f Cls1 Nov Gd2 Hdl soft	£17,085

Suffered at the hands of the handicapper since winning a novice handicap chase at Ayr in 2017 but steadily coming down the weights and ran well when sixth in the Scottish National back at that course last season (first run beyond 3m2f); best on good ground.

Lady Buttons
8 b m Beneficial - Lady Chapp (High Chaparral)

Philip Kirby   Mrs Jayne Sivills

PLACINGS: 1544P/P3111P/214414-   RPR **148**+c

Starts	1st	2nd	3rd	4th	Win & Pl
21	8	2	1	5	£66,175

	2/18	Newc	2m¹/₂f Cls2 Nov Ch heavy	£11,711
	11/17	Bang	2m1¹/₂f Cls1 Nov List Ch soft	£14,238
125	3/17	Donc	2m¹/₂f Cls3 106-125 Hdl Hcap good	£5,697
113	1/17	Sthl	2m4¹/₂f Cls4 97-113 Hdl Hcap soft	£3,249
106	11/17	Newc	2m Cls4 84-110 Hdl Hcap soft	£3,249
	10/14	Worc	2m Cls4 Nov Hdl gd-sft	£3,249
	2/14	Weth	2m Cls6 NHF 4-6yo heavy	£1,643
	12/13	Weth	1m4¹/₂f Cls6 NHF 3yo gd-sft	£1,711

Won her first two novice chases last season, looking particularly impressive at Newcastle; had reverted to hurdles in between with trainer convinced she can also win a good handicap hurdle; fair fourth when stepped up to a Grade 1 novice chase at Aintree.

Lalor (Ger)
6 b g It's Gino - Laviola (Waky Nao)

Kayley Woollacott   DG Staddon

PLACINGS: 1211/23201-   RPR **148+h**

Starts	1st	2nd	3rd	4th	Win & Pl
9	4	3	1	-	£90,177
	4/18	Aint	2m¹/₂f Cls1 Nov Gd1 Hdl soft		£56,130
	4/17	Aint	2m1f Cls1 Gd2 NHF 4-6yo good		£25,322
	3/17	Winc	1m7¹/₂f Cls6 Mdn NHF 4-6yo heavy		£1,949
	12/16	Winc	1m7¹/₂f Cls6 NHF 4-6yo soft		£1,625

Seems suited by sharp tracks and has won at Aintree's Grand National meeting for the last two years, most recently when winning a 2m Grade 1 novice hurdle; hadn't won over hurdles previously but may have been helped by wind surgery; regarded as a future chaser.

Last Goodbye (Ire)
7 b g Millenary - Welsh Ana (Welsh Term)

Liz Doyle (Ir)   Last Goodbye Syndicate

PLACINGS: 81111/026157/0100-   RPR **154+c**

Starts	1st	2nd	3rd	4th	Win & Pl
15	6	1	-	-	£94,349
135	2/18	Leop	2m5f 124-152 Ch Hcap soft		£52,212
	12/16	DRoy	2m4f Ch soft		£6,331
130	3/16	Cork	2m3f 107-131 Hdl Hcap heavy		£13,566
	1/16	Navn	2m4f Nov Hdl sft-hvy		£8,118
	10/15	Wxfd	2m Mdn Hdl 4yo soft		£5,616
	9/15	Rosc	2m NHF 4yo good		£4,814

Inconsistent last season but ran away with a big handicap at Leopardstown, confirming the promise of his fifth in the novice handicap chase at the 2017 Cheltenham Festival (badly hampered); below par when well fancied back there for the Plate.

Laurina (Fr)
5 b m Spanish Moon - Lamboghina (Alkalde)

Willie Mullins (Ir)   Sullivan Bloodstock

PLACINGS: F2/1111-   RPR **154+h**

Starts	1st	2nd	3rd	4th	Win & Pl
6	4	-	-	-	£131,254
	4/18	Fair	2m4f Nov Gd1 Hdl sft-hvy		£52,212
	3/18	Chel	2m1f Cls1 Nov Gd2 Hdl soft		£51,255
	1/18	Fair	2m2f Nov Gd3 Hdl heavy		£17,058
	12/17	Tram	2m Mdn Hdl heavy		£5,791

Unbeaten in four runs since joining Willie Mullins from France and particularly impressive when

ON THE FIGURES
LAURINA Unbeaten for current connections and was hugely impressive in landing Grade 1 mares' hurdles at Cheltenham and Fairyhouse. Should prove tough to beat against her own sex and probably good enough to mix it with the best around. [Steve Mason, Racing Post Ratings]

winning the mares' novice hurdle at last season's Cheltenham Festival by 18 lengths; has the scope to jump fences but could have a massive future over hurdles first.

Le Breuil (Fr)
6 ch g Anzillero - Slew Dancer (Fabulous Dancer)

Ben Pauling   Miss Emma Collins

PLACINGS: 1411P/52015-   RPR **143h**

Starts	1st	2nd	3rd	4th	Win & Pl
10	4	1	-	1	£23,270
139	4/18	Asct	2m4f Cls3 113-139 Hdl Hcap gd-sft		£7,213
	3/17	Newb	2m4¹/₂f Cls4 Nov Hdl soft		£4,549
	11/16	Sedg	2m4f Cls4 Nov Hdl gd-sft		£3,899
	5/16	Wrck	2m Cls6 NHF 4-6yo gd-sft		£1,625

Yet to live up to trainer's extremely high opinion of him, with foot problems not helping, but won a handicap hurdle at Fakenham last season to add to two novice successes; well beaten in stronger company at Cheltenham and Sandown in the spring; could go novice chasing.

Le Patriote (Fr)
6 b g Poliglote - Sentosa (Kaldounevees)

Dr Richard Newland   Canard Vert Racing Club

PLACINGS: 3/161/589741P-   RPR **135+h**

Starts	1st	2nd	3rd	4th	Win & Pl
11	3	-	1	1	£74,266
127	2/18	Asct	2m3¹/₂f Cls2 123-149 Hdl Hcap soft		£28,152
	3/17	Comp	2m2f Hdl soft		£19,692
	11/16	Engh	2m2f Hdl 4yo heavy		£16,941

Bought from France last season and immediately pitched into several big handicap hurdles, winning well at Ascot on his third run in Britain; pulled up when well fancied for the Imperial Cup on his final run; had looked a non-stayer over 2m5f in the Lanzarote Hurdle.

Le Prezien (Fr)
7 br g Blue Bresil - Abu Dhabi (Saint Cyrien)

Paul Nicholls   John P McManus

PLACINGS: 211212/21138P/2381P-   RPR **161+c**

Starts	1st	2nd	3rd	4th	Win & Pl
19	6	5	3		£183,155
150	3/18	Chel	2m¹/₂f Cls1 Gd3 139-154 Ch Hcap soft		£62,645
	12/16	Extr	2m1¹/₂f Cls2 Ch soft		£12,512
	11/16	Chel	2m Cls1 Nov Gd2 Ch soft		£19,078
	3/16	Kels	2m2f Cls1 Nov Gd2 Hdl soft		£21,356
	1/16	Donc	2m¹/₂f Cls4 Nov Hdl soft		£3,249
	12/15	Ludl	2m Cls4 Mdn Hdl soft		£3,899

Knocking on the door in good Cheltenham handicaps last season and finally broke through when winning the Grand Annual; ideally suited by 2m on soft ground having found that trip too sharp on a quicker surface, but come up just short over further; may find life tough after 7lb rise.

Lil Rockerfeller (USA)

7 ch g Hard Spun - Layounne (Mt. Livermore)

Neil King   Davies, Smith, Govier & Brown

PLACINGS: 2317/322420/31620P2-   RPR **153h**

Starts	1st	2nd	3rd	4th	Win & Pl
26	5	7	7	2	£365,687
	11/17 Asct	2m3¹/₂f Cls1 Gd2 Hdl gd-sft			£56,950
	2/16 Font	2m3f Cls1 Gd2 Hdl gd-sft			£45,560
146	12/15 Sand	2m Cls1 List 125-147 Hdl Hcap soft			£34,170
133	4/15 Sand	2m Cls2 111-137 Hdl 4yo Hcap gd-sft			£31,280
125	3/15 Asct	1m7¹/₂f Cls2 120-142 Hdl 4yo Hcap gd-sft			£25,992

Tough staying hurdler who has run well in many top races in recent seasons, notably when second in the Stayers' Hurdle at Cheltenham in 2017; not quite at that level last season but still won the Ascot Hurdle in November and was second in two more Grade 2 contests.

Limini (Ire)

7 ch m Peintre Celebre - Her Grace (Spectrum)

Willie Mullins (Ir)   Mrs S Ricci

PLACINGS: 1113/213/   RPR **158h**

Starts	1st	2nd	3rd	4th	Win & Pl
7	4	1	2	-	£116,541
	2/17 Punc	2m4f List Hdl heavy			£17,083
	3/16 Chel	2m1f Cls1 Nov Gd2 Hdl good			£42,713
	1/16 Fair	2m2f Nov Gd3 Hdl heavy			£16,728
	5/15 Punc	2m Mdn Hdl good			£6,419

Very smart mare who won at the Cheltenham Festival in 2016 but was only third there the following year when a beaten favourite at Grade 1 level for the third time; missed last season through injury and was twice a beaten favourite when running on the Flat during the Galway festival, finishing second and third, although not beaten far either time.

Lostintranslation (Ire)

6 b g Flemensfirth - Falika (Hero's Honor)

Colin Tizzard   Taylor & O'Dwyer

PLACINGS: 4/221672-   RPR **151+h**

Starts	1st	2nd	3rd	4th	Win & Pl
6	1	3	-	-	£30,501
	12/17 Newb	2m¹/₂f Cls3 Mdn Hdl soft			£6,498

Ran a huge race when a close second to Black Op in a Grade 1 novice hurdle at Aintree last season, benefiting from the step up to 2m4f after a staying-on seventh in the Supreme at Cheltenham (should get further again); likely to go novice chasing.

Louis' Vac Pouch (Ire)

6 b g Oscar - Coming Home (Exit To Nowhere)

Philip Hobbs   The Vacuum Pouch Company

PLACINGS: 03/4641F11/6100-   RPR **148+h**

Starts	1st	2nd	3rd	4th	Win & Pl
13	4	-	1	2	£32,878
132	11/17 Aint	3m¹/₂f Cls2 126-152 Hdl Hcap soft			£12,512
125	4/17 MRas	2m4¹/₂f Cls3 105-130 Hdl Hcap good			£12,512
	3/17 MRas	2m¹/₂f Cls4 Nov Hdl good			£3,249
	1/17 Sthl	1m7¹/₂f Cls4 Nov Hdl soft			£3,249

Hugely progressive in 2017 and was winning for the third time in four races when landing what proved to be a red-hot handicap at Aintree last season; put away for the Pertemps Final after that but disappointed at Cheltenham and Aintree; may prefer quicker ground.

facebook.com/racingpost

Mala Beach (Ire)

10 b g Beneficial - Peppardstown (Old Vic)

Gordon Elliott (Ir)   C Jones

PLACINGS: 231/214/F22FP/21P12-   RPR **159 + c**

Starts	1st	2nd	3rd	4th	Win & Pl
24	6	7	2	1	£166,449

	3/18	DRoy	3m2f Ch heavy £10,903
148	11/17	Navn	3m 121-149 Ch Hcap sft-hvy £50,427
	12/14	Punc	2m6f Ch gd-yld £6,900
	1/14	Gowr	3m Gd2 Hdl soft £21,667
	3/13	Fair	2m4f Nov Gd2 Hdl soft £21,138
	1/13	Leop	2m4f Mdn Hdl heavy £6,171

Returned from more than 18 months out in outstanding form last season and won the Troytown at Navan on his second run back; pulled up in the Irish Gold Cup next time but bounced back to finish first and second in small-field conditions races in the spring; needs soft ground.

Malaya (Fr)

4 b f Martaline - Clarte D'Or (Kendor)

Paul Nicholls   Mrs Johnny De La Hey

PLACINGS: 12/1212218-   RPR **131 + h**

Starts	1st	2nd	3rd	4th	Win & Pl
9	4	4	-	-	£104,009

134	3/18	Asct	1m7¹/₂f Cls2 108-134 Hdl 4yo Hcap soft £25,024
	11/17	Weth	2m Cls1 List Hdl 3yo gd-sft £11,390
	5/17	Autl	2m1¹/₂f List Hdl 3yo v soft £34,872
	3/17	Pari	1m7f Hdl 3yo good £8,205

Looked a tearaway when beaten at odds-on in a fillies' Listed hurdle at Aintree last season but showed true colours when much more tractable after a break, finishing second to Redicean in a Grade 2 and winning a handicap at Ascot; disappointing when up to Grade 1 level next time.

Mall Dini (Ire)

8 b g Milan - Winsome Breeze (Glacial Storm)

Pat Kelly (Ir)   Philip J Reynolds

PLACINGS: 314331/333235/5452P-   RPR **153 + c**

Starts	1st	2nd	3rd	4th	Win & Pl
21	3	3	7	3	£92,570

139	3/16	Chel	3m Cls1 List 135-154 Hdl Hcap good £51,255
	12/15	Thur	2m6¹/₂f Mdn Hdl sft-hvy £6,953
	3/15	Cork	2m NHF 4-7yo heavy £4,814

Cheltenham Festival regular who won the Pertemps Final in 2016 and has gone close in the last two runnings of the Kim Muir, notably when a half-length second to Missed Approach last season; still a novice over fences but capable of winning good staying races.

Maria's Benefit (Ire)

6 b m Beneficial - Youngborogal (Anshan)

Stuart Edmunds   P D Wells

PLACINGS: 1210/2111114-   RPR **148 + h**

Starts	1st	2nd	3rd	4th	Win & Pl
10	6	2	-	1	£77,613

	1/18	Donc	2m1¹/₂f Cls1 Gd2 Hdl soft £28,475
	12/17	Tntn	2m¹/₂f Cls1 Nov List Hdl soft £11,390
127	12/17	Ludl	2m Cls2 114-140 Hdl Hcap gd-sft £12,660
117	11/17	Sand	2m Cls3 114-131 Hdl Hcap gd-sft £12,512
	10/17	NAbb	2m1f Cls4 Nov Hdl 4-6yo good £4,549
	3/17	Hntg	2m Cls6 NHF 4-6yo gd-sft £1,819

Went from strength to strength as a novice hurdler last season, winning five in a row including a Grade 2 against older mares at Doncaster; below her best when fourth at the Cheltenham Festival (taken on in front); point-to-point winner with more to offer over fences.

Limini: high-class mare should prove a force in her division when returning to action over jumps this season

Master Blueyes (Ire)
5 gr g Mastercraftsman - Miss Blueyes (Dushyantor)

Alan King   The Legends Partnership

PLACINGS: **422110/**   RPR **141**h

Starts	1st	2nd	3rd	4th	Win & Pl
6	2	2		1	£30,741

2/17	Kemp	2m Cls1 Gd2 Hdl 4yo good	£17,085
2/17	Ludl	2m Cls4 Hdl 4yo soft	£5,198

Has improved with practice over hurdles and produced one of the best juvenile performances of two seasons ago when landing the Adonis at Kempton by 11 lengths; finished lame when tenth in that season's Triumph Hurdle and missed last season but back in training this summer.

Master Dee (Ire)
9 b g King's Theatre - Miss Lauren Dee (Montelimar)

Fergal O'Brien   Paul & Clare Rooney

PLACINGS: **1133/3/2212112/3321-**   RPR **160+c**

Starts	1st	2nd	3rd	4th	Win & Pl
21	7	7	7		£125,195

145	2/18	Kemp	3m Cls1 Gd3 132-152 Ch Hcap good	£56,950
139	10/16	Asct	2m3f Cls3 Nov 123-139 Ch Hcap good	£9,747
133	10/16	Ludl	2m4f Cls3 Nov 122-133 Ch Hcap gd-fm	£9,729
130	8/16	NAbb	2m5f Cls3 Nov 120-134 Ch Hcap good	£7,913
	12/14	Sedg	2m3f Cls4 Nov Hdl soft	£3,509
	11/14	Muss	3m¹/₂f Cls5 Mdn Hdl good	£2,663
	1/14	Sedg	2m1f Cls6 Mdn NHF 4-6yo heavy	£1,560

Very lightly raced last season owing to preference for good ground but made his mark on a rare opportunity when winning the Betdaq Chase at Kempton; saw out the longer trip well on first run over 3m since being caught late at Warwick in September 2016.

Master Tommytucker
7 b g Kayf Tara - No Need For Alarm (Romany Rye)

Paul Nicholls   AG Fear

PLACINGS: **11-**   RPR **143+h**

Starts	1st	2nd	3rd	4th	Win & Pl
2	2	-	-	-	£8,772

4/18	Extr	2m5¹/₂f Cls4 Nov Hdl soft	£4,224
2/18	Extr	2m2¹/₂f Cls4 Nov Hdl soft	£4,549

Hugely impressive in winning both novice hurdles at Exeter near the end of last season, especially when stepped up in trip; described as big and backward by his trainer and had reportedly taken a long time to come right at home; likely to go novice chasing.

Melon
6 ch g Medicean - Night Teeny (Platini)

Willie Mullins (Ir)   Mrs J Donnelly

PLACINGS: **122/1352F-**   RPR **166+h**

Starts	1st	2nd	3rd	4th	Win & Pl
8	2	3	1	-	£191,521

11/17	DRoy	2m Gd2 Hdl soft	£25,214
1/17	Leop	2m Mdn Hdl good	£6,833

Long held in high regard and finally fulfilled that promise when running a massive race in last season's Champion Hurdle, pushing Buveur D'Air to a neck; had generally been too keen prior to that, with sole win since his maiden coming at 2-5 at Down Royal.

Mengli Khan (Ire)
5 b g Lope De Vega - Danielli (Danehill)

Gordon Elliott (Ir)   Gigginstown House Stud

PLACINGS: **24/1110233-**   RPR **151**h

Starts	1st	2nd	3rd	4th	Win & Pl
9	3	2	2	1	£98,936

12/17	Fair	2m Nov Gd1 Hdl soft	£42,863
11/17	Navn	2m Nov Gd3 Hdl sft-hvy	£17,083
9/17	Navn	2m Mdn Hdl yield	£7,108

Not far off the best 2m novice hurdlers last season, though probably flattered by Grade 1 win in the Royal Bond; put in his place by Getabird soon after but beaten only two lengths when third in the Supreme and filled the same spot at Punchestown next time.

Mia's Storm (Ire)
8 b m September Storm - Letitia's Gain (Zaffaran)

Alan King   The Maple Street Partnership

PLACINGS: **1/24P/11591/111FF-**   RPR **154+c**

Starts	1st	2nd	3rd	4th	Win & Pl
13	6	1	-	1	£59,051

11/17	MRas	3m Cls1 List Ch gd-sft	£17,319
10/17	Chep	2m7¹/₂f Cls3 Nov Ch good	£6,498
126	5/17	Hayd	2m7f Cls2 125-150 Hdl Hcap good	£18,768
121	1/17	Donc	2m3¹/₂f Cls4 97-121 Hdl Hcap good	£3,899
	5/16	NAbb	2m5¹/₂f Cls4 Nov Hdl good	£4,549
	5/16	Weth	2m3¹/₂f Cls4 Nov Hdl good	£3,411

Looked a top novice chaser early last season,

Facebook.com/racingpost

winning first two races over fences; reportedly unsuited by soft ground when disappointing at Kempton in a Grade 1 over Christmas (favourite but beaten when falling) but flopped again on good ground at Ayr.

Mick Jazz (Fr)
7 b g Blue Bresil - Mick Maya (Siam)

Gordon Elliott (Ir)				George P Mahoney
PLACINGS: 6232/P/1231/35133-				RPR **162h**

Starts	1st	2nd	3rd	4th	Win & Pl
14	3	3	5	-	£160,404
	12/17	Leop	2m Gd1 Hdl soft		£50,427
	2/17	Punc	2m Nov List Hdl soft		£17,083
	10/16	Clon	2m¹/₂f Mdn Hdl good		£4,522

Much improved last season and ran a huge race to finish third at 25-1 in the Champion Hurdle behind Buveur D'Air and Melon; proved with that mighty effort that his earlier Grade 1 win at Leopardstown was no fluke having been widely seen as a fortunate winner because of Faugheen under-performing; likely to find rich pickings in Graded races on home soil during the autumn and winter.

Midnight Shadow
5 b g Midnight Legend - Holy Smoke (Statoblest)

Sue Smith				Mrs Aafke Clarke
PLACINGS: 127/1222U71-				RPR **139+h**

Starts	1st	2nd	3rd	4th	Win & Pl
10	3	4	-	-	£80,804
134	4/18	Ayr	2m Cls1 Gd2 134-154 Hdl Hcap good		£59,798
	10/17	Uttx	2m Cls4 Nov Hdl 4-6yo soft		£3,899
	12/16	Newc	1m6¹/₂f Cls6 NHF 3yo soft		£1,884

Relished the move into handicap company when winning the Scottish Champion Hurdle in April; had been steadily progressive in Graded company without winning, finishing second in a Grade 2 at Haydock and a fair seventh behind Lalor in a Grade 1 at Aintree.

Might Bite (Ire)
9 b g Scorpion - Knotted Midge (Presenting)

Nicky Henderson				The Knot Again Partnership
PLACINGS: 311/517/21F111/1121-				RPR **174c**

Starts	1st	2nd	3rd	4th	Win & Pl
16	10	2	1	-	£593,724
	4/18	Aint	3m1f Cls1 Gd1 Ch gd-sft		£106,745
	12/17	Kemp	3m Cls1 Gd1 Ch soft		£128,138
	11/17	Sand	3m Cls1 List Ch gd-sft		£17,085
	4/17	Aint	3m1f Cls1 Nov Gd1 Ch good		£56,130
	3/17	Chel	3m¹/₂f Cls1 Nov Gd1 Ch gd-sft		£99,663
	2/17	Donc	3m Cls4 Nov Ch gd-sft		£4,758
	12/16	Donc	2m3f Cls4 Nov Ch good		£5,908
138	3/16	Kemp	2m5f Cls2 127-128 Hdl Hcap good		£20,645
	4/15	Chel	2m4¹/₂f Cls2 Nov Hdl good		£10,102
	3/15	Newb	2m4¹/₂f Cls4 Nov Hdl gd-sft		£3,422

Massive talent who took an age to grow up

(wayward RSA Chase win in 2017 came more than a year after first attempt at chasing) but looked much more the finished article last term, winning the King George and the Bowl either side of gallant Cheltenham Gold Cup second; with Native River he sets a high standard.

Min (Fr)
7 b g Walk In The Park - Phemyka (Saint Estephe)

Willie Mullins (Ir)				Mrs S Ricci
PLACINGS: 43/112/11/11d1224-				RPR **176c**

Starts	1st	2nd	3rd	4th	Win & Pl
13	6	4	1	2	£336,067
	2/18	Leop	2m1f Gd2 Ch soft		£52,212
	11/17	Gowr	2m4f Ch heavy		£10,530
	12/16	Leop	2m1f Nov Gd1 Ch yield		£39,044
	11/16	Navn	2m1f Ch yld-sft		£7,235
	1/16	Punc	2m Nov Gd2 Hdl heavy		£18,529
	12/15	Punc	2m2f Mdn Hdl soft		£5,349

Big reputation slightly dented last season but proved himself a top-class chaser; won easily at Leopardstown in February and lost nothing in defeat the next twice (second to Altior in the Champion Chase and beaten a neck by Politologue when just too keen over 2m4f at Aintree).

Mind's Eye (Ire)
6 b g Stowaway - Joleen (Bob's Return)

Henry de Bromhead (Ir)				Gigginstown House Stud
PLACINGS: 2/22/11004-				RPR **135h**

Starts	1st	2nd	3rd	4th	Win & Pl
8	2	3	-	1	£31,467
125	12/17	Leop	2m4f Nov 106-130 Hdl Hcap soft		£15,769
	3/17	Fair	2m Mdn Hdl sft-hvy		£5,791

Promising novice hurdler last season; won twice, most impressively when stepped up to 2m4f in a handicap at Leopardstown, and got back on track with a fair fourth in a 2m Grade 1 at Aintree (travelled notably well); described as a real chaser by his trainer.

Minella Awards (Ire)
7 b g Oscar - Montys Miss (Presenting)

Harry Fry				Masterson Holdings
PLACINGS: 2/25/211/P7-2				RPR **157+h**

Starts	1st	2nd	3rd	4th	Win & Pl
8	2	3	-	-	£87,462
134	4/17	Punc	3m 123-142 Hdl Hcap gd-yld		£30,256
128	3/17	Sand	2m4f Cls1 Nov Gd3 116-132 Hdl 4-7yo Hcap soft		£36,576

Missed much of last term, returning from a long absence in the final week of the season at Punchestown, but bounced back to form when a close second at Galway this summer; had been a smart novice in 2016-17 and still open to further progress.

Minella Fair (Ire)

7 b g Flemensfirth - Bell Walks Run (Commanche Run)

Noel Meade (Ir)   Mrs Patricia Hunt

PLACINGS: 2/221/1531-   RPR **147+h**

Starts	1st	2nd	3rd	4th	Win & Pl
7	3	2	1	-	£27,770

			Win & Pl
3/18	Clon	2m6f Nov Hdl heavy	£10,903
11/17	Punc	2m6f Mdn Hdl sft-hvy	£7,897
12/16	Limk	2m2f NHF 4-7yo sft-hvy	£4,296

Won two novice hurdles last season and hugely impressive on second occasion, getting back on track after two defeats (suffered a knock at Limerick and then found 2m3f not far enough); held in high regard by connections and seen as a future chaser.

Minella Rocco (Ire)

8 b g Shirocco - Petralona (Alleged)

Jonjo O'Neill   John P McManus

PLACINGS: /11/3P621/3FU2/4P4F-   RPR **160+c**

Starts	1st	2nd	3rd	4th	Win & Pl
15	3	2	2	2	£212,650

				Win & Pl
3/16	Chel	4m Cls1 Nov List	Am Ch gd-sft	£59,960
2/15	Newb	2m4¹/₂f Cls4 Nov Hdl soft		£3,249
2/15	Kemp	2m5f Cls4 Nov Hdl soft		£3,249

Second to Sizing John in the Cheltenham Gold Cup in 2017 having beaten Native River in the National Hunt Chase 12 months earlier; well below that form last season, though often unsuited by soft ground; late Grand National withdrawal and may have a future in staying handicaps.

Minella Rocco: Jonjo O'Neill's pride and joy could do well in staying handicap chases this season

Facebook.com/racingpost

Missed Approach (Ire)
8 b g Golan - Polly's Dream (Beau Sher)

Warren Greatrex   Alan & Andrew Turner

PLACINGS: 3/1P2/413U28/P6321P-   RPR **149+c**

Starts		1st	2nd	3rd	4th	Win & Pl
18		5	3	3	1	£108,840
138	3/18	Chel	3m2f Cls2 119-145 Am Ch Hcap soft			£41,972
	1/17	Ling	2m7½f Cls4 Nov Ch heavy			£3,899
123	11/15	Newb	3m Cls3 120-142 Hdl Hcap soft			£9,384
	11/14	Ffos	2m4f Cls5 Mdn Hdl soft			£1,949
	10/14	Uttx	2m Cls6 NHF 4-6yo good			£1,560

Won last season's Kim Muir at the Cheltenham Festival, building on a terrific run at the meeting 12 months earlier when second to Tiger Roll in the NH Chase; largely disappointing in between but benefited from wind op just before Cheltenham.

Mister Whitaker (Ire)
6 b g Court Cave - Benbradagh Vard (Le Bavard)

Mick Channon   TP Radford

PLACINGS: 26343/31211-   RPR **147+c**

Starts		1st	2nd	3rd	4th	Win & Pl
10		3	2	3	1	£71,466
137	3/18	Chel	2m4½f Cls1 Nov List 137-145 Ch Hcap soft			£39,865
129	1/18	Chel	2m5f Cls2 Nov 128-147 Ch Hcap soft			£17,204
118	11/17	Carl	2m4f Cls3 Nov 115-134 Ch Hcap gd-sft			£7,798

Massively progressive in novice handicap chases, winning three out of four (second to Hell's Kitchen in between) including at the Cheltenham Festival; potentially better than that bare form (didn't get a clear run) and could also be suited by going up to 3m.

Modus: talented performer but needs to bounce back from below-par runs at Cheltenham and Aintree

Misterton
7 gr g Sagamix - Mighty Splash (Cape Cross)

Harry Fry　　　　　　　　Wilkin, Orr, Boileau & Sim

PLACINGS: 422/11P21/129-　　　　　RPR **144h**

Starts	1st	2nd	3rd	4th	Win & Pl
11	4	4	-	1	£50,302

130	10/17	Chep	2m Cls2 118-140 Hdl Hcap good	£12,996
124	3/17	Winc	2m4f Cls3 Nov 110-125 Hdl Hcap gd-sft	£6,330
	11/16	Tntn	2m¹/₂f Cls4 Nov Hdl good	£4,549
	10/16	NAbb	2m1f Cls5 NHF 4-6yo good	£2,738

Lightly raced hurdler who may well have a big 2m handicap in him judged on last season's neck second to subsequent Champion Hurdle fifth Elgin in the Greatwood at Cheltenham; ran only once after that when disappointing in the Betfair Hurdle.

Modus
8 ch g Motivator - Alessandra (Generous)

Paul Nicholls　　　　　　　　John P McManus

PLACINGS: 11300/327165/11F185-　　RPR **156+c**

Starts	1st	2nd	3rd	4th	Win & Pl
23	8	2	3	-	£138,635

	2/18	Kemp	2m4¹/₂f Cls2 Ch gd-sft	£12,512
	11/17	Winc	2m4f Cls1 Nov Gd2 Ch soft	£19,936
	10/17	Bang	2m4¹/₂f Cls4 Nov Ch good	£4,549
145	1/17	Kemp	2m5f Cls1 List 127-153 Hdl Hcap gd-sft	£22,780
	11/15	Newb	2m¹/₂f Cls3 Nov Hdl soft	£6,279
	11/15	Tntn	2m3f Cls3 Nov Hdl good	£5,697
	1/14	Chel	1m6f Cls1 List NHF 4yo soft	£11,888
	10/13	Extr	1m5f Cls6 NHF 3yo gd-sft	£1,560

Talented horse who was second in the 2015 Champion Bumper and won the 2017 Lanzarote Hurdle having come close in other big handicaps over shorter trips; won three of his first four races over fences last season but flopped at Cheltenham and Aintree.

Mohaayed
6 b g Intikhab - Reyaada (Daylami)

Dan Skelton　　　　　　　　Mrs June Watts

PLACINGS: 24173/10231-　　　　　RPR **145+h**

Starts	1st	2nd	3rd	4th	Win & Pl
10	3	2	2	1	£99,068

139	3/18	Chel	2m1f Cls Gd3 133-154 Hdl Hcap soft	£56,950
	5/17	MRas	2m¹/₂f Cls4 Hdl good	£4,874
	2/17	Tntn	2m¹/₂f Cls4 Nov Hdl good	£4,549

Surprise winner of last season's County Hurdle, coping with soft ground much better than connections had expected; maintained fine record in big fields with a novice win, Scottish Champion Hurdle third and County fifth (in 2017) in only runs against 13 or more rivals.

Momella (Ire)
6 ch m Sholokhov - Missing Link (Elusive Quality)

Harry Fry　　　　Holt, Clark, Macnabb, Nugent & Robinson

PLACINGS: 41/11213-　　　　　　RPR **140h**

Starts	1st	2nd	3rd	4th	Win & Pl
5	3	1	1	-	£47,366

134	12/17	Chel	2m4¹/₂f Cls2 118-139 Hdl Hcap soft	£18,768
	10/17	Fknm	2m4f Cls4 Nov Hdl good	£4,431
	5/17	NAbb	2m5¹/₂f Cls3 Nov Hdl good	£7,115

Won three times over hurdles last season and twice placed at Graded level, including when third behind Black Op at Aintree on his final run for Dan Skelton; has since joined Harry Fry and could be one to go novice chasing (has won a point-to-point).

Monalee (Ire)
7 b g Milan - Tempest Belle (Glacial Storm)

Henry de Bromhead (Ir)　　　　　Barry Maloney

PLACINGS: 12/212124/1F12F-　　　RPR **163+c**

Starts	1st	2nd	3rd	4th	Win & Pl
12	4	5	-	1	£162,494

	2/18	Leop	2m5f Nov Gd1 Ch soft	£52,212
	11/17	Punc	2m4f Ch sft-hvy	£7,371
	2/17	Clon	3m Nov Gd3 Hdl heavy	£19,712
	11/16	Punc	2m6f Mdn Hdl soft	£6,331

Won the Flogas Novice Chase last season and may well have won two more Grade 1 races had he stood up, especially at Punchestown (going well when fell two out before late carnage caused by Al Boum Photo); fine second in the RSA Chase behind Presenting Percy.

Monbeg Notorious (Ire)
7 b g Milan - Borleagh Princess (Presenting)

Gordon Elliott (Ir)　　　　　Gigginstown House Stud

PLACINGS: F14/31121/2211182-　　RPR **155+c**

Starts	1st	2nd	3rd	4th	Win & Pl
13	6	4	1	1	£131,456

	2/18	Navn	3m Nov Gd2 Ch sft-hvy	£22,190
137	1/18	Gowr	3m1f 131-159 Ch Hcap heavy	£52,212
	12/17	Punc	3m1¹/₂f Ch sft-hvy	£7,371
	3/17	Navn	2m6¹/₂f Nov Hdl heavy	£9,477
	11/16	DRoy	2m6f Mdn Hdl good	£6,331
	10/16	Tipp	2m4f NHF 5-7yo yld-sft	£4,070

Progressed rapidly over fences last season and defied lack of experience to run away with the Thyestes in just his fourth chase; raised 13lb for that victory but remains capable off that sort of mark judged on subsequent Grade 2 win and Grade 1 second back in novice company.

Mont Des Avaloirs (Fr)

5 b g Blue Bresil - Abu Dhabi (Saint Cyrien)

Paul Nicholls | Mrs Johnny De La Hey

PLACINGS: 2/1F13414-   RPR **140h**

Starts	1st	2nd	3rd	4th	Win & Pl
8	3	1	1	2	£27,517

4/18	MRas	2m¹/₂f Cls4 Nov Hdl soft	£4,660
12/17	Aint	2m1f Cls3 Nov Hdl heavy	£7,507
10/17	Chep	2m Cls4 NHF 4-6yo good	£3,249

Won two novice hurdles last season when making virtually all but paid the price for tearaway tendencies at a higher level; reacted well to far more restrained tactics when a close fourth in the novice handicap final at Sandown in April; could go novice chasing.

Moon Racer (Ire)

9 b g Saffron Walden - Angel's Folly (Wesaam)

David Pipe | Professor Caroline Tisdall & Bryan Drew

PLACINGS: 1/11/211P6/091-   RPR **145+h**

Starts	1st	2nd	3rd	4th	Win & Pl
11	6	1	-	-	£136,505

I39	4/18	Ayr	2m5¹/₂f Cls2 128-154 Hdl Hcap good £12,996
	11/16	Chel	2m¹/₂f Cls1 Nov Gd2 Hdl soft £17,085
	9/16	Prth	2m Cls4 Nov Hdl soft £3,249
	3/15	Chel	2m¹/₂f Cls1 Gd1 NHF 4-6yo good £34,170
	10/14	Chel	2m Cls4 NHF 4-6yo gd-sft £4,549
	4/14	Fair	2m NHF 4-5yo gd-yld £49,167

Blighted by injuries since winning the Champion Bumper at Cheltenham in 2015 but won for the first time in nearly 18 months at Ayr in April, relishing step up in trip; had been unsuited by soft ground in two previous runs; could go novice chasing.

Mount Mews (Ire)

7 b g Presenting - Kneeland Lass (Bob Back)

Donald McCain | Trevor Hemmings

PLACINGS: 1/112112/361230-   RPR **145c**

Starts	1st	2nd	3rd	4th	Win & Pl
13	6	3	2	-	£72,028

1/18	Donc	2m3f Cls4 Nov Ch soft	£4,614
3/17	Kels	2m2f Cls1 Nov Gd2 Hdl heavy	£24,687
1/17	Donc	2m¹/₂f Cls4 Nov Hdl good	£3,899
12/16	Kels	2m Cls4 Nov Hdl gd-sft	£3,249
5/16	Kels	2m Cls5 NHF 4-6yo good	£2,599
4/16	MRas	2m¹/₂f Cls6 Mdn NHF 4-6yo soft	£1,560

Finished second in a Grade 1 novice hurdle two seasons ago but unable to win off his handicap mark last season, gaining only win when finding an easy opportunity on his first run over fences;

also beaten twice in that sphere and reverted to hurdles at the Cheltenham Festival; has since left Ruth Jefferson.

Movewiththetimes (Ire)

7 ch g Presenting - Dare To Venture (Darazari)

Paul Nicholls | John P McManus

PLACINGS: 1/1512/423P-   RPR **147+c**

Starts	1st	2nd	3rd	4th	Win & Pl
9	2	2	1	1	£52,469

12/16	Winc	1m7¹/₂f Cls4 Nov Hdl gd-sft	£3,249
10/16	Font	2m1¹/₂f Cls4 Nov Hdl gd-sft	£5,198
4/16	Winc	1m7¹/₂f Cls6 NHF 4-6yo gd-sft	£1,625

Finished second in the 2017 Betfair Hurdle and showed fair form in defeat in novice chases last season, including a second to Finian's Oscar; laid out for the Plate at Cheltenham but stumbled and pulled up when still in contention; likely to be aimed at more big handicaps.

Mr Adjudicator

4 b g Camacho - Attlongglast (Groom Dancer)

Willie Mullins (Ir) | David Bobbett

PLACINGS: 1122-   RPR **147h**

Starts	1st	2nd	3rd	4th	Win & Pl
4	2	2	-	-	£103,636

2/18	Leop	2m Gd1 Hdl 4yo soft	£52,212
12/17	Leop	2m Mdn Hdl 3yo soft	£7,897

Proved himself one of last season's leading

Facebook.com/racingpost

juvenile hurdlers, winning a Grade 1 at Leopardstown on his second run over hurdles before finishing second in the Triumph Hurdle and another Grade 1 at Punchestown; trainer expects improvement on quicker ground, and looks a surefire candidate to do well in Graded races in Ireland this season.

Mr Antolini (Ire)
8 b g Catcher In The Rye - Victory Run (Old Vic)

Nigel Twiston-Davies				Alan & Sally Coney
PLACINGS: 7532F17/64940631212-				RPR **139+h**

Starts	1st	2nd	3rd	4th	Win & Pl
20	4	4	2	2	£77,964
130	3/18	Sand	2m Cls1 Gd3 126-152 Hdl Hcap soft £42,203
119	1/18	Leic	1m7¹/₂f Cls3 99-124 Hdl Hcap heavy £6,438
	9/16	Gowr	2m Mdn Hdl good £5,426
	3/16	Dpat	2m2f NHF 4-7yo good £4,070

Seemed largely moderate in Ireland but proved much better in just four runs for Nigel Twiston-Davies last season, most notably when winning the Imperial Cup; went close off 6lb higher in the Sussex Champion Hurdle despite apparent preference for right-handed tracks.

Mr Big Shot (Ire)
7 br g Flemensfirth - Une Etoile (Un Desperado)

David Pipe				Prof Caroline Tisdall
PLACINGS: 1/11/01-				RPR **150+h**

Starts	1st	2nd	3rd	4th	Win & Pl
5	4				£53,249
138	4/18	Aint	3m¹/₂f Cls1 Gd3 134-145 Hdl Hcap soft £42,203
	4/17	Carl	2m1f Cls4 Nov Hdl gd-sft £3,899
	1/17	Weth	2m Cls4 Nov Hdl soft £3,249
	3/16	Uttx	2m Cls4 NHF 4-6yo soft £3,899

Has been hard to train but has won four out of five under rules; suffered only defeat when returning from a long absence in the Martin Pipe at Cheltenham and took a big step forward from that run when winning at Aintree next time; likely to go novice chasing.

Mr Whipped (Ire)
5 br g Beneficial - Dyrick Daybreak (Ali-Royal)

Nicky Henderson				Grech & Parkin
PLACINGS: 1/1112P-				RPR **148h**

Starts	1st	2nd	3rd	4th	Win & Pl
5	3	1	-	-	£32,122
	1/18	Wwck	2m5f Cls1 Nov Gd2 Hdl soft £19,933
	12/17	Newb	2m4¹/₂f Cls4 Nov Hdl 4-6yo good £4,549
	11/17	Kemp	2m Cls4 Nov Hdl gd-sft...............£3,899

Added to win in sole point-to-point by landing first three novice hurdles last season, most notably in a Grade 2 at Warwick, before a fair second when stepped up to 3m at Musselburgh; described as a big baby by connections and found Cheltenham too much next time.

Ms Parfois (Ire)
7 ch m Mahler - Dolly Lewis (Sir Harry Lewis)

Anthony Honeyball				MR Chapman
PLACINGS: 11/743131/3111222-				RPR **151c**

Starts	1st	2nd	3rd	4th	Win & Pl
14	6	3	3	1	£108,185
	1/18	Wwck	3m Cls1 Nov List Ch soft...............£14,238
	12/17	Newb	2m7¹/₂f Cls1 Nov List Ch soft...............£14,238
123	12/17	Chel	2m5f Cls3 99-126 Ch Hcap soft £7,798
	3/17	Font	2m5¹/₂f Cls4 Nov Hdl gd-sft...............£3,899
	1/17	Wwck	2m5f Nov Hdl soft...............£4,549
	4/16	Uttx	2m Cls5 NHF 4-6yo heavy £2,599

Tough and consistent mare who went from strength to strength over fences last season, winning three in a row before finishing second three times at a higher level; proved her stamina for extreme trips when beaten just half a length in the National Hunt Chase at Cheltenham.

Mulcahys Hill (Ire)
6 b g Brian Boru - Belsalsa (Kingsalsa)

Warren Greatrex				McNeill Family & Prodec Networks
PLACINGS: 1/27/1124P-				RPR **147h**

Starts	1st	2nd	3rd	4th	Win & Pl
7	2	2	-	1	£17,431
	11/17	Ffos	2m4f Cls4 Mdn Hdl soft...............£3,899
	5/17	Strf	2m¹/₂f Cls5 NHF 4-6yo gd-sft £2,599

Went close to winning last season's Challow Hurdle at Newbury (pushed into a clear lead a long way out and nearly hung on) but failed to come close to that form otherwise, including when pulled up in the Albert Bartlett at Cheltenham; likely to go novice chasing.

Native River (Ire)
8 ch g Indian River - Native Mo (Be My Native)

Colin Tizzard				Brocade Racing
PLACINGS: 19/3113321/21113/11-				RPR **178c**

Starts	1st	2nd	3rd	4th	Win & Pl
21	11	2	5	-	£844,421
	3/18	Chel	3m2¹/₂f Cls1 Gd1 Ch soft...............£369,822
	2/18	Newb	2m7¹/₂f Cls1 Gd2 Ch soft...............£28,475
	2/17	Newb	2m7¹/₂f Cls1 Gd2 Ch soft...............£28,475
155	12/16	Chep	3m5¹/₂f Cls1 Gd3 139-155 Ch Hcap soft...............£85,425
155	11/16	Newb	3m2f Cls1 Gd3 140-166 Ch Hcap gd-sft...............£113,900
	4/16	Aint	3m1f Cls1 Nov Gd1 Ch gd-sft...............£56,319
	11/15	Newb	2m7¹/₂f Cls1 Nov Gd2 Ch gd-sft...............£20,284
	11/15	Extr	3m Cls2 Nov Ch soft...............£12,974
	2/15	Extr	2m1f Cls1 Nov List Hdl gd-sft...............£11,390
	11/14	Newc	2m6f Cls2 Nov Hdl soft...............£11,261
	10/14	Strf	2m6f Cls5 Mdn Hdl good...............£2,599

Superb staying chaser who seemed to benefit from a quieter campaign last season, triumphing on the biggest stage as a gutsy winner of the Cheltenham Gold Cup when outstaying Might Bite with a great front-running performance; had finished third in the race in 2017 after winning the Hennessy Gold Cup and Welsh National that season; set to start off in the Betfair Chase at Haydock before heading to Kempton for the

King George and back to Cheltenham in a bid to retain his crown and have a crack at the £1 million bonus for winning all three races.

Next Destination (Ire)

6 b g Dubai Destination - Liss Alainn (Flemensfirth)

Willie Mullins (Ir)   Malcolm C Denmark

PLACINGS: **1/142/11131-**   RPR **152+h**

Starts	1st	2nd	3rd	4th	Win & Pl
8	5	1	1	1	£151,778
4/18	Punc	3m Nov Gd1 Hdl yield.....................			£52,212
1/18	Naas	2m4f Nov Gd1 Hdl sft-hvy...............			£46,991
12/17	Navn	2m4f Nov Gd2 Hdl heavy................			£21,432
11/17	Naas	2m3f Mdn Hdl sft-hvy....................			£6,844
1/17	Fair	2m NHF 5-7yo soft......................			£4,070

Won four out of five in novice hurdles last season, including two Grade 1 races; looked short of pace when a fast-finishing third in the Ballymore at Cheltenham and duly relished the step up to 3m when winning at Punchestown next time; likely to go novice chasing.

No Comment

7 br g Kayf Tara - Dizzy Frizzy (Loup Sauvage)

Philip Hobbs   John P McManus

PLACINGS: **22/1U2111722/36-**   RPR **137+c**

Starts	1st	2nd	3rd	4th	Win & Pl
13	4	5	1	-	£54,086
1/17	Plum	2m4¹/₂f Cls3 Nov Hdl 4-7yo soft......			£6,498
12/16	Plum	2m4¹/₂f Cls4 Nov Hdl gd-sft...........			£3,249
11/16	MRas	2m2¹/₂f Cls4 Nov Hdl gd-sft...........			£3,249
4/16	Punc	2m2f NHF 5-7yo yield...................			£5,426

Progressive over hurdles two seasons ago but missed much of last term; highly tried in two

runs late in the campaign when pitched straight into Grade 1 company to finish third in the Scilly Isles and then coming sixth in the National Hunt Chase (looked a non-stayer).

Noble Endeavor (Ire)

9 b g Flemensfirth - Old Moon (Old Vic)

Gordon Elliott (Ir)   C Jones

PLACINGS: **/22125/2312F/P54136/**   RPR **160c**

Starts	1st	2nd	3rd	4th	Win & Pl
21	5	5	2	2	£147,991
143	12/16	Leop	3m¹/₂f 123-150 Ch Hcap yield.......		£76,838
	12/15	DRoy	2m4f Ch heavy.......................		£7,488
	1/15	Punc	2m4f Hdl soft.......................		£6,953
	2/14	Punc	2m4f Mdn Hdl heavy..................		£6,325
	12/13	Leop	2m NHF 4yo soft.....................		£5,049

Landed a big gamble when winning the Paddy Power Chase at Leopardstown at the end of 2016 and ran well in other big staying handicaps that season, finishing third in the Ultima and fourth in the Troytown; missed last season through injury.

Now McGinty (Ire)

7 b g Stowaway - Western Whisper (Supreme Leader)

Stuart Edmunds   The Garratt Family

PLACINGS: **64/45343/33P00112-**   RPR **144h**

Starts	1st	2nd	3rd	4th	Win & Pl
15	2	1	4	3	£27,949
120	3/18	Wwck	2m5f Cls4 97-120 Hdl Hcap soft.....		£4,419
110	3/18	Wwck	2m5f Cls4 94-117 Hdl Hcap heavy....		£4,549

Initially looked moderate when sent hurdling last season but made astonishing strides in the spring, rising 33lb in the handicap in just three runs;

nearly completed a hat-trick when taking a sharp rise in class at Aintree; likely to go novice chasing.

Nube Negra (Spa)
4 br g Dink - Manly Dream (Highest Honor)

Dan Skelton				T Spraggett

PLACINGS: 12135-				RPR **135h**

Starts	1st	2nd	3rd	4th	Win & Pl
5	2	1	1	-	£22,909
	1/18	Donc	2m¹/₂f Cls4 Nov Hdl soft		£4,094
	11/17	MRas	2m¹/₂f Cls4 Hdl 3yo gd-sft		£3,899

Beaten only by Apple's Shakira in first three runs over hurdles last season and made a bold bid to justify favouritism in the Fred Winter at Cheltenham, finishing third having travelled strongly into the lead two out; well beaten when stepped up to Grade 1 level at Aintree.

O O Seven (Ire)
8 b g Flemensfirth - Kestral Heights (Eagle Eyed)

Nicky Henderson				Christopher Hanbury

PLACINGS: 11218/213154/3450P3-				RPR **156c**

Starts	1st	2nd	3rd	4th	Win & Pl
20	6	3	3	2	£103,256
148	1/17	Hntg	2m4f Cls3 Nov 129-148 Ch Hcap gd-sft		£6,498
	11/16	Chel	2m4¹/₂f Cls2 Nov Ch good		£15,698
	2/16	Muss	3m Cls2 Hdl soft		£14,389
	12/15	Sand	2m Cls3 Nov Hdl soft		£6,498
	11/15	Hntg	2m Cls5 Mdn Hdl gd-sft		£2,599
	12/14	Hntg	2m Cls6 NHF 4-6yo gd-sft		£1,560

Unsuccessful since a novice handicap chase at Huntingdon in January 2017 despite often proving popular in the market; has made the frame in good handicaps at Aintree and Ascot

Off You Go (Ire)
5 b g Presenting - Ozzy Oscar (Oscar)

Charles Byrnes (Ir)				John P McManus

PLACINGS: 406311-				RPR **135h**

Starts	1st	2nd	3rd	4th	Win & Pl
6	2	-	1	1	£60,129
123	2/18	Leop	2m 122-147 Hdl Hcap soft		£52,212
107	12/17	Limk	2m4f 98-120 Hdl Hcap heavy		£6,581

since then and easily forgiven poor runs on unsuitably heavy ground last season.

Switched to handicaps after running in three maiden hurdles last season and soon made rapid progress, hacking up by 13 lengths at Limerick and easily defying a 16lb rise to follow up in a far more valuable contest at Leopardstown; may still have more to offer.

Ok Corral (Ire)
8 b g Mahler - Acoola (Flemensfirth)

Nicky Henderson				John P McManus

PLACINGS: 1/2/12125-				RPR **151h**

Starts	1st	2nd	3rd	4th	Win & Pl
7	3	3	-	-	£44,304
	2/18	Kemp	2m5f Cls4 Nov Hdl soft		£4,094
	5/17	Kemp	2m Cls4 Nov Hdl good		£3,249
	2/15	Kemp	2m Cls5 Mdn NHF 4-6yo soft		£2,274

Off the track for more than two years but soon made up for lost time last season, winning two novice hurdles before a second in the Albert Bartlett at Cheltenham on his first attempt at 3m; regarded as an old-fashioned chasing type.

Ok Corral (4): could develop into a useful novice chaser

Old Guard

7 b g Notnowcato - Dolma (Marchand De Sable)

Paul Nicholls   The Brooks, Stewart Families & J Kyle

PLACINGS: P14347747/713154174-   RPR **157**h

Starts	1st	2nd	3rd	4th	Win & Pl
27	8	1	3	6	£303,148

	2/18	Font	2m3f Cls1 Gd2 Hdl gd-sft		£45,560
149	12/17	Newb	2m4¹/₂f Cls2 123-149 Hdl Hcap gd-sft		£25,992
	10/17	Kemp	2m Cls5 List Hdl good		£17,165
	10/16	Extr	2m1¹/₂f Cls4 Ch good		£6,498
	12/15	Chel	2m1f Cls1 Gd2 Hdl soft		£74,035
145	11/15	Chel	2m¹/₂f Cls1 Gd3 128-154 Hdl Hcap gd-sft		£56,950
137	10/15	Chel	2m¹/₂f Cls3 116-139 Cond Hdl Hcap good		£6,256
	11/14	Newb	2m¹/₂f Cls3 Hdl 3yo soft		£6,498

Had largely struggled since winning a couple of big 2m hurdles at Cheltenham in 2015 but was superbly placed to win three times last season, most notably in the Grade 2 National Spirit Hurdle at Fontwell; hasn't run over fences since unconvincing novice win in 2016, and his trainer might well try that route again and is also keen to exploit options on the Flat.

On The Blind Side (Ire)

6 b g Stowaway - Such A Set Up (Supreme Leader)

Nicky Henderson   AD Spence

PLACINGS: 1/1116-   RPR **152**+h

Starts	1st	2nd	3rd	4th	Win & Pl
4	3	-	-	-	£40,586

	12/17	Sand	2m4f Cls1 Nov Gd2 Hdl gd-sft		£17,085
	11/17	Chel	2m5f Cls1 Nov Gd2 Hdl soft		£17,165
	10/17	Aint	2m4f Cls4 Mdn Hdl gd-sft		£5,005

Looked a top-class prospect in novice hurdles early last season, winning a really strong Grade 2 at Cheltenham and defying a penalty at the same level at Sandown; missed the Cheltenham Festival after a setback and disappointed at Aintree; likely to go novice chasing and it's not hard to imagine him doing well in that sphere.

One For Arthur (Ire)

9 b g Milan - Nonnetia (Trempolino)

Lucinda Russell   Two Golf Widows

PLACINGS: 33111P/1335243/1511/   RPR **160**c

Starts	1st	2nd	3rd	4th	Win & Pl
19	7	3	5	1	£638,938

148	4/17	Aint	4m2¹/₂f Cls1 Gd3 143-161 Ch Hcap gd-sft		£561,300
137	1/17	Wwck	3m5f Cls1 Gd3 129-152 Ch Hcap soft		£34,170
127	10/16	Kels	3m2f Cls3 109-135 Ch Hcap gd-sft		£11,047
	10/15	Kels	2m7¹/₂f Cls4 Nov Ch good		£4,549
	3/15	Ayr	3m¹/₂f Cls4 Nov Ch soft		£3,899
120	2/15	Ayr	3m¹/₂f Cls4 Nov 94-120 Hdl Hcap soft		£3,574
	1/15	Hayd	2m3f Cls4 Nov Hdl 4-7yo heavy		£3,899

Brilliant winner of the Grand National in 2017, doing remarkably well to make up a huge amount of ground in the final mile when the leaders weren't stopping; was progressing sharply but missed last season through injury; making progress on the sidelines and will surely be aimed at an Aintree repeat.

Out Of The Loop

5 b g Shantou - Sparron Hawk (Hawker's News)

Padraig Roche (Ir)   John P McManus

PLACINGS: 5/31511-   RPR **143**+h

Starts	1st	2nd	3rd	4th	Win & Pl
6	3	1	-	-	£30,762

127	2/18	Fair	2m4f 109-135 Hdl Hcap soft		£13,606
118	12/17	Fair	2m4f 105-125 Hdl Hcap soft		£9,477
	10/17	Dpat	2m3f Mdn Hdl yield		£5,791

Moved into handicap company straight after landing maiden hurdle and won twice more, most notably in a competitive contest at Leopardstown; form looks strong with well-beaten runner-up finishing fourth in the Martin Pipe at Cheltenham off 9lb higher.

Outlander (Ire)

10 b g Stowaway - Western Whisper (Supreme Leader)

Gordon Elliott (Ir)   Gigginstown House Stud

PLACINGS: F2/22F210P/61332PP8-   RPR **168**c

Starts	1st	2nd	3rd	4th	Win & Pl
30	10	7	3	-	£377,497

	11/17	DRoy	3m Gd1 Ch soft		£70,598
	12/16	Leop	3m Gd1 Ch yield		£65,074
	2/16	Leop	2m5¹/₂f Nov Gd1 Ch sft-hvy		£36,875
	12/15	Limk	2m3¹/₂f Nov Gd2 Ch heavy		£21,163
	11/15	Punc	2m4f Ch soft		£6,953
	1/15	Leop	2m4f Nov Gd2 Hdl yield		£19,903
	11/14	Fair	2m Mdn Hdl sft-hvy		£4,600
	2/13	Naas	2m NHF 4-7yo sft-hvy		£7,573
	12/12	Leop	2m NHF 4-7yo soft		£6,325
	11/12	Fair	2m NHF 4yo soft		£4,888

Has won Grade 1 staying chases in Ireland in each of the last two seasons, just beating Road To Respect at Down Royal last November; has also suffered physical problems (operated on for a back problem before that win) and his form again tailed off last spring; could do well over a distance in the early part of the season in Ireland.

Ozzie The Oscar (Ire)

7 b g Oscar - Private Official (Beneficial)

Philip Hobbs   Bradley Partnership

PLACINGS: 3111/21P430/51321-1   RPR **157**+c

Starts	1st	2nd	3rd	4th	Win & Pl
16	7	2	3	1	£81,812

148	5/18	Wwck	2m Cls2 132-158 Ch Hcap good		£18,768
142	4/18	Wwck	2m Cls2 Nov 121-145 Ch Hcap gd-sft		£15,640
	11/17	Wwck	2m Cls3 Nov Ch gd-sft		£9,445
	10/16	Weth	2m Cls3 Nov Hdl good		£5,523
	4/16	Ludl	2m Cls4 Nov Hdl gd-sft		£3,899
	4/16	Newb	2m¹/₂f Cls4 Nov Hdl good		£4,549
	3/16	Tntn	2m¹/₂f Cls4 Mdn Hdl soft		£3,249

Missed much of last term due to preference for good ground (had twice disappointed on soft after winning debut over fences) but returned to win well in the final week of the season and followed up the following month, both over 2m at Warwick; lightly raced and open to further progress.

Pacific De Baune (Fr)
5 gr g Al Namix - Perle De Baune (En Calcat)

Nicky Henderson Mr & Mrs Sandy Orr

PLACINGS: 2/1712- RPR **145+h**

Starts	1st	2nd	3rd	4th	Win & Pl
4	2	1	-		£10,692
3/18	Newb	2m¹/₂f Cls4 Nov Hdl soft			£4,809
12/17	Newb	2m¹/₂f Cls4 Mdn Hdl soft			£4,549

Long-term chasing prospect who won twice in novice hurdles last season; beaten at odds-on on final run but faced tough task conceding 12lb to a useful rival; had been found out by a step up in class and trip on bad ground when only seventh in a Grade 2 at Cheltenham.

Pairofbrowneyes (Ire)
9 b g Luso - Frankly Native (Be My Native)

Willie Mullins (Ir) Fibbage Syndicate

PLACINGS: 311/3352232206/801F- RPR **148+c**

Starts	1st	2nd	3rd	4th	Win & Pl
27	5	4	6	2	£163,188
137	3/18	Gowr	2m7f 120-140 Ch Hcap heavy		£52,212
122	12/15	Limk	2m3¹/₂f 112-140 Ch Hcap heavy		£23,256
116	11/15	Cork	2m1f 103-131 Ch Hcap heavy		£12,093
114	11/14	Punc	2m 114-125 Hdl Hcap soft		£12,188
	1/14	Fair	2m4f Mdn Hdl sft-hvy		£4,600

Placed in several good handicaps for Barry John Murphy and looked to have improved again on first run for Willie Mullins last spring, winning comfortably at Gowran; sent off favourite for the Irish Grand National next time but fell at the fifth.

Paisley Park (Ire)
6 b g Oscar - Presenting Shares (Presenting)

Emma Lavelle Andrew Gemmell

PLACINGS: 2/1220- RPR **145+h**

Starts	1st	2nd	3rd	4th	Win & Pl
5	1	3	-	-	£13,821
12/17	Hrfd	2m3¹/₂f Cls4 Nov Hdl soft			£4,549

Highly promising young stayer who made a successful hurdling debut last season and was unlucky not to add to that, finishing a length second to Mr Whipped in a Grade 2 and narrowly failing to concede 7lb to a useful rival next time; well beaten in the Albert Bartlett.

Pallasator
9 b g Motivator - Ela Athena (Ezzoud)

Gordon Elliott (Ir) Qatar Racing Limited

PLACINGS: 54115- RPR **151+h**

Starts	1st	2nd	3rd	4th	Win & Pl
5	2	-	-	1	£35,884
4/18	Fair	2m4f Nov Gd2 Hdl sft-hvy			£26,106
3/18	Leop	2m4f Mdn Hdl soft			£7,359

Temperamental but high-class stayer on the Flat,

winning up to Group 2 level; typically mixed record when sent over hurdles last season but showed he could translate his ability when winning a Grade 2 at Fairyhouse over Easter.

Paloma Blue (Ire)
6 br g Stowaway - Court Leader (Supreme Leader)

Henry de Bromhead (Ir) C Jones

PLACINGS: 12/321340- RPR **150+h**

Starts	1st	2nd	3rd	4th	Win & Pl
8	2	2	2	1	£46,101
12/17	Leop	2m Mdn Hdl yield			£7,371
1/17	Fair	2m NHF 5-7yo soft			£4,731

Largely disappointing over hurdles last season, including when beaten at 4-11 in a maiden hurdle, but clearly talented on his day; had been second in a Grade 1 bumper in 2017 and finally reproduced that form when fourth in the Supreme at Cheltenham.

Penhill
7 b g Mount Nelson - Serrenia (High Chaparral)

Willie Mullins (Ir) Tony Bloom

PLACINGS: 161114112/12- RPR **162+h**

Starts	1st	2nd	3rd	4th	Win & Pl
11	7	2	-	1	£388,650
3/18	Chel	3m Cls1 Gd1 Hdl soft			£192,707
3/17	Chel	3m Cls1 Nov Gd1 Hdl good			£71,188
12/16	Limk	3m Nov Gd2 Hdl sft-hvy			£19,305
10/16	Tipp	2m Nov Gd3 Hdl soft			£14,697
9/16	List	2m Nov Hdl yield			£9,949
7/16	Gway	2m¹/₂f Nov Hdl gd-yld			£11,305
5/16	Tram	2m Mdn Hdl good			£4,522

Did remarkably well to win last season's Stayers' Hurdle after a long injury layoff, showing a terrific turn of foot in a slowly run race; loves Cheltenham having also won the Albert Bartlett in 2017 but has twice failed to follow up at Punchestown (well beaten by Faugheen last time).

Petit Mouchoir (Fr)
7 gr g Al Namix - Arnette (Denham Red)

Henry de Bromhead (Ir) Gigginstown House Stud

PLACINGS: 113482/23F113/12324- RPR **161c**

Starts	1st	2nd	3rd	4th	Win & Pl
17	5	4	4	2	£302,848
10/17	Punc	2m Ch yld-sft			£7,634
1/17	Leop	2m Gd1 Hdl yield			£55,470
12/16	Leop	2m Gd1 Hdl yield			£43,382
11/15	Thur	2m Mdn Hdl 4yo soft			£5,349
4/15	Punc	2m NHF 4-5yo gd-yld			£45,736

Dual Grade 1 winner over hurdles but didn't quite hit the heights expected when sent novice chasing last season, albeit having suffered an early-season setback and then come up against Footpad; let down by headstrong tendencies when beaten at odds-on at Aintree.

Pingshou (Ire)

8 b g Definite Article - Quest Of Passion (Saumarez)

Colin Tizzard   Ann & Alan Potts Limited

PLACINGS: 8/414013/   RPR **149h**

Starts	1st	2nd	3rd	4th	Win & Pl
7	2	-	1	2	£73,162
4/17	Aint	2m¹/₂f Cls1 Nov Gd1 Hdl good			£56,130
12/16	Chel	2m1f Cls3 Nov Hdl good			£7,798

Surprise 16-1 winner of a Grade 1 novice hurdle at Aintree in 2017 having flopped in the Supreme and backed that up with another solid effort at Punchestown; had looked a non-stayer on only run over 2m4f; missed last season through injury.

Pleasant Company (Ire)

10 b g Presenting - Katie Flame (Alderbrook)

Willie Mullins (Ir)   Malcolm C Denmark

PLACINGS: 4/43/3413P/1419/0P2-   RPR **158c**

Starts	1st	2nd	3rd	4th	Win & Pl
17	4	1	4	4	£276,807
	2/17	Fair	3m1f Gd3 Ch heavy		£22,692
139	4/16	Punc	3m1f 120-145 Ch Hcap yield		£26,029
	12/15	Punc	3m1f Ch heavy		£6,953
	11/13	Asct	1m7¹/₂f Cls4 NHF 4-6yo gd-sft		£3,128

Laid out for a second crack at the Grand National last season (had gone well until a bad mistake six out in 2017) and very nearly got up for a stunning win when beaten a head by Tiger Roll; lightly raced otherwise, running just six times in the last two seasons.

Poetic Rhythm (Ire)

7 ch g Flemensfirth - Sommer Sonnet (Taipan)

Fergal O'Brien   The Yes No Wait Sorries

PLACINGS: 333U1/5115330/13107-   RPR **152h**

Starts	1st	2nd	3rd	4th	Win & Pl
12	4	-	3	-	£66,330
12/17	Newb	2m4¹/₂f Cls1 Nov Gd1 Hdl heavy			£22,887
10/17	Chep	2m3¹/₂f Cls1 Nov Gd2 Hdl good			£19,933
11/16	Chel	2m¹/₂f Cls1 List NHF 4-6yo soft			£11,390
10/16	Chep	2m Cls4 NHF 4-6yo good			£3,249

Made the most of his status as a second-season novice hurdler when winning good races in the first half of last season, most notably a weak running of the Grade 1 Challow Hurdle; flattered

ON THE FIGURES

PRESENTING PERCY The 2017 Pertemps Hurdle winner made it back-to-back Cheltenham Festival wins when bolting up in the RSA Chase in March and looks the most likely of last season's staying novices to make the step up to genuine Gold Cup contender. [Steve Mason, Racing Post Ratings]

by that win on balance of other form, twice flopping at Cheltenham in the spring.

Politologue (Fr)

7 gr g Poliglote - Scarlet Row (Turgeon)

Paul Nicholls   J Hales

PLACINGS: 1U210/11214F/111241-   RPR **173+c**

Starts	1st	2nd	3rd	4th	Win & Pl
18	9	4	-	2	£454,456
	4/18	Aint	2m4f Cls1 Gd1 Ch soft		£140,985
	12/17	Kemp	2m Cls1 Gd2 Ch soft		£52,854
	12/17	Sand	1m7¹/₂f Cls1 Gd1 Ch gd-sft		£85,827
154	11/17	Extr	2m1f Cls1 Gd2 142-162 Ch Hcap soft		£37,192
	2/17	Kemp	2m4¹/₂f Cls2 Ch gd-sft		£12,512
	12/16	Asct	2m5f Cls1 Nov Gd2 Ch gd-sft		£18,224
	11/16	Hayd	2m5¹/₂f Cls2 Nov Ch soft		£16,245
	2/16	Extr	2m1f Cls1 Nov List Hdl heavy		£11,524
	6/15	Autl	2m2f Hdl 4yo soft		£17,860

Took advantage of Altior's absence to dominate the first half of last season over 2m, with victory in the Tingle Creek the best of three wins; twice beaten subsequently but may not be a Cheltenham horse and bounced back at Aintree with fine Melling Chase win over Min.

Portrush Ted (Ire)

6 b g Shantou - Village Queen (King's Theatre)

Warren Greatrex   McNeill Family

PLACINGS: 1/2P21-1   RPR **133+b**

Starts	1st	2nd	3rd	4th	Win & Pl
6	3	2	-	-	£35,100
8/18	Prth	3m Cls4 Nov Hdl good			£4,431
4/18	Aint	2m1f Cls1 Gd2 NHF 4-6yo soft			£25,322
3/17	Uttx	2m Cls4 NHF 4-6yo soft			£3,249

Reportedly very fragile and took a long time to build on debut bumper win (even pulled up at Ascot last season) but proved himself a big talent when winning a Grade 2 at Aintree in April; stayed on well that day and has already won over 3m on hurdling debut.

Presenting Percy

7 b g Sir Percy - Hunca Munca (Presenting)

Pat Kelly (Ir)   Philip J Reynolds

PLACINGS: 21/741154116/131121-   RPR **170+c**

Starts	1st	2nd	3rd	4th	Win & Pl
17	9	2	1	2	£258,466
	3/18	Chel	3m1¹/₂f Cls1 Nov Gd1 Ch soft		£100,132
	1/18	Gowr	3m Gd2 Hdl heavy		£23,496
145	12/17	Fair	3m5f 117-145 Ch Hcap soft		£25,214
	10/17	Gway	2m6¹/₂f Ch heavy		£10,003
146	3/17	Chel	3m Cls1 List 137-147 Hdl Hcap good		£54,103
130	2/17	Fair	2m4f 108-138 Hdl Hcap heavy		£13,667
115	11/16	Punc	2m Nov 90-121 Hdl Hcap soft		£7,235
	10/16	Gway	2m Mdn Hdl 4-5yo yield		£5,879
	4/16	Baln	2m1f NHF 4-7yo soft		£4,296

Hugely exciting staying chaser who easily won last season's RSA Chase to claim a second Festival victory; thorough stayer who had previously won a big handicap over 3m5f at Fairyhouse but also showed smart form in defeat over 2m4f.

facebook.com/racingpost

follow us:

STRATFORD-ON-AVON RACECOURSE

2019 **FIXTURE LIST**

Monday, March 11th	Sunday, July 14th
Saturday March 30th	Sunday, July 21st
Sunday, April 14th	Thursday, August 1st
Sunday, May 19th	Thursday, August 22nd
Friday Evening, May 31st	Saturday, September 7th
Saturday Evening, June 1st	Monday, October 7th
Monday, June 10th	Saturday, October 19th
Tuesday, June 18th	Thursday, October 31st
Tuesday Evening, July 2nd	Monday, November 11th

Tel: 01789 267949 · Email: info@stratfordracecourse.net

www.stratfordracecourse.net

Rather Be (Ire)
7 b g Oscar - Irish Wedding (Bob Back)

Nicky Henderson				Matt & Lauren Morgan

PLACINGS: U129/112U18/1U12-   RPR **153c**

Starts	1st	2nd	3rd	4th	Win & Pl
14	3	-	-		£81,612

	2/18	Fknm	2m¹/₂f Cls3 Nov Ch soft	£7,408
	12/17	Towc	2m Cls3 Nov Ch gd-sft	£6,330
136	4/17	Aint	2m4f Cls1 Gd3 130-146 Hdl Hcap good	£39,389
	12/16	Hntg	2m3¹/₂f Cls4 Nov Hdl gd-sft	£3,249
	10/16	Hrfd	2m Cls4 Nov Hdl 4-6yo good	£3,899
	12/15	Ludl	1m6f Cls4 NHF 4-5yo soft	£3,899

Given a quiet campaign in low-grade novice chases last season until producing a massive run when a head second in the novice handicap at the Cheltenham Festival; confirmed liking for big-field handicaps having won a 22-runner hurdle race at Aintree in 2017.

Rathvinden (Ire)
10 b g Heron Island - Peggy Cullen (Presenting)

Willie Mullins (Ir)				RA Bartlett

PLACINGS: 11F23/P/2113112BU14-   RPR **159c**

Starts	1st	2nd	3rd	4th	Win & Pl
18	8	3	2	1	£189,774

	3/18	Chel	4m Cls1 Nov Gd2 Am Ch soft	£74,950
	10/17	Tipp	2m4f Nov Gd3 Ch heavy	£17,083
	9/17	List	2m4f Nov Ch heavy	£11,038
	8/17	Gway	2m2f Nov Gd3 Ch yield	£25,214
	7/17	Wxfd	3m1f Ch good	£6,581
	12/13	Cork	2m NHF 4-7yo sft-hvy	£5,610
	11/13	Cork	2m NHF 4-7yo soft	£5,610
	6/13	Dpat	2m2f NHF 4-7yo gd-fm	£3,927

Ran just once in three years after finishing third to Faugheen in the Neptune in 2014 but made up for lost time last season when stepped up to a marathon trip, beating Ms Parfois in the National Hunt Chase.

Red River (Ire)
5 ch g Beneficial - Socker Toppen (Great Palm)

Kim Bailey				The Red River Syndicate

PLACINGS: 2/131-   RPR **148+h**

Starts	1st	2nd	3rd	4th	Win & Pl
3	2	-	1	-	£19,667

	2/18	Muss	3m Cls2 Nov Hdl soft	£12,558
	10/17	Winc	2m5¹/₂f Cls4 Nov Hdl good	£3,899

Won two out of three in novice hurdles and found to require a wind operation after sole defeat at Sandown (stopped quickly after travelling well); bounced back after surgery when claiming a notable scalp in Mr Whipped at Musselburgh; likely to go novice chasing.

Redicean
4 b g Medicean - Red Halo (Galileo)

Alan King				Mrs David Thompson

PLACINGS: 1116-   RPR **141+h**

Starts	1st	2nd	3rd	4th	Win & Pl
4	3	-	-	-	£35,430

	2/18	Kemp	2m Cls1 Gd2 Hdl 4yo good	£17,085
	1/18	Kemp	2m Cls4 Hdl 4yo soft	£4,159
	12/17	Kemp	2m Cls2 Hdl 3yo soft	£12,512

Easy winner of first three runs over hurdles last season, all at Kempton, taking a big leap forward with seven-length victory in the Adonis Hurdle; well-beaten sixth in the Triumph when trainer blamed the ground (won twice on soft but Adonis win came on good).

Regal Encore (Ire)
10 b g King's Theatre - Go On Eileen (Bob Back)

Anthony Honeyball				John P McManus

PLACINGS: 3F1PPP/2PP1P8/03P1P-   RPR **156+c**

Starts	1st	2nd	3rd	4th	Win & Pl
30	6	4	2	3	£186,590

150	2/18	Asct	3m Cls1 List 135-152 Ch Hcap soft	£42,713
144	12/16	Asct	3m Cls1 List 134-155 Ch Hcap gd-sft	£56,950
	12/15	Plum	2m1f Cls3 Nov Ch soft	£6,498
129	2/15	Extr	2m7f Cls2 127-153 Hdl Hcap gd-sft	£12,512
	11/13	Plum	2m Cls4 Nov Hdl gd-sft	£3,249
	10/12	Chep	2m Cls6 NHF 4-6yo gd-sft	£1,754
	2/12	Sthl	2m Cls5 NHF 4-6yo std-slw	£1,437

Prone to running a stinker (pulled up in eight races out of 14 since the start of 2016) but has also won Listed handicap chases at Ascot in each of the last two seasons; eyecatching eighth in the 2017 Grand National but missed last season's race after a late setback.

Regal Flow
11 b g Erhaab - Flow (Over The River)

Bob Buckler				Mrs CJ Dunn

PLACINGS: 1552/794U12/3912110-   RPR **149+c**

Starts	1st	2nd	3rd	4th	Win & Pl
36	7	6	4	2	£137,295

135	3/18	Uttx	4m2f Cls1 List 121-144 Ch Hcap heavy	£70,338
129	3/18	Tntn	3m4¹/₂f Cls3 124-136 Ch Hcap heavy	£9,357
123	12/17	Winc	3m1f Cls3 99-125 Ch Hcap heavy	£12,777
115	3/17	Wwck	3m Cls3 115-130 Ch Hcap soft	£7,798
118	10/15	Chel	3m1f Cls3 99-125 Am Ch Hcap good	£7,195
103	1/15	Plum	2m3¹/₂f Cls4 Nov 100-118 Ch Hcap heavy	£3,899
100	10/14	Tntn	3m Cls5 85-100 Hdl Hcap firm	£2,738

Getting on in years but showed astonishing improvement last season (just his second since moving to Bob Buckler); won three handicap chases, the last two on his first runs beyond

200 EXPERTS IN YOUR HAND

RACING POST
WHEN YOU BET ON RACING, YOU CAN BET ON RACING POST.
Available on the App Store   Available at racingpost.com/android

 facebook.com/racingpost

3m1f, including the Midlands National at Uttoxeter; most effective on heavy ground.

Relegate (Ire)

5 b m Flemensfirth - Last Of The Bunch (Silver Patriarch)

Willie Mullins (Ir)					Paul McKeon
PLACINGS: 1117-				RPR **135+b**	

Starts	1st	2nd	3rd	4th	Win & Pl
4	3	-	-	-	£88,421

	3/18	Chel	2m½f Cls1 Gd1 NHF 4-6yo soft	£42,713
	2/18	Leop	2m Gd2 NHF 4-7yo soft	£39,159
	1/18	Punc	2m NHF 5-7yo sft-hvy	£6,550

Remarkable winner of last season's Champion Bumper at Cheltenham, completing a hat-trick by storming through in the straight having struggled to go the pace in rear; looks a strong stayer on that evidence; only seventh when attempting to follow up at Punchestown.

Rene's Girl (Ire)

8 b m Presenting - Brogella (King's Theatre)

Dan Skelton					Andy & Sharon Measham
PLACINGS: 4/31127/P21/2F13112-				RPR **149c**	

Starts	1st	2nd	3rd	4th	Win & Pl
17	6	4	2	1	£113,524

	2/18	Hntg	2m4f Cls1 List Ch soft	£43,466
	1/18	Donc	2m4½f Cls1 List Ch soft	£17,085
	10/17	Worc	2m4f Cls4 Nov Ch good	£4,431
123	4/17	Ludl	3m Cls3 119-125 Hdl Hcap good	£9,495
	12/15	Ludl	2m5f Cls4 Nov Hdl soft	£5,848
	11/15	Wwck	2m5f Cls6 NHF gd-sft	£3,249

Massive improver when sent over fences last season, hacking up at 20-1 on her chase debut

and winning twice more, both times in Listed mares' chases; fine second against the boys in a 2m4f Grade 1 at Aintree on her final outing when run down late by Finian's Oscar.

Rhinestone (Ire)

5 b g Montjeu - Apticanti (Aptitude)

Joseph O'Brien (Ir)					John P McManus
PLACINGS: 2129-				RPR **140+b**	

Starts	1st	2nd	3rd	4th	Win & Pl
4	1	2	-	-	£19,934

	12/17	Thur	2m NHF 4-7yo heavy	£5,528

Won just one of his four bumpers last season but ran a cracker when second to the smart Blackbow in a Grade 2 at Leopardstown, pulling 15 lengths clear of the third; below that form when a well-beaten ninth in the Champion Bumper at Cheltenham.

River Wylde (Ire)

7 b g Oscar - Clarin River (Mandalus)

Nicky Henderson					Grech & Parkin
PLACINGS: 23/1011135/12-				RPR **149+c**	

Starts	1st	2nd	3rd	4th	Win & Pl
10	5	-	2	-	£57,000

	11/17	Uttx	2m Cls3 Ch gd-sft	£6,330
	2/17	Kemp	2m Cls1 Nov Gd2 Hdl good	£17,085
	1/17	Ludl	2m Cls4 Nov Hdl soft	£3,899
	12/16	Ludl	2m Cls4 Mdn Hdl gd-sft	£3,899
	5/16	Wwck	2m Cls6 NHF 4-6yo gd-sft	£1,949

High-class novice hurdler two seasons ago, beating Elgin in a Grade 2 at Kempton and

Rather Be: put up a fine effort on his final start last season and sure to be a force in 2m handicaps once again

finishing third in the Supreme Novices' Hurdle (raced keenly and led turning for home); won on his chasing debut last term but missed the rest of the season after disappointing next time.

Road To Respect (Ire)

7 ch g Gamut - Lora Lady (Lord America)

Noel Meade (Ir)   Gigginstown House Stud

PLACINGS: 3135/01432211/12143-   RPR **169c**

Starts	1st	2nd	3rd	4th	Win & Pl
19	6	5	4	2	£322,212
	12/17	Leop	3m Gd1 Ch yield		£75,641
	10/17	Punc	3m1f Gd3 Ch soft		£20,171
	4/17	Fair	2m4f Nov Gd1 Ch gd-yld		£50,427
145	3/17	Chel	2m5f Cls1 Gd3 133-158 Ch Hcap good		£59,798
	11/16	Naas	2m3f Ch yld-sft		£6,105
	2/16	Thur	2m6½f Mdn Hdl heavy		£4,522

Improving chaser who did brilliantly to win last

season's Leopardstown Christmas Chase over Balko Des Flos; also produced a big run when fourth in the Cheltenham Gold Cup on ground softer than ideal and may not have fully recovered when only third at Punchestown.

Robin Waters (Fr)

5 b g Irish Wells - Skandia (Robin Des Champs)

Dan Skelton   Colm Donlon

PLACINGS: 13316-   RPR **142h**

Starts	1st	2nd	3rd	4th	Win & Pl
4	1	-	2	-	£8,251
	2/18	Weth	2m5½f Cls4 Nov Hdl heavy		£4,327

Thrown in at the deep end when running in the Albert Bartlett at Cheltenham after winning only a maiden hurdle but even looked a threat until

Robinsfirth (right): likely to do well in staying handicap chases after a winning performance at Cheltenham last December

stamina gave way, still finishing a fine sixth; should get 3m on a better surface; has won a point-to-point and could go novice chasing.

Robinsfirth (Ire)
9 b g Flemensfirth - Phardester (Phardante)

Colin Tizzard   Christine Knowles & Wendy Carter

PLACINGS: 1/4/124/21U/421-   RPR **149+c**

Starts	1st	2nd	3rd	4th	Win & Pl
11	4	3	-	3	£56,908

142	12/17	Chel	3m2f Cls1 Gd3 127-148 Ch Hcap soft	£25,628
	1/17	Extr	2m3f Cls3 Ch soft	£7,798
	12/14	Extr	2m1f Cls4 Nov Hdl 4-6yo gd-sft	£3,574
	4/13	Winc	1m7¹/₂f Cls6 NHF 4-6yo good	£1,625

Lightly raced chaser who was held in very high regard as a novice hurdler before missing nearly two years; steadily progressive over fences since

coming back and gained his biggest win in a good staying handicap at Cheltenham on his final run last season.

Rock The Kasbah (Ire)
8 ch g Shirocco - Impudent (In The Wings)

Philip Hobbs   Mrs Diana L Whateley

PLACINGS: P/21100/1324126/1P2-   RPR **155c**

Starts	1st	2nd	3rd	4th	Win & Pl
22	8	6	2	1	£173,568

142	10/17	Chep	2m7¹/₂f Cls2 134-160 Ch Hcap gd-sft	£19,494
	2/17	Chep	2m7¹/₂f Cls3 Nov Ch soft	£6,498
	10/16	Chep	2m3¹/₂f Cls2 Nov Ch good	£19,494
144	1/16	Asct	2m3¹/₂f Cls1 Gd3 125-151 Hdl Hcap soft	£28,475
136	11/15	Hayd	2m3f Cls2 121-139 Hdl Hcap soft	£25,024
	3/15	Newb	2m4¹/₂f Cls3 Nov Hdl gd-sft	£5,848
	11/14	Font	2m3f Cls4 Nov Cond Hdl soft	£3,119
	10/14	Ffos	2m Cls6 Mdn NHF 4-6yo soft	£1,643

Progressive staying chaser who won for the third

time at Chepstow on his return last season but was ruled out of the Welsh National there owing to heavy ground when well fancied; bumped into a handicap blot when a fine second in the bet365 Gold Cup at Sandown.

Rocklander (Ire)
9 b g Oscar - Rua Lass (Beau Sher)

Tom George   D O'Donohoe, J Cavanagh & S Nelson

PLACINGS: 334/22112220/1U13F-P   RPR **149c**

Starts	1st	2nd	3rd	4th	Win & Pl
19	5	4	4	1	£45,619

l39	12/17	Newb	2m6¹/₂f Cls3 Nov 124-140 Ch Hcap heavy £7,214
	11/17	Ludl	2m4f Cls4 Ch gd-sft.. £6,657
l20	11/16	Leic	1m7¹/₂f Cls4 94-120 Hdl Hcap gd-sft.................... £6,330
l10	11/16	Chep	2m Cls4 97-114 Hdl Hcap good............................ £5,198

Proved a talented but erratic novice chaser last season when let down by his jumping several times but compiling a good record when completing; won twice and finished third in the novice handicap chase at the Cheltenham Festival; has strong placed form over 3m.

Roksana (Ire)
6 b m Dubai Destination - Talktothetail (Flemensfirth)

Dan Skelton   Mrs Sarah Faulks

PLACINGS: 4/31112-   RPR **144h**

Starts	1st	2nd	3rd	4th	Win & Pl
6	3	1	1		£51,197

l30	3/18	Newb	2m4¹/₂f Cls1 Nov Gd2 115-135 Hdl Hcap soft...... £22,780
	12/17	Font	2m3f Cls4 Nov Hdl heavy................................... £3,249
	11/17	Plum	2m4¹/₂f Cls4 Nov Hdl good................................ £3,249

Completed a hat-trick when winning last season's EBF Mares' Final at Newbury on her handicap debut; ran another cracker when stepped up to 3m for a Grade 1 at Aintree, chasing home Santini; likely to be aimed at the Mares' Hurdle at Cheltenham.

Rolling Dylan (Ire)
7 ch g Indian River - Easter Saturday (Grand Plaisir)

Philip Hobbs   Miss ID Du Pre

PLACINGS: /1223/212P2/51P2312-   RPR **149c**

Starts	1st	2nd	3rd	4th	Win & Pl
16	4	7	2	-	£37,105

l32	2/18	Chep	2m7¹/₂f Cls3 Nov Ch soft £7,882
	11/17	Worc	2m4f Cls3 124-140 Ch Hcap gd-sft..................... £7,507
	11/16	Uttx	2m4f Cls4 Nov Hdl soft...................................... £3,899
	12/15	Winc	1m7¹/₂f Cls6 Mdn NHF 4-6yo soft £1,625

Generally progressive in novice chases last

season, albeit kept to an ordinary grade; won twice and finished second conceding 6lb to a useful opponent on his final run when stepping up to 3m for the first time over fences (beaten a head on only run over that far over hurdles).

Saglawy (Fr)
4 b g Youmzain - Spasha (Shamardal)

Willie Mullins (Ir)   Sullivan Bloodstock

PLACINGS: 3113-95   RPR **144h**

Starts	1st	2nd	3rd	4th	Win & Pl
6	2	-	2	-	£43,658

	4/18	Fair	2m Gd2 Hdl 4yo soft £22,190
	3/18	Gowr	2m Mdn Hdl 4-5yo heavy £7,087

Smart recruit off the Flat in France (placed at Listed level) who struggled back in his native country this summer but had progressed well over hurdles prior to that; won a Grade 2 at Fairyhouse on his third run before finishing third in a Grade 1 at Punchestown.

Saint Calvados (Fr)
5 b g Saint Des Saints - Lamorrese (Pistolet Bleu)

Harry Whittington   A Brooks

PLACINGS: 1116/1114-   RPR **165+c**

Starts	1st	2nd	3rd	4th	Win & Pl
8	6	-	-	1	£106,059

	2/18	Wwck	2m Cls1 Nov Gd2 Ch soft.................................. £22,780
l47	1/18	Newb	2m¹/₂f Cls3 Nov 135-147 Ch Hcap soft £7,343
l43	12/17	Newb	2m¹/₂f Cls3 Nov 127-143 Ch Hcap heavy £8,656
	3/17	Autl	2m2f Hdl 4yo v soft £28,718
	12/16	Cagn	2m1¹/₂f Hdl 3yo soft £15,882
	11/16	Fntb	2m2f Hdl 3yo heavy... £8,118

Hugely exciting recruit from France who won his first three chases last season by wide margins, destroying a couple of smart novices in the Kingmaker at Warwick; much better than he showed in the Arkle at Cheltenham when taken on in front and going far too fast.

Saldier (Fr)
4 b g Soldier Hollow - Salve Evita (Monsun)

Willie Mullins (Ir)   Mrs S Ricci

PLACINGS: 1531-   RPR **150+h**

Starts	1st	2nd	3rd	4th	Win & Pl
4	2	-	1	-	£66,306

	4/18	Punc	2m Gd1 Hdl 4yo yld-sft.................................... £52,212
	2/18	Gowr	2m Mdn Hdl 4yo heavy...................................... £7,359

Smart Flat horse (competed up to Group 2 level

in 2017) who got better with practice after starting his hurdling career late last season; finished fifth in the Triumph Hurdle on just his second run and comprehensively reversed that form when winning at Punchestown.

Sam Spinner
6 b g Black Sam Bellamy - Dawn Spinner (Arctic Lord)

Jedd O'Keeffe   Caron & Paul Chapman

PLACINGS: 12/1211/21153-   RPR **164+h**

Starts	1st	2nd	3rd	4th	Win & Pl
11	6	3	1	-	£170,584

	12/17	Asct	3m¹/₂f Cls1 Gd1 Hdl gd-sft	£56,950
139	11/17	Hayd	2m7f Cls3 Gd3 130-156 Hdl Hcap heavy	£56,950
	2/17	Catt	2m3¹/₂f Cls4 Nov Hdl 4-7yo soft	£3,899
	1/17	Catt	2m3¹/₂f Cls4 Nov Hdl gd-sft	£3,899
	11/16	Newc	2m¹/₂f Cls4 Nov Hdl gd-sft	£6,498
	2/16	Catt	1m7¹/₂f Cls6 Mdn NHF 4-6yo soft	£1,949

Outstanding in the first half of last season, graduating to the top level when winning the Long Walk Hurdle after a big handicap victory at Haydock; susceptible to speedier horses having not gone fast enough in the Stayers' Hurdle and below his best again at Aintree.

Sam's Gunner
5 ch g Black Sam Bellamy - Falcon's Gunner (Gunner B)

Michael Easterby   Falcon's Line

PLACINGS: 044/2121P-   RPR **137+h**

Starts	1st	2nd	3rd	4th	Win & Pl
8	2	2	-	2	£49,934

125	3/18	Sand	2m4f Cls1 Nov Gd3 122-139 Hdl 4-7yo Hcap soft	£42,203
	2/18	Catt	2m3¹/₂f Cls4 Nov Hdl gd-sft	£4,484

Progressive novice hurdler last season, winning the EBF Final at Sandown last season by seven lengths; looked a strong stayer that day and had found 2m too sharp when second on previous run; pulled up when stepped up into a 3m Grade I at Aintree.

Sam Spinner: high-class and lightly raced staying hurdler

Samcro (Ire)
6 ch g Germany - Dun Dun (Saddlers' Hall)

Gordon Elliott (Ir) Gigginstown House Stud

PLACINGS: 1/111/1111F- RPR **159+h**

Starts	1st	2nd	3rd	4th	Win & Pl
8	7	-	-	-	£177,057

3/18	Chel	2m5f Cls1 Nov Gd1 Hdl soft	£71,188
2/18	Leop	2m Nov Gd1 Hdl soft	£52,212
11/17	Navn	2m4f Nov Gd3 Hdl sft-hvy	£21,432
10/17	Punc	2m Mdn Hdl yld-sft	£6,844
4/17	Navn	2m NHF 4-7yo gd-yld	£8,424
12/16	Navn	2m List NHF 4-7yo sft-hvy	£12,436
11/16	Punc	2m NHF 4yo soft	£4,522

Unbeaten when completing under rules and in point-to-points and was the outstanding novice hurdler of last season; justified long-term aim of the Ballymore Hurdle by easily beating a stellar field at Cheltenham but had also shown speed for 2m with Grade 1 win at Leopardstown; fell at the Punchestown festival when holding every chance; connections split on whether he stays hurdling or goes chasing, but sure to prove a force in whichever direction he is sent.

San Benedeto (Fr)
7 ch g Layman - Cinco Baidy (Lure)

Paul Nicholls PJ Vogt

PLACINGS: 1423U311113/224542-3 RPR **165c**

Starts	1st	2nd	3rd	4th	Win & Pl
32	9	7	7	3	£270,169

150	4/17	Aint	2m Cls1 Nov Gd1 Ch good	£56,793
145	4/17	Asct	2m1f Cls2 Nov 124-150 Ch Hcap good	£29,675
140	3/17	Donc	2m½f Cls2 128-145 Ch Hcap soft	£18,768
140	2/17	Muss	2m Cls3 127-141 Ch Hcap good	£14,296
	6/16	Worc	2m4f Cls4 Nov Ch good	£4,549
	5/16	Sedg	2m3½f Cls4 Nov Ch gd-fm	£4,029
130	11/15	Winc	2m4f Cls3 114-134 Hdl Hcap heavy	£7,596
	5/15	Strf	2m½f Cls4 Nov Hdl good	£3,249
	3/15	Winc	1m7½f Cls4 Nov Hdl good	£3,249

Flattered by Grade 1 novice chase win at Aintree in 2017 and came up predictably short at that level last season; often ran well in defeat, notably when second in the Haldon Gold Cup and the Celebration Chase; best on good ground.

Santini
6 b g Milan - Tinagoodnight (Sleeping Car)

Nicky Henderson Mr & Mrs R Kelvin-Hughes

PLACINGS: 1/1131- RPR **153+h**

Starts	1st	2nd	3rd	4th	Win & Pl
4	3	-	1	-	£95,526

4/18	Aint	3m½f Cls1 Nov Gd1 Hdl soft	£56,224
1/18	Chel	2m4½f Cls1 Nov Gd2 Hdl heavy	£18,224
12/17	Newb	2m4f Cls3 Nov Hdl soft	£6,498

High-class staying novice hurdler last season, winning three times including a Grade 1 at Aintree; given plenty to do when suffering only defeat in the Albert Bartlett at Cheltenham, running on for third; looks every inch a chaser and may well prove even better over fences.

Sayar (Ire)
5 b g Azamour - Seraya (Danehill)

Willie Mullins (Ir) Mrs Audrey Turley

PLACINGS: 117- RPR **133+h**

Starts	1st	2nd	3rd	4th	Win & Pl
3	2	-	-	-	£23,138

10/17	Tipp	2m Nov Gd3 Hdl sft-hvy	£17,083
8/17	Kbgn	2m Mdn Hdl gd-yld	£6,055

Missed much of last season through injury but had looked a terrific prospect when winning first two starts over hurdles, including a Grade 3 at Tipperary; well beaten in a Grade 2 at Fairyhouse on first run after a six-month layoff; should stay beyond 2m.

Sayo
4 gr g Dalakhani - Tiyi (Fairy King)

Willie Mullins (Ir) Palmerstown Racing Partnership

PLACINGS: 213- RPR **144h**

Starts	1st	2nd	3rd	4th	Win & Pl
3	1	1	1	-	£24,769

1/18	Naas	2m Mdn Hdl 4yo sft-hvy	£7,087

Moved to Willie Mullins after finishing second on his hurdling debut in France last season and proved a revelation when third in the Triumph Hurdle on his second run for the yard having jumped poorly when winning at Naas; open to significant improvement.

Scarlet Dragon
5 b g Sir Percy - Welsh Angel (Dubai Destination)

Alan King HP Racing Scarlet Dragon

PLACINGS: 29- RPR **134+h**

Starts	1st	2nd	3rd	4th	Win & Pl
2	-	1	-	-	£6,611

High-class Flat horse (rated 109 and beaten a head at Group 3 level) who took well to hurdles when second in a Grade 2 at Kempton first time out last season; disappointed on only other outing when unsuited by soft ground at Aintree; could be a top novice.

Scarpeta (Fr)
5 b g Soldier Of Fortune - Sanada (Priolo)

Willie Mullins (Ir) Thurloe Thoroughbreds Ireland Limited

PLACINGS: 3143P- RPR **149h**

Starts	1st	2nd	3rd	4th	Win & Pl
5	-	-	2	1	£19,015

1/18	Gowr	2m Mdn Hdl heavy	£7,359

Bought off the Flat in 2016 (useful staying handicapper for Mark Johnston) and was highly tried in novice hurdles last season for his new trainer, finishing fourth in the Ballymore after landing his maiden by 17 lengths; going well when badly hampered two out and pulled up at Punchestown.

Sceau Royal (Fr)

6 b g Doctor Dino - Sandside (Marchand De Sable)

Alan King   Simon Munir & Isaac Souede

PLACINGS: 211106/114369/12111-   RPR **166+c**

Starts	1st	2nd	3rd	4th	Win & Pl
20	10	3	1	1	£188,271
	1/18	Donc	2m¹/₂f Cls1 Nov Gd2 Ch soft		£19,933
	12/17	Sand	1m7¹/₂f Cls1 Nov Gd1 Ch gd-sft		£29,810
	11/17	Wwck	2m cls3 Nov Ch 4-5yo gd-sft		£9,384
	10/17	Wwck	2m cls4 Nov Ch good		£5,198
149	11/16	Winc	1m7¹/₂f Cls1 Gd2 133-149 Hdl Hcap good		£35,772
	10/16	Chel	2m¹/₂f Cls2 Hdl 4yo good		£21,977
	1/16	Hntg	2m Cls2 Hdl 4yo soft		£12,512
	12/15	Chel	2m1f Cls2 Hdl 3yo soft		£12,628
	11/15	Wwck	2m Cls4 Hdl 3yo gd-sft		£3,249
	3/15	Bord	2m¹/₂f Hdl 3yo v soft		£7,814

Smart performer over hurdles but proved even better over fences last season despite missing big spring targets through injury; most impressive when winning the Grade 1 Henry VIII Novices' Chase at Sandown and battled home under a penalty at Doncaster on ground softer than ideal.

Seeyouatmidnight

10 b g Midnight Legend - Morsky Baloo (Morpeth)

Sandy Thomson   Mrs David Thompson

PLACINGS: 13/27/311173/1P2/30-   RPR **140c**

Starts	1st	2nd	3rd	4th	Win & Pl
17	7	2	4	-	£141,665
	10/16	Carl	2m4f Cls1 List Ch gd-sft		£15,661
	2/16	Newc	2m¹/₂f Cls2 Nov Ch gd-sft		£12,660
	1/16	Chel	2m5f Cls1 Nov Gd2 Ch heavy		£18,224
	12/15	Kels	2m7¹/₂f Cls3 Nov Ch heavy		£10,222
	2/14	Hayd	2m7f Cls1 Gd2 Hdl heavy		£20,787
	2/14	Muss	3m¹/₂f Cls2 Hdl soft		£12,996
	12/13	Hexm	2m Cls4 Nov Hdl soft		£3,119

Plagued by injuries since finishing third as a novice in the 2016 Scottish National; showed enough on return from a year absence (third over inadequate 2m4f at Newbury) to go off at 11-1 for last season's Grand National but faded from third-last to finish 11th.

Shaneshill (Ire)

9 b g King's Theatre - Darabaka (Doyoun)

Willie Mullins (Ir)   Andrea & Graham Wylie

PLACINGS: /F233F1P0/13224P3-38   RPR **154h**

Starts	1st	2nd	3rd	4th	Win & Pl
31	9	8	6	2	£453,850
	5/17	Autl	2m5¹/₂f Gd2 Hdl v soft		£67,308
	1/17	Gowr	3m Gd2 Hdl soft		£22,692
	1/16	Naas	2m Nov Ch heavy		£10,037
	11/15	Thur	2m2f Ch soft		£5,884
	4/15	Fair	2m4f Nov Gd2 Hdl heavy		£21,415
	11/14	Fair	2m4f Mdn Hdl sft-hvy		£4,600
	4/14	Punc	2m Gd1 NHF 4-7yo gd-yld		£48,750
	11/13	Fair	2m NHF 4-7yo gd-yld		£5,610
	11/13	Naas	2m NHF 4yo gd-sft		£4,488

Finished second at three successive Cheltenham

Festivals from 2014 to 2016 among five runner-up finishes at the top level in total; largely below that level last season but ran well on return from a four-month layoff when third to Faugheen at Punchestown.

Shantou Flyer (Ire)

8 b g Shantou - Carrigmorna Flyer (Bob Back)

Richard Hobson   Carl Hinchy

PLACINGS: PF/529142P/5PP2222P-   RPR **162+c**

Starts	1st	2nd	3rd	4th	Win & Pl
38	6	12	2	3	£210,817
149	1/17	Chel	2m5f Cls1 Gd3 134-159 Ch Hcap soft		£34,170
	11/15	Punc	2m6f Nov Gd2 Ch sft-hvy		£20,155
	10/15	Chel	3m¹/₂f Cls2 Nov Ch good		£12,512
	9/15	Slig	2m5f Ch yield		£7,756
	7/15	Gway	2m6¹/₂f Ch good		£8,023
	5/14	Dpat	2m5¹/₂f Mdn Hdl good		£4,600

Has climbed to a career-high mark without winning since a New Year's Day handicap chase at Cheltenham in 2017 but keeps threatening to score, especially back at Cheltenham; finished second there three times last season, including when beaten a neck in the Ultima.

Shantou Rock (Ire)

6 b g Shantou - Cool Cool (Anabaa)

Dan Skelton   Mr & Mrs Gordon Pink

PLACINGS: 42/2721211F/12223-   RPR **155c**

Starts	1st	2nd	3rd	4th	Win & Pl
13	4	6	1	-	£57,892
	10/17	NAbb	2m¹/₂f Cls3 Nov Ch good		£7,280
125	4/17	Ludl	2m Cls3 122-133 Hdl Hcap gd-sft		£7,798
	3/17	Ludl	2m Cls4 Nov Hdl soft		£5,198
	2/17	Ludl	2m Cls4 Mdn Hdl soft		£3,899

Ran consistently well in Graded novice chases last season, chasing home Cyrname and Sceau Royal before finishing third behind Diego Du Charmil at Aintree; had looked particularly exciting on chase debut on only run on good ground, with subsequent defeats on soft; looks open to improvement.

Sharjah (Fr)

5 b g Doctor Dino - Saaryeh (Royal Academy)

Willie Mullins (Ir)   Mrs S Ricci

PLACINGS: 11F7846-31   RPR **158+h**

Starts	1st	2nd	3rd	4th	Win & Pl
9	3	-	1	1	£179,275
146	8/18	Gway	2m 135-146 Hdl Hcap soft		£156,637
	11/17	Gowr	2m Nov Hdl 4yo heavy		£8,161
	9/17	Gowr	2m Mdn Hdl 4yo heavy		£6,844

Struggled to build on a hugely encouraging start over hurdles last season (won his first two runs and looked sure to add a Grade 1 at Leopardstown over Christmas until falling at the last); bounced back with a brilliant win in the Galway Hurdle and still has Grade 1 potential.

Shattered Love (Ire)

7 b m Yeats - Tracker (Bustino)

Gordon Elliott (Ir)   Gigginstown House Stud

PLACINGS: 13/1221107/11211125-   RPR **159+c**

Starts	1st	2nd	3rd	4th	Win & Pl
17	9	4	1		£245,144

3/18	Chel	2m4f Cls1 Nov Gd1 Ch soft	£85,425
12/17	Leop	3m Nov Gd1 Ch yld-sft	£42,863
12/17	Cork	2m¹/₂f Nov Gd3 Ch heavy	£20,763
11/17	Clon	2m2f Ch soft	£7,371
10/17	Fair	2m5f Ch gd-yld	£6,318
2/17	Fair	2m2f Nov Gd3 Hdl sft-hvy	£18,397
12/16	Thur	2m Nov List Hdl soft	£15,827
10/16	Tipp	2m Mdn Hdl yld-sft	£4,522
3/16	Naas	2m NHF 4-7yo sft-hvy	£4,522

Top-class mare who capped a stellar season by beating Terrefort in the JLT at the Cheltenham Festival; had also won a 3m Grade 1 at Leopardstown during a run of five wins out of six over fences; not quite at her best subsequently but still second in the Ryanair Gold Cup.

Silver Streak (Ire)

5 gr g Dark Angel - Happy Talk (Hamas)

Evan Williams   L Fell

PLACINGS: 432114/12U6-1   RPR **137+h**

Starts	1st	2nd	3rd	4th	Win & Pl
11	4	2	1	2	£114,772

132	5/18	Hayd	1m7¹/₂f Cls1 Gd3 130-156 Hdl Hcap good	£56,950
122	10/17	Chep	2m Cls2 120-135 Hdl 4yo Hcap gd-sft	£12,996
116	3/17	Muss	1m7¹/₂f Cls4 100-122 Hdl Hcap good	£4,549
96	12/16	Tntn	2m¹/₂f Cls5 74-102 Hdl Hcap good	£3,899

Deserved big handicap success at Haydock in May; had finished second in a valuable handicap at Ascot last season and unlucky when sixth in the Imperial Cup on ground much softer than ideal; raised 6lb but should remain competitive.

Silverhow (Ire)

7 br g Yeats - Monte Solaro (Key Of Luck)

Colin Tizzard   Swallowfield Racing

PLACINGS: 2/35971216/F421231-   RPR **137+c**

Starts	1st	2nd	3rd	4th	Win & Pl
16	4	4	2		£51,925

124	4/18	Sand	2m4f Cls2 Nov 124-139 Ch Hcap gd-sft	£21,896
119	2/18	Winc	2m4f Cls3 117-128 Ch Hcap heavy	£9,495
121	4/17	Chel	2m1f Cls3 121-137 Cond Hdl Hcap good	£6,256
108	3/17	Sand	2m Cls4 95-115 Am Hdl Hcap soft	£4,367

Half-brother to Altior; unlikely to get close to those heights but took a big step forward when encountering good to soft ground for the first time over fences at Sandown in April, winning a good novice handicap; had won on heavy but best hurdles form came on good.

Simply Ned (Ire)

11 ch g Fruits Of Love - Bishops Lass (Marju)

Nicky Richards   David & Nicky Robinson

PLACINGS: 6/14253P/22397/2412-   RPR **160c**

Starts	1st	2nd	3rd	4th	Win & Pl
37	9	10	5	4	£263,098

12/17	Leop	2m1f Gd1 Ch yield	£50,427
10/15	Kels	2m1f Cls2 131-157 Ch Hcap gd-fm	£13,986
157	10/14	Kels	2m1f Cls2 132-157 Ch Hcap gd-sft	£14,115
138	1/14	Donc	2m¹/₂f Cls2 130-153 Ch Hcap gd-sft	£14,076
130	11/13	Ayr	1m7¹/₂f Cls3 109-130 Ch Hcap soft	£7,798
127	2/13	Ayr	2m Cls3 112-133 Hdl Hcap soft	£5,523
117	12/11	Muss	1m7¹/₂f Cls3 95-121 Hdl Hcap gd-sft	£6,498
	11/11	Sedg	2m1f Cls4 Nov Hdl 4-6yo good	£2,534
	10/11	Kels	2m Cls5 Mdn Hdl gd-sft	£1,819

As good as ever last season despite advancing years and gained the biggest win of his career when rightly awarded a Grade I at Leopardstown after interference from Min; no match for that peak-form rival at the same course next time but still ran another good race in second.

Singlefarmpayment

8 b g Milan - Crevamoy (Shardari)

Tom George   NT Griffith & HM Haddock

PLACINGS: /2211P/321B2/2F5P52-   RPR **152+c**

Starts	1st	2nd	3rd	4th	Win & Pl
22	3	8	1	2	£82,780

12/16	Chel	3m1¹/₂f Cls2 Nov Ch good	£15,640
125	1/16	Chel	3m Cls2 125-144 Hdl Hcap heavy	£12,512
12/15	Sthl	3m Cls4 Nov Hdl soft	£3,899

Long thought capable of winning a big handicap chase but has been beaten a short head at Cheltenham in each of the last two seasons, including in the Ultima in 2017; generally below his best last term but bounced back with his latest near miss in April.

Sizing Codelco (Ire)

9 b g Flemensfirth - La Zingarella (Phardante)

Colin Tizzard   Ann & Alan Potts Limited

PLACINGS: 2U/38P24011/P6PP48-2   RPR **162+c**

Starts	1st	2nd	3rd	4th	Win & Pl
29	4	5	4	2	£125,493

150	4/17	Punc	3m¹/₂f 127-150 Ch Hcap gd-yld	£30,256
139	4/17	Aint	3m1f Cls1 List 131-148 Ch Hcap good	£39,423
	9/15	List	2m1f Ch yld-sft	£8,023
	1/14	Fair	2m Mdn Hdl sft-hvy	£4,600

Showed much-improved form to win at Aintree and Punchestown and again came good in the spring this year after a largely disappointing campaign; finished a good fourth behind Might Bite at Aintree on his first run at Grade 1 level and beaten just half a length at Uttoxeter in May.

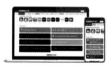
facebook.com/racingpost

Sizing Granite (Ire)
10 br g Milan - Hazel's Tisrara (Mandalus)

Colin Tizzard   Ann & Alan Potts Limited

PLACINGS: 1/25P2/P5P51/PP136-0   RPR **162c**

Starts	1st	2nd	3rd	4th	Win & Pl
24	7	3	2	-	£200,569

132	3/18	Newb	2m¹/₂f Cls2 120-135 Hdl Hcap soft £9,747
146	4/17	Punc	2m4f 127-155 Ch Hcap gd-yld £50,427
	4/15	Aint	2m Cls1 Nov Gd1 Ch good £61,897
	2/15	Leop	2m1f Nov Ch soft £10,581
	1/15	Naas	2m Nov Ch soft £10,078
	11/14	Naas	2m Ch yield £8,050
	3/14	Gowr	2m Mdn Hdl soft £5,750

Pulled up on his first two runs last season but got back on track after wind surgery, winning over hurdles at Newbury and running well in Grade 1 chases at Aintree and Punchestown; would have been much closer on first run over 3m in latter race but for bad mistake two out.

Sizing John
8 b g Midnight Legend - La Perrotine (Northern Crystal)

Jessica Harrington (Ir)   Ann & Alan Potts Limited

PLACINGS: 13/211223/321111/17-   RPR **173+c**

Starts	1st	2nd	3rd	4th	Win & Pl
20	9	5	3	1	£776,805

12/17	Punc	2m4f Gd1 Ch heavy £42,863
4/17	Punc	3m¹/₂f Gd1 Ch gd-yld £126,068
3/17	Chel	3m2¹/₂f Cls1 Gd1 Ch good £327,463
2/17	Leop	3m¹/₂f Gd1 Ch soft £72,436
1/17	Thur	2m4f Gd3 Ch yld-sft £22,692
11/15	Punc	2m Nov Gd2 Ch sft-hvy £21,163
10/15	Punc	2m Ch yield £7,488
12/14	Leop	2m Nov Gd1 Hdl heavy £43,333
11/14	Naas	2m Mdn Hdl 4yo yield £5,750

Cheltenham Gold Cup win the highlight of a stunning treble in 2017 as he also won at Leopardstown and Punchestown, proving himself the dominant staying chaser of the season; hasn't run since a woeful effort over Christmas, though, missing Cheltenham after a setback.

Sizing Tennessee (Ire)
10 ch g Robin Des Champs - Jolivia (Dernier Empereur)

Colin Tizzard   Ann & Alan Potts Limited

PLACINGS: /81F0/234P/2FU1233P-   RPR **155c**

Starts	1st	2nd	3rd	4th	Win & Pl
22	5	3	3	2	£86,858

12/17	Chel	3m1¹/₂f Cls2 Nov Ch soft £17,373
1/16	Navn	2m Hdl sft-hvy £11,471
12/13	Navn	2m Mdn Hdl yield £7,293
1/13	Gowr	2m NHF 4-7yo heavy £7,293
12/12	Punc	2m NHF 4yo heavy £4,600

Has won only once since starting late over fences two seasons ago but has run several fine races in defeat, especially at Cheltenham, and nearly added to sole victory when a neck second to Yanworth in the Dipper last season; trainer feels he'll improve on good ground, and he is lightly raced.

Slate House (Ire)
6 b g Presenting - Bay Pearl (Broadway Flyer)

Colin Tizzard   Eric Jones, Geoff Nicholas & John Romans

PLACINGS: 5/1/1145F8-   RPR **145h**

Starts	1st	2nd	3rd	4th	Win & Pl
6	2	-	-	1	£26,424

11/17	Chel	2m¹/₂f Cls1 Nov Gd2 Hdl soft £17,085
10/17	Chel	2m¹/₂f Cls3 Mdn Hdl good £6,256

Looked a top novice hurdler early last season, even beating Summerville Boy at Cheltenham; went off the boil subsequently but trainer's horses were wrong for a period and wouldn't have been beaten far in the Supreme but for falling at the last; likely to go novice chasing.

Snow Falcon (Ire)
8 b g Presenting - Flocon De Neige (Kahyasi)

Noel Meade (Ir)   Mrs Patricia Hunt

PLACINGS: F1/11F32538/2315UP-4   RPR **156+c**

Starts	1st	2nd	3rd	4th	Win & Pl
28	7	6	4	1	£156,321

12/17	Leop	2m5f Ch yield £7,897
11/16	Navn	2m4f Gd2 Hdl yld-sft £18,438
8/16	Rosc	3m¹/₂f Hdl good £8,366
2/16	Navn	2m5f Gd2 Hdl heavy £19,522
11/15	Naas	2m4f Hdl yield £10,078
1/15	Navn	2m4f Mdn Hdl soft £5,349
10/14	Fair	2m NHF 4-7yo good £4,313

Smart dual-purpose performer who won two Grade 2 staying hurdles in 2016 and has soon reached a similar standard over fences (fourth in the Galway Plate this summer); had been unlucky in the spring when unseating his rider in the Irish National and bleeding from the nose at Aintree.

Soul Emotion (Fr)
5 b g Martaline - Second Emotion (Medaaly)

Nicky Henderson   Mr & Mrs JD Cotton

PLACINGS: 1435/PF11-   RPR **150+h**

Starts	1st	2nd	3rd	4th	Win & Pl
8	3	-	1	1	£49,364

137	4/18	Sand	2m4f Cls2 126-143 Hdl Hcap gd-sft £21,896
125	3/18	Sand	2m4f Cls3 118-134 Hdl Hcap soft £9,384
	5/16	Comp	2m Hdl 3yo v soft £7,765

Joined Nicky Henderson from France last season and won both subsequent starts in 2m4f handicap hurdles at Sandown; could go further over hurdles but more likely to go chasing according to his trainer (fell and pulled up in two attempts in France).

'Smart dual-purpose performer was unlucky in the spring when unseating in the Irish National and bleeding at Aintree'

facebook.com/racingpost

Speak Easy
5 b g Beneficial - For Bill (Presenting)

Joseph O'Brien (Ir)   John P McManus

PLACINGS: 1/1532-   RPR **147+h**

Starts	1st	2nd	3rd	4th	Win & Pl
4	1	1	1	-	£21,388
	12/17	Navn	2m Mdn Hdl 4yo soft		£6,844

Exciting chasing prospect who did well over hurdles despite failing to add to debut win at Navan; well beaten at Grade 1 level next time but wasn't beaten far in a Grade 2 at Naas and finished a fine second under a big weight in the novice handicap final at Fairyhouse.

Special Tiara
11 b g Kayf Tara - Special Choice (Bob Back)

Henry de Bromhead (Ir)   Mrs S Rowley-Williams

PLACINGS: 31/423/631512/3F3P4-   RPR **164c**

Starts	1st	2nd	3rd	4th	Win & Pl
33	7	5	9	4	£655,279
	3/17	Chel	2m Cls1 Gd1 Ch gd-sft		£208,300
	12/16	Kemp	2m Cls1 Gd2 Ch good		£46,981
	4/15	Sand	1m7¹/₂f Cls1 Gd1 Ch good		£71,188
	12/14	Kemp	2m Cls1 Gd2 Ch soft		£46,096
	4/13	Aint	2m Cls1 Nov Gd1 Ch good		£62,190
	9/12	Baln	2m1f Ch yld-sft		£4,600
	7/12	Kbgn	2m Mdn Hdl 4-5yo yield		£4,313

Brilliant chaser over many seasons and finally won the Champion Chase in 2017 having been third in the race in the previous two years; hasn't won since then but still ran to a good level of form when third behind the likes of Fox Norton, Min and Altior last season.

Speredek (Fr)
7 b/br g Kapgarde - Sendamagic (Sendawar)

Nigel Hawke   Kapinhand

PLACINGS: 46P126/PP111/1212P8-   RPR **160c**

Starts	1st	2nd	3rd	4th	Win & Pl
20	7	3	1	2	£97,421
135	1/18	Sand	1m7¹/₂f Cls2 127-150 Ch Hcap heavy	£18,768
129	11/17	Extr	2m1f Cls3 120-134 Hdl Hcap soft	£7,798
129	3/17	Ludl	2m Cls2 129-142 Ch Hcap soft	£12,512
122	2/17	Sand	1m7¹/₂f Cls3 113-135 Ch Hcap soft	£7,507
115	2/17	Tntn	2m2f Cls4 Nov 106-120 Ch Hcap soft	£5,697
107	2/17	Extr	2m7f Cls4 93-114 Hdl Hcap gd-sft	£3,249
	3/15	Carl	2m1f Cls6 NHF 4-6yo soft	£1,560

Sharply progressive in 2017 when dropped in trip; completed a four-timer when reverting to

hurdles on his reappearance last season before also winning back over fences at Sandown; second to Un De Sceaux in the Clarence House Chase but well beaten next twice.

Splash Of Ginge
10 b g Oscar - Land Of Honour (Supreme Leader)

Nigel Twiston-Davies   JD Neild

PLACINGS: 306/44612500/417P82-   RPR **148c**

Starts	1st	2nd	3rd	4th	Win & Pl
41	6	4	4	7	£295,950
134	11/17	Chel	2m4¹/₂f Cls1 Gd3 129-154 Ch Hcap soft	£91,120
132	12/16	Hayd	2m7f Cls3 114-132 Hdl Hcap soft	£6,498
145	1/15	Chel	2m5f Cls1 Gd3 129-155 Ch Hcap soft	£28,475
	10/14	Chel	2m4f Cls2 Nov Ch gd-sft	£12,512
134	2/14	Newb	2m1¹/₂f Cls1 Gd3 124-150 Hdl Hcap heavy	£86,849
	12/13	Aint	2m11f Cls4 Mdn Hdl soft	£5,198

Very inconsistent but rarely in the handicapper's grip for long and has a habit of running well in big Cheltenham handicaps when down to a good mark; enjoyed a third course win in last season's BetVictor Gold Cup and was second in the Plate.

Squouateur (Fr)
7 gr g Martaline - Samansonnienne (Mansonnien)

Gordon Elliott (Ir)   John P McManus

PLACINGS: 21176/578P2U/6303BP-   RPR **141c**

Starts	1st	2nd	3rd	4th	Win & Pl
19	3	2	2	1	£59,257
128	2/16	Fair	2m4f 120-136 Ch Hcap heavy	£10,853
120	12/15	Leop	2m4f Nov 109-128 Hdl Hcap heavy	£13,605
	11/15	Fair	2m Mdn Hdl 4yo yield	£5,349

Has bled punters dry with a string of defeats when well fancied for major handicaps in recent seasons but little wrong with his efforts when third in the Paddy Power Chase and the Kim Muir last season; seems best over those longer trips these days.

Step Back (Ire)
8 ch g Indian River - Stepitoutmary (Roselier)

Mark Bradstock   Cracker & Smodge Partnership

PLACINGS: 3F2/5121/119/2311-   RPR **153+c**

Starts	1st	2nd	3rd	4th	Win & Pl
6	3	1	1	-	£96,636
135	4/18	Sand	3m5f Cls1 Gd3 135-161 Ch Hcap gd-sft	£84,405
	4/18	Fknm	3m Cls4 Nov Ch gd-sft	£5,592
	2/17	Ludl	3m Cls4 Mdn Hdl Hcap soft	£3,899

Stunning winner of last season's bet365 Gold

Twitter @RacingPost

Cup at Sandown, making most of the running as just one rival finished within 25 lengths; had run only three times over fences under rules prior to that but has plenty of experience from point-to-points.

Stormy Ireland (Fr)

4 b f Motivator - Like A Storm (Ultimately Lucky)

Willie Mullins (Ir)   Sullivan Bloodstock Limited

PLACINGS: 2/21FU-13   RPR **140+h**

Starts	1st	2nd	3rd	4th	Win & Pl
7	2	2	1	-	£58,301
	5/18	Klny	2m1f List Hdl yield.............................£16,327
	12/17	Fair	2m Mdn Hdl 3yo heavy.......................£6,055

Stunning 58-length winner on Irish debut last season when making all at a good pace but hasn't quite been able to pull off similar tactics in top company, including when falling at the last (held in third) in the Triumph Hurdle; again made all in a Listed hurdle at Killarney in May.

Style De Garde (Fr)

4 b g Kapgarde - Anowe De Jelois (Red Guest)

Nicky Henderson   Highclere Thoroughbred Racing – Style

PLACINGS: 3/1142P-   RPR **138h**

Starts	1st	2nd	3rd	4th	Win & Pl
6	2	1	1	1	£37,996
	12/17	Newb	2m¹/₂f Cls4 Hdl 3yo soft.....................£4,549
	10/17	Stra	2m1¹/₂f Hdl 3yo soft..........................£8,615

Bought after winning in France last season and made a big impression when scoring on his British debut at Newbury; flopped twice after that (fourth at odds-on and pulled up in a Grade I at Aintree) but ran a big race at Cheltenham in between when second in the Fred Winter.

Sub Lieutenant (Ire)

9 b g Brian Boru - Satellite Dancer (Satco)

Henry de Bromhead (Ir)   Gigginstown House Stud

PLACINGS: 1P/3113222/353454-51   RPR **163c**

Starts	1st	2nd	3rd	4th	Win & Pl
35	7	8	6	6	£299,492
	8/18	Gway	2m6¹/₂f Ch good.............................£13,606
	11/16	DRoy	2m3¹/₂f Gd2 Ch good........................£21,691
	10/16	Limk	2m3¹/₂f Ch yield............................£11,305
	3/16	Naas	2m4f Nov Gd3 Ch heavy....................£14,697
	2/15	Thur	2m4f Nov Gd2 Hdl heavy...................£20,155
	11/14	Fair	2m2f Mdn Hdl yld-sft.........................£5,750
	10/14	Thur	2m NHF 4-7yo good...........................£4,313

Former Ryanair Chase runner-up who was out of sorts for much of last season but did much better in the spring, following a more promising fifth in the Bowl at Aintree by finishing fourth in the Punchestown Gold Cup; confirmed his revival by winning at Galway this summer.

Summerville Boy (Ire)

6 b g Sandmason - Suny House (Carroll House)

Tom George   RS Brookhouse

PLACINGS: 122311-   RPR **156+h**

Starts	1st	2nd	3rd	4th	Win & Pl
6	3	2	1		£113,818
	3/18	Chel	2m¹/₂f Cls1 Nov Gd1 Hdl heavy...........£71,188
	1/18	Sand	2m Cls1 Nov Gd1 Hdl heavy...............£28,475
	5/17	Klny	2m1f NHF 5-7yo soft..........................£5,265

Took time to find his feet last season but ended up completing a Grade I double, adding to the Tolworth Hurdle with a remarkable win in the Supreme Novices' Hurdle (just recovered from late blunders); gained both those wins on heavy ground and something to prove on quicker.

Sumos Novios (Ire)

10 b g Flemensfirth - Gaelic Million (Strong Gale)

Liam Burke (Ir)   WJ Burke

PLACINGS: /421/1B7/143/22811P-   RPR **155c**

Starts	1st	2nd	3rd	4th	Win & Pl
16	5	3	2	2	£82,358
	4/18	Cork	3m Gd3 Ch sft-hvy............................£17,688
144	3/18	Wxfd	2m6f 116-144 Ch Hcap heavy.............£14,150
129	1/17	Cork	2m4f 101-129 Ch Hcap heavy..............£9,199
124	12/15	Punc	2m6f 116-141 Ch Hcap heavy.............£12,093
	2/15	Thur	3m Ch yld-sft...................................£5,884

Lightly raced for his age (had run just 12 times in five years prior to last season) and flourished under a busier campaign, peaking with a Grade 3 win at Cork; pulled up when tried at Grade I level at Punchestown but may have found ground too quick (most effective on heavy).

Supasundae

8 b g Galileo - Distinctive Look (Danehill)

Jessica Harrington (Ir)   Ann & Alan Potts Limited

PLACINGS: 9317/4812412/321221-   RPR **165h**

Starts	1st	2nd	3rd	4th	Win & Pl
20	7	5	2	2	£489,830
	4/18	Punc	2m Gd1 Hdl soft...........................£143,584
	2/18	Leop	2m Gd1 Hdl soft..............................£75,000
148	3/17	Chel	2m5f Cls1 Gd3 136-156 Hdl Hcap gd-sft...........£54,103
	12/16	Punc	2m4f Hdl soft...................................£9,044
	12/15	Leop	2m Mdn Hdl heavy.............................£7,488
	12/14	Asct	1m7¹/₂f Cls1 List NHF 4-6yo soft..........£11,390
	3/14	Weth	2m Cls6 NHF 4-6yo good.....................£1,711

Dual 2m Grade I winner last season despite

having his campaign geared towards the Stayers' Hurdle; probably better over the minimum trip given he has yet to score over 3m and was outstayed in a slowly run race at Cheltenham, although flattered by big-race wins (main rivals fell or disappointed).

Sussex Ranger (USA)
4 b g Hat Trick - Purple (Royal Academy)

Gary Moore — The Tongdean Partnership

PLACINGS: 1127- — RPR **135+h**

Starts	1st	2nd	3rd	4th	Win & Pl
4	2	1	-	-	£27,430

12/17	Sand	2m Cls2 Hdl 3yo gd-sft	£12,512
10/17	Font	2m1¹/₂f Cls4 Hdl 3yo good	£3,899

Won his first two starts over hurdles last season and emerged with lots of credit when second in the Finale Hurdle at Chepstow (pushed We Have A Dream close and pulled clear of rest); raced too keenly when flopping in the Triumph Hurdle.

Sutton Place (Ire)
7 b g Mahler - Glebe Beauty (Good Thyne)

Gordon Elliott (Ir) — John P McManus

PLACINGS: 3111/11P/1P- — RPR **141+c**

Starts	1st	2nd	3rd	4th	Win & Pl
9	6	-	1	-	£84,691

1/18	Fair	2m5f Ch heavy	£7,632
2/17	Navn	2m5f Gd2 Hdl sft-hvy	£22,692
1/17	Naas	2m Gd3 Hdl yld-sft	£17,083
3/16	Fair	2m Nov Gd2 Hdl yld-sft	£19,522
3/16	Naas	2m Nov List Hdl sft-hvy	£12,436
1/16	Fair	2m NHF 5-7yo heavy	£4,566

Has been pulled up in two runs at Grade 1 level, most recently when joint-favourite for the Flogas Novice Chase last season, but otherwise unbeaten since his debut under rules; beat Kemboy impressively on his first run over fences and retains Grade 1 potential.

Talkischeap (Ire)
6 b g Getaway - Carrigmoorna Oak (Milan)

Alan King — Charles Dingwall

PLACINGS: 1011233/1141P- — RPR **140+h**

Starts	1st	2nd	3rd	4th	Win & Pl
9	4	2	2	1	£21,979

133	2/18	Newb	3m Cls2 123-145 Hdl Hcap soft	£12,512
	5/17	Wwck	2m3f Cls4 Nov Hdl good	£5,198
	5/17	Font	2m3f Cls5 Mdn Hdl gd-fm	£2,599

Triple point-to-point winner who progressed well over hurdles last season, winning three times including a Newbury handicap; did particularly well to win that day given preference for faster ground and failed to cope with similar conditions in stronger company in the Albert Bartlett.

Tea For Two
9 b g Kayf Tara - One For Me (Tragic Role)

Jane Williams — Mrs Jane Williams & Len Jakeman

PLACINGS: 7113/5241U1/943P76-P — RPR **168c**

Starts	1st	2nd	3rd	4th	Win & Pl
28	9	4	3	2	£277,198

	4/17	Aint	3m1f Cls1 Gd1 Ch good	£84,365
	2/17	Extr	3m Cls2 Ch soft	£13,898
	12/15	Kemp	3m Cls1 Nov Gd1 Ch gd-sft	£39,865
	12/15	Extr	2m3f Cls2 Nov Ch heavy	£12,686
134	1/15	Kemp	2m5f Cls1 List 129-155 Hdl Hcap soft	£25,628
	12/14	Towc	2m Cls4 Nov Hdl 4-6yo gd-sft	£3,249
	10/14	Kemp	2m5f Cls4 Nov Hdl gd-sft	£3,899
	4/14	Extr	2m1f Cls6 NHF 4-6yo good	£1,625
	4/13	Winc	1m7¹/₂f Cls6 NHF 4-6yo good	£1,625

Loves a flat, sharp three miles and won the Betway Bowl at Aintree in 2017 as well as finishing third and fourth in the last two runnings of the King George at Kempton, doing much better there than in four runs at Cheltenham; well below that level in all other races last season but likely to remain a force given his ideal conditions.

Terrefort (Fr)
5 gr g Martaline - Vie De Reine (Mansonnien)

Nicky Henderson — Simon Munir & Isaac Souede

PLACINGS: 28/5226/13131121- — RPR **164+c**

Starts	1st	2nd	3rd	4th	Win & Pl
14	5	4	2	-	£192,532

	4/18	Aint	3m1f Cls1 Nov Gd1 Ch soft	£56,337
	2/18	Sand	2m4f Cls1 Nov Gd1 Ch soft	£31,323
137	1/18	Hntg	2m4f Cls3 Nov 120-137 Ch Hcap soft	£7,798
	9/17	Claf	2m2f Hdl 4yo heavy	£9,436
	8/17	Claf	2m3¹/₂f Ch 4yo heavy	£14,769

French recruit who became probably the leading British-trained staying novice chaser last season; narrow winner of the Scilly Isles and a good second in the JLT at Cheltenham before improving for the step up to 3m1f when winning impressively at Aintree.

Testify (Ire)
7 b g Witness Box - Tanya Thyne (Good Thyne)

Donald McCain — Trevor Hemmings

PLACINGS: 2/12129/1110P- — RPR **150+c**

Starts	1st	2nd	3rd	4th	Win & Pl
10	5	2	-	-	£47,961

1/18	Hayd	2m4f Cls1 Nov Gd2 Ch heavy	£19,936
12/17	Hayd	1m7¹/₂f Cls3 Nov Ch heavy	£7,820
12/17	Bang	2m1¹/₂f Cls2 Nov Ch soft	£6,410
2/17	Bang	2m7f Cls3 Nov Hdl soft	£7,798
12/16	Carl	2m1f Cls4 Nov Hdl soft	£3,249

Looked a very useful novice chaser when winning his first three starts last season, albeit all in small fields (no bigger than four runners); twice below that level in the spring, though, despite getting similar conditions (all five wins over jumps on soft or heavy ground); lightly raced and open to further improvement.

The Dutchman (Ire)

8 b g King's Theatre - Shivermetimber (Arctic Lord)

Colin Tizzard — Sprayclad UK

PLACINGS: /212P/132F227/261PU- — RPR 153+c

Starts	1st	2nd	3rd	4th	Win & Pl
16	3	6	1	-	£88,796

I35	1/18	Hayd	3m1¹/₂f Cls1 Gd2 133-153 Ch Hcap heavy	£42,914
	11/16	Weth	1m7f Cls4 Nov Ch gd-sft	£3,899
	1/16	Weth	2m Cls4 Nov Hdl heavy	£3,574

Looked much improved when switched to Colin Tizzard and stepped up in trip last season, winning the Peter Marsh at Haydock in first chase for the yard; broke blood vessels when pulled up next time; still in touch when unseating his rider at the 23rd in the Grand National.

The Last Samuri (Ire)

10 ch g Flemensfirth - Howaboutthis (Oscar)

Harry Fry — Paul & Clare Rooney

PLACINGS: U12/3112/5320/2243P- — RPR 163c

Starts	1st	2nd	3rd	4th	Win & Pl
24	8	7	3	1	£397,539

I49	3/16	Donc	3m2f Cls2 132-155 Ch Hcap soft	£34,536
I40	12/15	Kemp	3m Cls2 127-145 Ch Hcap gd-sft	£25,992
I32	3/15	Kels	3m2f Cls2 125-150 Ch Hcap gd-sft	£16,245
	1/15	Ayr	3m¹/₂f Cls4 Nov Ch soft	£4,029
	11/14	Bang	3m Cls3 Nov Ch soft	£8,406
	1/14	Catt	3m1¹/₂f Cls4 Nov Hdl soft	£3,249
	11/13	Bang	2m3¹/₂f Cls4 Nov Hdl soft	£3,249
	11/13	Kels	2m6¹/₂f Cls4 Nov Hdl gd-sft	£3,899

Second in the 2016 Grand National but has boiled over before the last two runnings of the race and disappointed; has failed to win in that time but has run well in other big handicaps, notably when second and third in the last two Becher Chases; has been switched from Kim Bailey.

The New One (Ire)

10 b g King's Theatre - Thuringe (Turgeon)

Nigel Twiston-Davies — S Such & CG Paletta

PLACINGS: 214F/121534/142210P- — RPR 165+h

Starts	1st	2nd	3rd	4th	Win & Pl
38	20	7	2	3	£1,048,354

	1/18	Hayd	1m7¹/₂f Cls1 Gd2 Hdl heavy	£42,713
I60	10/17	Ffos	2m Cls2 140-160 Hdl Hcap good	£28,256
	1/17	Hayd	1m7¹/₂f Cls1 Gd2 Hdl soft	£43,215
	12/16	Chel	2m1f Cls1 Gd2 Hdl soft	£74,035
	1/16	Hayd	1m7¹/₂f Cls1 Gd2 Hdl heavy	£42,713
	10/15	Kemp	2m Cls1 List Hdl good	£17,085
	1/15	Hayd	2m Cls1 Gd2 Hdl heavy	£42,713
	12/14	Chel	2m1f Cls1 Gd2 Hdl gd-sft	£74,035
	11/14	Hayd	2m Cls2 Hdl soft	£61,900
	10/14	Kemp	2m Cls1 List Hdl gd-sft	£14,238
	4/14	Aint	2m4f Cls1 Gd1 Hdl good	£112,540
	12/13	Chel	2m1f Cls1 Gd2 Hdl good	£74,035
	10/13	Kemp	2m Cls1 List Hdl gd-sft	£14,238
	3/13	Chel	2m5f Cls1 Nov Gd1 Hdl gd-sft	£68,340
	1/13	Wwck	2m5f Cls1 Nov Gd2 Hdl soft	£15,735
	10/12	Chel	2m5f Cls2 Nov Hdl gd-sft	£10,635
	10/12	NAbb	2m2¹/₂f Cls4 Nov Hdl soft	£2,924
	4/12	Aint	2m1f Cls2 Gd2 NHF 4-6yo good	£14,238
	1/12	Chel	1m6f Cls1 List NHF 4yo gd-sft	£7,133
	11/11	Wwck	1m6f Cls6 NHF 3yo good	£2,053

Major force in British 2m hurdles in recent seasons, winning four successive Champion

Hurdle Trials at Haydock and two International Hurdles at Cheltenham (also second last season); form tailed off in the spring, including when stepped up to 3m for the first time in the Stayers' Hurdle.

The Storyteller (Ire)

7 ch g Shantou - Bally Bolshoi (Bob Back)

Gordon Elliott (Ir) — Mrs P Sloan

PLACINGS: 24/21F211/2137151- — RPR 161+c

Starts	1st	2nd	3rd	4th	Win & Pl
15	6	4	1	1	£153,447

	4/18	Punc	3m¹/₂f Nov Gd1 Ch yld-sft	£52,212
I47	3/18	Chel	2m5f Cls1 Gd3 137-155 Ch Hcap soft	£62,645
	12/17	Fair	2m5f Ch soft	£7,634
	1/17	Thur	2m6¹/₂f Nov Hdl yld-sft	£7,622
	12/16	DRoy	2m3¹/₂f Mdn Hdl soft	£5,879
	5/16	Dpat	2m2f NHF 4-7yo good	£4,070

Steadily progressive over last two seasons and won the Plate at last season's Cheltenham Festival; hugely fortunate to get a Grade 1 win after that following Paul Townend's blunder on Al Boum Photo at Punchestown but still did enough to show he's equally effective at 3m.

The Worlds End (Ire)

7 b g Stowaway - Bright Sprite (Beneficial)

Tom George — McNeill Family

PLACINGS: F1/3111F1/84474- — RPR 154h

Starts	1st	2nd	3rd	4th	Win & Pl
12	5	-	1	3	£103,469

	4/17	Aint	3m¹/₂f Cls1 Nov Gd1 Hdl good	£56,141
	2/17	Hayd	2m7f Cls1 Nov Gd2 Hdl gd-sft	£16,972
	1/17	Chep	2m3¹/₂f Cls4 Nov Hdl soft	£3,249
	12/16	Chep	2m3¹/₂f Cls3 Mdn Hdl gd-sft	£6,498
	4/16	Chep	2m Cls6 NHF 4-6yo gd-sft	£1,949

Top-class staying novice hurdler two seasons ago, winning a Grade 1 at Aintree having fallen when challenging in the Albert Bartlett; came up short in open company last season but never got preferred good ground and still not beaten far in Long Walk and Stayers' Hurdles.

Theinval (Fr)

8 b g Smadoun - Kinevees (Hard Leaf)

Nicky Henderson — Mr & Mrs Sandy Orr

PLACINGS: 1334132227/4F364241- — RPR 154c

Starts	1st	2nd	3rd	4th	Win & Pl
39	8	8	6	7	£216,397

I44	4/18	Ayr	2m1¹/₂f Cls1 List 128-154 Ch Hcap good	£22,780
	12/16	Plum	2m1f Cls3 Nov Ch gd-sft	£6,498
	5/16	Uttx	2m4f Cls4 Ch good	£4,431
I44	4/15	Aint	2m4f Cls1 Gd3 127-149 Hdl Hcap gd-sft	£28,135
I34	3/15	Kemp	2m5f Cls2 115-135 Hdl Hcap good	£22,743
I19	11/14	Kemp	2m Cls3 105-129 Cond Hdl Hcap soft	£5,393

Standing dish in top 2m handicap chases over the last two seasons and finally landed a big one at Ayr in April; still improving on that evidence and may be more versatile regarding ground than

facebook.com/racingpost

was felt to be the case given previous second on soft in the Red Rum at Aintree.

Thistlecrack
10 b g Kayf Tara - Ardstown (Ardross)

Colin Tizzard				John & Heather Snook

PLACINGS: 151/211111/11112/54-   RPR **165**c

Starts	1st	2nd	3rd	4th	Win & Pl
21	13	2	1	1	£657,985

12/16	Kemp	3m Cls1 Gd1 Ch good	£119,026
11/16	Newb	2m7¹/₂f Cls1 Nov Gd2 Ch gd-sft	£20,167
11/16	Chel	3m¹/₂f Cls2 Nov Ch gd-sft	£16,025
10/16	Chep	2m7¹/₂f Cls3 Nov Ch gd-sft	£7,798
4/16	Aint	3m¹/₂f Cls1 Gd1 Hdl soft	£84,405
3/16	Chel	3m Cls1 Gd1 Hdl good	£170,850
1/16	Chel	3m Cls1 Gd2 Hdl heavy	£34,170
12/15	Asct	3m¹/₂f Cls1 Gd1 Hdl gd-sft	£56,950
11/15	Newb	3m Cls1 Gd2 Hdl soft	£25,628
4/15	Aint	3m¹/₂f Cls1 Nov Gd1 Hdl gd-sft	£56,437
2/15	Asct	1m7¹/₂f Cls2 Nov Hdl soft	£9,384
1/15	Winc	1m7¹/₂f Cls4 Nov Hdl heavy	£3,899
4/14	Winc	1m7¹/₂f Cls6 NHF 4-6yo good	£1,625

Had the world at his feet when winning the 2016 King George as a novice, carrying on his outstanding hurdles form, but has run just three times since due to injury; showed some promise in a close fourth in last season's King George only to suffer another setback.

Thomas Campbell
6 b g Yeats - Hora (Hernando)

Nicky Henderson				Mrs Van Geest & Mrs Kelvin Hughes

PLACINGS: 7/1115547/11560P-   RPR **157+**h

Starts	1st	2nd	3rd	4th	Win & Pl
14	5	-	-	1	£58,281

148	11/17	Chel	3m1¹/₂f Cls1 List 127-150 Hdl Hcap soft	£17,085
138	10/17	Chel	3m Cls2 123-149 Hdl Hcap good	£15,640
	11/16	Asct	1m7¹/₂f Cls3 Hdl gd-sft	£7,148
	10/16	Chel	2m¹/₂f Cls3 Mdn Hdl good	£6,256
	5/16	Kels	2m Cls5 NHF 4-6yo good	£2,599

Progressive staying hurdler in the first half of last season, winning two handicaps at Cheltenham on contrasting ground; came up just short at the top level when fifth in the Long Walk Hurdle next time and form tailed off subsequently; likely to go novice chasing.

Thomas Patrick (Ire)
6 b g Winged Love - Huncheon Siss (Phardante)

Tom Lacey				David Kellett

PLACINGS: 7/43PP1/0021281411-   RPR **153+**c

Starts	1st	2nd	3rd	4th	Win & Pl
10	4	2	-	1	£68,009

139	4/18	Aint	3m1¹/₂f Cls1 Gd3 129-155 Ch Hcap soft	£42,203
131	3/18	Newb	3m2f Cls3 129-140 Ch Hcap soft	£12,762
	2/18	Chep	2m7¹/₂f Cls4 Nov Ch heavy	£4,614
114	11/17	Extr	2m¹/₂f Cls4 98-117 Hdl Hcap soft	£4,224

Began last season in novice hurdles but soon switched to fences in the new year and proved rapidly progressive as he won three out of four; won a big handicap chase at Aintree's Grand

National meeting and should go well in more top chases despite going up 9lb.

Tiger Roll (Ire)
8 b g Authorized - Swiss Roll (Entrepreneur)

Gordon Elliott (Ir)				Gigginstown House Stud

PLACINGS: P114U2221331P/2P511-   RPR **160**c

Starts	1st	2nd	3rd	4th	Win & Pl
30	9	5	3	3	£800,446

150	4/18	Aint	4m2¹/₂f Cls1 Gd3 142-161 Ch Hcap heavy	£500,000
	3/18	Chel	3m6f Cls2 Ch soft	£40,261
	3/17	Chel	4m Cls1 Nov Gd2 Am Ch gd-sft	£71,952
138	10/16	Limk	3m 131-144 Ch Hcap yield	£43,382
	6/16	Kbgn	2m4f Nov Ch good	£6,331
	5/16	Baln	2m1f Ch good	£5,200
	10/14	Chel	2m¹/₂f Cls2 Hdl 4yo gd-sft	£18,768
	3/14	Chel	2m1f Cls1 Gd1 Hdl 4yo good	£68,340
	11/13	MRas	2m¹/₂f Cls4 Hdl 3yo soft	£3,899

Remarkable horse who won last season's Grand National after collecting a third Cheltenham Festival success in the Cross Country Chase; value for much more than the winning margin at Aintree (didn't get home on soft ground) so may not be handicapped out of a repeat.

Tombstone (Ire)
8 ch g Robin Des Champs - Connaught Hall (Un Desperado)

Gordon Elliott (Ir)				Gigginstown House Stud

PLACINGS: 24/31038/2121263626-   RPR **153**c

Starts	1st	2nd	3rd	4th	Win & Pl
22	6	6	4	1	£135,510

12/17	Navn	2m1f Nov Gd3 Ch soft	£19,712
11/17	DRoy	2m3¹/₂f Ch soft	£7,897
2/17	Gowr	2m Gd3 Hdl heavy	£22,692
11/15	Fair	2m4f Mdn Hdl sft-hvy	£6,419
10/15	DRoy	2m NHF 4-7yo yld-sft	£6,953
1/15	Naas	2m3f NHF 5-7yo soft	£4,279

Highly rated but largely disappointing since finishing fourth in the Supreme three seasons ago, notably when a well-beaten favourite in the 2017 Coral Cup; won two novice chases early last season but increasingly inconsistent as campaign progressed.

Top Gamble (Ire)
10 ch g Presenting - Zeferina (Sadler's Wells)

Kerry Lee				Walters Plant Hire & James & Jean Potter

PLACINGS: /P3311/53346/P24438-   RPR **155+**c

Starts	1st	2nd	3rd	4th	Win & Pl
28	8	3	5	3	£183,260

	3/16	Fair	2m1f Gd2 Ch yield	£18,438
	2/16	Chel	2m1f Gd2 Ch soft	£28,475
	4/15	Ayr	2m4¹/₂f Cls1 Nov Gd2 Ch good	£27,197
143	1/15	Newb	2m¹/₂f Cls3 125-144 Ch Hcap soft	£6,498
135	12/14	Wwck	2m Nov 124-135 Ch Hcap soft	£6,498
	11/14	Weth	1m7f Cls4 Ch soft	£4,106
	2/13	Ffos	2m Cls4 Nov Hdl heavy	£3,899
	12/12	Ffos	2m Cls6 Mdn NHF 4-6yo heavy	£1,430

Hasn't won since a couple of Grade 2 novice chases in early 2016 but dropped 11lb in the handicap last season and looked slightly unlucky not to take advantage when third in the Grand Annual (hampered twice); equally effective up to 2m5f; needs soft ground.

Top Notch (Fr)
7 b g Poliglote - Topira (Pistolet Bleu)

Nicky Henderson   Simon Munir & Isaac Souede

PLACINGS: 22515/3111123/31141-   RPR **171+c**

Starts	1st	2nd	3rd	4th	Win & Pl
23	13	4	3	1	£365,122

4/18	Sand	2m6¹/₂f Cls1 Gd2 Ch gd-sft	£31,470
12/17	Tntn	2m5¹/₂f Cls1 Gd2 Ch soft	£28,475
11/17	Asct	2m5f Cls1 Gd2 Ch gd-sft	£39,865
2/17	Sand	2m4f Cls1 Nov Gd1 Ch soft	£28,475
12/16	Asct	2m5f Cls2 Ch gd-sft	£15,640
11/16	Plum	2m1f Cls3 Nov Ch gd-sft	£6,498
11/16	Wwck	2m Cls3 Nov Ch 4-5yo soft	£9,384
2/16	Kels	2m2f Cls2 Hdl heavy	£16,245
2/15	Hayd	1m7¹/₂f Cls2 Hdl 4yo soft	£9,747
1/15	Asct	1m7¹/₂f Cls3 Hdl 4yo soft	£6,498
12/14	Newb	2m¹/₂f Cls3 Hdl 3yo gd-sft	£6,498
4/14	Engh	2m¹/₂f Hdl 3yo v soft	£19,200
3/14	Bord	2m¹/₂f Hdl 3yo heavy	£8,400

Triple Grade 2 winner from 2m5f to 2m6f last season; well beaten on his only run in a Grade 1 behind Waiting Patiently but wasn't right afterwards (missed Cheltenham and Aintree) and had looked well up to the top level when thrashing King George second Double Shuffle at Ascot.

Topofthegame (Ire)
6 ch g Flemensfirth - Derry Vale (Mister Lord)

Paul Nicholls   Chris Giles & Mr & Mrs PK Barber

PLACINGS: 1/142/F412-   RPR **155+h**

Starts	1st	2nd	3rd	4th	Win & Pl
7	2	2	-	2	£94,055

142	2/18	Sand	2m7¹/₂f Cls1 Gd3 123-147 Hdl Hcap soft	£56,270
	12/16	Asct	2m5¹/₂f Cls3 Mdn Hdl gd-sft	£7,798

Said to have chaser written all over him by his trainer but reverted to hurdles after falling first time out last season at Newbury; made good progress to win a big staying handicap at Sandown before dropping in trip to finish a close second in the Coral Cup.

Tornado Flyer (Ire)
5 b g Flemensfirth - Mucho Macabi (Exceed And Excel)

Willie Mullins (Ir)   TFP Partnership

PLACINGS: 131-   RPR **143b**

Starts	1st	2nd	3rd	4th	Win & Pl
3	2	1	-		£65,688

4/18	Punc	2m1¹/₂f Gd1 NHF 4-7yo yield	£52,212
1/18	Fair	2m NHF 5-7yo soft	£5,451

Top-class bumper performer last season; fine third in the Champion Bumper at Cheltenham on just his second run and stepped up to win a Grade 1 at Punchestown despite still looking green; looks a strong stayer for novice hurdles.

Total Recall (Ire)
9 b g Westerner - Augest Weekend (Dr Massini)

Willie Mullins (Ir)   Slaneyville Syndicate

PLACINGS: 7619/PF4U105/111FPP-   RPR **160+c**

Starts	1st	2nd	3rd	4th	Win & Pl
22	6	-	2	3	£262,858

125	2/18	Leop	3m 117-145 Hdl Hcap soft	£39,159
147	12/17	Newb	3m2f Cls1 Gd3 139-165 Ch Hcap gd-sft	£142,375
129	10/17	Limk	3m 128-145 Ch Hcap soft	£50,427
	12/16	Navn	2m4f Nov Ch sft-hvy	£7,235
123	3/16	Naas	2m3f 115-135 Hdl Hcap sft-hvy	£11,305
	2/15	Punc	2m4f Mdn Hdl soft	£6,419

Improved massively for the switch to Willie Mullins last season and won three big handicaps, most notably the Ladbrokes Trophy before reverting to hurdles at Leopardstown; still in contention when falling three out in the Cheltenham Gold Cup but twice pulled up subsequently.

Tower Bridge (Ire)
5 b g High Chaparral - Walkamia (Linamix)

Joseph O'Brien (Ir)   John P McManus

PLACINGS: 4/1104153-   RPR **146h**

Starts	1st	2nd	3rd	4th	Win & Pl
8	3	-	1	2	£78,844

2/18	Leop	2m6f Nov Gd1 Hdl soft	£52,212
7/17	Bell	2m1¹/₂f NHF 4-7yo good	£6,055
5/17	Baln	2m1¹/₂f NHF 4yo good	£5,265

Possibly flattered by Grade 1 win at Leopardstown last season (got up on the line in a modest race for the grade) but proved he wasn't far off the best staying novice hurdlers when fifth in the Albert Bartlett at Cheltenham and third in the Sefton at Aintree.

Traffic Fluide (Fr)
8 b g Astarabad - Petale Rouge (Bonnet Rouge)

Gary Moore   Galloping On The South Downs Partnership

PLACINGS: 113/3/46632/4575011-   RPR **151+c**

Starts	1st	2nd	3rd	4th	Win & Pl
22	5	2	4	3	£149,613

140	4/18	Chel	2m5f Cls1 Gd2 135-160 Ch Hcap good	£34,170
	4/18	Plum	2m4¹/₂f Cls4 Nov Hdl heavy	£5,003
135	3/15	Sand	1m7¹/₂f Cls3 Nov 122-140 Ch Hcap good	£6,498
129	2/15	Plum	2m1f Cls3 Nov 129-145 Ch Hcap gd-sft	£7,988
	10/14	Stra	2m4f Ch 4yo heavy	£8,800

Hasn't quite gone as anticipated since winning

ON THE FIGURES

TOPOFTHEGAME Strapping sort who fell on his chasing debut but went on to prove himself a high-class hurdler who was just touched off in the Coral Cup. Not hard to envisage him developing into a leading novice chaser this season. [Steve Mason, Racing Post Ratings]

facebook.com/racingpost

two novice chases in early 2015 but has been very highly tried (next 11 runs at Grade 1 or Grade 2 level); benefited from more realistic placing last spring, including when getting up late to win a good handicap at Cheltenham.

Trainwreck (Ire)

6 b g Stowaway - Trail Storm (Supreme Leader)

Henry de Bromhead (Ir)   Gigginstown House Stud

PLACINGS: 1/42/61210-   RPR **142+h**

Starts	1st	2nd	3rd	4th	Win & Pl
7	2	2	-	1	£25,451
126	12/17	Leop	2m 116-144 Hdl Hcap soft		£14,981
	11/17	Clon	2m½f Mdn Hdl soft		£5,791

Progressive novice hurdler last season, winning a

fiercely competitive contest at Leopardstown over Christmas on his handicap debut and then coming a fair tenth behind Samcro in the Ballymore; likely to go novice chasing.

Tully East (Ire)

8 b g Shantou - Ghillie's Bay (King's Ride)

Alan Fleming (Ir)   Barry Connell

PLACINGS: 2/16164/1621P/463-80   RPR **149c**

Starts	1st	2nd	3rd	4th	Win & Pl
18	4	3	1	2	£82,222
138	3/17	Chel	2m4½f Cls1 Nov List 137-142 Ch Hcap gd-sft		£39,865
	12/16	Thur	2m2f Ch yield		£4,974
120	11/15	Punc	2m Nov 96-120 Hdl Hcap soft		£8,558
	9/15	List	2m Mdn Hdl 5yo heavy		£6,953

Won the novice handicap chase at the

Top Notch: classy chaser scored with three Grade 2 victories last season

Cheltenham Festival in 2017; never got ideal conditions last season (even pulled out of Cheltenham because of the ground) and ran a couple of good races in the circumstances, notably when third in a big handicap at Leopardstown.

Two Taffs (Ire)

8 b g Flemensfirth - Richs Mermaid (Saddlers' Hall)

Dan Skelton   Walters Plant Hire & James & Jean Potter

PLACINGS: 1/32341/1722331/2-   RPR **152+c**

Starts	1st	2nd	3rd	4th	Win & Pl
14	4	4	4	1	£74,978

142	4/17	Ayr	2m4¹/₂f Cls1 List 130-148 Ch Hcap gd-sft	£28,475
	10/16	Carl	2m4f Cls4 Nov Hdl gd-sft	£3,249
129	4/16	Ayr	2m5¹/₂f Cls2 124-150 Hdl Hcap gd-sft	£12,996
	3/15	MRas	2m¹/₂f Cls6 Mdn NHF 4-6yo good	£1,560

Promising novice chaser two seasons ago, finally getting off the mark in a Listed handicap at Ayr in April 2017 after several good runs in defeat (third in the Cheltenham Festival novice handicap); ran only once last season when second at Cheltenham in October.

Ucello Conti (Fr)

10 b g Martaline - Gazelle Lulu (Altayan)

Gordon Elliott (Ir)   Simon Munir & Isaac Souede

PLACINGS: /1P/6236/74724U/2PU-   RPR **153c**

Starts	1st	2nd	3rd	4th	Win & Pl
34	8	7	2	3	£364,179

6/14	Rost	2m1f Ch gd-fm	£6,000
8/12	Roya	1m6¹/₂f NHF	£6,667
2/12	Ange	2m1f Hdl 4yo gd-sft	£10,400
11/11	Engh	2m1f List Ch 3yo v soft	£35,172
9/11	Autl	2m1¹/₂f Ch 3yo v soft	£23,172
7/11	Sabl	1m5¹/₂f NHF 3yo gd-sft	£6,034
7/11	Claf	2m1f Hdl 3yo soft	£13,241
5/11	Nanc	2m1f Hdl 3yo gd-fm	£8,276

Yet to win since moving from France but has run well in many top handicaps, including when runner-up in the Paddy Power Chase at Leopardstown for the second time last season; placed twice in the Thyestes but has unseated his rider in the last two Grand Nationals.

Ultragold (Fr)

10 b/br g Kapgarde - Hot D'Or (Shafoun)

Colin Tizzard   Brocade Racing, JP Romans & Terry Warner

PLACINGS: 512/651B6791/392P01-   RPR **152+c**

Starts	1st	2nd	3rd	4th	Win & Pl
40	8	3	3	6	£277,740

141	4/18	Aint	2m5f Cls1 Gd3 126-152 Ch Hcap good	£78,582
136	4/17	Aint	2m5f Cls1 Gd3 131-157 Ch Hcap good	£67,356
136	11/16	Newb	2m1¹/₂f Cls2 125-145 Ch Hcap gd-sft	£21,896
129	4/16	Newb	2m1¹/₂f Cls3 112-129 Ch Hcap good	£6,498
120	2/16	Winc	1m7¹/₂f Cls2 120-141 Ch Hcap soft	£12,628
119	12/14	Extr	2m3f Cls3 119-137 Ch Hcap gd-sft	£15,640
	4/13	Autl	2m6f Ch 5yo v soft	£21,463
	3/13	Sbri	2m2f Ch 5yo heavy	£6,634

Has developed into a real specialist over the

Grand National fences, winning the last two runnings of the Topham and finishing second in the Grand Sefton in between; less effective on conventional courses last season but has won two good handicaps at Newbury.

Un De Sceaux (Fr)

10 b g Denham Red - Hotesse De Sceaux (April Night)

Willie Mullins (Ir)   Edward O'Connell

PLACINGS: /1F122/161112/11211-   RPR **173+c**

Starts	1st	2nd	3rd	4th	Win & Pl
29	22	4	-	-	£1,318,699

4/18	Punc	2m Gd1 Ch yld-sft	£143,584
4/18	Fair	2m4f Gd2 Ch heavy	£41,770
1/18	Asct	2m1f Cls1 Ch soft	£86,430
12/17	Cork	2m¹/₂f Gd2 Ch heavy	£30,256
3/17	Chel	2m5f Cls1 Gd1 Ch good	£170,850
1/17	Chel	2m¹/₂f Cls1 Gd1 Ch soft	£40,053
12/16	Sand	1m7¹/₂f Cls1 Gd1 Ch gd-sft	£84,405
5/16	Autl	2m5¹/₂f Gd2 Hdl v soft	£57,904
1/16	Asct	2m1f Cls1 Ch soft	£71,188
4/15	Punc	2m Nov Gd1 Ch yield	£53,488
3/15	Chel	2m Cls1 Gd1 Ch gd-sft	£85,425
1/15	Leop	2m1f Nov Gd1 Ch yld-sft	£37,209
12/14	Fair	2m Ch soft	£6,900
4/14	Autl	2m3¹/₂f Gd2 Hdl heavy	£65,625
3/14	Autl	2m3¹/₂f Gd3 Hdl v soft	£50,625
2/14	Gowr	2m Gd2 Hdl heavy	£21,667
1/14	Navn	2m Hdl soft	£10,833
12/13	Thur	2m Hdl soft	£8,695
4/13	Punc	2m Nov Hdl heavy	£11,890
2/13	Punc	2m Mdn Hdl sft-hvy	£4,207
10/12	Sbri	1m4f NHF 4yo v soft	£4,167
2/12	Mchl	1m4f NHF 4yo gd-sft	£4,167

Remarkable chaser who has won nine Grade 1 chases from 2m to 2m5f, including a third successive Clarence House Chase last season; finished only second in the Ryanair Chase having won that Cheltenham Festival contest the previous year but returned to winning ways at Punchestown, relishing unusually soft ground for the time of year; all those races sure to be on his agenda again this season.

Un Temps Pour Tout (Ire)

9 b g Robin Des Champs - Rougedespoir (Bonnet Rouge)

David Pipe   Professor Caroline Tisdall & Bryan Drew

PLACINGS: 1/3363/122414/10361/   RPR **163c**

Starts	1st	2nd	3rd	4th	Win & Pl
26	8	3	10	2	£498,350

155	3/17	Chel	3m1f Cls1 Gd3 134-155 Ch Hcap gd-sft	£59,798
	11/16	Aint	2m4f Cls2 Hdl gd-sft	£19,230
148	3/16	Chel	3m1f Cls1 Gd3 131-153 Ch Hcap gd-sft	£56,950
	6/15	Autl	3m1¹/₂f Gd1 Hdl v soft	£129,070
	2/14	Asct	2m3¹/₂f Cls2 Nov Hdl heavy	£15,640
	9/13	Autl	2m2f Gd3 Hdl 4yo v soft	£49,390
0	5/13	Autl	2m3¹/₂f List Hdl 4yo Hcap heavy	£34,756
	5/13	Bord	2m2¹/₂f Hdl 4yo gd-sft	£8,585

Dual winner of the Ultima at Cheltenham, though probably not required to improve on his 2016 win as a novice to follow up off top weight in a weaker renewal in 2017; has struggled to match that form before the spring but being aimed at an autumn return having missed last season through injury.

Unowhatimeanharry
10 b g Sir Harry Lewis - Red Nose Lady (Teenoso)

Harry Fry   John P McManus

PLACINGS: 7P/11111/11131/1230-   RPR **163h**

Starts	1st	2nd	3rd	4th	Win & Pl
27	11	2	8	2	£447,031

	11/17	Aint	2m4f Cls2 Hdl soft..£28,152
	4/17	Punc	3m Gd1 Hdl gd-yld...£126,068
	1/17	Chel	3m Cls1 Gd2 Hdl soft..£34,170
	12/16	Asct	3m¹/₂f Cls1 Gd1 Hdl gd-sft......................................£56,950
	11/16	Newb	3m Cls1 Gd2 Hdl soft..£28,475
	3/16	Chel	3m Cls1 Nov Gd1 Hdl good......................................£68,340
138	2/16	Extr	2m7f Cls2 124-139 Hdl Hcap heavy......................£11,617
	12/15	Chel	3m Cls1 Nov Gd2 Hdl soft.......................................£17,165
123	11/15	Newb	2m4¹/₂f Cls4 Nov 109-123 Hdl Hcap soft..............£6,498
123	11/15	Chel	2m5f Cls3 118-125 Cond Hdl Hcap gd-sft.............£7,507
	2/13	Font	2m1¹/₂f Cls6 NHF 4-6yo soft.....................................£1,625

Made it ten wins in 11 races for Harry Fry when making a winning return at Aintree last season, with sole defeat in the 2017 Stayers' Hurdle (reversed form with the winner, Nichols Canyon, at Punchestown); form tailed off subsequently, though, and something to prove now.

Up For Review (Ire)
9 br g Presenting - Coolsilver (Good Thyne)

Willie Mullins (Ir)   Andrea & Graham Wylie

PLACINGS: /1/120/3114P1/2148-1   RPR **148c**

Starts	1st	2nd	3rd	4th	Win & Pl
14	6	2	2	1	£68,940

5/18	Klny	2m6¹/₂f Nov Ch yield...£7,904
3/18	Gowr	2m4f Ch heavy...£8,177
4/16	Prth	3m Cls2 Nov Hdl good...£11,261
12/15	Punc	3m Nov Gd2 Hdl heavy..£21,163
11/15	Fair	2m4f Mdn Hdl heavy..£5,349
12/14	Leop	2m NHF 4-6yo soft...£5,175

Returned from nearly two years out towards the end of last season and soon managed to win two novice chases, dominating modest fields both times; twice well beaten in stronger company in between but was a Grade 2 winner over hurdles and could reach a similar level.

Uppertown Prince (Ire)
6 b g Strategic Prince - Tarrawarra (Kayf Tara)

Donald McCain   TG Leslie

PLACINGS: 61/12214-   RPR **142h**

Starts	1st	2nd	3rd	4th	Win & Pl
5	2	2		1	£20,496

3/18	Ayr	2m4¹/₂f Cls4 Nov Hdl soft...£4,260
12/17	Bang	2m3¹/₂f Cls4 Nov Hdl soft...£3,249

Described as every inch a chaser by his trainer but did well in novice hurdles last season; won twice and made the frame twice at Graded level,

most notably when fourth behind Santini in the Sefton at Aintree.

Valseur Lido (Fr)
9 b g Anzillero - Libido Rock (Video Rock)

Henry de Bromhead (Ir)   Gigginstown House Stud

PLACINGS: 36/12FU22/14/55538-0   RPR **155c**

Starts	1st	2nd	3rd	4th	Win & Pl
26	8	5	2	1	£357,820

11/16	DRoy	3m Gd1 Ch good..£60,735
4/15	Punc	3m1f Nov Gd1 Ch gd-yld...£44,186
11/14	Fair	2m4f Nov Gd1 Ch yld-sft...£40,625
11/14	Punc	2m4f Ch yield...£6,900
4/14	Fair	2m Nov Gd2 Hdl soft...£21,667
12/13	Navn	2m Nov Hdl sft-hvy...£7,293
11/13	Cork	2m Mdn Hdl 4yo sft-hvy...£5,610
11/12	Pari	1m4f NHF 3yo v soft...£12,500

Three-time Grade 1 winner, most recently at Down Royal in November 2016; missed a year after picking up a knock later that season and below his best last term; slipped down the handicap, though, and shaped with promise when eighth in the Grand National.

Value At Risk
9 b g Kayf Tara - Miss Orchestra (Orchestra)

Dan Skelton   DM Huglin

PLACINGS: 5/FF921/4175/271651-   RPR **149h**

Starts	1st	2nd	3rd	4th	Win & Pl
23	7	4	1	1	£114,052

130	4/18	Ayr	2m4¹/₂f Cls1 List 130-145 Ch Hcap good...............£28,475
140	12/17	Donc	2m3¹/₂f Cls3 123-140 Hdl Hcap good.......................£5,630
	10/16	Bang	2m4¹/₂f Cls4 Nov Ch good..£5,198
	3/16	Fair	2m4f Gd2 Hdl yld-sft...£26,029
	12/14	Newb	2m3f Cls4 Nov Hdl 4-6yo soft...................................£3,899
	12/13	Leop	2m NHF 4-7yo soft...£6,171
	12/13	Fair	2m NHF 4yo gd-yld...£4,768

Classy hurdler (won off 140 last season) who has always looked cut out for fences but took an age to take to them; made a potential breakthrough when winning at Ayr on his final run of last season, though, and still on a lower mark than over hurdles despite 8lb rise.

Veneer Of Charm (Ire)
4 b g Fast Company - Nova Tor (Trans Island)

Gordon Elliott (Ir)   M J Wasylocha & George P Mahoney

PLACINGS: 127164-   RPR **135+h**

Starts	1st	2nd	3rd	4th	Win & Pl
6	2	1	-	1	£57,731

129	3/18	Chel	2m¹/₂f Cls1 Gd3 126-139 Hdl 4yo Hcap soft........£45,560
	12/17	Punc	2m Mdn Hdl 3yo sft-hvy...£6,844

Relished running in a big-field handicap for the

only time when landing last season's Fred Winter at Cheltenham at 33-1 with plenty to spare (ran around in front but won by three lengths); best run apart from that when beaten nine lengths in a Grade 2 at Fairyhouse.

Verdana Blue (Ire)

6 b m Getaway - Blue Gallery (Bluebird)

Nicky Henderson — Crimbourne Stud

PLACINGS: 6/0214U1143/51300- — RPR **150+h**

Starts	1st	2nd	3rd	4th	Win & Pl
15	4	1	2	2	£59,640

136	11/17	Asct	1m7½f Cls2 117-137 Hdl Hcap gd-sft	£18,768
	2/17	Tntn	2m3f Cls4 Nov Hdl good	£6,330
	1/17	Hrfd	2m Cls4 Nov Hdl gd-sft	£3,379
	7/16	Klny	2m1f NHF 4-7yo good	£4,748

Smart mare who ran well in good handicap hurdles at Ascot last season, winning in November; has won a novice hurdle over 2m3f but reported to need the bare minimum by his trainer and didn't seem to get home when faced with a gruelling test over the trip in the Betfair Hurdle.

Vicente (Fr)

9 b g Dom Alco - Ireland (Kadalko)

Paul Nicholls — Trevor Hemmings

PLACINGS: 1131451/F669F1/2UP5- — RPR **159+c**

Starts	1st	2nd	3rd	4th	Win & Pl
28	7	4	3	2	£327,702

146	4/17	Ayr	4m Cls1 Gd3 127-148 Ch Hcap good	£122,443
146	4/16	Ayr	4m Cls1 Gd3 135-155 Ch Hcap gd-sft	£119,595
	11/15	Chel	3m½f Cls2 Nov Ch gd-sft	£14,588
	5/15	Winc	3m1f Cls4 Nov Ch gd-fm	£3,994
	4/15	NAbb	2m5f Cls4 Ch gd-fm	£4,328
	10/14	Chel	2m5f Cls2 Nov Hdl good	£10,635
126	3/14	Winc	2m4f Cls3 113-129 Cond Hdl Hcap gd-sft	£6,330

Won the Scottish Grand National in 2016 and 2017, bouncing back to form on preferred good ground both times; fair fifth in the same race last season off a higher mark; had also run in the Grand National in 2017 but fell at the first.

Vieux Lion Rouge (Fr)

9 ch g Sabiango - Indecise (Cyborg)

David Pipe — Prof Caroline Tisdall & John Gent

PLACINGS: 90/111U267/116/4749- — RPR **147c**

Starts	1st	2nd	3rd	4th	Win & Pl
26	11	1	2	2	£225,508

146	2/17	Hayd	3m4½f Cls1 Gd3 132-152 Ch Hcap gd-sft	£42,713
142	12/16	Aint	3m2f Cls1 Gd3 133-159 Ch Hcap gd-sft	£78,582
139	11/15	Hayd	3m Cls2 128-145 Ch Hcap soft	£21,896
	6/15	MRas	2m3f Cls4 Nov Ch good	£3,861
	5/15	Towc	2m5½f Cls4 Nov Ch gd-sft	£3,769
	2/14	Sedg	2m1f Cls4 Nov Hdl heavy	£3,379
	1/14	Winc	1m7½f Cls3 Nov Hdl heavy	£5,523
	1/14	Winc	1m7½f Cls4 Nov Hdl heavy	£3,899
	2/13	Extr	2m1f Cls6 NHF 4-6yo heavy	£1,625
	1/13	Newb	1m4½f Cls6 NHF 4yo soft	£1,643
	12/12	Ffos	2m Cls6 NHF 3-5yo heavy	£1,430

Won two big staying handicaps two seasons ago, including the Becher Chase over the Grand National fences, but has failed to make a mark in three attempts at the National itself, finishing no better than sixth; out of sorts last term but has dropped to last winning handicap mark.

Vinndication (Ire)

5 b g Vinnie Roe - Pawnee Trail (Taipan)

Kim Bailey — Moremoneythan

PLACINGS: 1111- — RPR **152+h**

Starts	1st	2nd	3rd	4th	Win & Pl
4	4	-	-	-	£33,589

	2/18	Hntg	2m3½f Cls1 Nov List Hdl soft	£17,085
	1/18	Asct	2m5½f Cls3 Nov Hdl 4-7yo soft	£6,758
	12/17	Leic	2m4½f Cls3 Nov Hdl soft	£6,498
	11/17	Ludl	2m Cls4 NHF 4-6yo good	£3,249

Unbeaten after winning three novice hurdles (all on soft ground) and a bumper last season, most notably beating Western Ryder in a Listed race at Huntingdon; missed the spring as felt to be too weak and immature; likely to go novice chasing.

Vinnie Lewis (Ire)

7 b g Vinnie Roe - Ballyann Lewis (Sir Harry Lewis)

Harry Whittington — The Racing Demon Partnership

PLACINGS: /3F33/1417342/3411P- — RPR **144+c**

Starts	1st	2nd	3rd	4th	Win & Pl
11	2	1	3	3	£25,817

127	1/18	Plum	3m4½f Cls3 108-136 Ch Hcap heavy	£18,134
113	11/17	Sedg	3m2½f Cls4 88-117 Ch Hcap soft	£3,899

Relished stepping up in trip in testing conditions over fences last season, winning twice including a decisive victory in the Sussex National at Plumpton in just his fourth chase; sent off favourite for the Eider next time but pulled up.

Vintage Clouds (Ire)

8 gr g Cloudings - Rare Vintage (Germany)

Sue Smith — Trevor Hemmings

PLACINGS: 222P/222F3F7/124233- — RPR **149c**

Starts	1st	2nd	3rd	4th	Win & Pl
23	3	10	4	1	£104,887

132	10/17	Aint	3m1f Cls3 Nov 120-133 Ch Hcap gd-sft	£9,097
	11/15	Hayd	2m3f Cls3 Nov Hdl 4-7yo soft	£6,498
	1/15	Weth	2m Cls6 NHF 4-6yo soft	£1,643

Has won only once in two seasons over fences (in a novice handicap at the start of last term) but has been placed in a string of big handicaps; third in the Ultima Handicap Chase and the

'He was out of sorts last term but has dropped to his last winning handicap mark'

Scottish Grand National last spring, proving effectiveness on all types of ground.

Virgilio (Fr)

9 b g Denham Red - Liesse De Marbeuf (Cyborg)

Dan Skelton   CJ Edwards, D Futter & AH Rushworth

PLACINGS: 111P5/11P223/18PF-11   RPR **159+c**

Starts	1st	2nd	3rd	4th	Win & Pl
21	9	2	1	2	£179,395
149	7/18	Uttx	3m2f Cls1 List 123-149 Ch Hcap good		£42,203
145	5/18	Aint	3m1f Cls2 122-145 Ch Hcap good		£15,562
142	5/17	Aint	3m1f Cls2 121-146 Ch Hcap good		£13,928
	10/16	NAbb	2m5f Cls2 Ch good		£21,270
	5/16	Wwck	2m4f Cls4 Nov Ch gd-sft		£3,899
138	12/15	Aint	2m4f Cls2 125-144 Hdl Hcap good		£13,763
125	5/15	Aint	2m4f Cls2 125-146 Hdl Hcap good		£11,574
118	5/15	Wwck	2m3f Cls3 118-133 Hdl Hcap soft		£6,498
	10/13	Sabl	2m1f Hdl 4yo v soft		£9,756

Has won the same 3m1f handicap chase at Aintree in May for the last two years; achieved little in between but had wind surgery after two disappointing efforts last winter and has already gone in again at Uttoxeter in July; laid out for the Grand National back at Aintree but only got as far as the sixth.

Vision Des Flos (Fr)

5 b g Balko - Marie Royale (Turgeon)

Colin Tizzard   Ann & Alan Potts Limited

PLACINGS: 1/3421622-   RPR **150h**

Starts	1st	2nd	3rd	4th	Win & Pl
8	2	3	1	1	£111,024
	2/18	Extr	2m1f Cls1 Nov List Hdl heavy		£14,238
	4/17	Punc	2m NHF 4-5yo-gd-yld		£50,427

Improved massively following wind surgery midway through last season and ran well at all three major spring festivals; didn't quite get home after travelling strongly in the Ballymore at Cheltenham and dropped to 2m to finish second at Aintree and Punchestown.

Vyta Du Roc (Fr)

9 gr g Lion Noir - Dolce Vyta (Grand Tresor)

Nicky Henderson   Simon Munir & Isaac Souede

PLACINGS: 242/12155/36P52/501-   RPR **151+c**

Starts	1st	2nd	3rd	4th	Win & Pl
22	7	4	2	1	£176,134
138	1/18	Chel	3m2¹/₂f Cls2 124-144 Ch Hcap heavy		£15,784
	2/16	Asct	3m Cls1 Nov Gd2 Ch soft		£22,887
	12/15	Bang	2m1¹/₂f Cls4 Nov Ch heavy		£4,660
	12/14	Sand	2m4f Cls1 Nov Gd2 Hdl soft		£17,085
	11/14	Chel	2m1¹/₂f Cls1 Nov Gd2 Hdl soft		£17,085
	6/14	Hexm	2m Cls3 Nov Hdl good		£5,817
	5/14	Uttx	2m Cls5 Mdn Hdl good		£2,339

Thorough stayer who has run well in some top staying handicap chases, notably when beaten a head in the bet365 Gold Cup in 2017; looked better than ever when winning at Cheltenham on New Year's Day and was a leading Grand National contender until suffering a setback.

Waiting Patiently (Ire)

7 b g Flemensfirth - Rossavon (Beneficial)

Ruth Jefferson   Richard Collins

PLACINGS: 221/111/111-   RPR **174+c**

Starts	1st	2nd	3rd	4th	Win & Pl
9	7	2	-	-	£163,074
	2/18	Asct	2m5f Cls1 Gd1 Ch soft		£85,827
	1/18	Kemp	2m4¹/₂f Cls1 List Ch gd-sft		£22,780
	11/17	Carl	2m4f Cls1 List Ch gd-sft		£17,085
	1/17	Hayd	2m4f Cls1 Nov Gd2 Ch soft		£18,546
	12/16	Newc	2m¹/₂f Cls3 Nov Ch soft		£6,498
123	11/16	Sedg	2m¹/₂f Cls3 Nov 115-130 Ch Hcap soft		£6,498
	1/16	Sedg	2m4f Cls4 Nov Hdl gd-sft		£3,798

Exciting, lightly raced chaser who has won all six starts over fences, most notably last season's Ascot Chase when beating Cue Card before missing Aintree through injury; said to need soft ground by connections and hasn't raced on good since last defeat over hurdles; would be interesting stepped up to 3m.

Wakanda (Ire)

9 b g Westerner - Chanson Indienne (Indian River)

Sue Smith   MB Scholey & The Late RH Scholey

PLACINGS: /111PP/752P3/2521P0-   RPR **154+c**

Starts	1st	2nd	3rd	4th	Win & Pl
31	8	8	2	3	£243,920
145	1/18	Donc	3m Cls1 List 131-157 Ch Hcap soft		£45,560
151	12/15	Asct	3m Cls1 List 137-158 Ch Hcap soft		£56,950
145	11/15	Newc	2m7¹/₂f Cls1 List 128-153 Ch Hcap soft		£34,170
139	10/15	Weth	2m3¹/₂f Cls1 List 132-145 Ch Hcap soft		£15,661
	1/15	Hayd	2m4¹/₂f Cls1 Nov Gd2 Ch heavy		£17,370
	12/14	Kels	2m7¹/₂f Cls3 Nov Ch soft		£10,128
120	10/14	Hexm	2m4f Nov 101-120 Ch Hcap good		£6,844
	7/13	Slig	2m Mdn Hdl 4yo good		£4,207

Ended a long losing run when winning the Sky Bet Chase at Doncaster last season; had previously landed a hat-trick of Listed handicaps at the end of 2015 and has run well in several other good staying chases, finishing second in the last two runnings of the Rowland Meyrick at Wetherby.

Warriors Tale

9 b g Midnight Legend - Samandara (Kris)

Paul Nicholls   Trevor Hemmings

PLACINGS: 2P205/13253115/U22P-   RPR **154c**

Starts	1st	2nd	3rd	4th	Win & Pl
25	5	7	2	1	£75,476
137	3/17	Newb	2m4f Cls2 125-143 Ch Hcap gd-sft		£12,660
130	3/17	Newb	2m4f Cls3 Nov 130-143 Ch Hcap soft		£6,498
	5/16	Prth	3m Cls4 Nov Ch gd-fm		£4,328
110	2/15	Kels	2m6¹/₂f Cls3 110-125 Ch Hcap gd-sft		£6,498
	1/15	Ayr	2m4¹/₂f Cls5 Mdn Hdl soft		£2,469

Three-time winner as a novice chaser two seasons ago and progressed again despite not winning last season, going close in good handicaps at Newbury and Doncaster; pulled up in the Grand National when running beyond 3m for the first time over fences.

We Have A Dream (Fr)
4 b g Martaline - Sweet Dance (Kingsalsa)

Nicky Henderson   Simon Munir & Isaac Souede

PLACINGS: 5/4411111-   RPR **147+h**

Starts	1st	2nd	3rd	4th	Win & Pl
8	5	-	-	2	£139,563

4/18	Aint	2m1f Cls1 Gd1 Hdl 4yo gd-sft	£56,141
2/18	Muss	1m7¹/₂f Cls1 List Hdl 4yo soft	£14,405
1/18	Chep	2m Cls1 Gd1 Hdl 4yo heavy	£28,810
12/17	Donc	2m¹/₂f Cls1 Gd2 Hdl 3yo good	£25,748
11/17	Wwck	2m Cls4 Hdl 3yo gd-sft	£4,549

Arguably last season's leading juvenile hurdler, going unbeaten in five races including a second Grade 1 victory by seven lengths at Aintree, but missed the Triumph Hurdle through sickness; seems to act on any ground; set to be aimed at the Champion Hurdle.

West Approach
8 b g Westerner - Ardstown (Ardross)

Colin Tizzard   John & Heather Snook

PLACINGS: 20/1235U3PP/131356P-   RPR **148+c**

Starts	1st	2nd	3rd	4th	Win & Pl
22	4	2	5	1	£70,842

12/17	Extr	2m3f Cls2 Nov Ch soft	£16,025
10/17	Ffos	2m5f Cls3 Ch soft	£9,097
5/16	NAbb	2m1f Cls2 Nov Hdl good	£9,495
1/15	Newb	2m¹/₂f Cls5 NHF 4-6yo heavy	£2,053

Smart staying hurdler who finished third in the Cleeve Hurdle in 2017; won twice when sent novice chasing last season but jumping was exposed in better races; trainer expected that to improve over extreme trips before he was pulled up in the Scottish National.

Western Ryder (Ire)
6 b g Westerner - Seesea (Dr Massini)

Warren Greatrex   Albatross Club/Bryan Drew & Friends

PLACINGS: 121253/U114265-   RPR **149+h**

Starts	1st	2nd	3rd	4th	Win & Pl
13	4	3	1	1	£56,328

12/17	Chel	2m1f Cls3 Nov Hdl 4-6yo soft	£7,798
11/17	Chep	2m Cls4 Nov Hdl heavy	£3,249
12/16	Asct	1m7¹/₂f Cls1 List NHF 4-6yo gd-sft	£17,085
5/16	Ffos	2m Cls4 NHF 4-6yo good	£3,249

Very useful performer in novice hurdles last season; ran well in the face of some stiff tasks in the spring, including when an unlucky sixth in the Supreme at Cheltenham (badly hampered two out); yet to win beyond 2m1f but has shown good form over further.

Whatswrongwithyou (Ire)
7 ch g Bienamado - Greenfield Noora (Topanoora)

Nicky Henderson   5 Hertford Street Racing Club

PLACINGS: 2/1012/2113-   RPR **139h**

Starts	1st	2nd	3rd	4th	Win & Pl
7	3	2	1	-	£26,005

2/18	Newb	2m¹/₂f Cls3 Nov Hdl soft	£6,758
1/18	Newb	2m¹/₂f Cls4 Nov Hdl soft	£4,549
3/17	Ludl	2m Cls4 NHF 4-6yo soft	£3,899

Started to make up for lost time in novice hurdles last season, winning twice; well backed into favouritism for the Imperial Cup but got little luck in running and plugged on into third; may do better on quicker ground.

Whiskey Sour (Ire)
5 b g Jeremy - Swizzle Stick (Sadler's Wells)

Willie Mullins (Ir)   Luke McMahon

PLACINGS: 114342-7   RPR **143h**

Starts	1st	2nd	3rd	4th	Win & Pl
7	2	1	1	2	£83,248

12/17	Leop	2m Nov Gd1 Hdl soft	£42,863
6/17	Tram	2m Mdn Hdl 4yo good	£5,791

Hugely flattered by Grade 1 novice hurdle win last Christmas (would have finished a distant third but for final-flight carnage) but wasn't hit hard by the handicapper and found his level when third in the County Hurdle; stays further and may well pick up a decent handicap.

Whisper (Fr)
10 b g Astarabad - Belle Yepa (Mansonnien)

Nicky Henderson   Walters Plant Hire

PLACINGS: 11/251/5P8/1122/125-   RPR **171+c**

Starts		1st	2nd	3rd	4th	Win & Pl
25		11	5	2	2	£402,790

	11/17	Kemp	2m4¹/₂f Cls2 Ch good	£12,512
	1/17	Chel	2m5f Cls1 Nov Gd2 Ch soft	£18,224
	12/16	Chel	2m5f Cls2 Nov Ch gd-sft	£15,698
	4/15	Aint	3m¹/₂f Cls1 Gd1 Hdl good	£67,582
	4/14	Aint	3m¹/₂f Cls1 Gd1 Hdl gd-sft	£67,524
153	3/14	Chel	2m5f Cls1 Gd3 135-154 Hdl Hcap good	£45,560
140	12/13	Newb	2m4¹/₂f Cls2 134-144 Hdl Hcap heavy	£11,574
	4/13	Chel	2m4¹/₂f Cls2 Nov Hdl gd-sft	£10,010
	2/13	Ffos	2m4f Cls4 Nov Hdl 4-7yo heavy	£3,574
	12/12	Ffos	2m4f Cls4 Nov Hdl heavy	£2,599
	4/12	Ffos	2m Cls6 NHF 4-5yo good	£1,848

Second in the Ladbrokes Trophy last season but flopped in the King George and missed the rest of the season; considered more of a Grand National type than a Grade 1 horse by his trainer, although he may be rated too high for Aintree.

facebook.com/racingpost

White Moon (Ger)
6 gr g Sholokhov - Westalin (Sternkoenig)

Colin Tizzard | Brocade Racing

PLACINGS: **5F/1117-** RPR **132+h**

Starts	1st	2nd	3rd	4th	Win & Pl
3	2	-	-	-	£7,472

11/17	Extr	2m5½f Cls4 Nov Hdl soft	£4,549
10/17	Winc	2m5½f Cls5 Mdn Hdl good	£2,924

Point-to-point winner who also landed his first two starts under rules last season over hurdles; under the weather when well beaten up in grade at Sandown next time and missed the rest of the season; described by his increasingly powerful trainer as one of his nicest horses.

Wholestone (Ire)
7 br g Craigsteel - Last Theatre (King's Theatre)

Nigel Twiston-Davies | Simon Munir & Isaac Souede

PLACINGS: **13F/112113/42612323-** RPR **159h**

Starts	1st	2nd	3rd	4th	Win & Pl
17	6	4	4	1	£199,338

1/18	Chel	2m4½f Cls1 Gd2 Hdl heavy	£28,475
1/17	Chel	2m4½f Cls1 Nov Gd2 Hdl soft	£17,085
12/16	Chel	3m Cls1 Nov Gd2 Hdl soft	£17,085
10/16	Chel	3m Cls3 Nov Hdl good	£6,256
9/16	Wwck	2m5f Cls4 Mdn Hdl good	£3,574
9/15	Worc	2m Cls6 NHF 4-6yo good	£1,625

Consistent performer in top staying hurdles last season, especially at Cheltenham, achieving a third course win in the Relkeel Hurdle on New Year's Day and finishing third in the Stayers' Hurdle; second for the third time over the campaign when going on to Aintree.

Wicklow Brave
9 b g Beat Hollow - Moraine (Rainbow Quest)

Willie Mullins (Ir) | Wicklow Bloodstock (Ireland)

PLACINGS: **6/F580P1/033/71/72-2** RPR **161h**

Starts	1st	2nd	3rd	4th	Win & Pl
23	7	3	2	-	£289,603

4/17	Punc	2m Gd1 Hdl gd-yld	£126,068
3/15	Chel	2m1f Cls1 Gd3 134-146 Hdl Hcap soft	£45,560
2/14	Punc	2m Nov List Hdl heavy	£16,250
1/14	Cork	2m Mdn Hdl 4-5yo heavy	£6,038
10/13	Tipp	2m NHF 4-7yo soft	£6,030
9/13	List	2m NHF 4-7yo soft	£7,854
7/13	Gway	2m NHF 4-7yo good	£4,488

(138)

Holds rare distinction of being a top-flight winner on the Flat and over hurdles; unable to add to his Grade 1 tally last season having been freshened up for a spring campaign but ran well when defending his Punchestown crown in April, finishing second to Supasundae.

··

'This point-to-point winner is described by his trainer as one of his nicest horses'

William Henry (Ire)
8 b g King's Theatre - Cincuenta (Bob Back)

Nicky Henderson | Walters Plant Hire

PLACINGS: **411/2121/P144-** RPR **155+h**

Starts	1st	2nd	3rd	4th	Win & Pl
11	5	2	-	3	£64,386

1/18	Kemp	2m5f Cls1 List 122-145 Hdl Hcap soft	£25,628
4/17	Chel	2m4½f Cls2 Nov Hdl good	£10,010
12/16	Newb	2m½f Cls4 Hdl gd-sft	£4,549
4/15	Ayr	2m Cls3 NHF 4-6yo good	£6,498
3/15	Kemp	2m Cls5 Mdn NHF 4-6yo good	£2,599

(145)

Ran well in top handicap hurdles last season, winning the Lanzarote Hurdle and finishing fourth in the Coral Cup and at Ayr; final effort suggested handicapper may have his measure but has option of switching back to fences (pulled up in only chase on reappearance last term).

Willoughby Court (Ire)
7 br g Court Cave - Willoughby Sue (Dabai)

Ben Pauling | Paul & Clare Rooney

PLACINGS: **3/115/2111/113-** RPR **157+c**

Starts	1st	2nd	3rd	4th	Win & Pl
11	7	1	2	-	£135,064

12/17	Newb	2m4f Cls1 Nov Gd2 Ch gd-sft	£23,048
11/17	Hntg	2m4f Cls3 Nov Ch good	£7,798
3/17	Chel	2m5f Cls1 Nov Gd1 Hdl gd-sft	£71,188
1/17	Wwck	2m5f Cls1 Nov Gd2 Hdl soft	£19,933
12/16	Wwck	2m5f Cls4 Mdn Hdl gd-sft	£3,574
12/15	Wwck	2m Cls6 NHF 4-6yo soft	£1,625
11/15	Sthl	1m7½f Cls3 NHF 4-6yo soft	£1,949

Won the Neptune Hurdle at Cheltenham in 2017 and looked set to take similarly high rank as a novice chaser last season when impressively beating Yanworth at Newbury; unsuited by heavy ground when third behind that rival next time and missed the rest of the season through injury.

Yala Enki (Fr)
8 b/br g Nickname - Cadiane (Cadoudal)

Venetia Williams | Hills Of Ledbury (Aga)

PLACINGS: **31P5/31441/P364F166-** RPR **157+c**

Starts	1st	2nd	3rd	4th	Win & Pl
32	8	5	4	5	£244,499

2/18	Hayd	3m4½f Cls1 Gd3 138-161 Ch Hcap heavy	£60,067
3/17	Kels	3m2f Cls2 125-147 Ch Hcap heavy	£17,545
12/16	Hayd	2m7f Cls2 120-139 Ch Hcap soft	£15,640
2/16	Asct	2m3½f Cls2 Nov Hdl soft	£15,640
1/16	Kemp	2m5f Cls1 List 127-153 Hdl Hcap soft	£22,780
11/15	Extr	2m5½f Cls3 Nov Hdl gd-sft	£5,523
2/14	Fntb	2m Ch 4yo v soft	£9,600
10/13	Pari	2m1f Ch 3yo gd-sft	£7,415

(146) (146) (139) (130)

Thrives on heavy ground and relished the most extreme test of stamina he has faced when galloping to a wide-margin win in desperate conditions in last season's Grand National Trial at Haydock; had also won the Tommy Whittle at that course on soft ground in 2016.

Yanworth
8 ch g Norse Dancer - Yota (Galetto)

Alan King | John P McManus

PLACINGS: 4/11112/111dis1/1F216- RPR **156h**

Starts	1st	2nd	3rd	4th	Win & Pl
19	12	3	-	1	£353,333

1/18	Chel	2m5f Cls1 Nov Gd2 Ch heavy	£20,167
10/17	Extr	2m1½f Cls3 Ch gd-sft	£7,473
4/17	Aint	3m½f Cls1 Gd1 Hdl good	£84,251
2/17	Winc	1m7½f Cls1 Gd2 Hdl soft	£34,170
12/16	Kemp	2m Cls1 Gd1 Hdl good	£56,950
11/16	Asct	2m3½f Cls1 Gd2 Hdl gd-sft	£56,950
1/16	Chel	2m4½f Cls1 Nov Gd2 Hdl heavy	£17,085
12/15	Asct	1m7½f Cls1 Nov Gd2 Hdl soft	£17,085
11/15	Wwck	2m Cls4 Nov Hdl gd-sft	£3,899
11/15	Extr	2m1f Cls3 Nov Hdl soft	£5,523
11/14	Newb	2m½f Cls6 NHF 4-6yo soft	£1,689
5/14	Winc	1m7½f Cls6 NHF 4-6yo gd-sft	£1,625

Beaten only by Yorkhill in first eight races over jumps but has thrown in some mixed efforts since being sent off favourite for the 2017 Champion Hurdle; won a 3m Grade 1 hurdle that year but never quite convinced over fences last term and disappointed in the Stayers' Hurdle.

Yorkhill (Ire)
8 ch g Presenting - Lightning Breeze (Saddlers' Hall)

Willie Mullins (Ir) | Andrea & Graham Wylie

PLACINGS: /11111/41112/86P8-69 RPR **141h**

Starts	1st	2nd	3rd	4th	Win & Pl
17	9	1	-	1	£300,645

3/17	Chel	2m4f Cls1 Nov Gd1 Ch good	£89,275
1/17	Leop	2m3f Nov Gd3 Ch good	£22,692
12/16	Fair	2m Ch sft-hvy	£6,331
4/16	Aint	2m4f Cls1 Nov Gd1 Hdl soft	£42,402
3/16	Chel	2m5f Cls1 Nov Gd1 Hdl good	£68,340
1/16	Sand	2m Cls1 Nov Gd1 Hdl heavy	£23,048
12/15	Punc	2m4f Mdn Hdl heavy	£6,419
4/15	Punc	2m NHF 4-7yo yield	£6,419
3/15	Gowr	2m2f NHF 4-7yo soft	£4,814

Massive talent who has won four times at Grade 1 level, including at two successive Cheltenham Festivals in 2016 and 2017; without a win since then, though, and showed little last season over hurdles and fences as well as a variety of trips.

Ziga Boy (Fr)
9 gr g Califet - Our Ziga (Linamix)

Alan King | Axom LI

PLACINGS: /81UP46/P3118/65U31/ RPR **152c**

Starts	1st	2nd	3rd	4th	Win & Pl
27	5	2	3	4	£134,672

137	1/17	Donc	3m Cls1 List 132-152 Ch Hcap good	£45,560
133	1/16	Donc	3m Cls1 List 133-159 Ch Hcap good	£45,560
117	12/15	Donc	3m Cls3 114-133 Ch Hcap gd-sft	£6,498
119	12/14	Winc	3m1f Cls3 102-122 Ch Hcap good	£9,384
	10/13	Mlns	2m2f Ch 4yo sft-hvy	£7,805

Won back-to-back runnings of the Sky Bet Chase at Doncaster but hasn't run since his second victory in the race in 2017 having been injured during his build-up to the Grand National that year (unseated over the fences in the Becher); back in training this summer.

KEY HORSES LISTED BY TRAINER

Kim Bailey
Charbel (Ire)
First Flow (Ire)
Red River (Ire)
Vinndication (Ire)

Enda Bolger
Ballyoisin (Ire)

Peter Bowen
Beggar's Wishes (Ire)

Mark Bradstock
Coneygree
Step Back (Ire)

Bob Buckler
Regal Flow

W Burke
Sumos Novios (Ire)

Charles Byrnes
Off You Go (Ire)

Mick Channon
Mister Whitaker (Ire)

Stuart Coltherd
Captain Redbeard (Ire)

Gavin Cromwell
Espoir D'Allen (Fr)

Denis W Cullen
A Great View (Ire)

Rebecca Curtis
Joe Farrell (Ire)

Henry de Bromhead
Balko Des Flos (Fr)
Calino D'Airy (Fr)
Chris's Dream (Ire)
Identity Thief (Ire)
Mind's Eye (Ire)
Monalee (Ire)
Paloma Blue (Ire)
Petit Mouchoir (Fr)
Special Tiara
Sub Lieutenant (Ire)
Trainwreck (Ire)
Valseur Lido (Fr)

Miss Elizabeth Doyle
Last Goodbye (Ire)

Sean Thomas Doyle
Crosshue Boy (Ire)

Michael Easterby
Sam's Gunner

Stuart Edmunds
Domesday Book (USA)
Maria's Benefit (Ire)
Now McGinty (Ire)

Gordon Elliott
A Toi Phil (Fr)
Apple's Jade (Fr)
Ball D'Arc (Fr)
Baltazar D'Allier (Fr)
Blow By Blow (Ire)
Champagne Classic (Ire)
Cracking Smart (Fr)
Delta Work (Fr)
Diamond Cauchois (Fr)
Doctor Phoenix (Ire)
Don Poli (Ire)
Dortmund Park (Fr)
Dounikos (Fr)
Empire Of Dirt (Ire)
Fagan
Farclas (Fr)
Felix Desjy (Fr)
Folsom Blue (Ire)
General Principle (Ire)
Getaway John (Ire)
Glenloe (Ire)
Jury Duty (Ire)
Mala Beach (Ire)
Mengli Khan (Ire)
Mick Jazz (Fr)
Monbeg Notorious (Ire)
Noble Endeavor (Ire)
Outlander (Ire)
Pallasator
Samcro (Ire)
Shattered Love (Ire)
Squouateur (Fr)
Sutton Place (Ire)
The Storyteller (Ire)
Tiger Roll (Ire)
Tombstone (Ire)
Ucello Conti (Fr)
Veneer Of Charm (Ire)

Brian Ellison
Definitly Red (Ire)
Forest Bihan (Fr)

Pat Fahy
Castlegrace Paddy (Ire)

Alan Fleming
Tully East (Ire)

Harry Fry
Acting Lass (Ire)
American (Fr)
Drumcliff (Ire)
Hell's Kitchen
If The Cap Fits (Ire)
Jolly's Cracked It (Fr)
Kylemore Lough
Minella Awards (Ire)
Misterton
Momella (Ire)
The Last Samuri (Ire)
Unowhatimeanharry

facebook.com/racingpost

Tom George
Black Op (Ire)
Double Shuffle (Ire)
God's Own (Ire)
Rocklander (Ire)
Singlefarmpayment
Summerville Boy (Ire)
The Worlds End (Ire)

Nick Gifford
Didtheyleaveuoutto (Ire)

Chris Gordon
Highway One O One (Ire)

Chris Grant
Donna's Diamond (Ire)

Warren Greatrex
Keeper Hill (Ire)
La Bague Au Roi (Fr)
1231 Missed Approach (Ire)
Mulcahys Hill (Ire)
Portrush Ted (Ire)
Western Ryder (Ire)

Mrs John Harrington
Forge Meadow (Ire)
Jetz (Ire)
Sizing John
Supasundae

Edward Harty
Coney Island (Ire)

Nigel Hawke
Speredek (Fr)

Nicky Henderson
Altior (Ire)
Apple's Shakira (Fr)
Beware The Bear (Ire)
Brain Power (Ire)
Buveur D'Air (Fr)
Call Me Lord (Fr)
Casablanca Mix (Fr)
Champ (Ire)
Charli Parcs (Fr)
Chef Des Obeaux (Fr)
Claimantakinforgan (Fr)
Constantine Bay
Dame De Compagnie (Fr)
Daphne Du Clos (Fr)
Diese Des Bieffes (Fr)
Divine Spear (Ire)
Gold Present (Ire)
Jenkins (Ire)
Might Bite (Ire)
Mr Whipped (Ire)
O O Seven (Ire)
Ok Corral (Ire)
On The Blind Side (Ire)
Pacific De Baune (Fr)
Rather Be (Ire)
River Wylde (Ire)

Santini
Soul Emotion (Fr)
Style De Garde (Fr)
Terrefort (Fr)
Theinval (Fr)
Thomas Campbell
Top Notch (Fr)
Verdana Blue (Ire)
Vyta Du Roc (Fr)
We Have A Dream (Fr)
Whatswrongwithyou (Ire)
Whisper (Fr)
William Henry (Ire)

Philip Hobbs
Defi Du Seuil (Fr)
Garde La Victoire (Fr)
Gumball (Fr)
Imperial Presence (Ire)
Louis' Vac Pouch (Ire)
No Comment
Ozzie The Oscar (Ire)
Rock The Kasbah (Ire)
Rolling Dylan (Ire)

Richard Hobson
Allysson Monterg (Fr)
Shantou Flyer (Ire)

Anthony Honeyball
Acey Milan (Ire)
Ms Parfois (Ire)
Regal Encore (Ire)

Iain Jardine
L'Inganno Felice (Fr)

Ruth Jefferson
Waiting Patiently (Ire)

Patrick Kelly
Mall Dini (Ire)
Presenting Percy

Alan King
Dingo Dollar (Ire)
Label Des Obeaux (Fr)
Master Blueyes (Ire)
Mia's Storm (Ire)
Redicean
Scarlet Dragon
Sceau Royal (Fr)
Talkischeap (Ire)
Yanworth
Ziga Boy (Fr)

Neil King
Lil Rockefeller (USA)

Philip Kirby
Lady Buttons

Tom Lacey
Thomas Patrick (Ire)

Emma Lavelle
Paisley Park (Ire)

Kerry Lee
Gino Trail (Ire)
Happy Diva (Ire)
Top Gamble (Ire)

Charlie Longsdon
Ballydine (Ire)
Bentelimar (Ire)

Tony Martin
Anibale Fly (Fr)

Nicky Martin
Beer Goggles (Ire)

Donald McCain
Cloudy Dream (Ire)
Mount Mews (Ire)
Testify (Ire)
Uppertown Prince (Ire)

Graeme McPherson
Ami Desbois (Fr)

Noel Meade
Bel Ami De Sivola (Fr)
Brace Yourself (Ire)
Disko (Fr)
Minella Fair (Ire)
Road To Respect (Ire)
Snow Falcon (Ire)

Gary Moore
Baron Alco (Fr)
Benatar (Ire)
Diakali (Fr)
Sussex Ranger (USA)
Traffic Fluide (Fr)

Mouse Morris
Alpha Des Obeaux (Fr)

Neil Mulholland
Kalondra (Ire)

Margaret Mullins
Debuchet (Fr)

Seamus Mullins
Chesterfield (Ire)

Willie Mullins
Acapella Bourgeois (Fr)
Al Boum Photo (Fr)
Annamix (Fr)
Bacardys (Fr)
Bachasson (Fr)
Ballyward (Ire)
Bamako Moriviere (Fr)
Bapaume (Fr)
Bellshill (Ire)
Benie Des Dieux (Fr)
Blackbow (Ire)
Bleu Berry (Fr)
Bleu Et Rouge (Fr)
Bonbon Au Miel (Fr)
Brahma Bull (Fr)

Cadmium (Fr)
Carefully Selected (Ire)
Carter McKay
Cilaos Emery (Fr)
Coquin Mans (Fr)
Douvan (Fr)
Draconien (Fr)
Duc Des Genievres (Fr)
Fabulous Saga (Fr)
Faugheen (Ire)
Footpad (Fr)
Getabird (Ire)
Great Field (Fr)
Invitation Only (Ire)
Isleofhopendreams
Kemboy (Fr)
Killultagh Vic (Ire)
Laurina (Fr)
Limini (Ire)
Melon
Min (Fr)
Mr Adjudicator
Next Destination (Ire)
Pairofbrowneyes (Ire)
Penhill
Pleasant Company (Ire)
Rathvinden (Ire)
Relegate (Ire)
Saglawy (Fr)
Saldier (Fr)
Sayar (Ire)
Sayo
Scarpeta (Fr)
Shaneshill (Ire)
Sharjah (Fr)
Stormy Ireland (Fr)
Tornado Flyer (Ire)
Total Recall (Ire)
Un De Sceaux (Fr)
Up For Review (Ire)
Whiskey Sour (Fr)
Wicklow Brave
Yorkhill (Ire)

Amy Murphy
Kalashnikov (Ire)

Olly Murphy
Hunters Call (Ire)

Richard Newland
Audacious Plan (Ire)
Le Patriote (Fr)

Paul Nicholls
Adrien Du Pont (Fr)
Art Mauresque (Fr)
Binge Drinker (Fr)
Black Corton (Fr)
Blu Cavalier
Capitaine (Fr)
Captain Cattistock

KEY HORSES LISTED BY TRAINER

Clan Des Obeaux (Fr)
Cliffs Of Dover
Cyrname (Fr)
Danny Kirwan (Ire)
Diego Du Charmil (Fr)
Dolos (Fr)
El Bandit (Ire)
Frodon (Fr)
Give Me A Copper (Ire)
Le Prezien (Fr)
Malaya (Fr)
Master Tommytucker
Modus
Mont Des Avaloirs (Fr)
Movewiththetimes (Ire)
Old Guard
Politologue (Fr)
San Benedeto (Fr)
Topofthegame (Ire)
Vicente (Fr)
Warriors Tale

Fergal O'Brien
Aye Aye Charlie
Barney Dwan (Ire)
Cap Soleil (Fr)
Master Dee (Ire)
Poetic Rhythm (Ire)

Joseph O'Brien
Edwulf
Rhinestone (Ire)
Speak Easy
Tower Bridge (Ire)

Jedd O'Keeffe
Sam Spinner

Jonjo O'Neill
Forza Milan (Ire)
Go Conquer (Ire)
Minella Rocco (Ire)

Ross O'Sullivan
Baie Des Iles (Fr)

Ben Pauling
Barters Hill (Ire)
Global Citizen (Ire)
Kildisart (Ire)
Le Breuil (Fr)
Willoughby Court (Ire)

David Pipe
Daklondike (Ire)
King's Socks (Fr)
Moon Racer (Ire)
Mr Big Shot (Ire)
Un Temps Pour Tout (Ire)
Vieux Lion Rouge (Fr)

Nicky Richards
Baywing (Ire)
Guitar Pete (Ire)
Simply Ned (Ire)

Padraig Roche
Out Of The Loop

Lucinda Russell
Big River (Ire)
One For Arthur (Ire)

Kevin Ryan
Beyond The Clouds

Oliver Sherwood
Euxton Lane (Ire)
Got Away (Fr)

Dan Skelton
Ch'Tibello (Fr)
Cobra De Mai (Fr)
Fair Mountain (Ger)
Mohaayed
Nube Negra (Spa)
Rene's Girl (Ire)
Robin Waters (Fr)

Roksana (Ire)
Shantou Rock (Ire)
Two Taffs (Ire)
Value At Risk
Virgilio (Fr)

Sue Smith
I Just Know (Ire)
Midnight Shadow
Vintage Clouds (Ire)
Wakanda (Ire)

Jamie Snowden
Hogan's Height (Ire)

Sandy Thomson
Seeyouatmidnight

Colin Tizzard
Ainchea (Ire)
Cyrus Darius
Elegant Escape (Ire)
Fox Norton (Fr)
Kilbricken Storm (Ire)
Lostintranslation (Ire)
Native River (Ire)
Pingshou (Ire)
Robinsfirth (Ire)
Silverhow (Ire)
Sizing Codelco (Ire)
Sizing Granite (Ire)
Sizing Tennessee (Ire)
Slate House (Ire)
The Dutchman (Ire)
Thistlecrack
Ultragold (Fr)
Vision Des Flos (Fr)
West Approach
White Moon (Ger)

Nigel Twiston-Davies
Ballyandy
Ballyarthur (Ire)

Ballymoy (Ire)
Ballyoptic (Ire)
Blaklion
Bristol De Mai (Fr)
Calett Mad (Fr)
Crievehill (Ire)
Flying Angel (Ire)
Foxtail Hill (Ire)
Mr Antolini (Ire)
Splash Of Ginge
The New One (Ire)
Wholestone (Ire)

Tim Vaughan
Debece

Ted Walsh
Any Second Now (Ire)

Harry Whittington
Bigmartre (Fr)
Saint Calvados (Fr)
Vinnie Lewis (Ire)

Evan Williams
Clyne
King's Odyssey (Ire)
Silver Streak (Ire)

Jane Williams
Tea For Two

Nick Williams
Agrapart (Fr)
Coo Star Sivola (Fr)

Venetia Williams
Aso (Fr)
Belami Des Pictons (Fr)
Yala Enki (Fr)

Kayley Woollacott
Lalor (Ger)

*Golden moment: Native River's trainer
and fans celebrate his Cheltenham success*

Facebook.com/racingpost

INDEX OF HORSES

INDEX OF HORSES

facebook.com/racingpost

INDEX OF HORSES

facebook.com/racingpost